GLOBE FEARON'S

Algebra 1

Globe Fearon Educational Publisher
A Division of Simon & Schuster
Upper Saddle River, New Jersey

REVIEWERS

We are grateful to the following educators. They served as reviewers during various stages of product development. Their valuable comments and suggestions served to enhance the quality of this book.

Ann Dixon, Special Education Teacher
Allegheny Intermediate Unit
South Park High School
Library, PA 15129

Ravi Kamat, Math Teacher
Dallas, TX 75203

Janet Thompson, Special Education Teacher
St. Louis, MO 63107

Linda White, Special Education Teacher
Riverview Learning Center
Daytona Beach, CA 32118

Credits

Project Editor:	Jennifer McCarthy
Senior Editor:	Stephanie Petron Cahill
Production Editor:	Suzanne Keezer
Designers:	Evelyn Bauer, Jennifer Visco
Editorial Assistants:	Marilyn Bashoff, Derrell Bradford, and Eileen O'Shea
Editorial Services:	provided by Publishers Resource Group, Inc.
Electronic Page Production:	Burmar, Sharon Ferguson
Cover Photo Design:	FPG

Photo Credits appear on page 477.

Printed in the United States of America
3 4 5 6 7 8 9 10 01 00 99

ISBN 0-835-93500-0

Globe Fearon Educational Publisher
A Division of Simon & Schuster
Upper Saddle River, New Jersey

Contents

Chapter 3
Solving Equations

Chapter 14
Rational Expressions and Equations   **356**

A Note to the Student

Welcome to algebra! The purpose of this book is to make your journey through algebra a success. Your journey will be comfortable and interesting. You will build new skills based on what you already know. You will make connections between algebra and problem solving skills. You will apply these new concepts and skills throughout the text. As you work through and review each topic, your algebra skills will grow.

Each lesson presents clear models and examples. The lessons give you a chance to try out your skills in **Try These.** Then, you go on and use the skills in **Practice.** From lesson to lesson, you share what you have learned with a partner in **Do It Together.**

Application lessons show you how you can apply what you know to science, geometry, statistics, and business. **Problem Solving** lessons show different ways to solve problems using what you have learned. **Calculator** lessons show you another tool you can use with your algebra skills.

Math Connections contain interesting information about people and careers. They also give interesting facts about math in other areas that you might study.

There are many other study aids in the book. At the beginning of every chapter, you will find **Learning Objectives.** They will help you focus on the important points covered in the chapter. You will also find **Words to Know.** This is a look ahead at new vocabulary you may find difficult. At the end of each chapter, you will find a **Chapter Review.** This will give you a review of what you have just learned. A **Unit Review** comes after each unit.

Everyone who put this book together worked hard to make it useful, interesting, and enjoyable. The rest is up to you.

We wish you well on your journey through algebra. Our success comes from your success.

Unit One

Chapter 1

Numbers for Algebra

Numbers are used everywhere. Positive and negative numbers are used as values for all kinds of things. Balloon pilots use them to keep track of air temperature, wind speed, and altitude.

Chapter Learning Objectives

- Graph integers on a number line.
- Find the absolute value of integers.
- Add, subtract, multiply, and divide with positive and negative numbers.
- Use a calculator to add, subtract, multiply, and divide positive and negative numbers.
- Guess, check, and revise to solve problems.
- Apply concepts and skills to find information from broken-line graphs.

Words to Know

positive numbers   the numbers to the right of zero on the number line

negative numbers   the numbers to the left of zero on the number line

integers   the numbers ... $^-3$, $^-2$, $^-1$, 0, 1, 2, 3, ...

absolute value   the distance between 0 and a number on the number line

opposites   numbers with the same absolute value on opposite sides of zero; One is negative and the other is positive; $^-3$ and 3 are opposites

expression   a number, or a group of numbers written with operation signs

simplify   perform the operations; Find the value

base   a factor; In 3^2, 3 is the base used as a factor 2 times

exponent   the number that tells how many times the base is used as a factor

power   the product when factors are the same; In $3^2 = 9$, 9 is the power

revise   change; to change a guess when you have more information

broken–line graph   a graph made up of pieces of straight lines; used to display information

In this chapter, you will graph integers and find their absolute value. You will add, subtract, multiply, and divide with positive and negative numbers. Then, you will use a calculator to work with these numbers. You will learn to guess, check, and revise to solve problems. You will apply what you know about positive and negative numbers to interpret information from broken–line graphs.

1.1 The Number Line

Look at the number line below. **Positive numbers** are to the right of 0. **Negative numbers** are to the left of 0. Zero is not positive or negative.

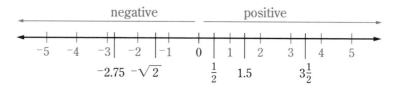

+ is a positive sign.
− is a negative sign.

Read $^+4$ as "positive four" or "four." 4 is the same as $^+4$. Read $^-5$ as "negative five."

The **integers** are the numbers...$^-3, ^-2, ^-1, 0, 1, 2, 3$... You can graph integers on a number line.

EXAMPLE 1 Graph $^-5$ on a number line.

Count 5 places to the left of zero.
Draw a dot.

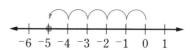

You can also use a number line to compare integers. Numbers increase in value to the right. Numbers decrease in value to the left.

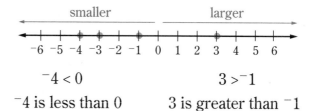

> means "is greater than."
< means "is less than."

$^-4 < 0$ $3 >^-1$

$^-4$ is less than 0   3 is greater than $^-1$

EXAMPLE 2 Compare $^-4$ and 3. Use > or <.

$^-4$ is to the left of 3 on the number line. $-4 < 3$

$^-4$ is less than 3.

EXAMPLE 3 Compare $^-1$ and $^-3$. Use > or <.

$^-1$ is to the right of $^-3$ on the number line. $^-1 >^-3$

$^-1$ is greater than $^-3$.

Graph on a number line.

1. ⁻6

Count 6 places to the ■ of 0.

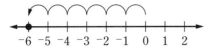

2. 5

Count 5 places to the ■ of 0.

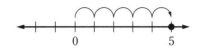

Compare. Use > or <.

3. ⁻7 and ⁻2

⁻7 is to the ■ of ⁻2 on the number line.

⁻7 is ■ than ⁻2.

⁻7 ■ ⁻2

4. 3 and ⁻5

3 is to the ■ of ⁻5 on the number line.

3 is ■ than ⁻5.

3 ■ ⁻5

Practice

Graph on a number line.

1. 2   **2.** ⁺5   **3.** ⁻7   **4.** ⁻1

5. 4   **6.** ⁻8   **7.** ⁻4   **8.** ⁻3

Compare. Use > or <.

9. 2 and ⁻1   **10.** ⁻4 and 0   **11.** ⁺3 and 4   **12.** ⁻8 and ⁻9

13. 1 and ⁻3   **14.** ⁻2 and 8   **15.** ⁻12 and 4   **16.** ⁻11 and 10

Do It Together!

17. Explain to a partner how to use a number line to compare the integers in number **9** in **Practice.**

18. Pick an integer between ⁻10 and 10. Have a partner graph the integer on a number line. Check the work.

1.2 Absolute Value

The **absolute value** of a number is its distance from 0.
Distance is never negative. It is zero or positive.

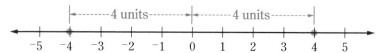

The absolute value of ⁻4 is 4. It is 4 units from 0.
The absolute value of ⁻4 is written as $|{}^-4|$.

The absolute value of 4 is 4. It is 4 units from 0.
The absolute value of 4 is written as $|4|$.

EXAMPLE 1 Find $|{}^-6|$.

⁻6 is 6 units from 0.

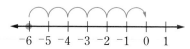

The absolute value of ⁻6 is 6.

EXAMPLE 2 Find $|0|$.

0 is 0 units from 0.

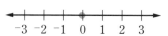

The absolute value of 0 is 0.

Opposites have the same absolute value. One is
positive and one is negative. The integers ⁻2 and 2 are
opposites.

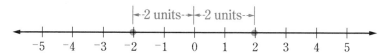

EXAMPLE 3 Find the opposite of ⁻3.

⁻3 is negative. The opposite is positive.

The opposite of ⁻3 is 3.

EXAMPLE 4 Find the opposite of 5.

5 is positive. The opposite is negative.

The opposite of 5 is ⁻5.

Find each absolute value.

1. $|8|$

8 is ■ units from 0.

$|8| = $ ■

2. $|{}^-12|$

$^-12$ is ■ units from 0.

$|12| = $ ■

Find the opposite of each integer.

3. $^-15$

$^-15$ is ■.

The opposite is ■.

The opposite of $^-15$ is ■.

4. 20

20 is ■.

The opposite is ■.

The opposite of 20 is ■.

Practice

Find the absolute value of each integer.

1. $|{}^-2|$ **2.** $|1|$ **3.** $|{}^-3|$ **4.** $|{}^-7|$

5. $|5|$ **6.** $|10|$ **7.** $|{}^-1|$ **8.** $|{}^-9|$

9. $|{}^-8|$ **10.** $|{}^+6|$ **11.** $|9|$ **12.** $|{}^-15|$

Find the opposite of each integer.

13. $^-5$ **14.** 10 **15.** 7 **16.** 4

17. $^-22$ **18.** 15 **19.** 0 **20.** $^-2$

Do It Together!

21. Explain to a partner how to use a number line to find the absolute value in number **4** in **Practice.**

22. Write a positive integer and a negative integer. Ask a partner to find the opposite of each. Check the work.

1.3 Addition

You can use a number line to add integers.
Move to the right to add positive numbers.

$$2 + 3 = 5$$

Move to the left to add negative numbers.

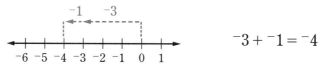

$$^-3 + {}^-1 = {}^-4$$

You can also add integers using absolute values.
When the signs of the integers are the same, add the
absolute values. The sign of the sum is the same as the
sign of the integers.

EXAMPLE 1   Add. $^-4 + {}^-2$

Find the absolute values. $|{}^-4| = 4$ $|{}^-2| = 2$
Add the absolute values. $4 + 2 = 6$
The sum is negative. $^-6$

$$^-4 + {}^-2 = {}^-6$$

When the signs of the integers are different, subtract
the smaller absolute value from the larger. Use the
sign of the integer with the larger absolute value.

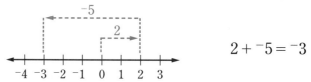

$$2 + {}^-5 = {}^-3$$

EXAMPLE 2   Add. $5 + {}^-7$

$^-7$ has the larger
absolute value.

Find the absolute values. $|5| = 5$ $|{}^-7| = 7$
Subtract the smaller from the larger. $7 - 5 = 2$
The sum is negative. $^-2$

$$5 + {}^-7 = {}^-2$$

Add.

1. $5 + {}^-5$

The signs are different.

Find the ■.

■ the absolute values.

Zero does not have a sign.

$5 + {}^-5 = $ ■

$5 + {}^-5$

$|5| = $ ■ $|{}^-5| = $ ■

$5 - 5 = $ ■

■

2. ${}^-3 + 4$

The signs are different.

Find the ■.

■ the absolute values.

■ has the larger absolute value.

${}^-3 + 4$

$|{}^-3| = $ ■ $|4| = $ ■

$4 - 3 = $ ■

${}^-3 + 4 = $ ■

Practice

Add.

1. $6 + {}^-3$

2. $4 + {}^-2$

3. ${}^-4 + {}^-5$

4. $8 + {}^-5$

5. $3 + {}^-9$

6. ${}^-5 + 7$

7. ${}^-1 + {}^-5$

8. ${}^-4 + 0$

9. $3 + 3$

10. $8 + {}^-8$

11. $0 + {}^-9$

12. ${}^-3 + {}^-2$

13. ${}^-4 + {}^-3$

14. ${}^-10 + 10$

15. ${}^-1 + 7$

Do It Together!

16. Explain to a partner how to add the integers in number **6** in **Practice.**

17. Write an addition problem with integers. Ask a partner to add the integers. Check the work with a number line.

1.4   Subtraction

You can use a number line to see how subtracting integers is like adding integers.

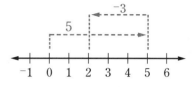

This shows the subtraction: $5 - 3 = 2$

This shows the addition: $5 + {}^-3 = 2$

3 is the opposite of ⁻3.

Subtracting 3 is the same as adding ⁻3.

Subtracting an integer is the same as adding its opposite. So, you can write all subtraction problems as addition.

EXAMPLE 1   Subtract. $^-2 - {}^-4$

Change to adding the opposite of ⁻4. $^-2 + {}^+4$

Find the absolute values. $|^-2| = 2 \quad |^+4| = 4$

Subtract the smaller from the larger. $4 - 2 = 2$

⁺4 has a larger absolute value. $^+2$

$^-2 - {}^-4 = 2$

EXAMPLE 2   Subtract. $^-3 - 6$

Change to adding the opposite of 6. $^-3 + {}^-6$

Find the absolute values. $|^-3| = 3 \quad |^-6| = 6$

Add the absolute values. $3 + 6 = 9$

⁻3 and ⁻6 are both negative. $^-9$

$^-3 - 6 = {}^-9$

EXAMPLE 3   Subtract. $5 - {}^-2$

Change to adding the opposite of ⁻2. $5 + {}^+2$

⁺2 is the same as 2.   **Add the integers.** $5 + 2 = 7$

$5 - {}^-2 = 7$

Subtract.

1. $^-1 - 4$

    Change to adding the opposite of 4. $^-1 + \blacksquare$

    Find the absolute values. $\left|^-1\right| = 1$
                                         $\left|^-4\right| = 4$

    $\blacksquare$ the absolute values. $4 \; \blacksquare \; 1 = \blacksquare$

    $^-1$ and $^-4$ are negative. $\blacksquare$

    $^-1 - 4 = \blacksquare$

2. $^-7 - \,^-3$

    Change to adding the opposite of $\blacksquare$. $^-7 + \blacksquare$

    Find the absolute values. $\left|^-7\right| = 7$
                                           $\left|\blacksquare\right| = 3$

    $\blacksquare$ the absolute values. $7 \; \blacksquare \; 3 = \blacksquare$

    $^-7$ has the larger absolute value. $\blacksquare$

    $^-7 - \,^-3 = \blacksquare$

Practice

Subtract.

1. $^-1 - \,^-3$ **2.** $6 - \,^-3$ **3.** $5 - 6$

4. $^-4 - \,^-5$ **5.** $8 - \,^-5$ **6.** $0 - 8$

7. $2 - \,^-4$ **8.** $^-3 - 1$ **9.** $4 - 6$

10. $7 - 7$ **11.** $0 - \,^-9$ **12.** $^-3 - \,^-11$

13. $^-10 - 13$ **14.** $^-20 - \,^-30$ **15.** $25 - \,^-25$

Do It Together!

16. Explain to a partner how to change the subtraction to addition in number **4** in **Practice.**

17. Write a negative and a positive number. Ask a partner to subtract the negative number from the positive number. Check your partner's work.

1.5 Multiplication

You can use repeated addition to multiply an integer by a whole number.

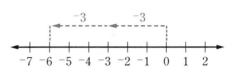

2(⁻3) means 2 times ⁻3.

Addition: $^-3 + ^-3 = ^-6$

Multiplication: $2(^-3) = ^-6$

The product of a positive and negative number is negative.

The product of two positive numbers is positive.
$(2)(3) = 6$

EXAMPLE 1   Multiply. $^-2 \bullet 4$

Find the absolute values.

Multiply the absolute values.

The product of a negative and a positive number is negative.

$^-2 \bullet 4 = ^-8$

$^-2 \bullet 4$
$|^-2| = 2 \quad |4| = 4$
$2 \bullet 4 = 8$

$^-2 \bullet 4 = ^-8$

Look at the pattern in these products to find the sign of the product of two negative numbers.

$$2 \bullet {}^-3 = {}^-6$$
$$1 \bullet {}^-3 = {}^-3$$
$$0 \bullet {}^-3 = 0$$
$${}^-1 \bullet {}^-3 = ?$$

$^-1 \bullet {}^-3$ is 3.

The product of two negative numbers is positive.

EXAMPLE 2   Multiply. $(^-4)(^-5)$

(⁻4)(⁻5) means ⁻4 times ⁻5.

Find the absolute values.

Multiply the absolute values.

The product of two negative numbers is positive.

$(^-4)(^-5) = 20$

$(^-4)(^-5)$
$|^-4| = 4 \quad |^-5| = 5$
$4 \bullet 5 = 20$

$(^-4)(^-5) = {}^+20$

Multiply.

1. $(^-7)(^-3)$

Multiply the absolute values.

The product of two negative numbers is ■.

$7 \bullet 3 = ■$

$(^-7)(^-3) = ■$

$(^-7)(^-3) = ■$

2. $^-4 \bullet 8$

Multiply the ■.

The product of a negative number and a ■ is ■.

$4 \bullet 8 = ■$

$^-4 \bullet 8 = ■$

$^-4 \bullet 8 = ■$

3. $(5)(^-6)$

Multiply the ■.

The product of a ■ and a negative number is ■.

$5 \bullet ■ = ■$

$(5)(^-6) = ■$

$(5)(^-6) = ■$

4. $(^-3)(0)$

Multiply the ■.

■ does not have a sign.

$■ \bullet 0 = ■$

$(^-3)(0) = ■$

$(^-3)(0) = ■$

Practice

Multiply.

1. $3 \bullet 5$

2. $(2)(^-5)$

3. $^-1 \bullet ^-7$

4. $(^-4)(^-3)$

5. $6 \bullet 3$

6. $^-6 \bullet 4$

7. $(9)(^-5)$

8. $^-2 \bullet 10$

9. $1 \bullet 6$

10. $2 \bullet ^-8$

11. $(^-9)(^-2)$

12. $^-11 \bullet 3$

13. $4 \bullet ^-7$

14. $9 \bullet 3$

15. $(^-10)(^-20)$

Do It Together!

16. Explain to a partner how to find the product in number **11** in **Practice.**

17. Write a positive number and a negative number. Have a partner find the product of the numbers. Check the work.

1.6 Division

You can use what you know about multiplying integers to divide integers.

$$(^+2)(^+3) = {}^+6 \quad \rightarrow \quad (^+6) \div (^+3) = {}^+2$$
$$(^+2)(^-3) = {}^-6 \quad \rightarrow \quad (^-6) \div (^-3) = {}^+2$$

The quotient of two negative numbers is positive.

EXAMPLE 1 Divide. $^-12 \div ^-4$

Find the absolute values. $\quad |^-12| = 12 \quad |^-4| = 4$

Divide the absolute values. $\quad 12 \div 4 = 3$

The quotient of two negative numbers is positive. $\quad {}^+3$

$$^-12 \div ^-4 = 3$$

Look at these products and quotients to find the sign of the quotient of a positive and negative number.

$$(^-2)(^-3) = {}^+6 \quad \rightarrow \quad (^+6) \div (^-3) = {}^-2$$
$$(^-2)(^+3) = {}^-6 \quad \rightarrow \quad (^-6) \div (^+3) = {}^-2$$

The quotient of a positive and a negative number is negative.

EXAMPLE 2 Divide. $\dfrac{^-49}{7}$

$\dfrac{^-49}{7}$ means $^-49 \div 7$.

Find the absolute values. $\quad |^-49| = 49 \quad |7| = 7$

Divide the absolute values. $\quad 49 \div 7 = 7$

The quotient of a positive integer and a negative integer is negative. $\quad \dfrac{^-49}{7} = {}^-7$

$$\dfrac{^-49}{7} = {}^-7$$

There are important and helpful facts to know when using division.

$\dfrac{0}{2}$ means $0 \div 2$.

Zero divided by any number is 0. $\quad \dfrac{0}{2} = 0$

You cannot divide by 0. $\quad \dfrac{3}{0}$ has no answer.

Any number divided by itself is 1. $\quad \dfrac{5}{5} = 1$

Divide.

1. $^-27 \div {}^-9$

Divide the absolute values.

$27 \div \blacksquare = \blacksquare$

The quotient of two negative numbers is $\blacksquare$.

$^-27 \div {}^-9 = \blacksquare$

$^-27 \div {}^-9 = \blacksquare$

2. $\frac{0}{23}$

Zero divided by a number is $\blacksquare$.

$\frac{0}{23} = \blacksquare$

$\frac{0}{23} = \blacksquare$

3. $24 \div {}^-6$

Divide the $\blacksquare$.

$\blacksquare \div \blacksquare = \blacksquare$

The quotient of a $\blacksquare$ number and a negative number is negative.

$24 \div {}^-6 = \blacksquare$

$24 \div {}^-6 = \blacksquare$

4. $\frac{-30}{5}$

Divide the $\blacksquare$.

$\blacksquare \div \blacksquare = \blacksquare$

The quotient of a negative number and a positive number is $\blacksquare$.

$\frac{-30}{5} = \blacksquare$

$\frac{-30}{5} = \blacksquare$

Practice

Divide.

1. $\frac{25}{5}$

2. $24 \div {}^-3$

3. $^-10 \div 10$

4. $^-9 \div 3$

5. $0 \div {}^-11$

6. $\frac{28}{-7}$

7. $\frac{32}{8}$

8. $\frac{-18}{0}$

9. $\frac{-8}{-4}$

10. $^-9 \div {}^-9$

11. $^-12 \div 4$

12. $72 \div 9$

13. $42 \div 0$

14. $\frac{-56}{8}$

15. $\frac{-24}{4}$

16. $\frac{-30}{-2}$

Do It Together!

17. Explain to a partner how to find the quotient in number **14** in **Practice.**

18. Pick an even number. Ask a partner to find the quotient of the even number divided by $^-2$.

1.7 More Adding and Subtracting Integers

A group of numbers written with operation signs, is called an **expression.** You **simplify** an expression when you do the addition, subtraction, multiplication, or division.

You can use the rules that you know about adding and subtracting to add and subtract more than two integers. Change subtraction to addition and add in groups of two.

EXAMPLE 1   Simplify. $^-28 + {}^-2 + 15$

Add $^-28$ and $^-2$.

Add $^-30$ and 15.

$$\underbrace{{}^-28 + {}^-2} + 15$$
$$\underbrace{{}^-30 + 15}$$
$${}^-15$$

$$^-28 + {}^-2 + 15 = {}^-15$$

EXAMPLE 2   Simplify. $^-3 - 7 + 8$

Rewrite subtraction as addition.

Add $^-3$ and $^-7$.

Add $^-10$ and 8.

$$\underbrace{{}^-3 + {}^-7} + 8$$
$$\underbrace{{}^-10 + 8}$$
$${}^-2$$

$$^-3 - 7 + 8 = {}^-2$$

Sometimes a minus sign is used in place of a plus sign and negative sign that are next to each other.

$$^-5 + {}^-8 = {}^-13$$
$$^-5 - 8 = {}^-13$$

Both mean $^-5$ plus $^-8$ equals $^-13$.

EXAMPLE 3   Simplify. $^-8 + 10 - 12$

Add $^-8$ and 10.

2 − 12 means 2 + (−12).   Add 2 and $^-12$.

$$\underbrace{{}^-8 + 10} - 12$$
$$\underbrace{2 - 12}$$
$${}^-10$$

$$^-8 + 10 - 12 = {}^-10$$

Simplify each expression.

1. $^-6 - {^-2} + 10$

    Rewrite as ■. $^-6 ■ 2 + 10$

    Add.   ■ $+ 10$

                          ■

    $^-6 - {^-2} + 10 = ■$

2. $^-11 - 15 + 6$

    Add $^-11$ and $^-15$. $^-11 + ■ + 6$

    Add $^-26$ and 6.   ■ $+ 6$

                          ■

    $^-11 - 15 + 6 = ■$

3. $^-5 - 15$

    Add $^-5$ and $^-15$. $^-5 + ■$

                          ■

    $^-5 - 15 = ■$

4. $^-12 - 8 + 14$

    Add $^-12$ and ■. $^-12 - 8 + 14$

    Add ■ and 14.   ■ $+ 14$

                          ■

    $^-12 - 8 + 14 = ■$

Practice

Simplify.

1. $2 - {^-3} + 10$

2. $^-5 - 1 + 6$

3. $6 - {^-10} + {^-4}$

4. $8 - 17 - 8$

5. $^-4 - {^-3} + {^-1}$

6. $^-3 + 9 - 12$

7. $^-8 + {^-8} - 16$

8. $0 + {^-5} - 3$

9. $^-5 - {^-12} - 16$

10. $^-3 + 10 - 9$

11. $^-7 - 4 + 11$

12. $^-8 - 4 + {^-10}$

13. $^-8 + 14$

14. $^-5 + 5$

15. $^-3 - 3$

16. $4 - 10 - 26$

17. $^-16 + 9 - 5$

18. $25 - 12 - 13$

Do It Together!

19. Explain to a partner how to simplify the expression in number **5** in **Practice.**

20. Write an expression adding two negative numbers. Have a partner simplify the expression. Check the work.

1.8 Exponents

There is a shorter way to show multiplication when the factors are the same.

$$4 \bullet 4 \bullet 4 = 4^3$$

base 4 is a factor
3 times

exponent
↓
$4^3 = 64$ ← power
↑
base

In 4^3, 4 is the **base,** and 3 is the **exponent.** The exponent tells how many times the base is used as a factor. The exponent also tells the **power** of the base. 64 is the third power of 4. You can use other numbers as exponents. Read these examples.

$$4^1 = 4 \qquad \qquad \text{4 is a factor 1 time.}$$
$$4^2 = 4 \bullet 4 = 16 \qquad \text{4 is a factor 2 times.}$$

EXAMPLE 1   Find the power. 6^2

Use 6 as a factor 2 times.

Multiply.

$6^2 = 36$

6^2
$6 \bullet 6$
36

Watch for the sign of the base. Parentheses are used to show the base.

$$-2^3 \qquad \qquad (-12)^2$$
$$\text{2 is the base.} \qquad -12 \text{ is the base.}$$

EXAMPLE 2   Find the power. -2^3

Use 2 as a factor 3 times.

Multiply.

$-2^3 = -8$

$-(2)^3$
$-(2 \bullet 2 \bullet 2)$
-8

EXAMPLE 3   Find the power. $(-12)^2$

The product of two negative numbers is positive.

Use -12 as a factor 2 times.

Multiply.

$(-12)^2 = 144$

$(-12)^2$
$(-12)(-12)$
144

Find the power.

1. $(-5)^3$

Use -5 as a factor ■ times.

Multiply.

$(-5)^3$

$(-5) \cdot (■) \cdot (■)$
■

$(-5)^3 = ■$

2. 3^4

Use ■ as a factor 4 times.

Multiply.

3^4

$■ \cdot ■ \cdot ■ \cdot ■$
■

$3^4 = ■$

Practice

Find the power.

1. 6^2	**2.** 8^2	**3.** 2^3	**4.** 5^3
5. -13^2	**6.** 50^2	**7.** $(-30)^3$	**8.** 5^4
9. 9^4	**10.** -10^4	**11.** $(-4)^2$	**12.** $(-11)^2$
13. $-(3)^3$	**14.** $(-7)^2$	**15.** $(-4)^3$	**16.** $(-10)^4$
17. 4^3	**18.** $-(5)^2$	**19.** $(-1)^4$	**20.** $(-1)^3$

Do It Together!

21. Explain to a partner how to find the power in number **10** in **Practice.**

22. Write a power with a negative number as the base and a positive number as the exponent. Make sure you use parentheses to show the base. Have a partner find the power. Check the work.

1.9 Calculator: Performing Operations

You can use a calculator to perform operations with positive and negative numbers. Follow the same rules you learned for adding, subtracting, multiplying, and dividing integers.

EXAMPLE 1   Add. $-53.62 + 180.8$

Find the absolute values.
$$|-53.62| = 53.62$$
$$|180.8| = 180.8$$

Subtract the smaller absolute value from the larger. $180.8 - 53.62$ **DISPLAY**

Enter 180.8 by pressing: [1][8][0][.][8]   180.8

Subtract 53.62 by pressing: [−][5][3][.][6][2][=]   127.18

The number with the larger absolute value is positive.

$$-53.62 + 180.8 = 127.18$$

EXAMPLE 2   Divide. $\dfrac{546}{-13}$

Find the absolute values.
$$|546| = 546$$
$$|-13| = 13$$

Divide the absolute values. $546 \div 13$ **DISPLAY**

Enter 546 by pressing: [5][4][6]   546

Divide by 13 by pressing: [÷][1][3][=]   42

The quotient of a positive number and a negative number is negative.

$$\frac{546}{-13} = -42$$

EXAMPLE 3   Subtract. $30 - 45$ **DISPLAY**

Enter 30 by pressing: [3][0]   30

Subtract 45 by pressing: [−][4][5][=]   -15

$$30 - 45 = -15$$

Practice

Use your calculator. Find the sum, difference, product, or quotient.

1. $-125 - 159$

2. $99 + (-54)$

3. $-100 + 76$

4. $-231 + 149$

5. $\frac{-598}{-23}$

6. $(-29)(-57)$

7. $-23(71)$

8. $\frac{-247}{13}$

MATH CONNECTION

Elevation

One way to describe a place is by its elevation. This tells how high a place is above *sea level*. Sea level is where the land meets the sea. Elevation can also tell you how far a place is below sea level.

Elevation can be shown on a map. At sea level, it is zero elevation. Like the points on a number line, elevation tells the distance from zero. Heights above sea level are like the positive numbers. Distances below sea level are like the negative numbers. Both tell the distance from zero, but in different directions.

The tallest mountain in the world is Mount Everest. It is 29,028 feet above sea level at the top. The floors of the oceans have deep trenches. Some trenches are more than 35,000 feet below sea level.

Elevation can affect how you live. In higher places, the air is thinner. If you go from a lower to a higher place, you might feel some changes. Your ears might "pop." You might find it hard to breathe, at first. You could even have trouble baking a cake! Knowing about elevation helps people adjust to these changes no matter where they live.

1.10 Problem Solving: Guess, Check, Revise

You can guess an answer to a problem and check to see if the guess is the correct answer. If the guess is not correct, **revise** or change your guess until you get the right answer.

EXAMPLE 1   José drove a total of 80 miles in two days. He drove 20 miles less on the first day than on the second day. How many miles did José drive on each day?

Guess for second day: 60
José drove 20 miles less on the first day. $60 - 20 = 40$
Check: **60 + 40 = 100** $100 > 80$
60 is too big!

Revise guess for second day: 40
Subtract 20 to find the miles on the first day. $40 - 20 = 20$
Check: **40 + 20 = 60** $60 < 80$
40 is too small.

Revise guess for second day: 50
Subtract 20 to find the miles on the first day. $50 - 20 = 30$
Check: **50 + 30 = 80** $80 = 80$
Correct!

José drove 30 miles on the first day and 50 miles on the second day.

EXAMPLE 2   The sum of the temperatures on Tuesday and Wednesday was $-8°$. The temperature was $-12°$ on Tuesday. What was the temperature on Wednesday?

Guess for Wednesday: 6°

Sum means add.

Check: **−12 + 6 = −6** $-6 > -8$
6 is too big.

Revise guess for Wednesday: 4°
Check: **−12 + 4 = −8** $-8 = -8$
Correct!

The temperature on Wednesday was $4°$.

1. Sue buys a shirt and jeans for $42.00. The jeans cost $14.00 more than the shirt. How much does each cost?

   Guess for shirt: $15
   Jeans cost $14 more: ■.
   Check: $15 + $29 = $44   Too big, but close!
   Revise guess for shirt: $14
   Jeans cost $14 more: ■.
   Check: $14 + ■ = $42   Correct!

   So, the jeans cost ■ and the shirt costs ■.

2. The product of two integers is 32. One integer is twice the other. What are the integers?

   Guess for first integer: 3
   Second integer is twice the first: ■.
   Check: 3 • ■ = 18   Too small!
   Revise guess for integer: 4
   Second integer: ■.
   Check: 4 • ■ = 32   Correct!

   So, the integers are ■ and ■.

Practice

Guess, check, and revise to solve each problem.

1. Alexandra put some money in her savings account in July. She put three times that amount into her savings account in August. She saved a total of $140.00 in July and August. How much did she save each month?

2. The sum of two integers is 9. The product of the integers is 14. What are the integers?

3. The drama club sold 240 tickets for admission to the play. They sold 20 more student tickets than adult tickets. How many of each type of ticket did they sell?

Do It Together!

4. Explain to a partner how to find the integers in number **2** in **Practice.**

5. Write a problem about the product of two integers. Make one integer three times the other. Find the product of the two integers. Ask a partner to find the two integers by looking only at the product.

1.11 Application: Information from Broken-Line Graphs

Information from graphs can be used to solve problems. The graph below is a **broken-line graph.** It shows a company's earnings over 6 months.

Negative earnings mean money lost.

Months	Earnings
January	5
February	6
March	−8
April	−6
May	−2
June	4

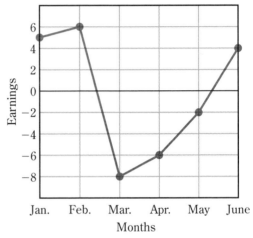

Earnings Over Six Months in Thousands of Dollars

EXAMPLE 1   What were the company's earnings in May?

Find the point above May.

Read across to the number to the left.   −2

The company's earnings were −$2,000 in May.
The company lost money in May.

EXAMPLE 2   Which month had the highest earnings?

Find the highest point.   The highest point is above February.

Find the earnings for February.

Read across to the number to the left.   6

The highest earnings were in February.
The company earned $6,000.

Use the graph about earnings to answer the questions.

1. Which month had the lowest earnings?

The lowest point is above ■.

Read across to the number to the left.   ■

■ has the lowest earnings.
Earnings were −$■,000.

2. What is the difference between the highest earnings and lowest earnings?

Find the highest point.   ■

Find the lowest point.   ■

Subtract.   ■ − ■

The difference between the highest and lowest earnings is $■,000.

Practice

Use this graph to answer the questions.

  1. Which month had the highest temperature?

  2. Which had the lowest?

  3. How much higher is the temperature in December than in February?

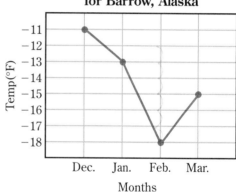

Monthly Normal Temperatures for Barrow, Alaska

Do It Together!

  4. Explain to a partner how to use the graph to answer number **3** in **Practice.**

  5. Ask a partner to find the total of the normal temperatures. Check the work.

Chapter 1 Summary

- Positive numbers are to the right of zero on the number line.
- Negative numbers are to the left of zero on the number line.
- The absolute value of a number is its distance from zero. Opposites have the same absolute value.
- To add two integers with the same sign, add their absolute values. Use the sign of the integers as the sign of the sum.
- To add integers with different signs, subtract the absolute values. Use the sign of the integer with the larger absolute value as the sign of the sum.
- To subtract an integer, add its opposite.
- The product or quotient of a positive integer and a negative integer is negative. The product or quotient of two negative integers is positive.
- You can use a calculator to perform operations.
- Guess, check, and revise is a way to solve problems.
- You can use a broken-line graph to find information.

Reviewing Vocabulary

Fill in each blank with the correct word.

positive numbers
negative numbers
integers
absolute value
opposites
expression
simplify
exponent
base
power
revise
broken-line graph

1. In 3^2, 3 is called the ?.
2. The ? are the numbers to the right of zero.
3. When you change a guess, you ?.
4. ? are the same distance from zero on opposite sides.
5. The ? are the numbers to the left of zero.
6. The distance of a number from 0 is called the ?.
7. The ? tells how many times the base is a factor.
8. A ? is a graph that is made up of pieces of straight lines.
9. The numbers ... $^-3, ^-2, ^-1, 0, 1, 2, 3, ...$ are ?.
10. Numbers with operation signs make an ?.
11. A ? is the result of multiplying when factors are the same.
12. To ? an expression, you perform the operations.

Chapter Quiz

Graph on a number line.

1. $^-5$ **2.** 3 **3.** $^-1$

Compare. Use > or < .

4. $^-10$ and $^-8$ **5.** 4 and $^-5$ **6.** 2 and 9

Find the absolute value of each integer.

7. $|7|$ **8.** $|^-10|$ **9.** $|0|$

Find the opposite of each integer.

10. $^+6$ **11.** $^-12$ **12.** 8

Simplify.

13. $^-5 + {}^-7$ **14.** $8 + {}^-10$ **15.** $^-2 - {}^-5$

16. $^-5 + 9$ **17.** $(^-2)(^-6)$ **18.** $(3)(^-9)$

19. $^-27 \div 3$ **20.** $^-6 \div {}^-6$ **21.** $(^-4)^2$

22. $^-5 + 9 - 14$ **23.** $^-2 - 2 - 4$ **24.** $9 - 15 + 6$

Guess, check, and revise to solve this problem.

25. The sum of two integers is 9 and their product is 18. What are the integers?

Use the graph of Alex's savings to answer the question.

26. How much more money did Alex have in savings in August than in June?

Six Months of Savings

Chapter 2

Tools for Algebra

Music uses tools and skills. To play an instrument, you learn how to read notes and keep a beat. Like music, algebra uses tools and skills. Algebra has its own symbols and rules that you will learn how to use.

Chapter Learning Objectives

- Simplify number expressions.
- Simplify variable expressions.
- Evaluate variable expressions.
- Identify an equation as *true* or *false*.
- Use a calculator to evaluate variable expressions.
- Solve problems by writing equations for word statements.
- Apply concepts and skills to using geometry formulas.

Words to Know

variable   a letter that represents a number

terms   parts of an expression separated by a + or − sign

constants   numbers, or quantities, that do not change

coefficient   a number that multiplies a variable

like terms   terms that have the same variables with the same exponents

evaluate   find the value of an expression

substitute   replace a variable with a number or expression

equivalent   having the same value; equal

equation   a statement that two expressions are equal

Commutative Property   the order of two numbers does not matter when you add or multiply

Associative Property   you can add or multiply more than two numbers in groups of two in any order

Identity Property   adding 0, or multiplying by 1, does not change a number

Addition Property of Opposites   the sum of a number and its opposite is 0

Zero Property of Multiplication   the product of any number and 0 is 0

Distributive Property   multiply a sum or difference by a number by multiplying each term of the sum or difference by the number

---

In this chapter, you will find the value of number expressions and variable expressions. You will learn about equations and properties of operations. You will see how to use a calculator to evaluate expressions. Writing equations from words is an important problem-solving skill. You will apply your skills to using geometry formulas.

2.1 Order of Operations

Numbers and operation signs are used to write expressions. You simplify an expression when you perform the operations and find the value. When there is more than one operation, you must follow the Order of Operations.

1. First, multiply and divide from left to right.
2. Then, add and subtract from left to right.

EXAMPLE 1 Simplify. $16 - 6 \bullet 2$

Multiply first. $16 - \underbrace{6 \bullet 2}$

Subtract next. $\underbrace{16 - 12}$

4

The value of $16 - 6 \bullet 2$ is 4.

EXAMPLE 2 Simplify. $2 + 12 \div 4 - 10$

Divide first. $2 + \underbrace{12 \div 4} - 10$

Add. $\underbrace{2 + 3} - 10$

Subtract. $\underbrace{5 - 10}$

-5

The value of $2 + 12 \div 4 - 10$ is -5.

Sometimes an expression contains a power. Find the value of the power first.

EXAMPLE 3 Simplify. $3 + 8 \div 2^2$

2^2 means $2 \bullet 2$.

Find the value of the power. $3 + 8 \div 2^2$

Divide. $3 + \underbrace{8 \div 4}$

Add. $\underbrace{3 + 2}$

5

The value of $3 + 8 \div 2^2$ is 5.

Simplify.

1. $3 \bullet 4 + 16 \div 2$

■ first.	$3 \bullet 4 + 16 \div 2$
Divide next.	$■ + 16 \div 2$
Add.	$■ + ■$
	$■$

The value of $3 \bullet 4 + 16 \div 2$ is ■.

2. $8 - 3^2$

Find the value of the ■.	$8 - 3^2$
Subtract.	$8 - ■$
	$■$

The value of $8 - 3^2$ is ■.

Practice

Simplify.

1. $3 \bullet 1 + 4$

2. $8 \div 4 + 4 \bullet 2$

3. $5 + 8 \bullet 3 + 2$

4. $14 \div 7 + 3$

5. $2 \bullet 4 - 9$

6. $10 \bullet 3 + 1 - 16$

7. $2 + 3^2$

8. $32 - 30 \div 10$

9. $-2 + 3 - 6 + 2$

10. $28 \div 7 \bullet 2$

11. $10 - 5 \bullet 3$

12. $10 \div 2 + 8$

13. $30 + 5 \div 5$

14. $9 + 15 \div 15 - 10$

15. $15 - 2 \bullet 2$

16. $2 + 12 \bullet 2 \div 6$

17. $5 \bullet 4 \div 2^2$

18. $24 - 25 \div 5^2$

19. $-9 \div 3 + 4 \bullet 7$

20. $5 + 2 \bullet 4^2 - 25$

21. $24 \div 4 - 6$

Do It Together!

22. Explain to a partner how to simplify the expression in number **16** in **Practice.**

23. Work with a partner to simplify $9 \bullet 5 \div 15 - 3$. Take turns doing the steps. Check each other's work.

2.2   Grouping Symbols

Sometimes, expressions contain parentheses. Be sure to do the operations inside the parentheses first.

EXAMPLE 1   Simplify. $4 \cdot (7-3)$

Do the subtraction in parentheses first. $4 \cdot \underbrace{(7-3)}$

Multiply. $\underbrace{4 \cdot 4}$

16

$4 \cdot (7-3)$ is 16.

EXAMPLE 2   Simplify. $2^3 - (2 \cdot 3) - 6$

Do the multiplication in parentheses first. $2^3 - \underbrace{(2 \cdot 3)} - 6$

2^3 means $2 \cdot 2 \cdot 2$.

Find the value of the power. $2^3 - 6 - 6$

Subtract from left to right. $\underbrace{8 - 6} - 6$

$2 - 6$ is the same as $2 + (-6)$.

$\underbrace{2 - 6}$

-4

$2^3 - (2 \cdot 3) - 6$ is -4.

EXAMPLE 3   Simplify. $(4+5) \div 3^2$

Do the addition in parentheses first. $\underbrace{(4+5)} \div 3^2$

3^2 means $3 \cdot 3$.

Find the value of the power. $9 \div 3^2$

Divide. $\underbrace{9 \div 9}$

1

$(4+5) \div 3^2$ is 1.

EXAMPLE 4   Simplify. $-(3-8) - 9$

Do the subtraction in parentheses first. $-\underbrace{(3-8)} - 9$

$-(-5) - 9$

$-(-5)$ means $-1(-5)$.

Multiply. $\underbrace{-1(-5)} - 9$

Subtract. $\underbrace{5 - 9}$

-4

$-(3-8) - 9$ is -4.

Simplify.

1. $20 - (8 - 4) \div 2$

Do ■ in parentheses.	$20 - (8 - 4) \div 2$
Divide.	$20 - \ \blacksquare \div 2$
Subtract.	$20 - \ \blacksquare$
	$\blacksquare$

$20 - (8 - 4) \div 2$ is ■.

2. $2^3 - (2 + 6)$

Do ■ in parentheses.	$2^3 - (2 + 6)$
Find the value of the ■.	$2^3 - \ \blacksquare$
Subtract.	$\blacksquare - \ \blacksquare$
	$\blacksquare$

$2^3 - (2 + 6)$ is ■.

Practice

Simplify.

1. $(5 + 3) \bullet 2$

2. $6 \div (6 - 3)$

3. $3(2 + 7) - 7$

4. $10 \div (5 \bullet 2)$

5. $12 + 2(9 - 5)$

6. $-6(1 - 3)$

7. $(9 - 5) \div 2$

8. $3^2 \div (4 - 3)$

9. $(5 - 6) \bullet 3$

10. $2(7 - 3)$

11. $-(4 - 6)$

12. $2^3(3 - 2)$

13. $3(4 + 6) \div 5$

14. $(4 + 16) \div 5 \bullet 2$

15. $14 - (8 - 4)$

16. $3(2 - 6) \div 2$

17. $9 - (4 - 2)$

18. $-2(3 \bullet 3)$

19. $4^2 - 3(2 + 1)$

20. $(12 - 8) \div 2 \bullet 3$

21. $4^3 \div 8(12 - 11)$

Do It Together!

22. Listen while a partner explains how to simplify the expression in number **13** in **Practice.** Follow the steps as your partner explains.

23. Simplify $6 - 4 \div 2$. Have a partner simplify $(6 - 4) \div 2$. Compare your answers. Why are they different?

2.3 Variable Expressions

A **variable** is a letter that stands for a number. Any letter can stand for any number. The letter t could be used to stand for a time like 4 hours, 8 hours, or any time.

You can write expressions with variables, operations, and numbers. The variable expressions below contain addition and subtraction.

$$4+t \qquad\qquad t-5 \qquad\qquad t+h$$

You can show multiplication in different ways.

$$3 \text{ times } a \rightarrow 3 \times a \quad \text{or} \quad 3 \bullet a \quad \text{or} \quad 3a \quad \text{or} \quad 3(a)$$
$$c \text{ times } d \rightarrow c \times d \quad \text{or} \quad c \bullet d \quad \text{or} \quad cd \quad \text{or} \quad c(d)$$

Show division with a fraction bar or a division sign.

$$4x \text{ divided by } 5 \rightarrow \frac{4x}{5} \quad \text{or} \quad 4x \div 5$$

EXAMPLE 1 Complete. xy means x ? y

xy means x times y.

xy means $x \bullet y$.

xy means x ? y

xy means $x \bullet y$

EXAMPLE 2 Complete. $3s^2$ means 3 ? s ? s

$3s^2$ means 3 times s^2.

s^2 means s times s.

$3s^2$ means $3 \bullet s \bullet s$.

$3s^2$ means 3 ? s^2

$3s^2$ means $3 \bullet s^2$

$3s^2$ means $3 \bullet s \bullet s$

EXAMPLE 3 Complete. $\dfrac{3x}{2}$ means 3 ? x ? 2

$3x$ means 3 times x.

$\dfrac{3x}{2}$ means $3x$ divided by 2.

$\dfrac{3x}{2}$ means $3 \bullet x \div 2$.

$\dfrac{3x}{2}$ means 3 ? x ? 2

$\dfrac{3x}{2}$ means $3 \bullet x$? 2

$\dfrac{3x}{2}$ means $3 \bullet x \div 2$

Complete. Replace ? with $+, -, \bullet$, or $\div$.

1. ab^2 means a ? b ? b.
ab^2 means a ■ b^2.
ab^2 means a ■ b ■ b.

2. $\dfrac{7a}{8} + 3$ means 7 ? a ? 8 ? 3.
$7a$ means 7 ■ a.
$\dfrac{7a}{8}$ means 7 ■ a ■ 8.
$\dfrac{7a}{8} + 3$ means 7 ■ a ■ 8 ■ 3.

Practice

Complete. Replace ? with $+, -, \bullet$, or $\div$.

1. $3y$ means 3 ? y.

2. $\dfrac{k}{4}$ means k ? 4.

3. $4b - 3$ means 4 ? b ? 3.

4. $7a^2$ means 7 ? a ? a.

5. $2d + 9$ means 2 ? d ? 9.

6. $3a^2 + 1$ means 3 ? a ? a? 1.

7. r^3 means r ? r ? r.

8. $-8n + 3$ means -8 ? n ? 3.

9. $\dfrac{2m}{4}$ means 2 ? m ? 4.

10. $3x^2 - 1$ means 3 ? x ? x ? 1.

11. $a + 4b$ means a ? 4 ? b.

12. $pq - 3$ means p ? q ? 3.

13. $\dfrac{6x}{y}$ means 6 ? x ? y.

14. $-6 + 3w$ means -6 ? 3 ? w.

15. $2x^2 + 3y$ means 2 ? x ? x ? 3 ? y.

16. $-8a - 2b^2$ means -8 ? a ? 2 ? b? b.

Do It Together!

17. Explain to a partner how to complete number **10** in **Practice**.

18. Write a variable expression using addition and multiplication. Have a partner write the meaning. Check the work.

2.4 Like Terms

The different parts of an expression are called the **terms** of an expression. They are the parts separated by addition or subtraction. Numbers alone are called **constants.**

$-4xy$	$x^2 - 16$	$-4y + 6x - xy$
one term	two terms	three terms

EXAMPLE 1   Name the terms and constant in $4x - 2x + 7$.

4x − 2x is the same as 4x + (−2x).

Look for the parts separated by + or −. $4x - 2x + 7$

There are three terms: $4x$, $-2x$, and 7.
7 is a constant.

A **coefficient** is a number that multiplies a variable.

$3x \rightarrow$	$3 \bullet x$	3 is the coefficient of x.
$a^2 \rightarrow$	$1 \bullet a^2$	1 is the coefficient of a^2.
$-y \rightarrow$	$-1 \bullet y$	-1 is the coefficient of y.

EXAMPLE 2   Name the coefficients in $3x^2 - x + 4$.

−x means −1 • x.

Look for the numbers that multiply variables. $3x^2 - 1x + 4$

The coefficients are 3 and -1.

Like terms have the same variables with the same exponents. All numbers are like terms.

yx is the same as xy.

Like terms	Unlike terms
$3xy$ and $-yx$	x and y
$4a$ and $3a$	a and ab
$-5x^2$ and $2x^2$	x and x^2

EXAMPLE 3   Are $3x^2y$ and yx^2 like or unlike?

Same variables with same exponents $3x^2y$ and yx^2

$3x^2y$ and yx^2 are like terms.

1. Name the terms in
$y^3 + 8x^2 - x + 12$.

Look for the parts separated by + or −.
There are ■ terms: ■, $8x^2$, ■, and 12.

2. Name the coefficients in
$5y - 10x + 3z$

Look for the numbers that ■ variables.
■ is the coefficient of y.
■ is the coefficient of x.
■ is the coefficient of z.

Are the terms like or unlike?

3. $-cd$ and $5dc$

Same variables with same exponents.
$-cd$ and $5dc$ are ■ terms.

4. $2p^3$ and $2p^4$

Variables have different exponents.
$2p^3$ and $2p^4$ are ■ terms.

Practice

Name the terms in each expression.

1. $3n + 4p + 2$

2. $-g^2 + 8k + 9$

3. $7a^3 b^2 c$

Name the coefficients in each expression.

4. $3a$

5. $x - 7y + 8$

6. $-ab + 9a$

7. $-2a^2 + 3a$

8. $y^2 - 2y - 15$

9. $x^2 + 2xy + y^2$

Are the terms like or unlike?

10. $3n$ and $3n^2$

11. $12wc$ and $12cw$

12. 10 and -2

Do It Together!

13. Explain to a partner how to decide if the terms are like or unlike in number **7** in **Practice.**

14. Write a variable expression with like terms. Have a partner name the terms, the coefficients, and the like terms. Check the work.

2.5 Combining Like Terms

You can simplify variable expressions by combining terms. You can only combine like terms.

$$\underbrace{2a}_{a+a} + \underbrace{3a}_{a+a+a} = \underbrace{5a}_{a+a+a+a+a}$$

So, $2a + 3a = 5a$

You combine like terms by adding the coefficients. For number terms, just add or subtract the numbers.

EXAMPLE 1 Simplify. $5n + n$

Look for like terms. $5n + n$

n means 1 • n.   **Add the coefficients.** $5n + \underbrace{1n}$
                                                              $6n$

$5n + n$ is the same as $6n$.

Sometimes, you need to combine more than two terms. Combine them two at a time. Combine all like terms in an expression.

EXAMPLE 2 Simplify. $6x^2 + x^2 - 9x^2$

Look for like terms. $6x^2 + x^2 - 9x^2$

Add the coefficients. $6\underbrace{x^2 + 1x^2} - 9x^2$
                                                  $\underbrace{7x^2 - 9x^2}$
                                                      $-2x^2$

$6x^2 + x^2 - 9x^2$ is the same as $-2x^2$

Some expressions contain like terms and unlike terms. Be sure to combine only the like terms.

EXAMPLE 3 Simplify. $3x - 6x - 2y + 8y$

Look for like terms. $3x - 6x - 2y + 8y$

$3x - 6x$ means $3x + (-6x)$. **Add the coefficients.** $\underbrace{3x - 6x}\underbrace{- 2y + 8y}$

−3x and 6y are unlike terms. $-3x \quad + \quad 6y$

$3x - 6x - 2y + 8y$ is the same as $-3x + 6y$.

Simplify by combining like terms.

1. $8x - 2x$

    Look for ■. $8x - 2x$

    Combine the coefficients. $8x - 2x$

                                    ■

2. $5y - 10y + 3y$

    Look for ■. $5y - 10y + 3y$

    Combine the coefficients.   ■ $+ 3y$

                                     ■

3. $7a - a - 9 - 5$

    Look for like terms. $7a - a - 9 - 5$

    Combine the $7a - 1a - 9 - 5$

    coefficients.

                             ■ $-$ ■

4. $c^2 + c^2 + c$

    Look for ■. $c^2 + c^2 + c$

    Combine the coefficients. $1c^2 + 1c^2 + c$

                                     ■ $+ c$

Practice

Simplify.

1. $3x^3 + 7x^3$

2. $12n - 2n$

3. $-5b - 6b$

4. $a + a + 2a$

5. $-7a + 10a$

6. $6x^2 - 8x^2$

7. $r + 2r + 3s$

8. $-4p^2 - 3p^2 + 5q + 2q$

9. $-5x + x + 8y^2 - 6y^2$

10. $4r - 3r$

11. $-6a + 2a + 5b - 2b$

12. $10n^2 + 4n^2 + 3n$

13. $5t - t + 2 + 8$

14. $c + 9c + 2$

15. $2x + x + 7x^2 - 10x^2$

16. $2y - 5y + 8 + 3$

Do It Together!

17. Explain to a partner how to simplify the expression in number **10** in **Practice.**

18. Write a variable expression with like terms. Have a partner simplify. Check the work.

2.6 Evaluating Variable Expressions

You **evaluate** a variable expression when you **substitute** numbers for the variables. You will then have a number expression. Then, find the value of the number expression.

EXAMPLE 1   Evaluate $a^2 + 3$ when a is 4.

Substitute 4 for *a*.	$a^2 + 3$

4^2 means $4 \bullet 4$.

Find the value of the power.	$4^2 + 3$
Add.	$16 + 3$
	19

The value of $a^2 + 3$ is 19 when a is 4.

EXAMPLE 2   Find the value of $3x$ when x is -2.

$3x$ means 3 times x.

Substitute -2 for *x*.	$3x$

Use parentheses around negative numbers.

Multiply.	$3(-2)$
	-6

The value of $3x$ is -6 when x is -2.

You can evaluate variable expressions with more than one variable.

EXAMPLE 3   Evaluate $2b - c$ when b is 3 and c is -4.

Substitute 3 for *b* and -4 for *c*.	$2b - c$

Follow the Order of Operations.

Multiply.	$2 \bullet 3 - (-4)$
	$6 - (-4)$
Add.	$6 + 4$
	10

The value of $2b - c$ is 10 when b is 3 and c is -4.

Evaluate each variable expression.

1. $\dfrac{6a}{4}$ when a is -2

Substitute ■ for a.

$$\dfrac{6a}{4}$$

Multiply.

$$\dfrac{6(-2)}{4}$$

Divide.

$$\dfrac{-12}{4}$$

$$■$$

The value of $\dfrac{6a}{4}$ is ■ when a is -2.

2. $3x^2 - y$ when x is 2 and y is -4

Substitute 2 for ■ and -4 for ■. $3x^2 - y$

Find the value of the power. $3 \bullet ■^2 - ■$

Multiply. $3 \bullet ■ - (-4)$

Add. $12 + ■$

$$■$$

The value of $3x^2 - y$ is ■ when x is 2 and y is -4.

Practice

Evaluate each variable expression.

1. $t + 5$ when t is 3

2. $9 + w$ when w is -7

3. $18 \div c$ when c is -2

4. $8x$ when x is 0

5. $4 - s^2$ when s is 4

6. $2r + r^2$ when r is 4

7. $\dfrac{5p}{-1} + q$ when p is -1 and q is 9

8. $8(a + b)$ when a is 5 and b is 3

9. $3m + 9 \div n$ when m is 4 and n is -3

10. $\dfrac{3x}{12}$ when x is 8

Do It Together!

11. Explain to a partner how to find the value of the variable expression in number **8** in **Practice.**

12. Pick three numbers for x. Ask a partner to evaluate $3(x - 1)$ for each of the numbers. Check the work.

2.7 Meaning of an Equation

When expressions have the same value, they are **equivalent.** You can write a statement that two expressions are equal. This is called an **equation.**

$$9 = 9 \qquad\qquad 7 - 9 = 2 - 4 \qquad\qquad 12 \div 3 = 4$$
$$\text{true} \qquad\qquad\qquad \text{true} \qquad\qquad\qquad\quad \text{true}$$

These equations are all true. Both sides of the equal sign have the same value. If the sides have different values, the equation is false.

EXAMPLE 1   Tell whether the equation $2 + 6 = 11 - 3$ is true or false.

Simplify each expression.
$$2 + 6 = 11 - 3$$
$$8 \;\; = \;\; 8 \;\; \text{true}$$

$2 + 6 = 11 - 3$ is true.

When an equation contains variables, you can substitute a value for the variable. Then, tell whether the number equation is true or false.

EXAMPLE 2   Tell whether the equation $2a = a + a$ is true or false when a is 3.

2a means 2 times a.

Substitute 3 for a.
$$2a = a + a$$

Simplify each side.
$$2(3) = 3 + 3$$
$$6 \;\; = \;\; 6 \;\; \text{true}$$

$2a = a + a$ is true when a is 3.

EXAMPLE 3   Tell whether $3(x + 2) = 3x + 2$ is true or false when x is -1.

Substitute −1 for x.
$$3(x + 2) = 3x + 2$$

Follow the Order of Operations to simplify.

Simplify each side.
$$3(-1 + 2) = 3(-1) + 2$$
$$3(1) \;\; = \;\; -3 + 2$$
$$3 = -1 \;\; \text{false}$$

$3(x + 2) = 3x + 2$ is false when $x = -1$.

1. Tell whether $\frac{4+6}{2} = 2 \bullet 5 - 5$ is true or false.

   Simplify each side. $\quad \frac{4+6}{2} = 2 \bullet 5 - 5$

   $$\frac{\blacksquare}{2} = \blacksquare - 5$$

   $$\blacksquare = \blacksquare$$

   $\frac{4+6}{2} = 2 \bullet 5 - 5$ is $\blacksquare$.

2. Tell whether $3x + 4 = 4x$ is true or false when $x = 5$.

   Substitute 5 for $\blacksquare$. $\quad 3x + 4 = 4x$

   Simplify each side. $\quad 3 \bullet \blacksquare + 4 = 4 \bullet \blacksquare$

   $$\blacksquare + 4 = \blacksquare$$

   $$\blacksquare = \blacksquare$$

   $3x + 4 = 4x$ is $\blacksquare$ when $x = 5$.

Practice

Tell whether the equation is true or false.

1. $24 \div 3 = 16 - 8$

2. $2 \bullet 4 = 10 - 4$

3. $3z + 2 = 5$ when z is 1

4. $x \bullet x = 2x$ when x is 3

5. $2k = 6$ when k is 3

6. $10 \div b = -5$ when b is -2

7. $a \div 5 = 6$ when a is 35

8. $3(x + 2) = 3x + 6$ when x is 1

9. $2(x - 5) = 3x - 5$ when x is 15

10. $5n + n = 30$ when n is 6

11. $\frac{b}{3} + 6 = 12$ when b is 12

12. $4a - 10 = -26$ when a is -4

13. $7y + 3y = 20$ when y is 2

14. $-16 = -4x - 8$ when x is 2

Do It Together!

15. Explain to a partner how to decide if the equation in number **3** in **Practice** is true or false.

16. Pick two values for k. Have your partner decide if $2(k - 1) = 2k - 2$ is true or false for each value of k.

2.8 Properties of Addition

There are rules called properties that are always true when adding numbers. These properties are also true for variables.

Commutative Property of Addition
The order of two numbers in addition does not matter.
$3+2=2+3$ true

Associative Property of Addition
With more than two numbers, you can add pairs in any order.
$(1+7)+4=1+(7+4)$ true

Identity Property of Addition
Adding 0 to any number does not change the number.
$0+(-5)=-5$ true

Addition Property of Opposites
The opposite of a positive number is negative.

The sum of a number and its opposite is 0.
$8+(-8)=0$ true

EXAMPLE 1   Name the property shown. $(2x+3)+5=2x+(3+5)$
The sum of three terms. $(2x+3)+5=2x+(3+5)$

Add pairs of terms in any order.

The Associative Property of Addition is shown.

EXAMPLE 2   Use a property to complete the equation. $-2n+?=0$
The sum of a number and its opposite is 0. $-2n+?=0$

The opposite of −2n is 2n. $-2n+2n=0$

Use the Addition Property of Opposites.

EXAMPLE 3   Use a property to complete the equation. $x-?=-10+x$
The sum of two terms. $x-?=-10+x$

Add terms in any order. $x-10=-10+x$

Use the Commutative Property.

1. Name the property shown.
   $0 + 8n = 8n$

   Adding ■ does not change the value of a number.

   $0 + 8n = 8n$

   $0 + 8n = 8n$ shows the ■.

2. Use a property to complete.
   $(b + 5) - 5 = b + (? - 5)$

   The ■ says you can add pairs of terms in any order.

   $(b + 5) - 5 = b + (? - 5)$

   The missing term is ■.

Practice

Name the property shown.

1. $3x + 5x^2 = 5x^2 + 3x$

2. $(-12 + 3) + 4 = -12 + (3 + 4)$

3. $7 - 7 = 0$

4. $2cd + 5 - 3cd = 2cd - 3cd + 5$

5. $10 + 0 = 10$

6. $7x + (2x + 3) = (7x + 2x) + 3$

Use a property to complete.

7. $3d + 1 = 1 + ?$

8. $4s + ? = 4s$

9. $-6m + ? = 0$

10. $(w^2 + 3w) + w = w^2 + (? + w)$

11. $x + 3k = 3k + ?$

12. $(a + b) + c = a + (b + ?)$

13. $-n + 3 = ? - n$

14. $5k = ? + 0$

Do It Together!

15. Explain to a partner how to use a property to complete number **11** in **Practice.**

16. Write a variable expression that shows one of the properties of addition. Have a partner name the property.

2.9 Properties of Multiplication

There are rules called properties that are always true when multiplying numbers. These properties are also true for variables.

Commutative Property of Multiplication
The order of two factors in multiplication does not matter.
$3 \bullet (-4) = (-4) \bullet 3$ true

Associative Property of Multiplication
With two or more numbers, you can multiply pairs in any order.
$(2 \bullet 4) \bullet 5 = 2 \bullet (4 \bullet 5)$ true

Identity Property of Multiplication
The product of any number and 1 is that number.
$21 \bullet 1 = 21$ true

Zero Property of Multiplication
The product of 0 and any number is 0.
$(-15) \bullet 0 = 0$ true

EXAMPLE 1   Name the property shown. $2 \bullet (3 \bullet a) = (2 \bullet 3) \bullet a$
The product of three terms. $2 \bullet (3 \bullet a) = (2 \bullet 3) \bullet a$

Multiply pairs of terms in any order.

The Associative Property of Multiplication is shown.

EXAMPLE 2   Use a property to complete the equation. $? \bullet c = c$
The value does not change. $? \times c = c$

Multiplying by 1 does not change a number. $1 \times c = c$

Use the Identity Property.

EXAMPLE 3   Use a property to complete the equation. $a \bullet ? = 3a$
Multiply two numbers in any order. $a \bullet ? = 3a$

                                                          $a \bullet 3 = 3a$

Use the Commutative Property.

Name the property shown.

1. $8x \cdot 1 = 8x$

Multiplying by ■ **does** $8x \cdot 1 = 8x$
not change the value
of a number.

$8x \cdot 1 = 8x$ shows the ■.

2. $0 \times x = 0$

The product of any $0 \times x = 0$
number and ■ **is 0.**

$0 \times x = 0$ shows the ■.

Use a property to complete.

3. $4 \cdot (5 \cdot b) = (4 \cdot ?) \cdot b$

The ■ **says** $4 \cdot (5 \cdot b) = (4 \cdot ?) \cdot b$
you can
multiply pairs of
terms in any order.

The missing factor is ■.

4. $?(-12) = -12b$

The ■ **says the**   ■$(-12) = -12b$
order does not
matter when
multiplying.

The missing factor is ■.

Practice

Name the property shown.

1. $(4x)(9x) = (9x)(4x)$

2. $0n = 0$

3. $(2 \cdot 8) \cdot 5 = 2 \cdot (8 \cdot 5)$

4. $ba = ab$

5. $1 \cdot 7 = 7$

6. $3y \cdot 4 = 4 \cdot 3y$

Use a property to complete.

7. $-8d \cdot 1 = 1 \cdot ?$

8. $yx = ?y$

9. $(l \cdot w) \cdot h = l \cdot (w \cdot ?)$

10. $-6k \cdot ? = 0$

11. $? \cdot 6 = 6$

12. $(3k)(2) = (?)(3k)$

Do It Together!

13. Explain to a partner how to use a property to complete number **8** in **Practice.**

14. Write a variable expression that shows one of the properties of multiplication. Have a partner name the property.

2.10   Distributive Property

The **Distributive Property** uses multiplication with addition or subtraction. You can multiply a sum or difference by another number or term.

$$2(3+4) = \underbrace{2 \bullet 3} + \underbrace{2 \bullet 4}$$
$$\underbrace{2(7)} \quad = \quad \underbrace{6 \;\; + \;\; 8}$$
$$14 \quad = \quad \quad 14 \;\; \text{true}$$

Multiply each term of the sum or difference by the number. You can use this property with variables.

EXAMPLE **1**   Simplify. $6(x+3)$

Multiply each term in the parentheses by 6. $6(x+3)$

Simplify the expression. $6 \bullet x + 6 \bullet 3$

$6x + 18$

EXAMPLE **2**   Simplify. $8(a-b)$

Multiply each term in the parentheses by 8. $8(a-b)$

Simplify the expression. $8 \bullet a - 8 \bullet b$

$8a - 8b$

EXAMPLE **3**   Simplify. $-(6n+5)$

$-(6n+5)$

$-(6n+5)$ means
$(-1)(6n+5)$.

Multiply each term in the parentheses by −1. $-1(6n+5)$

Simplify the expression. $(-1)6n + (-1)5$

$-6n - 5$

EXAMPLE **4**   Simplify. $-3(y-4)$

Multiply each term in the parentheses by −3. $-3(y-4)$

Simplify the expression. $(-3)(y) - (-3)(4)$

$-3y - (-12)$

$-3y + 12$

Use the Distributive Property to simplify.

1. $2(r-1)$

Multiply each term in the parentheses by ■.
Simplify the expression.

$2(r-1) = ■$

$2(r-1)$
$■ \cdot r + ■ \cdot (-1)$
$■ \, r + (-■)$
$■$

2. $4(a+c)$

Multiply each term in the parentheses by ■.
Simplify the expression.
$4(a+c) = ■.$

$4(a+c)$
$■ \cdot a + ■ \cdot c$
$■ \, a + ■ \, c$

Practice

Use the Distributive Property to simplify.

1. $7(2-y)$

2. $12(t+2)$

3. $2(-12+k)$

4. $5(r-8)$

5. $-5(3-x)$

6. $-(a+4)$

7. $4(a-7)$

8. $7(s+3)$

9. $-6(3-d)$

10. $2(l-4)$

11. $2(3-2n)$

12. $-(m-7)$

13. $2(x+k)$

14. $4(q+4r)$

15. $5(2w+4)$

Do It Together!

16. Explain to a partner how to use the Distributive Property to simplify number **11** in **Practice.**

17. Write a variable expression like one of the practice exercises. Have a partner use the Distributive Property to complete the equation.

2.11 Simplifying Expressions

Properties can help you simplify expressions. Use the Distributive Property to remove parentheses. Use the Commutative Property to rearrange terms.

EXAMPLE 1

$-x$ means $(-1)x$.

Simplify. $\quad 2x + 4y - x$

Look for like terms. Change the order. $\quad 2x + 4y - x$

Combine like terms.

$$\underbrace{2x - 1x} + 4y$$
$$x + 4y$$

EXAMPLE 2

Simplify. $\quad 5 + 2(x+3)$

Use the Distributive Property.

$$5 + 2(x+3)$$
$$5 + 2(x) + 2(3)$$

Look for like terms. Change the order. $\quad 5 + 2x + 6$

Combine like terms.

$$\underbrace{5 + 6} + 2x$$
$$11 + 2x$$

EXAMPLE 3

Simplify. $\quad -6x + 4(5-x)$

Use the Distributive Property.

$$-6x + 4(5-x)$$
$$-6x + 4(5) - 4(x)$$

Look for like terms. Change the order. $\quad -6x + 20 - 4x$

Combine like terms.

$$\underbrace{-6x - 4x} + 20$$
$$-10x + 20$$

EXAMPLE 4

Simplify. $\quad 2xy^2 + 8 - xy^2 + 4$

Look for like terms. Change the order. $\quad 2xy^2 + 8 - xy^2 + 4$

Combine like terms.

$$\underbrace{2xy^2 - xy^2} + \underbrace{8 + 4}$$
$$xy^2 \quad + \quad 12$$

Simplify the expressions.

1. $4(x-3)+5$

Use ■.	$4(x-3)+5$
	$■ \bullet x - ■ \bullet 3 + 5$
Combine like terms.	$4x - ■ + 5$
	$4x - ■$

$4(x-3)+5 = ■$

2. $8m - n - 3m + 12n$

Change the order.	$8m - n - 3m + 12n$
	$8m - 3m - ■ + 12n$
Combine like terms.	$■m + ■n$

$8m - n - 3m + 12n = ■$

Practice

Simplify the expressions.

1. $a + a + 2$

2. $5(t+8) - 6$

3. $-(r+2)$

4. $3(x-4)+6$

5. $6(y-8) - 10$

6. $7a + 3(a+4)$

7. $5b + 2(b-2)$

8. $10y + 4(1+3y)$

9. $5t + 8 - (t+2)$

10. $10 + 3(c+4)$

11. $2p + 2 + 9p - 2$

12. $6(h+2) + 3h$

13. $n + 3m - n$

14. $2k + 3 - 7k + 4k$

15. $x + 2(x-4)$

16. $2b + 4(b-5)$

17. $-5p + 2(p+4)$

18. $x - 3(x+2)$

19. $10 - (5+m)$

20. $-(2-x) - 8$

21. $-x + 4y - x + y$

Do It Together!

22. Explain to a partner how to simplify the expression in number **12** in **Practice.**

23. Write a variable expression containing parentheses. Have a partner simplify. Check the work.

2.12 Calculator: Finding the Value of Expressions

You can use your calculator to evaluate expressions when the values of the variable are large numbers. Be sure to follow the Order of Operations.

EXAMPLE 1   Use your calculator to find the value of the expression $7a + 3b - 21$ when a is 2.5 and b is .8.

Substitute 2.5 for *a* and .8 for *b*. $7a + 3b - 21$

$$7(2.5) + 3(.8) - 21 \quad \textbf{DISPLAY}$$

Enter 7 by pressing: $\boxed{7}$ 7

Multiply by 2.5 by pressing: $\boxed{\times}\,\boxed{2}\,\boxed{.}\,\boxed{5}\,\boxed{=}$ 17.5

Write 17.5 on your paper.

Enter 3 by pressing: $\boxed{3}$ 3

Multiply by .8 by pressing: $\boxed{\times}\,\boxed{.}\,\boxed{8}\,\boxed{=}$ 2.4

Write 2.4 on your paper.

The expression becomes $17.5 + 2.4 - 21$. Now, find the value of the expression.

Enter 17.5 by pressing: $\boxed{1}\,\boxed{7}\,\boxed{.}\,\boxed{5}$ 17.5

Add 2.4 by pressing: $\boxed{+}\,\boxed{2}\,\boxed{.}\,\boxed{4}\,\boxed{=}$ 19.9

Write 19.9 on your paper.

Subtract 21 by pressing: $\boxed{-}\,\boxed{2}\,\boxed{1}\,\boxed{=}$ -1.1

$7a + 3b - 21 = -1.1$ when $a = 2.5$ and $b = .8$.

Make sure you clear your calculator each time you start a calculation.

Practice

Find the value of each expression.

1. $8x - 42$ when x is 32

2. $72(z - 12)$ when z is 22

3. $\dfrac{21y}{9}$ when y is 3.3

4. $\dfrac{324v}{15t}$ when v is 10 and t is 72

5. $\dfrac{n}{24} - 21$ when n is 1,248

6. $50y - 92 + 36y$ when y is 8.7

7. $3y^2$ when y is 1.5

8. $4a - 7b$ when a is .02 and b is 1.9

MATH CONNECTION

Assembly Lines

Large machines like cars and airplanes are made of many smaller parts. Together, the parts make the machine work. How do you think these machines are made?

Many machines are made on assembly lines. Here, parts are put together, or *assembled*. An assembly line has tools, parts, and workers. They are placed in an order. Each part is added to the machine in order. Workers have the tools they need right next to them. This keeps the line moving quickly. Sometimes, a robot will attach or adjust a part too.

An assembly line must follow steps in the correct order. You cannot put the wheels on before the axle! Workers need the right tools and skills to do their jobs. Building a car on an assembly line is a lot like algebra. You need to have the right tools and skills. Then, you follow the steps in the right order.

2.13 Problem Solving: Writing Equations

You can translate simple word statements into variable equations. It is helpful to know other words for the four operations.

Addition	sum of 3 and 5	$3 + 5$
	3 increased by 5	
	5 more than 3	
Subtraction	subtract 3 from 5	$5 - 3$
	5 decreased by 3	
	3 less than 5	
Multiplication	product of 3 and 5	$3 \cdot 5$
	2 times 3	$2 \cdot 3$
Division	quotient of 10 and 2	$10 \div 2$

Note the order of the numbers is important.

When you begin, first pick variables for the numbers you do not know.

EXAMPLE 1   The perimeter of a square is 4 times the length of a side. Write an equation for the perimeter of a square.

Pick variables for perimeter and side.

The perimeter is 4 times a side.

$$P \qquad\qquad s$$

Translate "4 times." $P \ = \ 4 \ \cdot \ s$

Simplify. $P \ = \ 4s$

You can write $P = 4s$ for the perimeter of a square.

EXAMPLE 2   The price of a tape is $3 less than the price of a CD.

Pick variables for the prices of tape and CD.

Price of a tape is $3 less than a CD.

$$t \qquad\qquad c$$

Translate "3 less than" as −3.

$$t \ = \ c - 3$$

You can write $t = c - 3$ for the price of a tape.

1. Maria's score is twice Jon's score.
   Write a variable equation for Maria's score.

   Pick variables for Maria's score and Jon's score.

   Maria's score is twice Jon's score.
   $\downarrow$ $\downarrow$
   m j

   Translate "twice." $m = 2 \blacksquare j$

   You can write $m = 2 \blacksquare j$ for Maria's score.

2. The perimeter of a triangle is the sum of its 3 sides.
   Write a variable equation for the perimeter of a triangle.

   Pick variables for the perimeter and the sides.

   The perimeter of a triangle is the sum of its 3 sides.
   $\downarrow$ $\downarrow$
   P a, b, c

   Use *a*, *b*, and *c* for the 3 sides.

   Translate "sum." $P = a \blacksquare b \blacksquare c$

   You can write $P = a \blacksquare b \blacksquare c$.

Practice

Write a variable equation for each sentence.

1. The area of a rectangle is length times width.

2. Danika's new running route is 4 miles longer than her old route.

3. Today's temperature is 5 degrees less than yesterday's.

Do It Together!

4. Explain to a partner how to choose the variable in number **2** in **Practice.**

5. Write three word sentences. Have a partner write an equation for the sentences you wrote. Check the work.

2.14 Application: Geometry Formulas

You can use what you know about evaluating expressions to use a formula from geometry.

EXAMPLE 1 The perimeter of a triangle is the sum of its three sides. Use the formula $P=a+b+c$. Find the perimeter of a triangle when a is 4 in., b is 3 in., and c is 5 in.

Write the formula for perimeter.	$P=a+b+c$
Substitute 4 for a, 3 for b, and 5 for c.	$P=4+3+5$
Add.	$P=12$

The perimeter of the triangle is 12 in.

EXAMPLE 2 The area of a rectangle is its length times its width. Use the formula $A=lw$. Find the area of a rectangle when l is 6 cm and w is 3 cm.

Write the formula for area.	$A=lw$
Substitute 6 for l and 3 for w.	$A=6 \bullet 3$
Multiply.	$A=18$

The area of the rectangle is 18 square centimeters, or 18 cm^2.

EXAMPLE 3 The volume of a box is its length times its width times its height. Use the formula $V=lwh$. Find the volume of a box when l is 5 cm, w is 2 cm, and h is 4 cm.

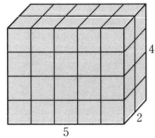

Write the formula for volume	$V=lwh$
Substitute 5 for l, 2 for w, and 4 for h.	$V=5 \bullet 2 \bullet 4$
Multiply.	$V=40$

The volume of the box is 40 cubic centimeters, or 40 cm^3.

1. Use the formula $P=a+b+c$. Find the perimeter of a triangle when a is 23 ft, b is 17 ft, and c is 34 ft.

   Write the formula for ■. $P=a+b+c$

   Substitute. $P=■+■+■$

   Add. $P=■$

   The perimeter of the triangle is ■.

2. Use the formula $A=lw$. Find the area of a rectangle when l is 24 yd and w is 14 yd.

   Write the formula for ■. $A=lw$

   Substitute. $A=24 • ■$

   Multiply. $A=■$

   The area of the rectangle is ■.

Practice

Use the formula $P=a+b+c$ to find the perimeter of each triangle.

1. a is 12 m, b is 13 m, c is 22 m

2. a is 11 in., b is 9 in., c is 12 in.

Use the formula $A=lw$ to find the area of each rectangle.

3. l is 12 in., w is 6 in.

4. l is 90 mm, w is 40 mm

5. l is 8 yd, w is 2 yd

6. l is 5 cm, w is 14 cm

Use the formula $V=lwh$ to find the volume of each box.

7. l is 4 cm, w is 3 cm, h is 1 cm

8. l is 2 yd, w is 10 yd, h is 8 yd

Do It Together!

9. Explain to a partner how to find the perimeter of number **2** in **Practice.**

10. Write a length, width, and height for a box. Ask a partner to use the formula for volume to find the volume of the box. Check the work.

Chapter 2 Summary

- Use the Order of Operations to find the value of an expression.
- Variable expressions contain terms with numbers and variables.
- You can simplify expressions by combining like terms.
- You can evaluate variable expressions by substituting numbers for variables.
- Two expressions that have the same value are equivalent.
- An equation is true if both sides of the equal sign have the same value.
- Properties help you simplify expressions.
- You can use a calculator to help find the value of expressions.
- To rewrite verbal statements into variable equations, translate the words into variables, numbers, and signs.
- You can evaluate geometry formulas.

Reviewing Vocabulary

variable
terms
constant
coefficient
like terms
evaluate
substitute
equivalent
equation
Commutative
  Property
Associative Property
Identity Property
Addition Property of
  Opposites
Zero Property of
  Multiplication
Distributive Property

1. The ? lets you add or multiply two numbers in any order.
2. Use the ? to help you multiply a sum by a number.
3. You ? an expression when you find its value.
4. A ? is a letter that represents any number.
5. Two expressions are ? when they have the same value.
6. The ? lets you add or multiply more than two numbers in groups of two in any order.
7. The ? of Multiplication tells you multiplying by 1 does not change the value of a number.
8. To ? means to replace a variable with a number.
9. The ? says the sum of any number and its opposite is zero.
10. A number that multiplies a variable is a(n) ? .
11. ? have the same variables with the same exponents.
12. ? are parts of an expression separated by a + or − sign.
13. A ? is a number or quantity that does not change value.
14. A statement that two expressions are equal is a(n) ?.
15. The ? says that the product of any number and 0 is 0.

Chapter Quiz

Simplify.

1. $10 - 4 \div 2$

2. $3 \cdot 4 + 7$

3. $8 \div 2 - 6 \cdot 0$

4. $12 \div (3 + 3) \cdot 6$

5. $20 - 2(16 - 4)$

6. $(5 + 8) \cdot 3 - 7$

Evaluate each variable expression.

7. $(15 \div a)a$ when a is 5

8. $s + 2s$ when s is 4

9. $-5s$ when s is 7

10. $6 + c$ when c is 13

Find the values of the expressions and tell whether the expressions are equivalent.

11. $3t + 8$ and 14 when t is 2

12. $3g - 3$ and $3(g - 1)$ when g is 2

Name the property shown.

13. $4(y + 2) = 4y + 8$

14. $-3 + 3 = 0$

15. $4x \cdot 2 = 2 \cdot 4x$

16. $(t + 2) + 4 = t + (2 + 4)$

Simplify each expression.

17. $4x + x + 3$

18. $3w + 4x - 7x - w$

19. $1 + 2b + 7b$

20. $4(y + 3)$

21. $-(a + 9)$

22. $6(x - 8)$

23. $3x + 5(4 + x)$

24. $12 - (c + 8)$

25. $16 - 4(n - 4)$

Write a variable equation for the sentence.

26. Marie-José's time is 29 seconds less than Inger's.

Use the formula $A = lw$ to find the area of each rectangle.

27. $l = 4$ in. and $w = 8$ in.

28. $l = 10$ yd and $w = 5$ yd

Chapter 3
Solving Equations

A gymnast uses balance to support himself. If his force on each side is not the same, he will fall. An equation also uses balance.

Chapter Learning Objectives

- Solve equations by adding, subtracting, multiplying, or dividing.
- Solve equations using more than one operation.
- Solve equations containing parentheses.
- Check solutions to equations by using a calculator.
- Solve problems about percents by writing and solving equations.
- Apply concepts and skills to find discounts and sale prices.

Words to Know

variable equation an equation containing a variable

solution a value of the variable that makes the equation true

equivalent equations equations with the same solutions

properties of equality adding, subtracting, multiplying, or dividing both sides of an equation by the same number gives an equivalent equation

inverse operations operations that "undo" each other; Addition and subtraction are inverse operations, and multiplication and division are inverse operations

solve find the solution of an equation

check substitute the solution for the variable

discount the amount you save when you buy an item on sale

sale price the regular price minus the discount

In this chapter, you will learn about variable equations. You will find equivalent equations by using the properties of equality and inverse operations. You will learn to solve an equation by using addition, subtraction, multiplication, and division. You will also solve equations with parentheses and with variables on both sides. You will see how you can use a calculator to check solutions. You will learn the useful tool of writing equations to solve percent problems. Finally, you will apply what you know about working with equations to find discounts and sale prices.

3.1 Solution of an Equation

A **variable equation** is an equation that contains a variable. The equation $x = 8$ is a variable equation. If you substitute 8 for x, you get $8 = 8$. This is a true equation. The **solution** is the value of the variable that makes the equation true. The solution of $x = 8$ is 8.

This scale shows the equation $x + 4 = 10$.

It is balanced when x is 6. Other amounts will not balance the scale. So, 6 is the solution of $x + 4 = 10$.

$x + 4 = 10$ $x + 4 = 10$ $x + 4 = 10$
$2 + 4 = 10$ false $6 + 4 = 10$ true $9 + 4 = 10$ false

The equation $x + 4 = 10$ is true when x is 6.

EXAMPLE 1   Tell whether -9 is the solution of $-4 = 5 + w$.

Substitute −9 for w.	$-4 = 5 + w$
Add.	$-4 = 5 + (-9)$
	$-4 = -4$ true

-9 is the solution of $-4 = 5 + w$.

EXAMPLE 2   Tell whether 20 is the solution of $15 = \frac{x}{2} - 5$.

Substitute 20 for x.	$15 = \frac{x}{2} - 5$
Divide.	$15 = \frac{20}{2} - 5$
Subtract.	$15 = 10 - 5$
	$15 = 5$ false

$\frac{x}{2}$ means $x \div 2$.

20 is not the solution of $15 = \frac{x}{2} - 5$.

1. Tell whether 8 is the solution of $5 - y = 3$.

Substitute ■ for y.	$5 - y = 3$
Subtract.	$5 - 8 = 3$
	■ $= 3$ false

8 ■ the solution of $5 - y = 3$.

2. Tell whether 5 is the solution of $2n - 4 = 6$.

Substitute 5 for ■.	$2n - 4 = 6$
Multiply.	$2(■) - 4 = 6$
Subtract.	■ $- 4 = 6$
	■ $= 6$ true

5 ■ the solution of $2n - 4 = 6$.

Practice

Tell whether the number is a solution of the equation.

1. 4; $a = 4$

2. 5; $6 + w = 12$

3. -3; $11 + c = 8$

4. -7; $c - 4 = 11$

5. 6; $2 - x = -4$

6. 8; $11 = 3y$

7. 6; $5x = 30$

8. -20; $\frac{n}{4} = -4$

9. -4; $2 - y = 6$

10. -4; $2x = -8$

11. 0; $12 = 3n + 9$

12. 1; $1 = -4 + 5s$

13. 6; $3x + 2 = 17$

14. -3; $2a + 5 = -1$

15. 4; $6 = -2 + 2y$

16. 4; $-7 + 5y = 10$

17. 5; $6 = 16 - 2x$

18. -3; $8 - 3x = 17$

19. 0; $3x + 17 = 16$

20. 10; $8 - b = -2$

21. 18; $\frac{w}{3} + 2 = 12$

Do It Together!

22. Explain to a partner how to tell whether 1 is the solution of the equation in number **12** in **Practice.**

23. Write the variable equation $3x + 5 = 11$. Then, write three integers that could be solutions to the equation. Ask a partner to check each integer to see if it is a solution of the equation.

3.2 Equivalent Equations

You can look at the equation $x=3$ to find the solution. The solution is 3. The solutions of $x-1=2$ and $x+1=4$ are not as easy to find. They also have 3 as a solution. You can **check** a solution. Substitute the solution for the variable in the equation. If the equation is true, the solution is correct.

$$x-1=2 \qquad\qquad\qquad x+1=4$$

Solution: 3   **Solution:** 3

Check: $x-1=2$ **Check:** $x+1=4$

           $3-1=2$ $3+1=4$

              $2=2$ true $4=4$ true

Equations with the same solution are **equivalent equations.** These are equivalent equations:

$$x=3 \qquad\qquad x-1=2 \qquad\qquad x+1=4$$

EXAMPLE 1   Show that $x=-3$ and $4=x+7$ are equivalent.

                       $x=-3$ $4=x+7$

Solution: -3 $\rightarrow$ **Substitute -3 for x.** $4=-3+7$

                                                      $4=4$ true

$x=-3$ and $4=x+7$ are equivalent.

EXAMPLE 2   Show that $12=y$ and $1=\dfrac{y}{4}-2$ are equivalent.

                     $12=y$ $1=\dfrac{y}{4}-2$

Solution: 12 $\rightarrow$ **Substitute 12 for y.** $1=\dfrac{12}{4}-2$

                                                $1=3-2$

                                                $1=1$ true

$12=y$ and $1=\dfrac{y}{4}-2$ are equivalent.

Show that each pair of equations is equivalent.

1. $x = -5$ and $2x + 6 = -4$

$$2x + 6 = -4$$

Substitute ■ $2(■) + 6 = -4$
for x.

$$■ + 6 = -4$$

$$■ = -4 \quad \text{true}$$

$x = -5$ and $2x + 6 = -4$ are equivalent.

2. $y = -4$ and $2 - 3y = 14$

$$2 - 3y = 14$$

Substitute ■ $2 - 3(■) = 14$
for y.

$$2 - (■) = 14$$

$$■ = ■ \quad \text{true}$$

$y = -4$ and $2 - 3y = 14$ are equivalent.

Practice

Show that each pair of equations is equivalent.

1. $a = 7$ and $10 - a = 3$

2. $n = 4$ and $9 = n + 5$

3. $x = -5$ and $7 = 12 + x$

4. $y = 11$ and $4 - y = -7$

5. $c = 6$ and $2c = 12$

6. $x = 30$ and $\frac{x}{6} = 5$

7. $y = 10$ and $-2y - 3 = -23$

8. $n = -15$ and $\frac{n}{5} - 6 = -9$

9. $b = 0$ and $8 + 6b = 8$

10. $w = 5$ and $-2 = 8 - 2w$

11. $-2 = n$ and $-3n + 1 = 7$

12. $x = -1$ and $1 + 5x = -4$

Do It Together!

13. Explain to a partner how to show that the two equations are equivalent in number **5** in **Practice**.

14. Write an equation equivalent to $d = 3$. Ask a partner to show the equations are equivalent.

3.3 Properties of Equality

The equations $x+4=7+4$ and $x-2=7-2$ are both equivalent to $x=7$. They all have 7 as a solution. These equations show the facts, or **properties of equality.**

$$x+4=7+4 \qquad\qquad\qquad x-2=7-2$$

Solution: 7   **Solution:** 7

Check: $7+4=7+4$ **Check:** $7-2=7-2$

$\qquad\qquad 11=11$ $\qquad\qquad 5=5$

Adding or subtracting the same number from both sides of an equation gives an equivalent equation. Later you will use these properties to solve equations.

EXAMPLE 1   Complete. $x-6=9$ is equivalent to $x-6+6=9+?$

6 is added to the left side. $x-6+6=9+?$

Add 6 to the right side. $x-6+6=9+6$

$x-6=9$ is equivalent to $x-6+6=9+6$.

The equations below are equivalent to $x=6$. They all have 6 as a solution.

$$5 \bullet x=5 \bullet 6 \qquad\qquad\qquad x \div 3=6 \div 3$$

Solution: 6   **Solution:** 6

Check: $5 \bullet 6=5 \bullet 6$ **Check:** $6 \div 3=6 \div 3$

$\qquad\qquad 30=30$ $\qquad\qquad 2=2$

Multiplying or dividing both sides of an equation by the same number gives an equivalent equation.

EXAMPLE 2   Complete. $-5x=25$ is equivalent to $-5x\,?-5=25 \div -5$

The right side is divided by -5 $-5x\,?-5=25 \div -5$

Divide the left side by -5. $-5x \div -5=25 \div -5$

$-5x=25$ is equivalent to $-5x \div -5=25 \div -5$.

Complete to make equivalent equations.

1. $x+5=-10$ and $x+5 \,?\, 5=-10-5$

5 is ■ from the right side.
■ 5 from the left side.
$$x+5 \,■\, 5=-10-5$$
$x+5=-10$ and $x+5 \,■\, 5=-10-5$ are equivalent.

2. $-9=\dfrac{y}{3}$ and $-9 \bullet \,?\, =\dfrac{y}{3} \bullet 3$

The right side is ■ by 3.
■ the left side by 3.
$$-9 \bullet \,■\, =\dfrac{y}{3} \bullet 3$$
$-9=\dfrac{y}{3}$ and $-9 \bullet \,■\, =\dfrac{y}{3} \bullet 3$ are equivalent.

Practice

Complete to make equivalent equations.

1. $a+5=7$
$a+5-?=7-5$

2. $6z=24$
$6z \div ?=24 \div 6$

3. $\dfrac{x}{10}=5$
$\dfrac{x}{10} \,?\, 10=5 \bullet 10$

4. $t-8=11$
$t-8 \,?\, 8=11+8$

5. $18=-3b$
$18 \div ?=-3b \div -3$

6. $\dfrac{w}{9}=2$
$\dfrac{w}{9} \,?\, 9=2 \bullet 9$

7. $-16=\dfrac{y}{4}$
$-16 \bullet 4=\dfrac{y}{4} \bullet ?$

8. $x+25=25$
$x+25 \,?\, 25=25-25$

9. $-6=n-2$
$-6+?=n-2+2$

Do It Together!

10. Explain to a partner how to complete the equation in number **5** in **Practice.**

11. Write the equation $a+5-5=-8-5$. Then, remove a number or an operation from the equation. Ask a partner to fill in the missing number or operation.

3.4 Inverse Operations

Adding and then subtracting the same number from 8 does not change 8.

$$\underbrace{(8-3)}+3 \qquad\qquad \underbrace{(8+6)}-6$$
$$\underbrace{5+3} \qquad\qquad\qquad \underbrace{14-6}$$
$$8 \qquad\qquad\qquad\qquad 8$$

Addition "undoes" subtraction. Subtraction "undoes" addition. Addition and subtraction are **inverse operations.** Inverse operations also work with variables. You will use inverse operations to solve equations.

EXAMPLE 1   Complete. $x+2\ ?\ 2=x$

Undo addition. $x+2\ ?\ 2=x$

Subtract 2. $x+2-2=x$

$x+2-2=x$

Multiplication and division are inverse operations. Division "undoes" multiplication. Multiplication "undoes" division.

$$\underbrace{8\bullet 4\div 4} \qquad\qquad \underbrace{8\div 2\bullet 2}$$
$$\underbrace{32\div 4} \qquad\qquad\qquad \underbrace{4\bullet 2}$$
$$8 \qquad\qquad\qquad\qquad 8$$

EXAMPLE 2   Complete. $-4y\ ?\ (-4)=y$

$-4y$ means $-4\bullet y$.

Undo multiplication. $-4y\ ?\ (-4)=y$

Divide by -4. $-4y\div(-4)=y$

$-4y\div(-4)=y$

Complete each equation with the missing operation.

1. $x + 4 \, ? \, 4 = x$

Undo addition.
■ 4.
$x + 4 \, \blacksquare \, 4 = x$

2. $y = \dfrac{y}{-6} \, ? \, (-6)$

Undo division.
■ by −6.
$y = \dfrac{y}{-6} \, \blacksquare \, (-6)$

Practice

Complete each equation with the missing operation.

1. $a + 4 \, ? \, 4 = a$

2. $z - 7 \, ? \, 7 = z$

3. $2b \, ? \, 2 = b$

4. $\dfrac{v}{9} \, ? \, 9 = v$

5. $10 \, ? \, 10 + x = x$

6. $y - 3 \, ? \, 3 = y$

7. $-8x \, ? \, (-8) = x$

8. $\dfrac{s}{2} \, ? \, (2) = s$

9. $11 \, ? \, 11 + y = y$

10. $\dfrac{r}{12} \, ? \, 12 = r$

11. $x - 25 \, ? \, 25 = x$

12. $-15b \, ? \, (-15) = b$

Do It Together!

13. Explain to a partner how to complete the equation in number **7** in **Practice.**

14. Write an expression with a variable and one operation. Ask a partner to write an expression that undoes that operation.

3.5 Solving Equations Using Subtraction

You can find the solution of the equation $x = 4$ just by looking at it. It is not as easy to find the solution of the equation $x + 3 = 7$. It contains addition.

You **solve** an equation when you find its solution. You can solve this equation by using subtraction to undo addition. That will give you an equivalent equation that is easy to solve.

EXAMPLE 1   Solve. Then, check the solution. $x + 3 = 7$

Subtracting the same number from both sides of an equation gives an equivalent equation.

Subtract to undo addition.	$x + 3 = 7$
Subtract 3 from both sides.	$x + 3 - 3 = 7 - 3$
Simplify each side.	$x + 0 = 4$
	$x = 4$

Solution: 4

Check: Substitute 4 for *x*.
$$x + 3 = 7$$
$$4 + 3 = 7$$
$$7 = 7 \quad \text{true}$$

The solution of $x + 3 = 7$ is 4.

The variable can also be on the right side of the equation. You still subtract to undo addition.

EXAMPLE 2   Solve. Then, check the solution. $-9 = 4 + y$

Subtract to undo addition.	$-9 = 4 + y$
Subtract 4 from both sides.	$-9 - 4 = 4 - 4 + y$
Simplify each side.	$-13 = 0 + y$
	$-13 = y$

Solution: -13

Check: Substitute -13 for *y*.
$$-9 = 4 + y$$
$$-9 = 4 + (-13)$$
$$-9 = -9 \quad \text{true}$$

The solution of $-9 = 4 + y$ is -13.

Solve. Then, check the solution.

1. $n + 8 = -3$

Subtract ■ from both sides.	$n + 8 - ■ = -3 - ■$
Simplify each side.	$n + 0 = ■$
	$n = ■$

Solution: ■

Check.	$n + 8 = -3$
Substitute ■ for *n*.	$■ + 8 = -3$
	$■ = ■$ true

2. $24 = t + 6$

Subtract ■ from both sides.	$24 - ■ = t + 6 - ■$
Simplify each side.	$■ = t + ■$
	$■ = t$

Solution: ■

Check	$24 = t + 6$
Substitute ■ for *t*.	$24 = ■ + 6$
	$■ = ■$ true

Practice

Solve. Then, check the solution.

1. $k + 0 = 6$

2. $r + 2 = 10$

3. $6 + n = 18$

4. $10 = x + 9$

5. $7 = s + 4$

6. $3 = z + 7$

7. $x + 4 = -11$

8. $-10 = y + 5$

9. $c + 12 = 4$

10. $1 = y + 0$

11. $7 + b = 3$

12. $5 + a = -20$

13. $-13 = b + 8$

14. $x + 6 = -10$

15. $y + 8 = 3$

Do It Together!

16. Explain to a partner how to solve the equation in number **8** in **Practice.**

17. Write the equation $y = 10$. Then, write a new equation by adding a number less than 10 to the left side of the equation. Ask a partner to solve the new equation. Check the solution.

3.6 Solving Equations Using Addition

You have solved equations containing addition. You subtracted to undo the addition. You solve equations that contain subtraction by adding to undo the subtraction.

EXAMPLE 1

Adding the same number to both sides of an equation gives an equivalent equation.

Solve. Then, check the solution. $x - 3 = 7$

Add to undo subtraction.

Add 3 to both sides.

Simplify each side.

$$x - 3 = 7$$
$$x - 3 + 3 = 7 + 3$$
$$x + 0 = 10$$
$$x = 10$$

Check: Substitute 10 for x.

$$x - 3 = 7$$
$$10 - 3 = 7$$
$$7 = 7 \quad \text{true}$$

The solution of $x - 3 = 7$ is 10.

EXAMPLE 2

Solve. Then, check the solution. $-5 = y - 9$

Add to undo subtraction.

Add 9 to both sides.

Simplify each side.

$$-5 = y - 9$$
$$-5 + 9 = y - 9 + 9$$
$$4 = y - 0$$
$$4 = y$$

Check: Substitute 4 for y.

$4 - 9$ means $4 + (-9)$

$$-5 = y - 9$$
$$-5 = 4 - 9$$
$$-5 = -5 \quad \text{true}$$

The solution of $-5 = y - 9$ is 4.

An equation can contain 0. Solve the equation the same way you solve other equations.

EXAMPLE 3

Solve. Then, check the solution. $b - 6 = 0$

Add to undo subtraction.

Add 6 to both sides.

Check:
$b - 6 = 0$
$6 - 6 = 0$
$0 = 0$

Simplify each side.

$$b - 6 = 0$$
$$b - 6 + 6 = 0 + 6$$
$$b + 0 = 6$$
$$b = 6$$

The solution of $b - 6 = 0$ is 6.

Solve. Then, check the solution.

1. $n - 5 = -15$

    Add ■ to both sides. $n - 5 + ■ = -15 + ■$

    Simplify each side. $n + ■ = ■$

                        $n = ■$

    Check: $n - 5 = -15$

    Substitute ■ for n. $■ - 5 = -15$

                     $■ = -15$ true

2. $6 = t - 4$

    Add ■ to both sides. $6 + ■ = t - 4 + ■$

    Simplify each side. $■ = t + ■$

                    $■ = t$

    Check: $6 = t - 4$

    Replace t with ■. $6 = ■ - 4$

                    $6 = ■$ true

Practice

Solve. Then, check the solution.

1. $k - 20 = 10$ **2.** $r - 2 = 12$ **3.** $21 = n - 6$

4. $0 = x - 9$ **5.** $16 = t - 4$ **6.** $z - 3 = 0$

7. $x - 4 = -15$ **8.** $-3 = y - 15$ **9.** $c - 2 = -8$

10. $y - 0 = 8$ **11.** $-13 = b - 7$ **12.** $20 = v - 5$

13. $k - 12 = 0$ **14.** $-5 = m - 9$ **15.** $x - 1 = -21$

16. $-10 = a - 10$ **17.** $x - 9 = -25$ **18.** $y - 15 = -7$

Do It Together!

19. Explain to a partner how to solve the equation in number **9** in **Practice.**

20. Write an equation that contains subtraction. Ask a partner to solve your equation. Check the solution.

3.7 Solving Equations Using Multiplication

You have solved equations containing addition and subtraction by undoing the addition or the subtraction. The equation $\frac{x}{2} = -8$ contains division. You solve division equations by multiplying to undo the division.

EXAMPLE 1   Solve. Then, check the solution. $\frac{x}{2} = -8$

$\frac{x}{2}$ means $x \div 2$.

Multiply to undo division. $\frac{x}{2} = -8$

Multiply both sides by 2. $\frac{2x}{2} = -8(2)$

Check:

$\frac{x}{2} = -8$

Simplify each side. $x = -16$

$\frac{-16}{2} = -8$

$-8 = -8$ true

The solution of $\frac{x}{2} = -8$ is -16.

EXAMPLE 2   Solve. Then, check the solution. $9 = \frac{y}{-3}$

Multiply to undo division. $9 = \frac{y}{-3}$

Multiply both sides by -3. $(-3)9 = \frac{-3y}{-3}$

Check:

$9 = \frac{y}{-3}$

Simplify each side. $-27 = 1y$

$9 = \frac{-27}{-3}$

$-27 = y$

$9 = 9$ true

The solution of $9 = \frac{y}{-3}$ is -27

EXAMPLE 3   Solve. Then, check the solution. $\frac{c}{5} = 0$

Multiply to undo division. $\frac{c}{5} = 0$

Multiply both sides by 5. $\frac{5c}{5} = 0(5)$

Check:

$\frac{c}{5} = 0$

Simplify each side. $1c = 0$

$\frac{0}{5} = 0$

$c = 0$

$0 = 0$ true

The solution of $\frac{c}{5} = 0$ is 0.

Solve. Then, check the solution.

1. $-7 = \dfrac{n}{-5}$

    Multiply both sides by ■. $■(-7) = \dfrac{■\, n}{-5}$

    Simplify. $■ = n$

    Check: $-7 = \dfrac{n}{-5}$

    Substitute ■ for *n*. $-7 = \dfrac{■}{-5}$

                       $-7 = ■$ true

2. $\dfrac{t}{-4} = -6$

    Multiply both sides by ■. $\dfrac{■\, t}{-4} = -6(■)$

    Simplify. $t = ■$

    Check: $\dfrac{t}{-4} = -6$

    Substitute ■ for *t*. $\dfrac{■}{-4} = -6$

                       $■ = -6$ true

Practice

Solve. Then, check the solution.

1. $\dfrac{k}{4} = 6$

2. $\dfrac{b}{2} = 5$

3. $3 = \dfrac{n}{6}$

4. $9 = \dfrac{x}{3}$

5. $-7 = \dfrac{s}{4}$

6. $0 = \dfrac{z}{2}$

7. $\dfrac{x}{4} = -5$

8. $-5 = \dfrac{y}{8}$

9. $\dfrac{c}{-12} = 2$

10. $\dfrac{x}{3} = 4$

11. $\dfrac{y}{5} = -10$

12. $\dfrac{a}{2} = -3$

13. $-8 = \dfrac{y}{-9}$

14. $\dfrac{b}{-1} = -13$

15. $-3 = \dfrac{a}{-5}$

16. $\dfrac{x}{-3} = 8$

17. $10 = \dfrac{n}{10}$

18. $0 = \dfrac{c}{11}$

Do It Together!

19. Explain to a partner how to solve the equation in number **9** in **Practice.**

20. Write an equation with $\frac{y}{3}$ on the left side. Use any number for the right side. Ask a partner to solve your equation. Check the solution.

3.8 Solving Equations Using Division

You have solved equations that contain division. You multiplied to undo the division. You can also solve equations that contain multiplication. You divide to undo multiplication.

EXAMPLE 1   Solve. Then, check the solution. $4x = -16$

Divide to undo multiplication. $4x = -16$

Divide both sides by 4. $\dfrac{4x}{4} = \dfrac{-16}{4}$

Simplify each side. $1x = -4$

$x = -4$

Check: Substitute −4 for x. $4x = -16$

$4(-4) = -16$

$-16 = -16$ true

The solution of $4x = -16$ is −4.

EXAMPLE 2   Solve. Then, check the solution. $-y = 12$

Divide to undo multiplication. $-y = 12$

−y means −1y   **Divide both sides by −1.** $\dfrac{-1y}{-1} = \dfrac{12}{-1}$

Check: **Simplify each side.** $1y = -12$
−y = 12
−(−12) = 12 $y = -12$
  12 = 12 true   The solution of $-y = 12$ is −12.

EXAMPLE 3   Solve. Then, check the solution. $-20 = -5b$

Divide to undo multiplication. $-20 = -5b$

Divide both sides by −5. $\dfrac{-20}{-5} = \dfrac{-5b}{-5}$

Check: **Simplify each side.** $4 = 1b$
−20 = −5b
−20 = −5(4) $4 = b$
−20 = −20 true   The solution of $-20 = -5b$ is 4.

Solve. Then, check the solution.

1. $-n = -30$

$-n$ means $-1 \cdot n$.

Divide both sides by -1.

Simplify each side.

Check:

Substitute ■ for n.

$-1n = -30$

$$\frac{-1n}{-1} = \frac{-30}{-1}$$

$n = ■$

$-n = -30$

$-(■) = -30$

$■ = -30$ true

2. $0 = 8y$

Divide both sides by ■.

Simplify each side.

Check:

Substitute ■ for y.

$$\frac{0}{8} = \frac{8y}{8}$$

$■ = y$

$0 = 8y$

$0 = 8(■)$

$0 = ■$ true

Practice

Solve. Then, check the solution.

1. $3x = 21$

2. $5r = 60$

3. $32 = 4n$

4. $49 = 7a$

5. $48 = -8c$

6. $0 = 2b$

7. $-9x = 45$

8. $-9b = -54$

9. $-a = 24$

10. $-80 = -y$

11. $35 = -7y$

12. $-4 = -4a$

13. $5x = 50$

14. $-12 = 4n$

15. $-9b = 9$

16. $-100 = -10x$

17. $-64 = 8y$

18. $56 = -7a$

Do It Together!

19. Explain to a partner how to solve the equation in number **8** in **Practice.**

20. Write an equation with $-2y$ on the left side. Use any even number for the right side. Ask a partner to solve your equation. Check the solution.

3.9 Solving Equations Using More Than One Operation

Sometimes, you need more than one operation to solve equations. To solve these equations, first undo addition or subtraction. Then, undo multiplication or division.

EXAMPLE 1 Solve. Then, check the solution. $5x-3=7$

Add to undo subtraction.	$5x-3=7$
Add 3 to both sides.	$5x-3+3=7+3$
Simplify each side.	$5x=10$
Divide to undo multiplication.	$\dfrac{5x}{5}=\dfrac{10}{5}$
Divide both sides by 5.	
Simplify each side.	$x=2$

Check: $5x-3=7$
$5(2)-3=7$
$10-3=7$
$7=7$ true

The solution of $5x-3=7$ is 2.

EXAMPLE 2 Solve. Then, check the solution. $\dfrac{y}{3}+2=-7$

Subtract to undo addition.	$\dfrac{y}{3}+2=-7$
Subtract 2 from both sides.	$\dfrac{y}{3}+2-2=-7-2$
Simplify each side.	$\dfrac{y}{3}=-9$
Multiply to undo division.	$\dfrac{3y}{3}=-9(3)$
Multiply both sides by 3.	
Simplify each side.	$y=-27$

Check: $\dfrac{y}{3}+2=-7$
$\dfrac{-27}{3}+2=-7$
$-9+2=-7$
$-7=-7$ true

The solution of $\dfrac{y}{3}+2=-7$ is -27.

EXAMPLE 3 Solve. Then, check the solution. $-5=-x+3$

Subtract to undo addition.	$-5=-x+3$
Subtract 3 from both sides.	$-5-3=-x+3-3$
Divide by -1.	$-8=-1x$
Simplify each side.	$\dfrac{-8}{-1}=\dfrac{-1x}{-1}$
	$8=x$

Check: $-5=-x+3$
$-5=-8+3$
$-5=-5$ true

The solution of $-5=-x+3$ is 8.

Solve. Then, check the solution.

1. $5y - 8 = 12$

Add ■ to both sides. $\qquad 5y - 8 + ■ = 12 + ■$

Simplify each side. $\qquad 5y = ■$

Divide both sides by ■. $\qquad \dfrac{5y}{■} = \dfrac{20}{■}$

Simplify each side. $\qquad y = ■$

Check: $\qquad 5y - 8 = 12$

Substitute ■ for y. $\quad 5(■) - 8 = 12$

$\qquad\qquad\qquad ■ - 8 = 12$

$\qquad\qquad\qquad ■ = 12 \;$ true

2. $14 = -\dfrac{v}{2} + 6$

■ 6 from both sides. $\quad 14 - ■ = -\dfrac{v}{2} + 6 - ■$

Simplify each side. $\qquad ■ = -\dfrac{v}{2}$

■ both sides by −2. $\qquad 8(■) = \dfrac{■v}{-2}$

Simplify each side. $\qquad ■ = v$

Check: $\qquad 14 = -\dfrac{-16}{2} + 6$

Substitute ■ for v. $\quad 14 = -(-8) + 6$

$\qquad\qquad\qquad 14 = ■ + 6$

$\qquad\qquad\qquad 14 = ■ \;$ true

Practice

Solve. Then, check the solution.

1. $10x - 4 = 16$

2. $10x + 8 = 18$

3. $7 = 2z - 7$

4. $-8y + 2 = 26$

5. $14 = -c - 14$

6. $-1 = -4c - 9$

7. $4u + 10 = 2$

8. $-11 = \dfrac{y}{3} - 4$

9. $\dfrac{x}{-5} + 3 = -2$

10. $-n + 7 = 12$

11. $\dfrac{m}{2} + 5 = -3$

12. $26 = -5y + 6$

Do It Together!

13. Explain to a partner how to choose the first step in solving number **6** in **Practice.**

14. Write the equation $2b = 24$. Think of an even number. Subtract it from the left side of the equation. Ask a partner to solve your equation. Check the solution.

3.10 Solving Equations Containing Parentheses

Some equations contain parentheses. Use the Distributive Property to remove the parentheses. Then, you will have an equation you know how to solve.

EXAMPLE 1 Solve. Then, check the solution. $2(y+6)=18$

Use the Distributive Property.
$$2(y+6)=18$$
$$2 \bullet y + 2 \bullet 6 = 18$$
Simplify.
$$2y+12=18$$
Subtract 12 from both sides.
$$2y+12-12=18-12$$
Simplify each side.
$$2y=6$$
Divide both sides by 2.
$$\frac{2y}{2}=\frac{6}{2}$$
Simplify each side.
$$y=3$$

The solution of $2(y+6)=18$ is 3.

Check:
$2(y+6)=18$
$2(3+6)=18$
$2(9)=18$
$18=18$ true

EXAMPLE 2 Solve. Then, check the solution. $-4(b-2)=-12$

Use the Distributive Property.
$$-4(b-2)=-12$$
$$(-4)b-(-4)(2)=-12$$
Simplify.
$$-4b+8=-12$$
Subtract 8 from both sides.
$$-4b+8-8=-12-8$$
Simplify each side.
$$-4b=-20$$
Divide both sides by -4.
$$\frac{-4b}{-4}=\frac{-20}{-4}$$
Simplify each side.
$$b=5$$

The solution of $-4(b-2)=-12$ is 5.

Check:
$-4(b-2)=-12$
$-4(5-2)=-12$
$-4(3)=-12$
$-12=-12$ true

EXAMPLE 3 Solve. Then, check the solution. $15=-(-x+10)$

Use the Distributive Property.
$$15=-(-x+10)$$
Multiply by -1.
$$15=(-1)(-x)+(-1)10$$
Simplify.
$$15=x-10$$
Add 10 to both sides.
$$15+10=x-10+10$$
Simplify each side.
$$25=x$$

The solution of $15=-(-x+10)$ is 25.

Check:
$15=-(-x+10)$
$15=-(-25+10)$
$15=-(-15)$
$15=15$ true

Solve. Then, check the solution.

1. $-5(s-4)=10$

$$-5(s-4)=10$$

Use the Distributive Property. $-5(s)-(-5)(4)=10$

Simplify. $-5\blacksquare+\blacksquare=10$

$\blacksquare$ 20 from both sides. $-5s+\blacksquare-\blacksquare=10-\blacksquare$

Simplify. $-5s=\blacksquare$

Divide both sides by $\blacksquare$. $\dfrac{-5s}{\blacksquare}=\dfrac{-10}{\blacksquare}$

Simplify. $s=\blacksquare$

Check: $-5(\blacksquare-4)=10$

Substitute $\blacksquare$ for s. $-5(\blacksquare)=10$

$\blacksquare=10$ true

2. $-8=4(n-3)$

$$-8=4(n-3)$$

Use the $\blacksquare$. $-8=4(n-3)$

$-8=4\blacksquare-\blacksquare(3)$

Simplify. $-8=\blacksquare-12$

Add $\blacksquare$ to both sides. $-8+\blacksquare=4n-12+\blacksquare$

Simplify. $\blacksquare=4n$

Divide both sides by $\blacksquare$. $\dfrac{4}{\blacksquare}=\dfrac{4n}{\blacksquare}$

Simplify. $\blacksquare=n$

Check: $-8=4(\blacksquare-3)$

Substitute $\blacksquare$ for n. $-8=4(\blacksquare)$

$-8=\blacksquare$ true

Practice

Solve. Then, check the solution.

1. $3(x+3)=18$

2. $16=2(y+7)$

3. $5(b+3)=-30$

4. $2(s-2)=6$

5. $-(x-1)=-12$

6. $16=-4(r+2)$

7. $-5(a+2)=30$

8. $27=-9(z-1)$

9. $-5(y-7)=-20$

Do It Together!

10. Explain to a partner how you use the Distributive Property to remove the parentheses in number **7** in **Practice.**

11. Write an equation that contains parentheses. Ask a partner to solve your equation. Check the solution.

3.11 Solving Equations with Variables on Both Sides

Sometimes equations have a variable on both sides of the equal sign. To solve these equations, get the variable on one side.

You can begin by subtracting the variable term with the smaller coefficient.

EXAMPLE 1   Solve. Then, check the solution. $7x = 5x + 8$

Get the variable on one side. $7x = 5x + 8$

Subtract 5x from both sides. $7x - 5x = 5x - 5x + 8$

Combine like terms. $2x = 8$

Divide both sides by 2. $\dfrac{2x}{2} = \dfrac{8}{2}$

Simplify each side. $x = 4$

Solution: 4

The solution of $7x = 5x + 8$ is 4.

Check:
$7x = 5x + 8$
$7(4) = 5(4) + 8$
$28 = 20 + 8$
$28 = 28$ true

When the smaller coefficient is negative, you can add the variable term to both sides.

EXAMPLE 2   Solve. Then, check the solution. $4y + 4 = -2y - 8$

Get the variable on one side. $4y + 4 = -2y - 8$

Add 2y to both sides. $4y + 2y + 4 = -2y + 2y - 8$

Combine like terms. $6y + 4 = -8$

Subtract 4 from both sides. $6y + 4 - 4 = -8 - 4$

Simplify each side. $6y = -12$

Divide both sides by 6. $\dfrac{6y}{6} = \dfrac{-12}{6}$

Simplify each side. $y = -2$

Solution: -2

The solution of $4y + 4 = -2y - 8$ is -2.

Check:
$4y + 4 = -2y - 8$
$4(-2) + 4 = -2(-2) - 8$
$-8 + 4 = 4 - 8$
$-4 = -4$ true

Solve.

1. $-6t = 14 + t$

Add ■ to both sides.	$-6t + ■ = 14 + t + ■$
Combine like terms.	$0 = 14 + ■$
Subtract ■ from both sides.	$0 - ■ = 14 - ■ + 7t$
Simplify each side.	$-14 = ■$
Divide by ■ on both sides.	$\dfrac{-14}{■} = \dfrac{7t}{■}$
Simplify each side.	$■ = t$

Solution: ■

2. $24 - 4k = -12k$

Add ■ to both sides.	$24 - 4k + ■ = -12k + ■$
Combine like ■.	$24 + ■ = 0$
Subtract ■ from both sides.	$24 - ■ + 8k = 0 - ■$
Simplify each side.	$8k = ■$
Divide by ■ on both sides.	$\dfrac{8k}{■} = \dfrac{-24}{■}$
Simplify each side.	$k = ■$

Solution: ■

Practice

Solve. Then, check the solution.

1. $2x = x + 3$

2. $7x = 3x + 24$

3. $30 + 6t = 11t$

4. $5 - 2t = 3t$

5. $z = 49 - 6z$

6. $5a - 9 = 2a$

7. $28 + 10r = 3r$

8. $4x = 7x + 33$

9. $-3y = -8y - 15$

10. $10x + 9 = 4x - 9$

11. $8x - 8 = -4x + 16$

12. $7w + 5 = 3w - 15$

Do It Together!

13. Explain to a partner how you solve the equation in number **6** in **Practice.**

14. Take turns with a partner to solve $2x = x + 3$.

3.12 Calculator: Checking Solutions

Some equations have decimals. You can use a calculator to check the solutions to these equations.

EXAMPLE 1

Is 17.04 the solution of $2.5(x-16.4)=1.6$?

Substitute 17.04 for x.

$$2.5(x-16.4)=1.6$$

$$2.5(17.04-16.4)=1.6$$

Use your calculator to simplify the left side.   DISPLAY

Perform the operations in the parentheses first.

Enter 17.04 by pressing: [1] [7] [.] [0] [4]   17.04

Subtract 16.4 by pressing: [−] [1] [6] [.] [4] [=]   .64

Multiply by 2.5 by pressing: [×] [2] [.] [5] [=]   1.6

$1.6=1.6$ is true. 17.04 is the solution of $2.5(x-16.4)=1.6$.

EXAMPLE 2

Check whether .56 is the solution of $11v+.456=19v$.

Substitute .56 for v.

$$11v+.456=19v$$

$$11(.56)+.456=19(.56)$$

Use your calculator to simplify each side.   DISPLAY

Enter 11 by pressing: [1] [1]   11

Multiply by .56 by pressing: [×] [.] [5] [6] [=]   6.16

Add .456 by pressing: [+] [.] [4] [5] [6] [=]   6.616

Enter 19 by pressing: [1] [9]   19

Multiply by .56 by pressing: [×] [.] [5] [6] [=]   10.64

The left side does not equal the right side. .56 is not the solution of $11v+.456=19v$.

Practice

Tell whether the number is a solution of the equation.

1. .28; $.1998 = .27(x + .46)$

2. 2.1; $12.2 = 11.5 + \frac{z}{3}$

3. 58; $.21y = .28y - 4.06$

4. 20.4; $14(v - .89) = 162.4$

5. 6.2; $.5(n + 4.9) = 5.55$

6. 7; $9.5y - 8.8 = 5.39y$

Keeping Things in Balance

Scientists use a tool called a balance. This tool lets them find the amounts of different things. To measure an amount, they use a balance with metal weights called *masses*.

The thing they want to measure goes on one side of the balance. Then, they put the masses on the other side. If it does not balance, they add or take away masses until it does. When the two sides balance, the sides are equal in amount. The number of masses tells the amount.

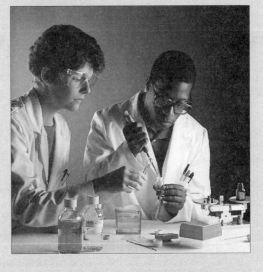

Some balances are large and use large masses. They measure larger items. Other kinds of balances are used to find very exact amounts. Scientists need to use just the right amount of chemicals. If too much is used, an experiment can go wrong!

3.13 Problem Solving: Writing Percent Equations

You will see many problems that ask you to find the percent of a number. You can write a variable equation for the problem. Begin by choosing a variable for the missing number. Use "=" for "is" and "•" for "of."

What number is 25% of 60?

don't know $= .25 • 60$

$25\% = .25 = .25$

Pick a letter to stand for the number. You can use n.

$n = .25 • 60$

$n = 15$

Solution: 15
15 is 25% of 60.

EXAMPLE 1   6% of 50 is what number?

6% of 50 is what number?

Write an equation. $.06 • 50 = $ don't know

$6\% = .06 = .06$

Use y for the variable. $.06 • 50 = y$

Solve for y. $3 = y$

$.06 • 50 = 3$

Solution: 3
6% of 50 is 3.

EXAMPLE 2   85% of the 300 seniors are going to college. How many seniors are going to college?

85% of seniors are going to college.

Write an equation. $.85 • 300 = $ don't know

$85\% = .85 = .85$

Use x for the variable. $.85 • 300 = x$

Solve for x. $255 = x$

$.85 • 300 = 255$

Solution: 255
85% of 300 is 255. 255 students are going to college.

Find the number.

1. What is 50% of 88?

Write an equation.   ? is 50% of 88

Use *w* as the variable.   ■ = .50 • 88

Solve for *w*. $w = ■$

Solution: ■

50% of 88 is 44.

2. 15% of 40 computers have a virus. How many have a virus?

Write an   15% of 40 have a virus.
equation.

Use *n* as the   .15 • 40 = ■
variable.

Solve for *n*.   ■ = n

Solution: ■

15% of 40 is 6.
6 computers have a virus.

Practice

Write an equation and solve each percent problem.

1. What is 55% of 80?

2. What is 20% of 50?

3. 25% of 100 is what number?

4. 40% of 65 is what number?

5. 5% of 160 teachers are retiring. How many teachers are retiring?

6. Megan scored in 80% of 20 games this season. In how many games did Megan score?

Do It Together!

7. Explain to a partner how you wrote the variable equation in number **6** in **Practice.**

8. Write a word sentence. Have a partner write a variable equation for what you wrote. Check the work.

3.14   Application: Consumer Math

When you buy something on sale, you pay less than the regular price. The money you save is the **discount.** You can find the discount by multiplying by the percent of the discount.

discount = percent of discount × regular price

EXAMPLE 1   A shirt costs $30.00. It is on sale for 20% off the regular price. Find the discount.

discount = percent of discount × regular price

discount = 20% • 30

discount = .2 • 30

discount = 6

$20\% = .20 = .2$

$$\begin{array}{r} 30 \\ \times\ \ .2 \\ \hline 6.0 \end{array}$$

The discount is $6.00.

Once you know the discount you can find the **sale price.** Subtract the discount from the regular price.

sale price = regular price − discount

EXAMPLE 2   A CD costs $15.00. It is on sale for 5% off the regular price. Find the sale price.

Find the discount.

discount = percent of discount × regular price

discount = 5% • 15

discount = .05 • 15

discount = .75

$5\% = .05$

The discount is $.75.

Find the sale price.

sale price = regular price − discount

sale price = 15 − .75

sale price = 14.25

$$\begin{array}{r} \$15.00 \\ -\ \ \ .75 \\ \hline \$14.25 \end{array}$$

The sale price is $14.25.

Solve.

1. Find the discount on a $24 shirt that is on sale for 25% off.

discount = percent of discount × regular price

discount = ■ • 24

discount = ■

The discount is ■.

2. Find the sale price of the $24 shirt.

sale price = ■ − discount

sale price = ■ − 6

sale price = ■

The sale price is ■.

Practice

Find the discount or the sale price.

1. Find the discount on a $15 T-shirt. It is on sale for 10% off.

2. Find the sale price of a $50 bookshelf that is on sale for 15% off.

3. A train set costs $120.00. Find the discount if it is on sale for 30% off.

4. What is the sale price of a $300 mountain bike that is on sale for 50% off?

5. Find the discount for a stereo that is on sale for 12% off. The original price is $200.00.

Do It Together!

6. Explain to a partner how you find the discount and the sale price for the item in number **2** in **Practice.**

7. Work with a partner. Think of the cost of an item. The item is on sale for 10% off. Ask your partner to find the amount that would be saved with the discount. Then have your partner find the sale price of the item.

Chapter 3 Summary

- The solution of an equation is the value of the variable that makes the equation true.
- Adding, subtracting, multiplying, or dividing both sides of an equation by the same number gives an equivalent equation.
- When you add, subtract, multiply, or divide both sides of an equation by the same number, you are using properties of equality.
- You can use inverse operations to solve an equation.
- You can use the Distributive Property to remove parentheses in equations.
- To solve an equation with variables on both sides, you can add or subtract the variable term from one side.
- You can use a calculator to check solutions that are decimals.
- To write a percent equation, use "=" for "is," "•" for "of," and a variable for the number you don't know. Write the percent as a decimal.
- You can find the sale price by subtracting the amount of the discount. You can find the discount by multiplying the regular price by the percent of the discount.

Reviewing Vocabulary

Fill in each blank with the correct word.

variable equation
solution
equivalent equations
properties of equality
inverse operations
solve
check
discount
sale price

1. The regular price minus the discount is called the ? .
2. ? are operations that "undo" other operations.
3. You can ? a solution when you substitute the solution for the variable.
4. The amount you save when you buy an item on sale is the ? .
5. Two equations are ? when they have the same solution.
6. A ? is an equation that contains a variable.
7. The ? is the value of the variable that makes a variable equation true.
8. An example of one of the ? is adding the same amount to both sides of an equation.
9. To ? an equation is to find the solution of the equation.

Chapter Quiz

Tell whether the number is the solution of the equation.

1. $-15; x+35=20$ **2.** $3; 2y+4=12$ **3.** $-2; 8=10+x$

Show that each pair of equations is equivalent.

4. $b=9$ and $3b=27$ **5.** $w=-14$ and $w+8=-6$ **6.** $2=b$ and $6b-3=9$

Complete to make equivalent equations.

7. $\frac{x}{4}=3$ **8.** $6+x=-11$ **9.** $-2y=14$

    $\frac{x}{4}?4=3 \bullet 4$ $6-?+x=-11-6$ $-2y \blacksquare (-2)=14 \div (-2)$

Complete each equation with the missing operation.

10. $x+3?3=x$ **11.** $-5y?(-5)=y$ **12.** $\frac{v}{10}?10=v$

Solve. Then, check the solution.

13. $x-4=20$ **14.** $a-13=-20$ **15.** $0=t-7$

16. $4t=-20$ **17.** $2=3x-13$ **18.** $\frac{y}{3}+6=-1$

19. $4(y+2)=28$ **20.** $-(w+3)=-15$ **21.** $4x=2x+6$

Find the number.

22. What is 30% of 150?

23. 40% of 250 students have part-time jobs. How many students have part-time jobs?

Find the discount or the sale price.

24. Find the discount for a $40.00 jacket that is on sale at 20% off.

25. Find the sale price of a $10.00 T-shirt. It is discounted 15%.

Unit One Review

Add, subtract, multiply, or divide.

1. $3 + (^-6)$ **2.** $(^-8) + (^-4)$ **3.** $9 + (^-8)$ **4.** $(^-11) - (^-4)$

5. $(4)(^-3)$ **6.** $(^-13)(^-1)$ **7.** $\dfrac{25}{-5}$ **8.** $\dfrac{-28}{-7}$

Simplify.

9. $-6 + 14 \div 2$ **10.** $4 - 8 \div 2^2$ **11.** $6(2+3) - 13$

12. $3x - 12x$ **13.** $4(a - 8)$ **14.** $12 - 3(y + 2)$

Evaluate each expression.

15. $3q - 8$ when q is 1 **16.** $\dfrac{s}{7}$ when s is 42 **17.** $-4a^2$ when a is -3

Tell whether the number is a solution of the equation.

18. $9; 13 = a + 4$ **19.** $-2; 3m + 4 = -2$ **20.** $5; \dfrac{x}{4} = 20$

Solve. Then, check the solution.

21. $x - 2 = 17$ **22.** $15 = y + 3$ **23.** $-2n = -16$

24. $-12 = \dfrac{p}{3}$ **25.** $3k + 3 = 27$ **26.** $5 = 2t + 15$

27. $25 = 7x - 3$ **28.** $2b = 18 - 4b$ **29.** $5(a - 4) = 10$

Find the number.

30. The product of a number and 4 is -36.

31. Twice the sum of a number and 1 is 8.

32. 10% of 30 is what number?

33. 25% of the 200 students in ninth grade are on the honor roll. How many students are on the honor roll?

Unit Two

Chapter 4
Introducing Functions

Chapter 5
Linear Equations and Functions

Chapter 6
Writing Linear Equations

Chapter 4

Introducing Functions

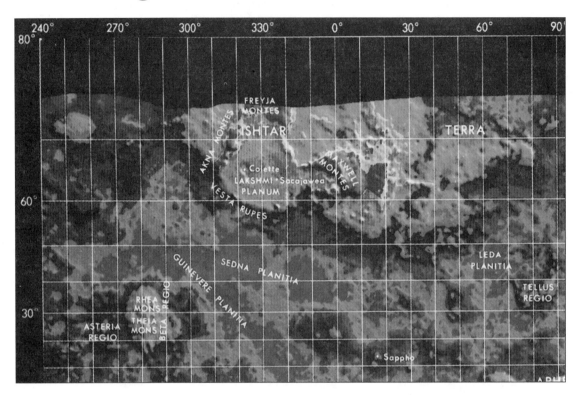

Maps can be used to find places anywhere, even on Venus. Maps use a grid system based on the directions north/south and east/west. Algebra uses a grid system, too, but on this grid you can plot values to find functions.

Chapter Learning Objectives

- Graph ordered pairs.
- Find ordered pairs from tables and equations.
- Identify a function.
- Use a calculator to find ordered pairs.
- Use a function shown as a table or equation to solve problems.
- Apply concepts and skills to use information in tables and bar graphs.

Words to Know

coordinate plane   plane with two perpendicular number lines

coordinate axes   perpendicular number lines

origin   the point where coordinate axes cross

ordered pairs   two numbers in a special order; Ordered pairs give the locations of points

graph of an ordered pair   a dot that shows the location of an ordered pair

function   a group of ordered pairs where no two ordered pairs have the same first number

vertical line test   a test you use on a graph to tell if the graph is a function

function notation   a way to write an equation to show it is a function

bar graph   a graph that uses bars to represent information

In this chapter, you will locate and graph ordered pairs on a coordinate plane. You will learn how to find ordered pairs from tables and equations. You will also learn what functions are and how to write them. You will use your calculator to find ordered pairs. By the end of the chapter, you will solve problems by choosing the best method and getting information from tables, equations, and bar graphs.

4.1   The Coordinate Plane

A **coordinate plane** has two perpendicular number lines called **coordinate axes.** The axis that goes left and right is the horizontal axis. It is called the *x*-axis. The axis that goes up and down is the vertical axis. It is called the *y*-axis. The axes cross at the **origin.**

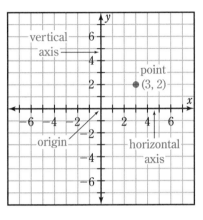

Ordered pairs give the locations of points on the coordinate plane. The first number tells the location in the horizontal direction. The second number gives the location in the vertical direction. The ordered pair for the origin is (0, 0). When you use the variables *x* and *y*, the ordered pair is (*x*, *y*).

EXAMPLE 1

Give the location of A at (4, −2).

Begin at the origin.

Positive numbers are right or up from the origin.

Move right 4 units.

Move down 2 units.

Negative numbers are left or down from the origin.

The location of A is right 4 units, down 2 units.

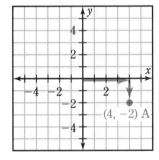

Sometimes, other letters are used to label the axes.

EXAMPLE 2

Give the location of B at (−3, −1).

Begin at the origin.

Move left 3 units.

Move down 1 unit.

The location of B is left 3 units, down 1 unit.

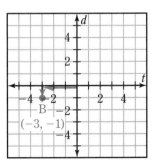

Give the location of each point.

1. A (2, 5)

   right 2 units, up ▧ units

2. B (−2, −3)

   left ▧ units, down 3 units

3. C (−4, 2)

   ▧ 4 units, up ▧ units

4. D (0, 3)

   up ▧ units from the origin

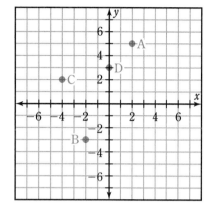

Practice

Give the location of each point.

1. A (1, 3)

2. B (−3, 3)

3. C (0, 2)

4. D (2, −1)

5. E (−4, 0)

6. F (3, 1)

7. G (−2, −5)

8. H (0, −3)

9. I (−5, −4)

10. J (3, −4)

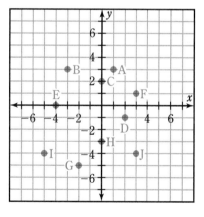

Do It Together!

11. Explain to a partner how to give the location of the point in number **5** in **Practice.**

12. Ask a partner to tell why A (1, 3) and F (3, 1) are not at the same location.

4.2 Graphing Ordered Pairs

You have used an ordered pair to find the location of a point. Now, you will graph an ordered pair on a coordinate plane. The **graph of an ordered pair** is a point.

EXAMPLE 1

Graph point A at $(3, -2)$

Begin at the origin.

3 means right 3 units.

Move right 3 units.

−2 means down 2 units.

Move down 2 units.

Draw a dot at this location.

Label it A (3, −2).

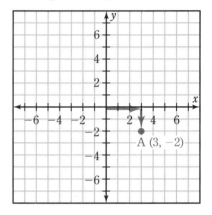

EXAMPLE 2

Graph point B at $(-4, 0)$

Begin at the origin.

−4 means left 4 units.

Move left 4 units.

0 means no units up or down.

Do not move up or down.

Draw a dot at this location.

Label it B (−4, 0).

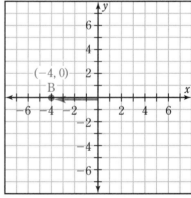

EXAMPLE 3

Graph point C at $(0, 3)$

Begin at the origin.

0 means no units left or right.

Do not move left or right.

3 means up 3 units.

Move up 3 units.

Draw a dot at this location.

Label it C (0, 3).

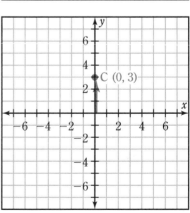

Graph and label each point.

1. P at $(-2, 1)$

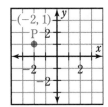

Begin at the origin.

Move left ■ units.

Move ■ 1 unit.

Draw a dot.

Label it P $(-2, 1)$.

2. Q at $(-4, -3)$

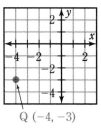

Begin at the origin.

Move ■ 4 units.

Move down ■ units.

Draw a dot.

Label it Q $(-4, -3)$.

Q $(-4, -3)$

Practice

Use graph paper. Draw coordinate axes. Graph and label each point on the same pair of axes.

1. A at $(4, 4)$

2. B at $(-2, 2)$

3. C at $(-2, -4)$

4. D at $(3, -2)$

5. E at $(2, 4)$

6. F at $(0, 3)$

7. G at $(-3, 1)$

8. H at $(1, -3)$

9. I at $(2, 2)$

10. J at $(-3, -2)$

11. K at $(-2, 0)$

12. L at $(5, 2)$

13. M at $(2, -1)$

14. N at $(-4, 3)$

15. O at $(-1, -1)$

Do It Together!

16. Explain to a partner how to graph and label the point in number **8** in **Practice.**

17. Write four ordered pairs. Ask a partner to graph each point on the coordinate axes. Check the work.

4.3 Tables and Ordered Pairs

You can show ordered pairs in tables. The first column of the table contains the first number of an ordered pair. The second column of the table contains the second number.

EXAMPLE 1 Write the ordered pairs from the table.

Write each row as an ordered pair.
(1, 2), (2, 4), (3, 6)

Time	Distance
1 second	2 feet
2 seconds	4 feet
3 seconds	6 feet

The ordered pairs are (1, 2), (2, 4), and (3, 6)

You can graph the ordered pairs. Use the heading of the first column for the horizontal axis. Use the heading of the second column for the vertical axis.

EXAMPLE 2 Write the ordered pairs from the table. Label the coordinate axes. Then, graph the ordered pairs

Minutes	°Celsius
4	−4
5	−2
6	0

Write each row as an ordered pair.
(4, −4), (5, −2), (6, 0)

Label the horizontal axis with the heading from the first column.

Label the vertical axis with the heading from the second column.

Graph the ordered pairs.

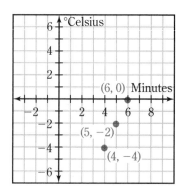

1. Write the ordered pairs from the table.

   Write the rows as ordered pairs. (1, ■)

   (2, ■)

   (■, ■)

   The ordered pairs are (1, ■), (2, ■), and (■, ■).

Hours	Feet
1	2
2	−2
3	−6

2. Label the axes. Graph the ordered pairs.

   Label the horizontal axis with the heading from the first column.

   Label horizontal axis: Hours.

   Label the vertical axis with the heading from the second column.

   Label vertical axis: ■.

   Graph the ordered pairs.

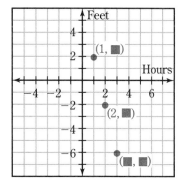

Practice

Write the ordered pairs from each table. Use graph paper. Label the axes. Then, graph the ordered pairs.

1.

Day	Temperature
1	−5
2	0
3	5

2.

Quarts	Pints
2	4
4	8
6	12

Do It Together!

3. Explain to a partner how to write the ordered pairs in number **2** in **Practice.**

4. Make a table containing three pairs of numbers. Ask a partner to write the ordered pairs. Be sure to put labels in the table.

4.4 Equations and Ordered Pairs

One way to find ordered pairs is from equations that have two variables. Substitute a value for one variable into the equation, and find the corresponding value for the other variable. Each pair of values forms an ordered pair.

EXAMPLE 1

Find four ordered pairs for $y = x - 3$.

The x-value is the first number in the ordered pair.

Let $x = -1$. Then, $y = (-1) - 3 = -4$. $(-1, -4)$

Let $x = 0$. Then, $y = (0) - 3 = -3$. $(0, -3)$

The y-value is the second number in the ordered pair.

Let $x = 1$. Then, $y = (1) - 3 = -2$. $(1, -2)$

Let $x = 2$. Then, $y = (2) - 3 = -1$. $(2, -1)$

Four ordered pairs for $y = x - 3$ are $(-1, -4)$, $(0, -3)$, $(1, -2)$, and $(2, -1)$.

You can use a table to show the ordered pairs. The columns show the values of each number in an ordered pair.

EXAMPLE 2

Make a table of values for $d = a^2 - 1$.

Write column headings from the equation.

Choose values for the variables that are easy to use.

Let $a = -1$. Substitute -1 for a. Simplify.

Let $a = 0$. Substitute 0 for a. Simplify.

Let $a = 1$. Substitute 1 for a. Simplify.

Let $a = 2$. Substitute 2 for a. Simplify.

a	$a^2 - 1$	d
-1	$(-1)^2 - 1$	0
0	$(0)^2 - 1$	-1
1	$(1)^2 - 1$	0
2	$(2)^2 - 1$	3

Write the ordered pairs.

Four ordered pairs for $d = a^2 - 1$ are $(-1, 0)$, $(0, -1)$, $(1, 0)$, and $(2, 3)$.

1. Find three ordered pairs for the equation $y = 3(x+1)$.

   Let $x = -1$.
   Then, $y = 3(-1+1) = \blacksquare \rightarrow (-1, \blacksquare)$.
   Let $x = 0$.
   Then, $y = 3(0+1) = \blacksquare \rightarrow (0, \blacksquare)$.
   Let $x = 1$.
   Then, $y = 3(\blacksquare + 1) = \blacksquare \rightarrow (\blacksquare, \blacksquare)$.
   Three ordered pairs for
   $y = 3(x+1)$ are $(-1, \blacksquare)$, $(0, \blacksquare)$, and $(\blacksquare, \blacksquare)$.

2. Make a table of values for $y = 2x + 4$.

   Write column headings from the equation.
   Let $x = -1$.
   Let $x = 0$.
   Let $x = 1$.

x	$\blacksquare$	y
-1	$2(-1) + 4$	$\blacksquare$
$\blacksquare$	$2(\blacksquare) + 4$	4
$\blacksquare$	$2(\blacksquare) + 4$	$\blacksquare$

   Three ordered pairs for $y = 2x + 4$ are $(-1, \blacksquare)$, $(\blacksquare, 4)$, and $(\blacksquare, \blacksquare)$.

Practice

Find three ordered pairs for each equation.

1. $y = 5x + 1$

2. $y = 10 - x$

3. $y = 2x$

Complete each table to show four ordered pairs for the equation.

4.

x	x^2	y
-1	$(-1)^2$	?
0	?	?
1	?	?
2	?	?

5.

x	$2(x-1)$	y
-1	$2(-1-1)$	?
0	?	?
1	?	?
2	?	?

Do It Together!

6. Explain to a partner how to find the last row in number 4 in **Practice.**

7. Write a simple equation. Ask a partner to find an ordered pair for your equation.

4.5 Functions

Some groups of ordered pairs are called **functions.** In a function, each value of x has only one value of y.

(2, 3), (4, 5), (6, 7), (8, 9)

x-values: 2, 4, 6, and 8

Each x-value has only one y-value.

This is a function.

(5, 8), (5, 9), (6, 10), (7, 11)

x-values: 5, 5, 6, and 7

5 has two y-values, 8 and 9

This is not a function.

EXAMPLE 1   Tell whether (2, −1), (3, −2), (4, 0), (3, 1) is a function.

List each x-value.   2, 3, 4, 3

Look for repeated numbers.   3 has two y-values, −2 and 1.

This group of ordered pairs is not a function.

You can look at a graph to see if the ordered pairs form a function. If a vertical line can cross the graph more than once, it is not a function. This is the **vertical line test.**

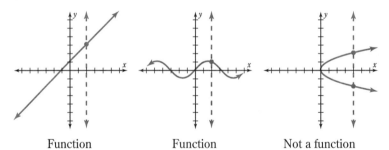

Function   Function   Not a function

EXAMPLE 2   Tell whether the graph is a function.

Draw a vertical line.
The line crosses the graph exactly once.

The graph is a function.

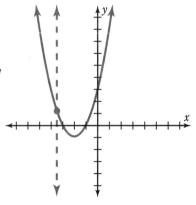

1. Tell without graphing whether (0, 2), (1, 3), (2, 4), (3, 4) is a function.

   List each *x*-value. 0, 1, 2, ■

   Look for repeated numbers. Each *x*-value has ■ *y*-value.

   This set of ordered pairs ■ a function.

2. Tell whether the graph is a function.

   A vertical line ■ this graph more than one time.

   This set of ordered pairs ■ a function.

   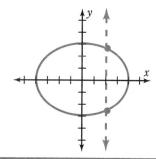

Practice

Tell without graphing whether each group of ordered pairs is a function.

1. (5, 1), (10, 2), (15, 3), (15, 4)   **2.** (2, 5), (3, 9), (4, 12), (5, 15)

Tell by using the vertical line test whether each graph is a function.

3. 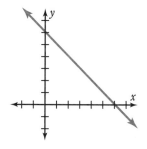   **4.** 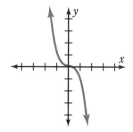   **5.**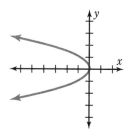

Do It Together!

6. Explain to a partner how to tell whether the group of ordered pairs is a function in number **2** in **Practice.**

7. Draw two graphs. Make one a function. Make the other not a function. Ask a partner to tell which one is the function.

4.6　Function Notation

Some equations are functions. Ordered pairs from these equations have only one y-value for each x-value. You can use **function notation** to show that an equation is a function. The symbol $f(x)$ means "the function of x."

You can say "*f* of *x*" for *f(x)*.

$$y = 2x + 4 \rightarrow f(x) = 2x + 4$$

A function is a rule for finding ordered pairs. It tells you how to find y when you know x.

$f(3)$ means the value of $f(x)$ when x is 3.

$$f(x) = 2x + 4$$
$$f(3) = 2(3) + 4$$
$$f(3) = 6 + 4$$
$$f(3) = 10 \rightarrow (3, 10) \text{ is an ordered pair for}$$
$$f(x) = 2x + 4.$$

EXAMPLE 1　Find $f(4)$ when $f(x) = -3x$.

$$f(x) = -3x$$

Substitute 4 for *x*.　　$f(4) = -3 \bullet 4$

Simplify.　　$f(4) = -12$

$f(4) = -12$ when $f(x) = -3x$.

EXAMPLE 2　Find $f(-1)$ when $f(x) = x^2$.

$$f(x) = x^2$$

$(-1)^2 = (-1)(-1)$　　**Substitute −1 for *x*.**　　$f(-1) = (-1)^2$

Simplify.　　$f(-1) = 1$

$f(-1) = 1$ when $f(x) = x^2$.

EXAMPLE 3　Find $f(0)$ when $f(x) = 2(x + 4)$.

$$f(x) = 2(x + 4)$$

Substitute 0 for *x*.　　$f(0) = 2(0 + 4)$

Simplify.　　$f(0) = 8$

$f(0) = 8$ when $f(x) = 2(x + 4)$.

Write using function notation.

1. $y = x + 2$

$$y = x + 2$$

Use $f(x)$ for y. $\blacksquare = x + 2$

2. $y = 6(x + x^2)$

$$y = 6(x + x^2)$$

Use $\blacksquare$ for y. $f(x) = \blacksquare$

Find the value of each function.

3. $f(-2)$ when $f(x) = 3 - x$

$$f(x) = 3 - x$$

Substitute -2 for x. $f(\blacksquare) = 3 - (-2)$

Simplify. $f(-2) = 3 + \blacksquare$

$$f(-2) = \blacksquare$$

$f(-2) = \blacksquare$ when $f(x) = 3 - x$.

4. $f(0)$ when $f(x) = 5(x + 4)$

$$f(x) = 5(x + 4)$$

Substitute $\blacksquare$ for x. $f(0) = 5(\blacksquare + 4)$

Simplify. $f(\blacksquare) = 5(\blacksquare)$

$$f(0) = \blacksquare$$

$f(0) = \blacksquare$ when $f(x) = 5(x + 4)$.

Practice

Each equation below is a function. Write with function notation.

1. $y = 4 + x$ **2.** $y = -x - 9$ **3.** $y = 3(x - 5)$

Find the value of each function.

4. $f(5)$ when $f(x) = 5 + x$

5. $f(0)$ when $f(x) = x - 9$

6. $f(-2)$ when $f(x) = 6x$

7. $f(8)$ when $f(x) = 4(x - 2)$

8. $f(3)$ when $f(x) = x^2 - 2$

9. $f(-3)$ when $f(x) = x + 2$

Do It Together!

10. Explain to a partner how to find the value in number **5** in **Practice.**

11. Write the function $f(x) = 6x - 10$. Think of an even number between 2 and 10. Ask a partner to find the value of the function for the number you chose.

4.7 Calculator: Finding Ordered Pairs

Some equations have large numbers. You can use a calculator to find ordered pairs for these equations.

EXAMPLE 1 Complete this table of ordered pairs for the equation $y = 25(x+3)$.

x	$25(x+3)$	y
.2	$25(.2+3)$	?
1.4	$25(1.4+3)$	?
.06	$25(.06+3)$	?

Use .2 for x.   DISPLAY

Remember to simplify the parentheses first.

		DISPLAY
Enter .2 by pressing:	$\boxed{.}\,\boxed{2}$	.2
Add 3 by pressing:	$\boxed{+}\,\boxed{3}\,\boxed{=}$	3.2
Multiply by 25 by pressing:	$\boxed{\times}\,\boxed{2}\,\boxed{5}\,\boxed{=}$	80

The first ordered pair is (.2, 80).

Use 1.4 for x.   DISPLAY

		DISPLAY
Enter 1.4 by pressing:	$\boxed{1}\,\boxed{.}\,\boxed{4}$	1.4
Add 3 by pressing:	$\boxed{+}\,\boxed{3}\,\boxed{=}$	4.4
Multiply by 25 by pressing:	$\boxed{\times}\,\boxed{2}\,\boxed{5}\,\boxed{=}$	110

The second ordered pair is (1.4, 110).

Use .06 for x.   DISPLAY

		DISPLAY
Enter .06 by pressing:	$\boxed{.}\,\boxed{0}\,\boxed{6}$	.06
Add 3 by pressing:	$\boxed{+}\,\boxed{3}\,\boxed{=}$	3.06
Multiply by 25 by pressing:	$\boxed{\times}\,\boxed{2}\,\boxed{5}\,\boxed{=}$	76.5

The third ordered pair is (.06, 76.5)

Practice

Complete each table of ordered pairs.

1. $y = 0.5x + 18$

x	$0.5x + 18$	y
2	$0.5(2) + 18$	?
4	?	?
6	?	?
8	?	?

2. $y = 10(x + 6)$

x	$10(x + 6)$	y
2	$10(2 + 6)$	?
4	?	?
6	?	?
8	?	?

MATH CONNECTION

Making Maps

There are all kinds of maps. Some maps show natural places like rivers and deserts. Others show things like streets and cities. Maps can be of large areas, such as continents. They also can be small, showing a town or even your school.

One thing maps have in common is how they are made. Mapmakers are also called *cartographers*. Cartographers start with a photograph of the place they are mapping. It may be taken from an airplane or even a satellite. They study the photographs carefully so they don't make mistakes. From the air, many things can look alike. A park and a forest need to be labeled correctly.

Labels make reading a map easier. Some maps are labeled with a special coordinate plane. One axis is numbered, and the other axis has a letter. A grid divides the map into squares. Each square on the map is located by its letter and number. This is like finding a point on a graph by its ordered pair.

4.8 Problem Solving: Choosing the Best Method

You plan to order CDs from a catalog. Each CD is $12.00. You have to pay $4.00 total for shipping. The total cost is a function of the number of CDs you buy. You can show this function with a table or an equation.

Let t be the total cost of the CDs you buy. Let c be the number of CDs you buy.

Table			Equation
c	$12c+4$	t	t is $12 for each c plus $4
1	$12(1)+4$	16	$t=12c+4$
2	$12(2)+4$	28	
3	$12(3)+4$	40	

You can choose to use the table or equation to solve a problem.

EXAMPLE 1   How much do 3 CDs cost?

Use the table.

3	$12(3)+4$	40

It costs $40.00 to order 3 CDs.

EXAMPLE 2   How much do 4 CDs cost?

Use the equation. $t=12c+4$

Substitute 4 for c. $t=12(4)+4$

Simplify. $t=52$

It costs $52.00 to order 4 CDs.

EXAMPLE 3   How much do 10 CDs cost?

Use the equation. $t=12c+4$

Substitute 10 for c. $t=12(10)+4$

Simplify. $t=124$

It costs $124.00 to order 10 CDs.

Answer each question using the table or equation.

1. How much do 100 CDs cost?

   Use the ■. $t = 12c + 4$

   Substitute 100 for c. $t = 12\,(■) + 4$

   Simplify. $t = ■ + 4$

                     $t = ■$

   100 CDs cost ■.

2. How much do 2 CDs cost?

   Use the ■. $12(■) + 4$

   2 CDs cost ■.

Practice

Tell whether you would use the table or equation. Then, answer the question.

1. How much does 1 CD cost?

2. How much do 8 CDs cost?

3. How much do 5 CDs cost?

4. How much do 50 CDs cost?

5. As the number of CDs you buy increases, what happens to the cost?

Do It Together!

6. Explain to a partner how to decide which method to use in number **3** in **Practice.**

7. Choose a number between 6 and 20. Ask a partner to find the cost to order that many CDs.

4.9 Application: Tables and Graphs

The table shows what kinds of music the students in a class like best. You can show the information from the table in a **bar graph.**

Kinds of Music	Number of Students
Alternative	5
Classical	2
Country	4
Rap	2
Oldies	4
Rock	6
Tejano	3

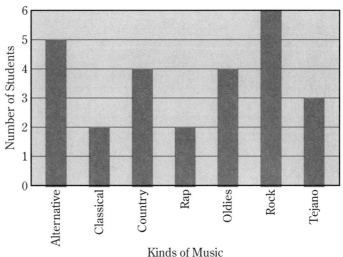

You can use either the table or the bar graph to answer questions about the information.

EXAMPLE 1   How many students chose Rock?

Use the table.

Rock	6

The number is 6.

Find "Rock" in the table, and read the number to the right.

Six students like Rock best.

EXAMPLE 2   What kinds of music were liked least? How many students chose each of these kinds of music?

The shortest bars represent the music students liked the least.   The Rap and Classical bars are the shortest.

Find the height by looking across to the vertical axis.   The height of the bars is 2.

Rap and Classical music were liked the least. Two students chose Rap, and two chose Classical.

Use the bar graph or table to answer each question.

1. What kind of music was liked second most? How many students chose this kind of music?

Find the second highest bar. The second highest bar represents Alternative.

Find the height by looking across to the vertical axis. The height of the bar is ■.

Alternative was liked second most.
■ students chose Alternative.

2. How many more students chose Rock than Oldies?

Use the table to find Rock. ■ students chose Rock.

Use the table to find Oldies. ■ students chose Oldies.

Find the difference. $■ - 4 = 2$

■ more students chose Rock than Oldies.

Practice

Use the bar graph or table to answer each question.

1. How many students chose Tejano?

2. How many students chose Country?

3. How many more students chose Alternative than Classical?

4. List the types of music from least liked to most liked.

Do It Together!

5. Explain to a partner how you find the number of students in number **1** in **Practice.**

6. Think of a question you can answer using the bar graph. Ask a partner your question.

Chapter 4 Summary

- You use coordinate axes to graph the locations of ordered pairs.
- You can use tables to show ordered pairs.
- You can find ordered pairs from equations that have two variables.
- You can use the vertical line test on a graph to tell if a set of ordered pairs is a function.
- You can use a calculator to find ordered pairs.
- To answer questions about a function, you can use an equation or a table of ordered pairs.
- You can use a bar graph to show information from a table.

Reviewing Vocabulary

Fill in each blank with the correct word.

coordinate axes

coordinate plane

origin

ordered pairs

graph of an ordered
 pair

function

vertical line test

function notation

bar graph

1. A dot that shows the location of a point is called a(n) ? .
2. Perpendicular number lines are called ? .
3. Coordinate axes cross at the ? .
4. ? give the location of points on the coordinate plane.
5. A(n) ? is a group of ordered pairs for which no two pairs have the same first number.
6. You use the ? to tell if the graph is a function.
7. A plane with two perpendicular number lines is called a(n) ? .
8. You use a(n) ? to show that an equation is a function.
9. A graph that uses bars to show information is called a(n) ? .

Chapter Quiz

Use graph paper. Draw coordinate axes. Graph and label each point.

1. A at $(3, -2)$ **2.** B at $(0, -5)$ **3.** C at $(-1, 3)$

4. Write the ordered pairs. Graph.

Seconds	°Celsius
1	-3
2	-1
3	1

5. Copy and complete the table.

x	$3(x-2)$	y
-1	$3(-1-2)$	?
0	?	?
1	?	?

Tell whether each group of ordered pairs is a function.

6. $(-1, 1)$, $(0, 1)$, $(1, 1)$, $(2, 4)$ **7.** $(-1, 2)$, $(0, 0)$, $(0, 5)$, $(2, 7)$

8.

9.

Find the value of each function.

10. $f(2)$ when $f(x) = 15 + x$ **11.** $f(0)$ when $f(x) = 2(x+6)$

Use the table or $d = 55t + 20$.

12. What is the distance when the time is 6 hours?

Time	Distance
1 hour	75 miles
2 hours	130 miles
3 hours	185 miles

Use the bar graph.

13. How many employees were there in 1993?

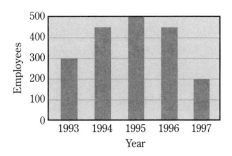

Chapter 5

Linear Equations and Functions

In a race, the distance you can travel in an hour varies with your speed. The faster you go, the farther you will travel. The relationship between distance and speed can be described in a linear equation.

Chapter Learning Objectives

- Graph linear equations using ordered pairs.
- Find the slope of a line.
- Find the intercepts of a line.
- Graph a line using the slope and a point.
- Use a calculator to find intercepts.
- Use slope to solve problems.
- Apply concepts and skills to using direct variation.

Words to Know

linear equation   an equation whose graph is a straight line

slope   a measure of the steepness of a straight line; Tells how fast one variable changes compared with the other

rise   the change between two points on a line in an up-and-down direction

run   the change between two points on a line in a left-to-right direction

x-intercept   the x-value of the ordered pair at the point where a line crosses the x-axis

y-intercept   the y-value of the ordered pair at the point where a line crosses the y-axis

slope-intercept form $y = mx + b$; m is the slope and b is the y-intercept

standard form $Ax + By = C$

direct variation $y = kx$; k is a positive number; As one variable increases, the other increases

---

In this chapter, you will learn how to graph linear equations. You will learn about the slope and the intercepts of a line. Then, you will learn to use these to graph a line. You will use your calculator to find the intercepts of linear equations that contain large numbers. You will use slope to solve problems. Then, you will solve problems about direct variation.

5.1 Equations with Two Variables

Some equations have two variables. The solutions are ordered pairs. You can substitute the first number of the ordered pair for x and the second number for y. If the ordered pair makes a true equation, the ordered pair is a solution.

$$y = 2x + 1 \text{ has 2 variables; } x \text{ and } y$$

The order of the variables is always (x, y)

$(1, 3)$ is one solution of $y = 2x + 1$.

$$3 = 2 \bullet 1 + 1$$
$$3 = 3 \quad \text{true}$$

The equation $y = 2x + 1$ has other solutions.

EXAMPLE 1   Tell whether $(1, -1)$ is a solution of $y = 2x - 3$.

Substitute 1 for x and -1 for y. $y = 2x - 3$

Simplify. $-1 = 2(1) - 3$

$$-1 = 2 - 3$$
$$-1 = -1 \quad \text{true}$$

$(1, -1)$ is a solution of $y = 2x - 3$.

EXAMPLE 2   Tell whether $(-2, 1)$ is a solution of $y = 2x - 3$.

$$y = 2x - 3$$

Substitute -2 for x and 1 for y. $1 = 2(-2) - 3$

Simplify. $1 = -4 - 3$

$$1 = -7 \quad \text{false}$$

$(-2, 1)$ is not a solution of $y = 2x - 3$.

EXAMPLE 3   Tell whether $(6, -2)$ is a solution of $y + x = 4$.

$$y + x = 4$$

Substitute 6 for x and -2 for y. $-2 + 6 = 4$

Simplify. $4 = 4 \quad \text{true}$

$(6, -2)$ is a solution of $y + x = 4$.

Tell whether each ordered pair is a solution of $y=1-4x$.

1. $(0, 2)$

$$y=1-4x$$
Substitute ■ **for** x $■=1-4(■)$
and ■ **for** y.
Simplify. $■=1-■$
   $■=■$ false

$(0, 2)$ ■ a solution of $y=1-4x$.

2. $(-3, 13)$

$$y=1-4x$$
Substitute ■ **for** x $■=1-4(■)$
and ■ **for** y.
Simplify. $■=1+■$
   $■=■$ true

$(-3, 13)$ ■ a solution of $y=1-4x$.

Practice

Tell whether each ordered pair is a solution of $y=2-3x$.

1. $(0, 2)$ **2.** $(1, -5)$ **3.** $(3, -7)$

4. $(-1, 5)$ **5.** $(-2, 8)$ **6.** $(-3, -3)$

Tell whether each ordered pair is a solution of $y=-\dfrac{x}{3}-2$.

7. $(3, -4)$ **8.** $(2, -6)$ **9.** $(-3, 4)$

10. $(0, -1)$ **11.** $(-6, 0)$ **12.** $(9, -4)$

Tell whether each ordered pair is a solution of $y=2x$.

13. $(0, 2)$ **14.** $(2, 4)$ **15.** $(15, 30)$

Do It Together!

16. Explain to a partner how you tell whether the ordered pair is a solution in number **5** in **Practice.**

17. Write an equation containing x and y. Think of an ordered pair. Have a partner tell whether the ordered pair is a solution. Check the work.

5.2 Graphing Linear Equations

The equation $y = 3x - 1$ is a **linear equation.** Solutions to the equation are ordered pairs. You can graph the ordered pairs. The graph is a straight line. It is a picture of the solutions of the equation.

$(-1, -4)$, $\left(\frac{1}{3}, 0\right)$, and $(2, 5)$ are points on the line. So, they are solutions.

$$-4 = 3(-1) - 1 \qquad 0 = 3\left(\tfrac{1}{3}\right) - 1 \qquad 5 = 3(2) - 1$$
$$-4 = -3 - 1 \qquad\quad 0 = 1 - 1 \qquad\qquad 5 = 6 - 1$$
$$-4 = -4 \;\; \text{true} \qquad 0 = 0 \;\; \text{true} \qquad\quad 5 = 5 \;\; \text{true}$$

To graph a linear equation, start by finding at least three ordered pairs. Choose values for x, then find y.

EXAMPLE 1   Graph. $y = 2x - 2$

x	$2x - 2$	y
-1	$2(-1) - 2$	-4
0	$2(0) - 2$	-2
2	$2(2) - 2$	2

Graph the ordered pairs.
Draw a line through the points.

EXAMPLE 2   Graph. $y = 3 - 3x$

x	$3 - 3x$	y
-1	$3 - 3(-1)$	6
0	$3 - 3(0)$	3
1	$3 - 3(1)$	0

Graph the ordered pairs.
Draw a line through the points.

Graph each equation.

1. $y=3-x$

x	$3-x$	y
-1	$3-(-1)$	■
0	$3-0$	■
1	$3-1$	■

Graph the ordered pairs (−1, ■), (0, ■), and (1, ■). Draw a line through the points.

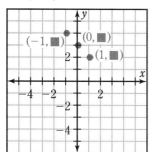

2. $y=\dfrac{x}{-2}$

x	$\dfrac{x}{-2}$	y
-2	$\dfrac{-2}{-2}$	■
0	$\dfrac{0}{-2}$	■
2	$\dfrac{2}{-2}$	■

Graph the ordered pairs (−2, ■), (0, ■), and (2, ■). Draw a line through the points.

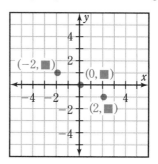

Practice

Graph each equation.

1. $y=x+3$

2. $y=3x-1$

3. $y=2x$

4. $y=2-x$

5. $y=\dfrac{x}{2}$

6. $y=\dfrac{x}{-1}$

Do It Together!

7. Explain to a partner how to graph the equation in number **3** in **Practice**.

8. Write an equation containing x and y. Work with a partner to graph the equation. Take turns finding points. Check each other's work.

5.3   Slope of a Line

Slope describes the steepness of a line. It also tells how fast the value of y is changing compared with x. The change in the y direction is called the **rise.** The change in the x direction is called the **run.**

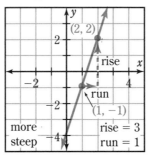 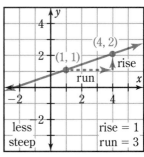

$$slope = \frac{rise}{run}$$

Pick two points on the line. To find the rise, subtract the y-values. To find the run, subtract the x-values in the same order. The slope is the rise divided by the run.

Slope can be positive or negative. A positive slope means that as x increases, y also increases.

EXAMPLE 1   Find the slope of the line that contains (1, 0) and (3, 1).

Find the rise. Subtract the y-values. (1, 0), (3, 1) $0-1=-1$

Find the run. Subtract the x-values. (1, 0), (3, 1) $1-3=-2$

Divide rise by run. $\dfrac{rise}{run} = \dfrac{-1}{-2} = \dfrac{1}{2}$

The slope of the line is $\frac{1}{2}$.

A negative slope means that as x increases, y decreases.

EXAMPLE 2   Find the slope of the line that contains (1, −6) and (−1, −4).

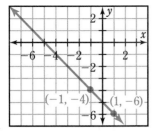

Find the rise. Subtract the y-values.
(1, −6), (−1, −4) $-6-(-4)=-2$

Find the run. Subtract the x-values.
(1, −6), (−1, −4) $1-(-1)=2$

Divide rise by run. $\dfrac{rise}{run} = \dfrac{-2}{2} = -1$

The slope of the line is −1.

Find the slope of the line that contains each pair of points.

1. $(-2, 5)$ and $(3, -3)$

Find the rise. Subtract the ■ values. $5 - ■ = ■$

Find the run. Subtract the ■ values. $-2 - ■ = ■$

Divide rise by run. $\dfrac{\text{rise}}{\text{run}} = \dfrac{■}{■}$

The slope of the line is ■.

2. $(0, -4)$ and $(3, 2)$

Find the rise. Subtract the ■ values. $-4 - ■ = ■$

Find the run. Subtract the ■ values. $0 - ■ = ■$

Divide rise by run. $\dfrac{\text{rise}}{\text{run}} = \dfrac{■}{■} = ■$

The slope of the line is ■.

Practice

Find the slope of the line that contains each pair of points.

1. $(5, 7)$ and $(3, 4)$

2. $(7, 6)$ and $(4, 3)$

3. $(-1, 3)$ and $(2, -2)$

4. $(0, -2)$ and $(4, 3)$

5. $(6, 0)$ and $(-3, 5)$

6. $(-4, -1)$ and $(1, 3)$

7. $(1, 3)$ and $(-4, -5)$

8. $(-5, -6)$ and $(-1, -5)$

9. $(4, 3)$ and $(6, 4)$

10. $(1, 4)$ and $(-2, 2)$

11. $(2, 3)$ and $(-4, 3)$

12. $(4, 5)$ and $(1, 6)$

13. $(4, 4)$ and $(7, 7)$

14. $(-4, 5)$ and $(5, -4)$

Do It Together!

15. Explain to a partner how you find the slope of the line in number **6** in **Practice.**

16. Write two points. Have a partner find the slope of the line that contains the two points. Check the work.

5.4 More About Slopes

Look at the lines below.

Vertical Line

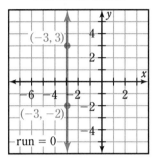

Horizontal Line

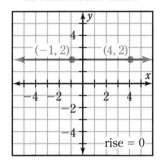

The x-values do not change. So, run $= 0$.

$$\text{Slope} = \frac{\text{rise}}{\text{run}} = \frac{\text{rise}}{0}$$

All vertical lines have no slope.

The y-values do not change. So, rise $= 0$.

$$\text{Slope} = \frac{\text{rise}}{\text{run}} = \frac{0}{\text{run}} = 0$$

All horizontal lines have 0 slope.

You cannot divide by 0.

EXAMPLE 1 Find the slope of the line that contains (2, 2) and (2, −1).

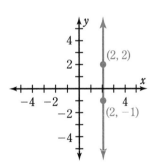

Find the rise. $\qquad 2 - (-1) = 3$

Find the run. $\qquad 2 - 2 = 0$

Divide rise by run. $\qquad \dfrac{\text{rise}}{\text{run}} = \dfrac{3}{0}$

You cannot divide by 0. No slope

The line has no slope. The line is vertical.

EXAMPLE 2 Find the slope of the graph.

The line is flat right and left.

The line is horizontal.

Horizontal lines have a slope of 0.

The slope is 0.

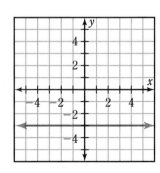

1. Find the slope of the line that contains the points $(-1, 8)$ and $(9, 8)$.

   Find the rise.   ■ $- 8 =$ ■

   Find the run.   ■ $-$ ■ $=$ ■

   Divide rise by run. $\dfrac{■}{■} =$ ■

   The slope of the line is ■.

2. Find the slope of the line from the graph.

   The line runs straight up and down.

   The line is ■.

   ■ lines have ■ slope.

   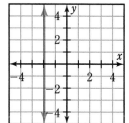

   The line has ■ slope.

Practice

Find the slope of each line from its graph.

1.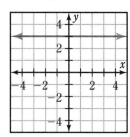

2.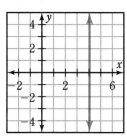

3.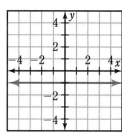

Find the slope of the line that contains each pair of points.

4. $(3, 5)$ and $(4, 5)$ 5. $(4, 3)$ and $(4, 7)$ 6. $(-3, -2)$ and $(-3, 8)$

7. $(0, 4)$ and $(0, -7)$ 8. $(-1, -2)$ and $(-9, -2)$ 9. $(6, 6)$ and $(-4, 6)$

Do It Together!

10. Explain to a partner how you use the graph to find the slope of the line in number **2** in **Practice.**

11. Draw a graph of a horizontal or vertical line. Have a partner find the slope of the line. Check the work.

5.5 Parallel and Perpendicular Lines

You can use slope to find parallel and perpendicular lines.

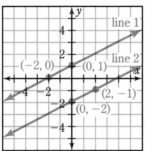
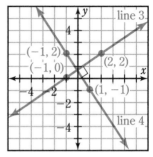

slope of line 1	slope of line 3
$\dfrac{0-1}{-2-0}=\dfrac{1}{2}$	$\dfrac{0-2}{-1-2}=\dfrac{2}{3}$
slope of line 2	slope of line 4
$\dfrac{-2-(-1)}{0-2}=\dfrac{1}{2}$	$\dfrac{2-(-1)}{-1-1}=-\dfrac{3}{2}$

$\frac{2}{3}$ and $\frac{3}{2}$ are reciprocals.

$\frac{2}{3}$ and $-\frac{3}{2}$ are negative reciprocals.

Lines 1 and 2 are parallel. They have the same slope.

Lines 3 and 4 are perpendicular. Their slopes are negative reciprocals of each other.

EXAMPLE 1 Show that the line that contains $(-2, -3)$ and $(1, 3)$ and the line that contains $(0, -4)$ and $(2, 0)$ are parallel.

Find the slope of the first line.
Divide rise by run.
$$\frac{-3-3}{-2-1}=\frac{-6}{-3}=2$$

Find the slope of the second line.
Divide rise by run.
$$\frac{-4-0}{0-2}=\frac{-4}{-2}=2$$

The slopes are equal. So, the lines are parallel.

EXAMPLE 2 Show that the line that contains $(1, -1)$ and $(0, 2)$ and the line that contains $(-1, 0)$ and $(2, 1)$ are perpendicular.

Find the slope of the first line.
Divide rise by run.
$$\frac{-1-2}{1-0}=\frac{-3}{1}=-3$$

Find the slope of the second line.
Divide rise by run.
$$\frac{0-1}{-1-2}=\frac{-1}{-3}=\frac{1}{3}$$

-3 and $\frac{1}{3}$ are negative reciprocals. So, the lines are perpendicular.

1. Tell whether the line containing $(-1, -2)$ and $(4, 4)$ and the line containing $(6, 3)$ and $(-1, -3)$ are parallel.

   Find the slope of the first line. $(-1, -2)$ and $(4, 4)$

   Divide rise by run. $\dfrac{\blacksquare - \blacksquare}{\blacksquare - \blacksquare} = \blacksquare$

   Find the slope of the second line. $(6, 3)$ and $(-1, -3)$

   Divide rise by run. $\dfrac{\blacksquare - \blacksquare}{\blacksquare - \blacksquare} = \blacksquare$

   $\blacksquare$ and $\blacksquare$ are not the same slope.

   The lines $\blacksquare$ parallel.

2. Tell whether the line containing $(-1, -2)$ and $(2, 7)$ and the line containing $(-1, 5)$ and $(-4, 4)$ are perpendicular.

   Find the slope of the first line. $(-1, -2)$ and $(2, 7)$

   Divide rise by run. $\dfrac{\blacksquare - \blacksquare}{\blacksquare - \blacksquare} = \blacksquare$

   Find the slope of the second line. $(-1, 5)$ and $(-4, 4)$

   Divide rise by run. $\dfrac{\blacksquare - \blacksquare}{\blacksquare - \blacksquare} = \blacksquare$

   $\blacksquare$ and $\blacksquare$ are not negative reciprocals.

   The lines $\blacksquare$ perpendicular.

Practice

Tell whether the lines containing each pair of points are parallel.

1. $(1, 3)(2, 4)$ and $(-2, 1)(-3, 0)$
2. $(-4, -3)(2, 4)$ and $(0, 2)(5, 9)$
3. $(3, 4)(1, 0)$ and $(6, 8)(4, 4)$
4. $(5, -2)(3, 2)$ and $(6, -1)(4, -3)$

Tell whether the lines containing each pair of points are perpendicular.

5. $(4, 5)(1, 3)$ and $(3, 7)(5, 4)$
6. $(-2, -3)(2, 5)$ and $(-4, -4)(-6, -3)$

Do It Together!

7. Explain to a partner how to tell whether the lines are perpendicular in number **6** in **Practice.**

8. Pick two points. Have a partner pick two points. Show whether the lines that connect the points are parallel or perpendicular. They may be neither.

5.6 Intercepts

The **x-intercept** is the value of x at the point where a line crosses the x-axis. This happens when $y = 0$.

The **y-intercept** is the value of y at the point where a line crosses the y-axis. This happens when $x = 0$.

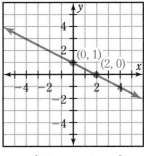

x-intercept → 2

y-intercept → 1

At the point where the line crosses the x-axis, $y = 0$. So, you can find the x-intercept of an equation without a graph. Substitute 0 for y. Then, solve for x.

EXAMPLE 1 Find the x-intercept. $y = -2x - 4$

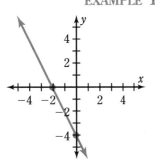

$$y = -2x - 4$$

Substitute 0 for y. $$0 = -2x - 4$$

Solve for x. $$4 = -2x$$

$$-2 = x$$

The x-intercept of $y = -2x - 4$ is -2.

You can also solve for the y-intercept. At the point of the y-intercept, $x = 0$. So, substitute 0 for x and solve for y.

EXAMPLE 2 Find the y-intercept. $y = -2x - 4$

$$y = -2x - 4$$

Substitute 0 for x. $$y = -2(0) - 4$$

Simplify. $$y = 0 - 4$$

$$y = -4$$

The y-intercept of $y = -2x - 4$ is -4.

1. Find the *x*-intercept. $y=3x+3.$
$y=3x+3$

Substitute ■ for *y*. $\blacksquare=3x+3$

Subtract ■ from $\blacksquare=3x$
both sides.

Divide both sides by ■. $\blacksquare=x$
The *x*-intercept of $y=3x+3$ is ■.

2. Find the *y*-intercept. $y=3x+3.$
$y=3x+3$

Substitute ■ for *x*. $y=3(\blacksquare)+3$

Simplify. $y=\blacksquare+3$

$y=\blacksquare$
The *y*-intercept of $y=3x+3$ is ■.

Practice

Use the graph to find the *x*-intercept and *y*-intercept of each line.

1.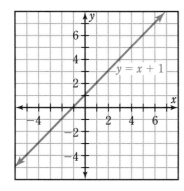

2.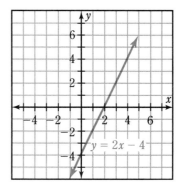

Find the *x*-intercept and *y*-intercept of each line.

3. $y=x-2$

4. $y=-3x+3$

5. $y=5x+10$

6. $y=-4x-4$

7. $y=\frac{1}{2}x-3$

8. $y=\frac{-1}{4}x+1$

9. $y=\frac{1}{5}x$

10. $y=-6x-12$

11. $y=3x+9$

Do It Together!

12. Explain to a partner how you find the *y*-intercept in number **8** in **Practice.**

13. Draw a line. Have a partner label the *x*-intercept and the *y*-intercept. Check the work.

5.7 Slope and a Point

You can graph a line using one point on the line and the slope. First, graph the point. Then, start at that point and use the slope to find another point.

EXAMPLE 1

Slope is $\frac{\text{rise}}{\text{run}}$.

$\frac{2}{3}$ means up 2, right 3.

Graph the line that contains (1, 3) and has a slope of $\frac{2}{3}$.

Graph (1, 3).

Move up 2 units.

Move right 3 units.

Draw a dot at (4, 5).

Draw a line through the points.

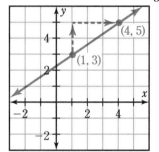

EXAMPLE 2

-3 means $\frac{-3}{1}$.

$\frac{-3}{1}$ means down 3, right 1.

Graph the line that contains $(-2, -1)$ and has a slope of -3.

Graph $(-2, -1)$.

Move down 3 units.

Move right 1 unit.

Draw a dot at $(-1, -4)$.

Draw a line through the points.

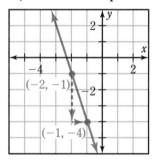

Sometimes, you are given an intercept for the point.

EXAMPLE 3

A *y*-intercept of 3 means the ordered pair (0, 3).

$-\frac{1}{2}$ means down 1, right 2.

Graph the line with a *y*-intercept of 3 and a slope of $-\frac{1}{2}$.

Graph (0, 3).

Move down 1 unit.

Move right 2 units.

Draw a dot at (2, 2).

Draw a line through the points.

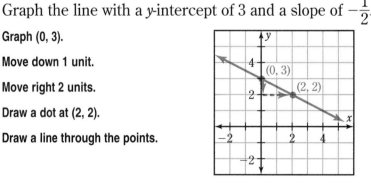

Graph each line.

1. y-intercept: -2; slope: 2

Graph (■, ■).
Move up ■ units.
Move right ■ unit.
Draw a dot at
(■, ■).
Draw a line through
the points.

2. (1, 1); slope: $-\dfrac{4}{3}$

Graph (■, ■).
Move down ■ units.
Move right ■ units.
Draw a point at
(■, ■).
Draw a line through
the points.

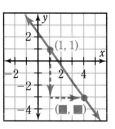

Practice

Graph the line that contains the point and has the given slope.

1. point: (2, 2); slope: $\dfrac{1}{2}$

2. point: $(-1, 3)$; slope: 3

3. point: $(3, -2)$; slope: $-\dfrac{3}{2}$

4. point: $(-2, -3)$; slope: -2

Graph the line that contains the y-intercept and has the given slope.

5. y-intercept: 1; slope: 2

6. y-intercept: 4; slope: $\dfrac{1}{3}$

7. y-intercept: -3; slope: $\dfrac{2}{5}$

8. y-intercept: -2; slope: -4

Do It Together!

9. Explain to a partner how to graph the line in number **5** in **Practice.**

10. Write an ordered pair and a slope. Have a partner graph the line. Check the work.

5.8 Slope-Intercept Form

Sometimes, you write equations so you can find the slope and y-intercept of a line just by looking at the equation.

Look at the equation of the line $y = \frac{1}{2}x + 2$

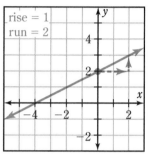

$$\underset{\text{slope}}{\uparrow} \quad \underset{y\text{-intercept}}{\uparrow}$$

This is called the **slope-intercept form** of an equation.

Sometimes, the slope-intercept form is written: $y = mx + b$. m is the coefficient of the x-term. It tells you the slope. b is a constant. It tells you the y-intercept.

EXAMPLE 1   Find the slope and y-intercept. $y = -x - 2$

Write the slope-intercept form. $y = mx + b$

$-x$ means $-1x$.
$-x - 2$ means $-x + (-2)$

Write the equation. $y = -x - 2$

Find m and b. m is -1 and b is -2.

The slope is -1 and the y-intercept is -2.

EXAMPLE 2   Find the slope and y-intercept. $y = 4 - \frac{x}{2}$

$\frac{x}{2}$ is the same as

Rearrange the terms. $y = -\frac{1}{2}x + 4$

$\frac{1x}{2}$ or $\frac{1}{2}x$.

Write the the slope-intercept form. $y = mx + b$

Find m and b. m is $-\frac{1}{2}$ and b is 4.

The slope is $-\frac{1}{2}$ and the y-intercept is 4.

EXAMPLE 3   Find the slope and y-intercept. $y = 2x$

If there is no b-term, the
y-intercept is 0.

Write the slope-intercept form. $y = mx + b$

Write the equation. $y = 2x + 0$

Find m and b. m is 2 and b is 0.

The slope is 2 and the y-intercept is 0.

Find the slope and y-intercept of each line.

1. $y=x+5$

$y=mx+b$
$y=x+5$
Find m and b. m is 1 and b is 5.
The slope is ■ and the y-intercept is ■.

2. $y=\frac{3}{2}x-1$

$y=mx+b$
$y=\frac{3}{2}x-1$
Find m and b. m is ■ and b is ■.
The slope is ■ and the y-intercept is ■.

3. $y=4x$

$y=mx+b$
$y=4x+$ ■
Find m and b. m is ■ and b is ■.
The slope is ■ and the y-intercept is ■.

4. $y=3-x$

Rearrange the terms. $y=-x+3$
$y=mx+b$
Find m and b. m is ■ and b is ■.
The slope is ■ and the y-intercept is ■.

Practice

Find the slope and y-intercept of each line.

1. $y=\frac{1}{2}x+3$

2. $y=4x-1$

3. $y=-\frac{2}{3}x+6$

4. $y=-5x-3$

5. $y=\frac{3}{4}x$

6. $y=5x-2$

7. $y=-4-2x$

8. $y=x-4$

9. $y=1+\frac{x}{3}$

10. $y=5x+3$

11. $y=3x+6$

12. $y=-x$

Do It Together!

13. Pick a problem from practice. Write an equation with the same y-intercept and a different slope. Explain your work to a partner.

14. Write an equation in slope-intercept form. Ask a partner to find the slope and y-intercept.

5.9 The Standard Form

Linear equations can be written in many ways. The **standard form** is one way.

$$\text{Standard form} \rightarrow Ax + By = C$$

You can rewrite an equation in standard form as an equation in slope-intercept form. Solve the equation for y.

EXAMPLE 1 Write in slope-intercept form. $4x + 2y = -8$

$$4x + 2y = -8$$

Subtract **4x** from both sides. $4x - 4x + 2y = -8 - 4x$

$$2y = -8 - 4x$$

To divide both sides of the equation, divide all terms by 2.

Divide both sides by 2. $\dfrac{2y}{2} = \dfrac{-8}{2} - \dfrac{4x}{2}$

Rearrange the terms. $y = -4 - 2x$

$$y = -2x - 4$$

You can write $4x + 2y = -8$ as $y = -2x - 4$.

EXAMPLE 2 Write in slope-intercept form. $3x - 2y = -6$

$$3x - 2y = -6$$

Subtract **3x** from both sides. $3x - 3x - 2y = -6 - 3x$

$$-2y = -6 - 3x$$

$\frac{3x}{2}$ means $\frac{3}{2}$ x.

Divide both sides by −2. $\dfrac{-2y}{-2} = \dfrac{-6}{-2} - \dfrac{3x}{-2}$

$$y = 3 + \frac{3}{2}x$$

Rearrange the terms. $y = \dfrac{3}{2}x + 3$

You can write $3x - 2y = -6$ as $y = \dfrac{3}{2}x + 3$.

EXAMPLE 3 Write in slope-intercept form. $x + y = 0$

$$x + y = 0$$

Subtract **x** from both sides. $x - x + y = 0 - x$

$$y = -x$$

You can write $x + y = 0$ as $y = -x$.

Write each equation in slope-intercept form.

1. $3x - 4y = 0$

$$3x - 4y = 0$$

Subtract ■ from both sides. $3x - ■ - 4y = 0 - ■$
$$-4y = -3x$$

Divide both sides by ■. $\dfrac{-4y}{-4} = \dfrac{-3x}{-4}$
$$y = ■$$

2. $4x - y = 4$

$$4x - y = 4$$

Subtract ■ from both sides. $4x - ■ - y = 4 - ■$
$$-y = 4 - 4x$$

Divide both sides by ■. $\dfrac{-y}{■} = \dfrac{4}{■} - \dfrac{4x}{■}$
$$y = ■ + ■$$
$$y = ■ - ■$$

Practice

Write each equation in slope-intercept form.

1. $6x + 2y = 2$

2. $x - y = 0$

3. $-5x - y = -10$

4. $-2x + 5y = -5$

5. $6x + y = 6$

6. $x - y = 4$

7. $-3x - y = -10$

8. $3x - 3y = 9$

9. $2x + 3y = 0$

10. $x - 4y = -8$

11. $2x + y = 3$

12. $2y - 6x = 0$

Do It Together!

13. Explain to a partner how you write the equation in number **2** in **Practice** in slope-intercept form.

14. Write an equation in standard form. Ask a partner to write it in slope-intercept form.

5.10 Calculator: Finding Intercepts

You can use your calculator to find the intercept of a line.

EXAMPLE 1 Find the x-intercept. $y = 17x + 119$

$$y = 17x + 119$$

The x-intercept is the value of x when $y = 0$.

Let $y = 0$. $\quad 0 = 17x + 119$

Subtract 119 from both sides. $\quad -119 = 17x$

Divide both sides by 17. $\quad \dfrac{-119}{17} = \dfrac{17x}{17}$

Use your calculator to simplify the left side.

DISPLAY

Make sure to clear your calculator before you start.

Enter 119 by pressing: [1][1][9]   119

$\dfrac{-119}{17} = -7.$

Divide by 17 by pressing: [÷][1][7][=]   7

Find the sign of a negative number divided by a positive number. -7

The x-intercept of $y = 17x + 119$ is -7.

EXAMPLE 2 Find the y-intercept. $9x - 4y = -96$

$$9x - 4y = -96$$

The y-intercept is the value of y when $x = 0$.

Let $x = 0$. $\quad 9(0) - 4y = -96$

Divide both sides by -4. $\quad \dfrac{-4y}{-4} = \dfrac{-96}{-4}$

Use your calculator to simplify the right side.

DISPLAY

Enter 96 by pressing: [9][6]   96

$\dfrac{-96}{-4} = 24.$

Divide by 4 by pressing: [÷][4][=]   24

Find the sign of a negative number divided by a negative number. $+24$

The y-intercept of $9x - 4y = -96$ is 24.

Practice

Find the *x*-intercept of each line.

1. $5y = 8x + 104$ **2.** $-3y = -19x + 114$ **3.** $-13x + 36y = -91$

Find the *y*-intercept of each line.

4. $63x + 12y = 168$ **5.** $-15x - 3y = -72$ **6.** $27x + 15y = -75$

7. $12y - 24x = 21.6$ **8.** $28.2y - 282 = 42.3x$ **9.** $5y - 9x = 160$

MATH CONNECTION

Evelyn Boyd Granville

Evelyn Boyd Granville was born in 1924. Growing up, she studied math in college. There, she got her first degree in math. Then, she went on to Yale for another degree. In 1949, she became the first African American woman to get a Ph.D. in math from Yale.

Dr. Granville's first job was with the space program. Her knowledge of math and science was a great combination. She studied the orbits for space probes and worked on Project Mercury. She also worked for IBM as a math and computer expert.

Later, she became a professor at a California university. Her goal was to improve the way math was taught. Teaching young students was part of her plan. She also ran an after-school enrichment program.

In 1984, she retired and moved to Texas with her husband. There, they have a farm to enjoy. Still, she teaches math and computer science at a local college.

5.11 Problem Solving: Using Slope

The distance you travel changes with the amount of time you travel. You can describe the change in distance compared with the change in time with slope.

EXAMPLE 1   Alison walks 4 miles by 9:00 A.M. She walks 8 miles by 11:00 A.M. If she continues at this rate, how far will she walk by 12:00 noon?

Write the information as ordered pairs.

(time, miles)	(time, miles)
(9, 4)	(11, 8)

Graph the ordered pairs.

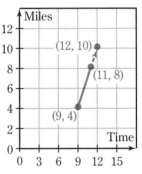

Find the slope.

$$\frac{\text{rise}}{\text{run}} = \frac{\text{difference in miles}}{\text{difference in time}} = \frac{4-8}{9-11} = 2$$

Use the slope to find the distance at 12:00 noon.

Start at (11, 8). Move up 2, right 1. Graph (12, 10).

By 12:00 noon, Alison will walk 10 miles.

EXAMPLE 2   The temperature is 32°C at 1:00 P.M. At 5:00 P.M., the temperature is 30°C. Find the temperature at 7:00 P.M. if the temperature continues to drop at the same rate.

Write the information as ordered pairs.

(time, temperature)	(time, temperature)
(1, 32)	(5, 30)

Graph the ordered pairs.

Find the slope.

$$\frac{\text{rise}}{\text{run}} = \frac{\text{difference in temperature}}{\text{difference in time}}$$

$$= \frac{32-30}{1-5} = -\frac{1}{2}$$

Use the slope to find the temperature at 7:00 P.M.

Start at (5, 30). Move down 1 and right 2. Graph (7, 29).

The temperature will drop to 29°C by 7:00 P.M.

1. During a race, Carolina passed the 3 mile mark at 24 minutes. She passed the 5 mile mark at 40 minutes. Find the slope to describe her rate.

   Write the information as ordered pairs.

   (time, miles)   (time, miles)

   (■, 3)   (40, ■)

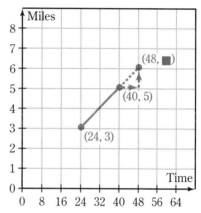

   Graph the ordered pairs.

   Find the slope. $\dfrac{\text{rise}}{\text{run}} = \dfrac{\text{difference in miles}}{\text{difference in time}} = \dfrac{3-5}{24-40} = \dfrac{■}{■}$

   Her rate is 1 mile in ■ minutes.

2. If Carolina continues at the same rate, where will she be at 48 minutes?

   Use the slope to find another point.

   Start at (40, 5),

   Move up ■ and right 8 .   Point is (48, ■).

   At 48 minutes, Carolina will be at the 6 mile mark.

Practice

Use slope to solve each problem.

1. Gracie earns $15 by 12:00 P.M. She earns $25 by 2:00 P.M. How much will she earn if she continues at the same rate until 5:00 P.M.?

2. Michael fixes computers. By 1:00 P.M., he has fixed 5 computers. By 3:00 P.M., 7 computers are fixed. How many will he fix by 6:00 P.M.?

3. A bus leaves a city at 6:00 A.M. It travels 150 miles by 9:00 A.M. How far will it travel by 12:00 noon?

Do It Together!

4. Explain to a partner how to use slope to solve the problem in number **2** in **Practice.**

5. Write a problem that can be solved using slope. Write the information as ordered pairs. Ask a partner to graph the ordered pairs and find the slope. Check the work.

5.12   Application: Direct Variation

Look at the graphs of lines 1, 2, and 3.

line 1: $y = 3x$ slope $= 3$

line 2: $y = x$ slope $= 1$

line 3: $y = \dfrac{x}{2}$ slope $= \dfrac{1}{2}$

$y = kx$ slope $= k$

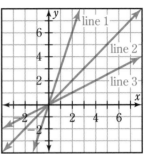

These equations are examples of **direct variation.** In direct variation, the slope, k, is always positive. Also, all the lines go through the point $(0, 0)$.

When an equation shows direct variation, you can say y varies directly with x. The equation is $y = kx$

You can use a graph of direct variation to find equations. Then, you can use the equation to solve problems.

EXAMPLE 1

Corey earned $20.00 in 4 hours. His pay varies directly with his hours. Find the equation for his pay.

Graph (0, 0) to show the money when he starts work.

Graph (4, 20) for 4 hours and $20.00.

Find the slope.

$$\frac{\text{rise}}{\text{run}} = \frac{20 - 0}{4 - 0} = 5$$

Write the equation.

Use P for pay and h for hours. $P = kh$

Substitute the slope for k. $P = 5h$

The equation for the graph is $P = 5h$.

EXAMPLE 2

Use the equation to find Corey's pay for 40 hours of work.

Write the equation. $P = 5h$

Substitute 40 for h. $P = 5(40)$

Simplify. $P = 200$

Corey earns $200.00 for 40 hours of work.

The cost of notebooks varies directly with the number of notebooks you buy. Three notebooks cost $9.00.

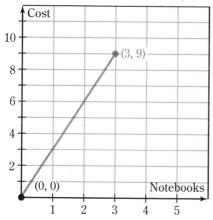

1. Find the equation for the cost of notebooks

   Graph the cost of 3 notebooks. (3, ■)

   Graph (0, 0).

   Find the slope. $\dfrac{\text{rise}}{\text{run}} = \dfrac{9-0}{3-0} = ■$

   Write the equation.

   Use *C* for cost and $C = kn$

   n for notebooks.

   Substitute the slope for *k*. $C = ■ n$

2. Find the cost of 15 notebooks.

   Write the equation. $C = ■ n$

   Substitute 15 for ■. $C = 3(■)$

   Simplify. $C = ■$

   Fifteen notebooks cost ■.

Practice

The cost of pens varies directly with the number of pens. One pen costs $2.00.

1. Find *k* in the equation for the cost of pens. Use $C = kp$.

2. Find the total cost of 12 pens.

Jasmine's pay varies directly with the hours she works. She earns $40.00 in 5 hours.

3. Find *k* in the equation for Jasmine's pay. Use $P = kh$.

4. Find her pay for 30 hours.

Do It Together!

5. Explain to a partner how to find the total cost in number **2** in **Practice.**

6. Draw the graph of a line that goes through the origin. Have a partner solve for *k* and write the equation. Check the work.

Chapter Review

Chapter 5 Summary

- Equations with two variables have solutions that are ordered pairs. A graph of the ordered pairs in a linear equation makes a straight line.
- The slope of a line is the change in the y-values divided by the change in the x-values.
- Horizontal lines have a slope of 0. Vertical lines have no slope.
- You can use slope to find parallel and perpendicular lines.
- Substituting 0 for y will give you the x-intercept. Substituting 0 for x will give you the y-intercept.
- You can graph a line when you have a point and the slope.
- The slope-intercept form of a linear equation lets you find the slope and y-intercept by looking at the equation.
- You can use a calculator to find intercepts.
- Using the slope can help you solve problems.
- Direct variation is a linear equation with positive slope that goes through the point $(0, 0)$.

Reviewing Vocabulary

Fill in each blank with the correct word.

linear equation

slope

rise

run

x-intercept

y-intercept

slope-intercept form

standard form

direct variation

1. _?_ is the change in the left-to-right direction between two points.
2. $Ax + By = C$ is a linear equation in _?_.
3. $y = mx + b$ is the _?_ of a linear equation.
4. An equation whose graph is a straight line is a _?_.
5. A _?_ is a linear equation in the form $y = kx$.
6. The y-value of the point where a line crosses the y-axis is called the _?_.
7. _?_ is the change in the up-and-down direction between two points.
8. The point where a line crosses the x-axis is called the _?_.
9. _?_ is the steepness of a straight line.

Chapter Quiz

Tell whether each ordered pair is a solution of the equation.

1. $(1, 5); y=2+3x$ **2.** $(0,-2); y=1-4x$ **3.** $(-4, 4); y=2-\frac{x}{2}$

Find three ordered pairs for each equation. Then, graph the equation.

4. $y=2x+3$ **5.** $y=4-x$ **6.** $x+y=0$

Find the slope of each line that contains the given pair of points.

7. $(2, 4)$ and $(1, 0)$ **8.** $(-2, 3)$ and $(4,-4)$ **9.** $(-1,-3)$ and $(-2,-5)$

10. $(2, 3)$ and $(1, 3)$ **11.** $(-1,-5)$ and $(2,-5)$ **12.** $(-1, 4)$ and $(-1, 3)$

Tell whether the line containing each pair of points are parallel or perpendicular.

13. $(1, 3)(-1, 0)$ and $(5, 0)(3,-3)$ **14.** $(-2,-4)(1, 5)$ and $(6, 2)(3, 3)$

Find the x-intercept and y-intercept of each line.

15. $5x+y=10$ **16.** $4x-4y=12$ **17.** $10x-5y=15$

Graph each line.

18. point: $(0, 3)$; slope: $-\frac{1}{4}$ **19.** y-intercept: 2; slope: $\frac{2}{3}$

20. $y=2x-6$ **21.** $y=x-4$ **22.** $y=-2x+10$

Write each equation in slope-intercept form.

23. $3x+2y=12$ **24.** $y-x=0$ **25.** $3x-y=7$

Find the slope to solve each problem.

26. Sue drives 200 miles by 1:00 P.M. She drives 350 miles by 4:00 P.M. If she continues at the same rate, how far will she drive by 5:00 P.M.?

27. Manny's pay varies directly with the number of lawns he mows. He earns $52.00 for mowing 4 lawns. Find k in the equation for Manny's pay. Use $P=kl$.

Chapter 6

Writing Linear Equations

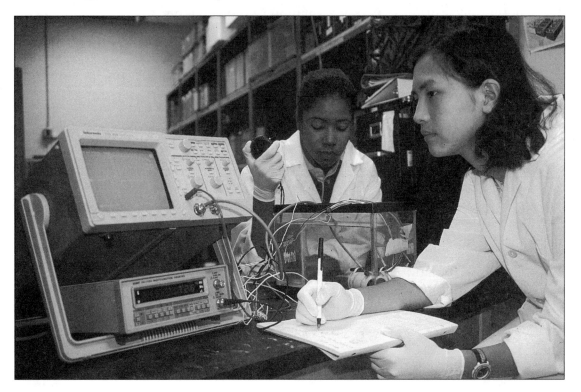

Scientists and researchers look for patterns and relationships in nature. They write equations to describe the relationships they find.

Chapter Learning Objectives

- Write an equation using the slope and *y*-intercept.
- Write an equation using a point and the slope.
- Write an equation using two points.
- Write equations of horizontal and vertical lines.
- Write equations of parallel and perpendicular lines.
- Use a calculator to check that a point is on a line.
- Solve problems by writing equations from patterns.
- Apply concepts and skills to writing equations in science.

Words to Know

slope-intercept form $y = mx + b$

horizontal lines lines with slope $= 0$

vertical lines lines with no slope

perpendicular lines two lines with slopes that are negative reciprocals

parallel lines lines that have the same slope

In this chapter, you will write equations for straight lines. First, you will use the slope and y-intercept of a line to write its equation. Then, you will use any point on a line and its slope. Finally, you will write an equation of a line using any two points on the line. You will look at horizontal and vertical lines and find their equations. You will also write equations for parallel and perpendicular lines. You can check equations with a calculator. You will solve problems by writing equations from patterns. Then, you will apply your skills to writing equations about science.

6.1 Using the Slope and Intercept

You have worked with the **slope-intercept form** of an equation. It is $y = mx + b$. Now, you will use the graph of a line to write an equation. First find the slope and y-intercept.

EXAMPLE 1   Write the equation of the line with slope $= \frac{3}{2}$ and y-intercept $= -2$.

m is the slope and b is the y-intercept.

Write the slope-intercept form.	$y = mx + b$
Substitute $\frac{3}{2}$ for *m*.	$y = \frac{3}{2}x + b$
Substitute -2 for *b*.	$y = \frac{3}{2}x + (-2)$
Simplify.	$y = \frac{3}{2}x - 2$

The equation of the line is $y = \frac{3}{2}x - 2$.

EXAMPLE 2   Write the equation of the line with slope $= -2$ and y-intercept $= 0$.

Write the slope-intercept form.	$y = mx + b$
Substitute -2 for *m*.	$y = -2x + b$
Substitute 0 for *b*.	$y = -2x + 0$
Simplify.	$y = -2x$

The equation of the line is $y = -2x$.

You can find the slope and y-intercept of a line from its graph.

EXAMPLE 3   Use the graph to write the equation of the line.

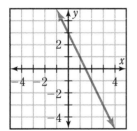

Find the slope by looking at rise over run.	$m = -\frac{2}{1} = -2$
Look at the graph to find the y-intercept.	$b = 3$
Write the slope-intercept form.	$y = mx + b$
Substitute -2 for *m* and 3 for *y*.	$y = -2x + 3$
Check: Pick a point on the line.	$(1, 1)$
Substitute 1 for *x* and 1 for *y*.	$1 = -2(1) + 3$
	$1 = 1$ true

The equation of the line is $y = -2x + 3$.

Write the equation of each line.

1. Slope $= \frac{1}{2}$ and y-intercept $= 1$

Write the slope-intercept form.	$y = mx + b$
Substitute ■ for m. Substitute ■ for b.	$y = ■x + ■$

The equation is $y = ■x + ■$.

2. Slope $= 3$ and y-intercept $= 0$

Write the slope-intercept form.	$y = mx + b$
Substitute ■ for m. Substitute ■ for b.	$y = ■x + ■$

The equation is $y = ■x$.

3.

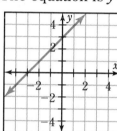

Find the slope.	$m = ■$
Find the y-intercept.	$b = ■$
Write the slope-intercept form.	$y = ■x + ■$
Substitute ■ for m and ■ for b.	$y = ■x + ■$

The equation is $y = ■x + ■$.

Practice

Write the equation of each line.

1. slope $= -4$ and y-intercept $= -3$

2. slope $= \frac{1}{2}$ and y-intercept $= 0$

Use the graph to write the equation of each line. Then, check by using a point.

3.

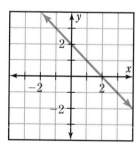

4.

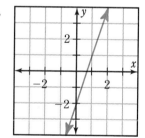

Do It Together!

5. Explain to a partner how to write the equation for number **3** in **Practice.**

6. Graph the line that passes through the points $(0, -2)$ and $(-4, 0)$. Have a partner write the equation of this line.

6.2 Using a Point and the Slope

You can write the equation of a line when you know any point on the line and the slope. Use the $y = mx + b$ form of the equation. Substitute the slope for m. Use the ordered pair to substitute for x and y. Then, solve for b.

EXAMPLE 1   Write the equation of the line that passes through the point (3, 0) and has slope $= -2$. Then, check the equation.

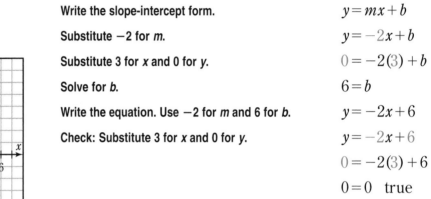

Write the slope-intercept form.	$y = mx + b$
Substitute -2 for m.	$y = -2x + b$
Substitute 3 for x and 0 for y.	$0 = -2(3) + b$
Solve for b.	$6 = b$
Write the equation. Use -2 for m and 6 for b.	$y = -2x + 6$
Check: Substitute 3 for x and 0 for y.	$y = -2x + 6$
	$0 = -2(3) + 6$
	$0 = 0$ true

The equation of the line is $y = -2x + 6$.

EXAMPLE 2   Write the equation of the line that passes through the point (6, 4) and has slope $= \frac{2}{3}$.

Write the slope-intercept form.	$y = mx + b$
Substitute $\frac{2}{3}$ for m.	$y = \frac{2}{3}x + b$
Substitute 6 for x and 4 for y.	$4 = \frac{2}{3}(6) + b$
Solve for b.	$4 = \frac{12}{3} + b$
	$4 = 4 + b$
	$0 = b$
Write the equation. Use $\frac{2}{3}$ for m and 0 for b.	$y = \frac{2}{3}x + 0$

Check: Use (6, 4)
$y = \frac{2}{3}x$
$4 = \frac{2}{3}(6)$
$4 = \frac{12}{3}$
$4 = 4$ true

The equation of the line is $y = \frac{2}{3}x$.

Find the equation of each line.

1. through (2, 3) and with slope $=\frac{1}{2}$

Write the slope-intercept form.	$y = mx + b$
Substitute ■ for *m*.	$y = ■x + b$
Substitute ■ for *x* and ■ for *y*.	$3 = ■(2) + b$
Solve for *b*.	$■ = b$
Write the slope-intercept form.	$y = mx + b$
Substitute ■ for *m* and ■ for *b*.	$y = \frac{1}{2}x + ■$

The equation of the line is ■.

2. through (2, 0) and with slope $= -3$

Write the slope-intercept form.	$y = mx + b$
Substitute ■ for *m*.	$y = ■x + b$
Substitute ■ for *x* and ■ for *y*.	$0 = ■(2) + b$
Solve for *b*.	$■ = b$
Write the slope-intercept form.	$y = mx + b$
Substitute ■ for *m* and ■ for *b*.	$y = -3x + ■$

The equation of the line is ■.

Practice

Find the equation of each line.

1. through (1, 1) and with slope $= -2$

2. through (2, −1) and with slope $= \frac{3}{2}$

3. through (2, 4) and with slope $= \frac{3}{2}$

4. through (2, 5) and with slope $= 5$

5. through (4, 3) and with slope $= \frac{1}{4}$

6. through (−3, 0) and with slope $= -2$

7. through (4, 4) and with slope $= 1$

8. through (3, 3) and with slope $= -1$

Do It Together!

9. Explain to a partner how to write the equation for number **4** in **Practice.**

10. Graph number **1** in **Practice.** Find a point on the graph other than the one given. Ask a partner to use that point to check your equation.

6.3 Using Two Points

You can find the slope of a line when you know two points. Then, you can write the equation of the line though these points. Use the ordered pairs to find the slope. Then, use one of the ordered pairs and the slope to find b in the $y = mx + b$ equation.

EXAMPLE 1

Find the equation of a line through points $(2, 4)$ and $(1, 1)$.

$\text{slope} = \dfrac{\text{rise}}{\text{run}}$

Find the slope. $\qquad m = \dfrac{4-1}{2-1} = \dfrac{3}{1} = 3$

Substitute 3 for m in $y = mx + b$. $\qquad y = 3x + b$

Use $(2, 4)$. Substitute 2 for x and 4 for y. $\qquad 4 = 3(2) + b$

Solve for b. $\qquad -2 = b$

Write the slope-intercept form. $\qquad y = mx + b$

Substitute 3 for m and -2 for b. $\qquad y = 3x - 2$

Check: Use the other point, $(1, 1)$.
Substitute 1 for x and 1 for y. $\qquad 1 = 3(1) - 2$

$1 = 1 \quad$ true

The equation of the line is $y = 3x - 2$.

EXAMPLE 2

Find the equation of a line through points $(3, 7)$ and $(2, 7)$.

Find the slope. $\qquad m = \dfrac{7-7}{3-2} = \dfrac{0}{1} = 0$

Substitute 0 for m in $y = mx + b$. $\qquad y = 0x + b$

Use $(3, 7)$. Substitute 3 for x and 7 for y. $\qquad 7 = 0(3) + b$

Solve for b. $\qquad 7 = b$

Write the slope-intercept form. $\qquad y = mx + b$

Substitute 0 for m and 7 for b. $\qquad y = 0x + 7$

Check: Use the other point, $(2, 7)$.
Substitute 2 for x and 7 for y. $\qquad y = 7$

$7 = 7 \quad$ true

The equation of the line is $y = 7$.

Find the equation for each line through the two points. Then, check the equation.

1. $(2, 5)$ and $(-1, -4)$

Find the slope. $\quad m = \dfrac{5-(-4)}{2-(-1)} = \blacksquare$

Substitute $\blacksquare$ for m. $\quad y = \blacksquare x + b$

Substitute 2 for x and $\blacksquare$ for y. $\quad \blacksquare = 3(2) + b$

Solve for b. $\quad \blacksquare = b$

Write the equation in slope-intercept form. $\quad y = 3x + \blacksquare$
$y = 3x - \blacksquare$

Check with the other point.

Substitute -1 for x and -4 for y. $\quad \blacksquare = 3(\blacksquare) - 1$
$\blacksquare = \blacksquare \quad$ true

The equation of the line is $\blacksquare$.

2. $(0, 4)$ and $(2, 3)$

Find the slope. $\quad m = \dfrac{4-3}{0-2} = \blacksquare$

Substitute $\blacksquare$ for m. $\quad y = \blacksquare x + b$

Substitute 0 for x and $\blacksquare$ for y. $\quad \blacksquare = -\frac{1}{2}(0) + b$

Solve for b. $\quad \blacksquare = b$

Write the equation in slope-intercept form. $\quad y = \blacksquare x + \blacksquare$

Check with the other point.

Substitute 2 for x and 3 for y. $\quad \blacksquare = -\frac{1}{2}(\blacksquare) + 4$
$3 = \blacksquare \quad$ true

The equation of the line is $\blacksquare$.

Practice

Find the equation for each line through the two points. Then, check the equation.

1. $(4, 3)$ and $(2, 4)$ **2.** $(5, -8)$ and $(2, -2)$ **3.** $(1, 9)$ and $(7, 3)$

4. $(6, -3)$ and $(8, -2)$ **5.** $(2, 6)$ and $(3, 6)$ **6.** $(4, 7)$ and $(3, 5)$

7. $(0, 0)$ and $(4, 2)$ **8.** $(2, 3)$ and $(0, 6)$ **9.** $(-1, -1)$ and $(2, 2)$

Do It Together!

10. Explain to a partner how to write the equation for number **6** in **Practice.**

11. Graph the two points in number **2** in **Practice.** Have a partner explain how to find the slope using the graph.

6.4 Equations of Horizontal and Vertical Lines

You can write the equations of **horizontal lines** and **vertical lines** by looking at their graphs.

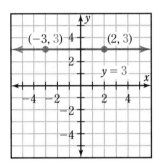

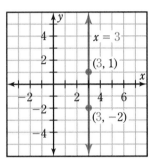

horizontal line   vertical line

In horizontal lines, all of the ordered pairs have the same value for y. In vertical lines, all of the ordered pairs have the same value for x.

EXAMPLE 1

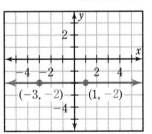

Write the equation of the line from the graph.

Find two ordered pairs on the line.	$(-3, -2)$ and $(1, -2)$
Find the y-value in the ordered pairs.	-2
Check: Pick another point on the line.	$(2, -2)$
Substitute.	$y = -2$
	$-2 = -2$ true

The equation of the line is $y = -2$.

EXAMPLE 2

Write the equation of the line from the graph.

Find two ordered pairs on the line.	$(4, 2)$ and $(4, -4)$
Find the x-value of the ordered pairs.	4

The equation of the line is $x = 4$.

Write the equation for each graph.

1. **Find two ordered pairs on line 1.**
   (■, 4) and (■, −2)
   Find the *x*-value of the ordered pairs. ■
   The equation of the line is $x = $ ■.

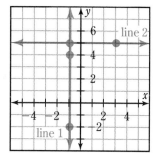

2. **Find two ordered pairs on line 2.**
   (−1, ■) and (3, ■)
   Find the *y*-value of the ordered pairs. ■
   The equation of the line is $y = $ ■.

Practice

Write the equation for each graph.

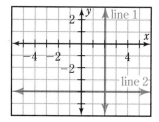
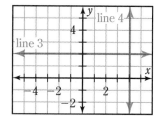

1. line 1   2. line 2   3. line 3   4. line 4

Do It Together!

5. Explain to a partner how to find the equation for number **2** in **Practice.**

6. Graph a vertical line and have a partner write the equation. Check the equation with a point on the graph.

6.5 Parallel and Perpendicular Lines

You know the slopes of **perpendicular lines** are negative reciprocals. You can use this to write the equation of a line perpendicular to another line.

EXAMPLE 1 Write the equation of the line with y-intercept $=3$ and perpendicular to $y=\frac{1}{2}x+4$.

Find the slope of $y=\frac{1}{2}x+4$. $\qquad\qquad\qquad \frac{1}{2}$

The slopes of perpendicular lines are negative reciprocals.

Find the negative reciprocal. $\qquad\qquad\qquad -\frac{2}{1}=-2$

Write the slope-intercept form. $\qquad\qquad\quad y=mx+b$

Substitute -2 for m. Substitute 3 for b. $\qquad y=-2x+3$

The line $y=-2x+3$ is perpendicular to $y=\frac{1}{2}x+4$.

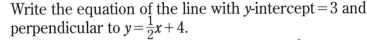

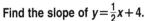

Graph with points labeled $(0, 3)$.

Parallel lines have the same slope. You can use this to write the equations of parallel lines.

EXAMPLE 2 Write the equation of the line through the point (1, 2) and parallel to $y=-x+1$.

Find the slope of $y=-x+1$. $\qquad\qquad\qquad\qquad -1$

Parallel lines have the same slope. $\qquad\qquad\quad \text{slope}=-1$

Write the slope-intercept form. $\qquad\qquad\qquad y=mx+b$

Substitute -1 for m. $\qquad\qquad\qquad\qquad\quad y=-1x+b$

Use the point (1, 2). Substitute 1 for x and 2 for y. $\quad 2=-1(1)+b$

Solve for b. $\qquad\qquad\qquad\qquad\qquad\qquad\quad 2=-1+b$

$\qquad\qquad\qquad\qquad\qquad\qquad\qquad\qquad\quad 3=b$

Write the equation. Use -1 for m and 3 for b. $\quad y=-1x+3$

The line $y=-x+3$ is parallel to $y=-x+1$.

Graph with point labeled $(1, 2)$.

Write the equation for each line described.

1. through the point (4, 1) and perpendicular to $y=-4x-1$

Find the slope of $y=-4x-1$. ■

Find the negative reciprocal of -4. ■

Write the slope-intercept form. $y=mx+b$

Substitute $\frac{1}{4}$ for m. $y=\blacksquare x+b$

Substitute 4 for x and 1 for y. $\blacksquare=\frac{1}{4}(\blacksquare)+b$

Solve for b. $1=1+b$

$\blacksquare=b$

The equation of the line is $y=\blacksquare$.

2. y-intercept $=-5$ and parallel to $y=-2x+4$

Find the slope of $y=-2x+4$. ■

Write the slope-intercept form. $y=mx+b$

Parallel lines have the same slope.

Substitute -2 for m and -5 for b. $y=\blacksquare x+(\blacksquare)$

$y=-2x-\blacksquare$

The equation of the line is $y=\blacksquare$.

Practice

Write the equation for each line.

1. y-intercept $=1$ and parallel to $y=4x-3$

2. through $(-1, 5)$ and parallel to $y=-x+1$

3. y-intercept $=-3$ and parallel to $y=-\frac{1}{2}x+2$

4. y-intercept $=9$ and perpendicular to $y=\frac{1}{5}x+4$

5. y-intercept $=-6$ and perpendicular to $y=-2x-3$

6. through $(2, 8)$ and perpendicular to $y=-\frac{1}{3}x-8$

Do It Together!

7. Work with a partner to check number **1** in **Practice** by graphing both lines.

8. Pick any point. Have a partner write the equation of the line through that point and perpendicular to the line $y=\frac{1}{3}x-2$. Check by graphing the equations.

6.6 Calculator: Is the Equation Correct?

You can write the equations of lines from their graphs. You can check whether the equation is correct with a calculator. Pick a point you know is on the line. Substitute the x- and y-values into the equation.

EXAMPLE **1**   Check that the graph of the equation $y = 4x - 9$ goes through the point $(3.5, 5)$.

Substitute 3.5 for x and 5 for y. $\qquad\qquad\qquad\qquad 5 = 4(3.5) - 9$

Use the calculator to simplify.   **DISPLAY**

Enter 4 by pressing:	$\boxed{4}$	4
Multiply by 3.5 by pressing:	$\boxed{\times}\,\boxed{3}\,\boxed{.}\,\boxed{5}\,\boxed{=}$	14
Subtract 9 by pressing:	$\boxed{-}\,\boxed{9}\,\boxed{=}$	5

$5 = 5$ is true. The equation is correct.

EXAMPLE **2**   Check that the graph of the equation $y = 7x + 80$ goes through the point $(1.8, 91)$.

Substitute 1.8 for x and 91 for y. $\qquad\qquad\qquad 91 = 7(1.8) + 80$

Use the calculator to simplify.   **DISPLAY**

Enter 7 by pressing:	$\boxed{7}$	7
Multiply by 1.8 by pressing:	$\boxed{\times}\,\boxed{1}\,\boxed{.}\,\boxed{8}\,\boxed{=}$	12.6
Add 80 by pressing:	$\boxed{+}\,\boxed{8}\,\boxed{0}\,\boxed{=}$	92.6

$91 = 92.6$ is not true. The equation is not correct.

EXAMPLE **3**   Check that the graph of the equation $y = 5.3x$ goes through the point $(2, 10.6)$.

Substitute x with 2 and y with 10.6. $\qquad\qquad\qquad 10.6 = 5.3(2)$

Use the calculator to simplify.   **DISPLAY**

Enter 5.3 by pressing:	$\boxed{5}\,\boxed{.}\,\boxed{3}$	5.3
Multiply by 2 by pressing:	$\boxed{\times}\,\boxed{2}\,\boxed{=}$	10.6

$10.6 = 10.6$ is true. The equation is correct.

Practice

Check the equation using the given point.

1. $y = 4.2x$
   given the point $(9, 37.8)$

2. $y = 1.9x + 2.3$
   given the point $(3, 8)$

3. $y = 56x - 39$
   given the point $(1.2, 29)$

4. $y = 38x + 5$
   given the point $(.7, 31.6)$

5. $y = 60x + 9.1$
   given the point $(4, 359.1)$

6. $y = 4.2x - 13$
   given the point $(5, 8)$

MATH CONNECTION

Luis Alvarez

Luis Alvarez was born in San Francisco. In 1936, he earned a Ph.D. in physics. He applied his physics and math skills to scientific research.

First, he worked on microwaves and radar. He made a special radar beam. It helped planes to land safely, even in very thick fog.

He was awarded the Nobel Prize in 1968. His work helped build the "bubble chamber." This is used to find very tiny subatomic particles. He found many unknown particles with his research.

In 1980, he wrote an article with his geologist son. They said that a giant asteroid struck the Earth 65 million years ago. It forced a thick cloud of dust up into the sky. This blocked out the sun for a very long time. They think this is what killed the dinosaurs. This theory has caused a lot of debate. As Dr. Alvarez said, "…only time will tell the real story."

6.7 Problem Solving: Looking for Number Patterns

Sometimes you can see a pattern in a table of ordered pairs. You can write an equation to show the pattern.

EXAMPLE 1   Find the pattern. Then, write the equation.

x	y
8	2
9	3
10	4

Look at the first pair of numbers. $8 \to 2$

How do you use 8 to find 2?   subtract 6 or divide by 4

Look at the next pair of numbers. $9 \to 3$

How do you use 9 to find 3?   subtract 6 or divide by 3

Look at the third pair of numbers. $10 \to 4$

How do you use 10 to find 4?   subtract 6

What is the common pattern?   subtract 6

Write the equation. $x - 6 = y$

EXAMPLE 2   Find the pattern. Then, write the equation.

Use _t_ for time and _d_ for distance

Time	Distance
1	2
2	4
3	6

Look at the first pair of numbers. $1 \to 2$

How do you use 1 to find 2?   multiply by 2 or add 1

Look at the next pair of numbers. $2 \to 4$

How do you use 2 to find 4?   multiply by 2 or add 2

Look at the third pair of numbers. $3 \to 6$

How do you use 3 to find 6?   multiply by 2 or add 3

What is the common pattern?   multiply by 2

Write the equation. $2t = d$

Find the pattern. Then, write the equation.

1.

x	y
$50	$10
40	8
30	6

First pair. ■ → 10
divide by 5 or subtract ■

Second pair. 40 → 8
divide by ■ or subtract 32

Third pair. 30 → 6
divide by ■ or subtract 24

The common pattern is ■.
The equation is $y = x$ ■ 5.

2.

Gallons (g)	Miles (m)
1	30
2	60
3	90

First pair. ■ → 30
multiply by 30 or add ■

Second pair. 2 → 60
multiply by ■ or add 58

Third pair. 3 → 90
multiply by ■ or add ■

The common pattern is ■.
The equation is $m =$ ■ g.

Practice

Find the pattern. Then, write the equation.

1.

x	y
28	25
30	27
32	29

2.

Quarts	Gallons
1	4
2	8
3	12

3.

Jo's Age	Mia's Age
3	9
4	10
5	11

Do It Together!

4. Explain to a partner how to find the pattern in number **3** in **Practice.**

5. Write a table using an addition pattern. Ask a partner to describe the pattern in your table and write an equation that gives the pattern.

6.8 Application: Writing Formulas

This graph shows how volume of a gas changes with its temperature. You can use this graph to write an equation or formula that describes this.

t	V
0	450
30	500
60	550
90	600
120	650
150	700

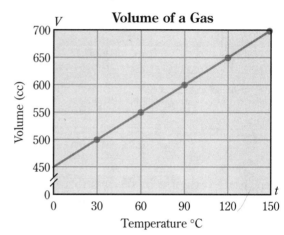

The broken line means a break in the vertical axis.

EXAMPLE 1   Write an equation to show how volume changes with temperature.

Pick variables for volume and temperature.

Use V for volume and t for temperature.

Find the slope.
Use (90, 600) and (30, 500).

$$\frac{\text{rise}}{\text{run}} = \frac{600-500}{90-30} = \frac{100}{60} = \frac{5}{3}$$

Find the y-intercept   450

Substitute $\frac{5}{3}$ for m and 450 for b in $V = mt + b$.

$$V = \frac{5}{3}t + 450$$

The formula for the volume of a gas is $V = \frac{5}{3}t + 450$.

EXAMPLE 2   Use the formula to find the volume of a gas when its temperature is 75°C.

Write the formula. $V = \frac{5}{3}t + 450$

Substitute 75 for t. $V = \frac{5}{3}(75) + 450$

Simplify. $V = 125 + 450$

                            $V = 575$

cc means cubic centimeters.
It is a measure of volume.

The volume of the gas is 575 cc at 75°C.

A spring stretches and gets longer as you put more mass on it.
The graph shows how the length of the spring changes with the mass.

1. Write a formula to describe how
   length changes with mass.

   Pick variables for   Use l for length
   length and mass.   and g for mass.

   Find the slope. Use $\dfrac{\text{rise}}{\text{run}} = \dfrac{81-79}{75-50} = \dfrac{2}{25}$
   (75, 81) and (50, 79).

   Find the y-intercept.   ■

   Substitute ■ for m $l = ■g + ■$
   and ■ for b in $l = mg + b$.

   The formula is $l = ■g + ■$.

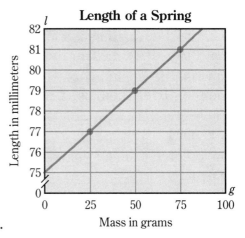

Length of a Spring

2. Use the formula to find the length of
   the spring when the mass is 100 grams.

   Write the formula. $l = \dfrac{2}{25}g + 75$

   Substitute 100 for g. $l = \dfrac{2}{25}■ + 75$

   Simplify. $l = ■$

   The length is ■ millimeters when the mass is 100 grams.

Practice

Use the formula $V = \dfrac{5}{3}t + 450$ to find the volume of a gas at each temperature.

1. 21°C   2. 45°C   3. 150°C   4. 180°C

Do It Together!

5. Explain to a partner how to find the volume in number 1 of **Practice.**

6. Pick a mass in grams. Have a partner use the formula $l = \dfrac{2}{25}g + 75$ to find the length of a spring.

Chapter Review

Chapter 6 Summary

- You can write the equation of a line if you know the slope and the y-intercept.
- To write the equation of a line when you know a point and the slope, substitute the coordinates for x and y and solve for b.
- To write the equation of a line when you know two points, first find the slope. Then, use a point on the line to find b.
- The ordered pairs for points on a vertical line have the same value for x.
- The ordered pairs for points on a horizontal line have the same value for y.
- The slopes of perpendicular lines are negative reciprocals.
- Parallel lines have the same slope.
- You can use a calculator to check if an equation is correct.
- You can describe a pattern with an equation.
- You can write formulas from graphs.

Reviewing Vocabulary

Fill in each blank with the correct word.

slope-intercept form
horizontal line
vertical line
perpendicular lines
parallel lines

1. _?_ have the same slope.

2. An equation written in $y = mx + b$ form is in _?_ .

3. A line with slope $= 0$ is a _?_ .

4. _?_ are two lines with slopes that are negative reciprocals.

5. A line with no slope is a _?_ .

Chapter Quiz

Write the equation of each line.

1. with slope $= -1$ and y-intercept $= 3$ **2.** with slope $= \frac{1}{2}$ and y-intercept $= 7$

3. with slope $= 2$ and y-intercept $= -6$ **4.** through (1, 1) and with slope $= 4$

5. through $(-4, 3)$ and with slope $= 0$ **6.** through (1, 6) and (3, 16)

7. through (1, 2) and (2, 0)   **8.** through (3, 5) and parallel to $y = x + 5$

9. with y-intercept $= -6$ and perpendicular to $y = 2x + 1$

Write the equation of each line.

10. 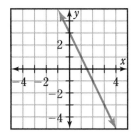   **11.** 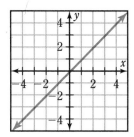   **12.**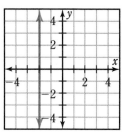

Find the pattern. Then, write the equation.

13.

Time	Distance
3	12
4	16
5	20

14.

x	y
15	11
16	12
17	13

Use the formula $l = \frac{2}{25}g + 75$ to answer the question. Use l for length and g for mass.

15. What is the length of a spring when the mass is 250 grams?

Unit Two Review

Tell whether each set of ordered pairs is a function.

1. (1, 3)
   (−2, 0)
   (4, 3)
   (2, 0)

2.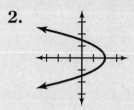

3.

Find the value of each function.

4. $f(-3)$ when $f(x) = -2x$ 5. $f(0)$ when $f(x) = 5x - 3$ 6. $f(4)$ when $f(x) = 3(x - 1)$

Tell whether the ordered pair is a solution of the equation.

7. $(1, 1)$; $y = 3x - 2$ 8. $(-6, 4)$; $y = 2 + \frac{x}{3}$ 9. $(2, -1)$; $y = 2x + 4$

Find the slope of each line that contains these pairs of points.

10. $(-1, 3)$ and $(2, 3)$ 11. $(-1, 0)$ and $(-1, 8)$ 12. $(-2, -5)$ and $(-5, -7)$

Find the x-intercept and y-intercept of each line.

13. $x + 2y = 8$ 14. $y = \frac{3}{2}x + 12$ 15. $y = 2x + 4$

Tell whether lines that contain these points are parallel or perpendicular.

16. $(2, 4)$ and $(1, 6)$;   17. $(1, -3)$ and $(-3, 3)$;   18. $(-1, -4)$ and $(2, 8)$;
    $(5, 3)$ and $(3, 2)$ $(-2, -5)$ and $(-5, -7)$ $(1, 3)$ and $(0, -1)$

Graph each line. Then, write the equation of the line.

19. slope: 2   20. slope: $\frac{-1}{3}$ 21. point: $(4, -5)$
    y-intercept: −3 y-intercept: 5   slope: 0

22. a line through   23. a line through   24. point: $(-1, -4)$
    $(-3, 6)$ and $(0, 4)$ $(-1, -1)$ and $(1, 3)$ parallel to $y = x + 4$

Unit Three

Chapter 7
Inequalities

Chapter 8
Systems of Linear Equations and Inequalities

Chapter 9
More about Data and Data Analysis

Chapter 7

Inequalities

Stocking a warehouse takes careful planning. The warehouse needs to keep enough items on the shelves to fill all the orders. The warehouse also must not order more than it can afford to keep in stock. Inequalities can be used to show this amount.

Chapter Learning Objectives

- Solve and graph the solution of an inequality with one variable.
- Solve an inequality with two variables.
- Graph the solution of an inequality with two variables.
- Use a calculator to check a solution of an inequality.
- Solve a problem by using an inequality.
- Apply concepts and skills to using solutions of inequalities.

Words to Know

graph of a solution   points on the number line or coordinate plane that show the solutions of an equation or inequality

inequality   a statement that shows "greater than," "greater than or equal to," "less than," or "less than or equal to"

$\leq$ the symbol for "is less than or equal to" also means "at most" or "no greater than"

$\geq$ the symbol for "is greater than or equal to" also means "at least" or "no less than"

In this chapter, you will learn how to graph solutions of inequalities on a number line and on the coordinate plane. Using addition, subtraction, multiplication, and division, you will learn how to solve inequalities. You will use your calculator to check solutions. Then, you will write inequalities for word statements. You will apply what you learn about graphing inequalities to get information from graphs.

7.1 Solutions on the Number Line

You can **graph a solution** to an equation with one variable on a number line.

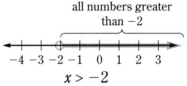

$x = -2$

The only solution is -2.

The statement $x > -2$ is an **inequality.** It means that x is greater than -2. You can also graph its solution.

all numbers greater than -2

$x > -2$

An open dot means -2 is not a solution of $x > -2$. Any point to the right of -2 is greater than -2. Any point to the right of -2 is a solution.

EXAMPLE 1   Graph the solution. $x < 4$

Place an open dot at 4.

Shade the number line to the left of 4.

The inequality $x \leq 1$ means x is less than or equal to 1.

1 and all numbers less than 1

$x \leq 1$

A solid dot means 1 is a solution of the inequality. Any point to the left of 1 is also a solution.

EXAMPLE 2   Graph the solution. $y \geq 3$

$y \geq 3$ means y is greater than or equal to 3.

Place a solid dot at 3.

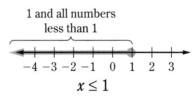

Shade the number line to the right of 3.

Graph the solution of each inequality.

1. $x \geq 4$

Place a ■ dot at 4.

Shade the number line to the ■ of 4.

2. $y < -3$

Place an ■ dot at −3.

Shade the number line to the ■ of −3.

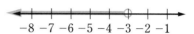

3. $p > 0$

Place an ■ dot at 0.

Shade the number line to the ■ of 0.

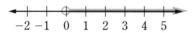

4. $w \leq 5$

Place a ■ dot at 5.

Shade the number line to the ■ of 5.

Practice

Graph the solution of each inequality on a number line.

1. $x > 5$

2. $y \leq -1$

3. $a \geq 2$

4. $t < 7$

5. $k \geq -6$

6. $m \leq 0$

7. $b > -4$

8. $x < 8$

9. $q \geq -5$

10. $y \geq 0$

11. $n \leq -9$

12. $z > 3$

13. $r > -7$

14. $w \geq 1$

15. $s \leq -8$

Do It Together!

16. Explain to a partner how to graph the solution of $y \geq 10$.

17. Write an inequality using integers. Ask a partner to graph the solution of the inequality. Check the work.

7.2 Solving Inequalities Using Addition and Subtraction

You have solved equations using addition and subtraction. You can follow the same steps to solve an inequality using addition and subtraction.

$$\text{greater than} \quad \rightarrow \qquad 7 > 4$$
$$7 - 2 \, ? \, 4 - 2$$
$$\text{stays greater than} \quad \rightarrow \qquad 5 > 2$$

Adding or subtracting the same number from both sides keeps the inequality true.

EXAMPLE 1 Solve. Then, graph. Check. $\quad x + 1 > 3$

$$x + 1 > 3$$

Subtract 1 from both sides. $\qquad x + 1 - 1 > 3 - 1$

Simplify. Then, graph. $\qquad\qquad\qquad x > 2$

Check: Substitute a number from the $\qquad x + 1 > 3$
shaded part into $x + 1 > 3$. Use 4. $\qquad 4 + 1 > 3$

$$5 > 3 \quad \text{true}$$

EXAMPLE 2 Solve. Then, graph. Check. $\quad y - 2 \le -3$

$$y - 2 \le -3$$

Add 2 to both sides. $\qquad\qquad y - 2 + 2 \le -3 + 2$

Simplify. Then, graph. $\qquad\qquad\qquad y \le -1$

Check: Substitute a number from the $\qquad y - 2 \le -3$
shaded part into $y - 2 \le -3$. Use -4. $\qquad -4 - 2 \le -3$

$$-6 \le -3 \quad \text{true}$$

EXAMPLE 3 Solve. Then, graph. Check. $\quad y + 3 \ge 0$

$$y + 3 \ge 0$$

Subtract 3 from both sides. $\qquad y + 3 - 3 \ge 0 - 3$

Simplify. Then, graph. $\qquad\qquad\qquad y \ge -3$

Check: Substitute a number from the $\qquad y + 3 \ge 0$
shaded part into $y + 3 \ge 0$. Use 0. $\qquad 0 + 3 \ge 0$

$$3 \ge 0 \quad \text{true}$$

Solve each inequality. Then, graph the solution.

1. $x - 4 > -3$

Add 4 to both sides. $x - 4 + \blacksquare > -3 + \blacksquare$

Simplify both sides. $x > \blacksquare$

```
←——+——+——⊕——+——+——+——+——+——→
   -1  0  1  2  3  4  5  6
```

2. $q + 4 \leq 5$

Subtract $\blacksquare$ from both sides. $q + 4 - \blacksquare \leq 5 - \blacksquare$

Simplify both sides. $q \leq \blacksquare$

```
←——+——+——+——+——+——+——●——+——+——→
  -4 -3 -2 -1  0  1  2  3
```

Practice

Solve each inequality. Then, graph the solution. Check with a point from the shaded part of the graph.

1. $y + 4 > 6$

2. $x + 3 \leq -4$

3. $b - 2 < 5$

4. $m - 1 \geq -2$

5. $s + 5 > 3$

6. $a - 6 \leq 3$

7. $x - 3 < -2$

8. $p - 2 \geq 8$

9. $w + 7 < -2$

10. $t + 2 > -7$

Do It Together!

11. Show a partner how to find the solution in number **10** in **Practice.**

12. Write an inequality that contains integers. Use addition or subtraction in the inequality. Ask a partner to solve the inequality. Check the work.

7.3 Solving Inequalities Using Multiplication and Division

You can use multiplication and division to solve inequalities. Watch what happens to the inequality sign.

Multiply by a positive number.	Multiply by a negative number.
$5 > 3$	$5 > 3$
$5(2) \ ? \ 3(2)$	$5(-2) \ ? \ 3(-2)$
$10 > 6$	$-10 < -6$
The inequality stays "is greater than."	The inequality changes to "is less than."

Multiplying both sides of an inequality by the same negative number changes the inequality.

EXAMPLE 1   Solve. Then, graph. $\dfrac{x}{4} < 3$

Multiply both sides by 4. Do not change the inequality.

Check: Use 8.

$\dfrac{x}{4} < 3$

$\dfrac{8}{4} < 3$

$2 < 3$ true

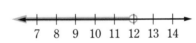

$\dfrac{x}{4} < 3$

$\dfrac{x}{4}(4) < 3(4)$

$x < 12$

Division works the same way.

$10 < 15$	$10 < 15$
$\dfrac{10}{5} \ ? \ \dfrac{15}{5}$	$\dfrac{10}{-5} \ ? \ \dfrac{15}{-5}$
$2 < 3$	$-2 > -3$
The inequality stays "is less than."	The inequality changes to "is greater than."

EXAMPLE 2   Solve. Then, graph. $-5x \geq 20$

Divide both sides by −5. Change the inequality.

Check: Use −5.

$-5x \geq 20$

$-5(-5) \geq 20$

$25 \geq 20$ true

$-5x \geq 20$

$\dfrac{-5x}{-5} \leq \dfrac{20}{-5}$

$x \leq -4$

Solve each inequality. Then, graph the solution.

1. $\dfrac{x}{-3} \le 2$

$\dfrac{x}{-3} \le 2$

Multiply both
sides by ■.

■ the inequality.

$\dfrac{x}{-3}(■) ■ 2(■)$

$x ■ -6$

2. $-6y > -18$

Divide both
sides by ■.

■ the inequality.

$-6y > -18$

$\dfrac{-6y}{■} ■ \dfrac{-18}{■}$

$y ■ 3$

Practice

Solve each inequality. Then, graph.

1. $\dfrac{x}{2} > 4$ **2.** $4b \ge 8$ **3.** $\dfrac{f}{6} < 6$ **4.** $8c > 24$

5. $\dfrac{m}{-5} \le 6$ **6.** $-3x < 0$ **7.** $\dfrac{x}{-4} \ge 5$ **8.** $-5d \le 30$

Solve each inequality.

9. $\dfrac{x}{-2} > 10$ **10.** $3b \ge 21$ **11.** $\dfrac{f}{9} < 0$ **12.** $-7c > 28$

13. $\dfrac{m}{5} \le 7$ **14.** $-8x < 40$ **15.** $\dfrac{x}{-6} \ge 5$ **16.** $11d \le 88$

Do It Together!

17. Explain to a partner how to solve the inequality in number **6** in **Practice.**

18. Write an inequality with $\dfrac{x}{3}$ on the left side. Write an integer on the right. Ask a partner to solve your inequality. Check the work.

7.4 Solving Inequalities Using More than One Step

Some inequalities contain more than one operation. You undo the operations the same way you undo them when solving equations. First, undo addition or subtraction. Then, undo multiplication or division.

EXAMPLE 1 Solve. Then, graph. $3x - 6 < 9$

Add 6 to both sides. $\qquad 3x - 6 + 6 < 9 + 6$

Simplify. $\qquad 3x < 15$

Divide both sides by 3. $\qquad \dfrac{3x}{3} < \dfrac{15}{3}$

Do not change the inequality. Simplify. $\qquad x < 5$

EXAMPLE 2 Solve. Then, graph. $-5a + 2 \geq 22$

Subtract 2 from both sides. $\qquad -5a + 2 - 2 \geq 22 - 2$

Simplify. $\qquad -5a \geq 20$

Divide both sides by −5. $\qquad \dfrac{-5a}{-5} \leq \dfrac{20}{-5}$

Change the inequality.

Simplify. $\qquad a \leq -4$

Check: Use −5.
$-5a + 2 \geq 22$
$-5(-5) + 2 \geq 22$
$25 + 2 \geq 22$
$27 \geq 22$ true

EXAMPLE 3 Solve. Then, graph. $\dfrac{m}{-4} + 3 < 0$

Subtract 3 from both sides. $\qquad \dfrac{m}{-4} + 3 - 3 < 0 - 3$

Simplify. $\qquad \dfrac{m}{-4} < -3$

Multiply both sides by −4. $\qquad \dfrac{m}{-4}(-4) > -3(-4)$

Change the inequality.

Simplify. $\qquad m > 12$

Check: Use 16.
$\dfrac{m}{-4} + 3 < 0$
$\dfrac{16}{-4} + 3 < 0$
$-4 + 3 < 0$
$-1 < 0$ true

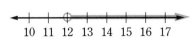

Solve each inequality. Then, graph the solution.

1. $\frac{x}{3} + 6 \geq 12$

$$\frac{x}{3} + 6 \geq 12$$

Subtract ■ from both sides. $\frac{x}{3} + 6 - \blacksquare \geq 12 - \blacksquare$

Simplify. $\frac{x}{3} \geq \blacksquare$

Multiply both sides by ■. Do not change the inequality. $\frac{x}{3}(3) \geq 6(3)$

Simplify. $x \geq \blacksquare$

Graph the inequality.

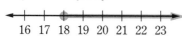

2. $-6y - 4 > -22$

$$-6y - 4 > -22$$

Add ■ to both sides. $-6y - 4 + \blacksquare > -22 + \blacksquare$

Simplify. $-6y > \blacksquare$

Divide both sides by ■. Change the inequality. $\frac{-6y}{-6} \blacksquare \frac{\blacksquare}{-6}$

Simplify. $y \blacksquare 3$

Graph the inequality.

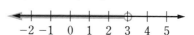

Practice

Solve each inequality. Then, graph the solution.

1. $2x - 8 > 16$

2. $2y + 6 < 18$

3. $-9x + 3 \geq 21$

4. $\frac{a}{3} + 2 > 3$

5. $\frac{m}{2} - 4 \geq -1$

6. $\frac{n}{5} + 4 \leq 7$

Solve each inequality.

7. $-3x + 15 < 0$

8. $-5g + 3 \geq 28$

9. $\frac{m}{-3} - 6 \leq 1$

10. $\frac{x}{-5} + 8 > 3$

11. $-8a + 19 > -5$

12. $\frac{x}{9} + 13 \geq 5$

Do It Together!

13. Explain to a partner how to solve the inequality in number **8** in **Practice.**

14. Write the inequality $2a \geq 20$. Think of an even number. Subtract it from the left side of $2a \geq 20$. Ask a partner to solve your inequality. Graph the solution. Then, check.

7.5 Solutions in the Coordinate Plane

You have graphed linear equations on a coordinate plane. You can also graph inequalities on a coordinate plane.

The shaded areas are graphs of the solutions of the inequalities. Substitute the x- and y-values of any ordered pair in the shaded area. You will have a true statement.

Points on the dotted line are not solutions.

Points on the solid line are solutions.

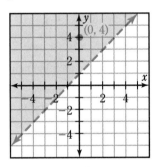

$y > x + 1$
Check $(0, 4)$.
$4 > 0 + 1$
$4 > 1$ true

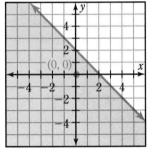

$y \leq -x + 2$
Check $(0, 0)$.
$0 \leq -0 + 2$
$0 \leq 2$ true

EXAMPLE 1

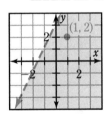

Tell whether $(1, 2)$ is a solution of $y < 2x + 3$.

$$y < 2x + 3$$

Substitute 1 for x and 2 for y. $2 < 2(1) + 3$

Simplify. $2 < 2 + 3$

$$2 < 5 \quad \text{true}$$

$(1, 2)$ is a solution of $y < 2x + 3$.

EXAMPLE 2

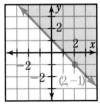

Tell whether $(2, -1)$ is a solution of $y \geq -x + 1$.

$$y \geq -x + 1$$

Substitute 2 for x and -1 for y. $-1 \geq -(2) + 1$

Simplify. $-1 \geq -2 + 1$

$$-1 \geq -1 \quad \text{true}$$

$(2, -1)$ is a solution of $y \geq -x + 1$.

Tell whether each point is a solution of the inequality.

1. $(-1, 0)$; $y < 2x + 2$

Substitute ■ for
x and ■ for y. $■ < 2(■) + 2$
Simplify. $■ < ■ + 2$
                          $■ < ■$ false

$(-1, 0)$ ■ a solution of $y < 2x + 2$.

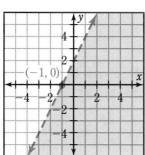

2. $(2, 3)$; $y \leq -x + 4$

Substitute ■ for
x and ■ for y. $■ \leq -(■) + 4$
Simplify. $■ \leq ■$ false

$(2, 3)$ ■ a solution of $y \leq -x + 4$.

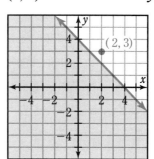

Practice

Tell whether each point is a solution of $y > x + 1$.

1. $(-1, 1)$ **2.** $(1, 2)$

3. $(2, -1)$ **4.** $(0, 0)$

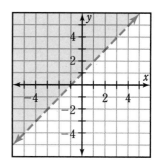

Tell whether each point is a solution of $y \geq -2x$.

5. $(-2, -1)$ **6.** $(-1, 2)$ **7.** $(0, 4)$ **8.** $(1, -1)$

Do It Together!

9. Explain to a partner how to solve number **2** in **Practice.**

10. Pick any three points. Have a partner tell whether they are solutions of $y > 3x$. Check the work.

7.6 Solving Inequalities with Two Variables

You can solve inequalities with two variables. First, graph the equation. Then, find the area that contains the solutions to the inequality. To find the area, pick a point on either side of the line. Substitute for x and y to see if it is in the solution.

EXAMPLE 1

x means 1x.

Graph the solution. $y < x + 2$

Graph $y = x + 2$.

Use y-intercept $= 2$ and slope $= 1$.

Draw a dotted line through the points to show $<$.

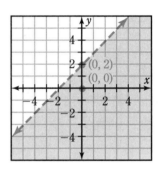

It is easiest to use (0, 0) if the line does not pass through the origin.

Pick a point on one side of the line.	$(0, 0)$
Substitute into the inequality.	$0 < 0 + 2$
Simplify.	$0 < 2$ true

Shade the side of the line that contains (0, 0).

EXAMPLE 2

Graph the solution. $y \leq -2x$

Graph the line $y = -2x$.

Use y-intercept $= 0$ and slope $= -2$.

Draw a solid line through the points to show $\leq$.

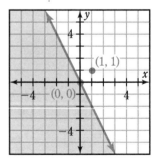

Pick a point on one side of the line.	$(1, 1)$
Substitute into the inequality.	$1 \leq -2(1)$
Simplify.	$1 \leq -2$ false

Shade the side of the line that does not contain (1, 1).

Graph the solution of each inequality.

1. $y \le \frac{2}{5}x - 2$

Graph $y = \frac{2}{5}x - 2$.
Use y-intercept = ■.
Use slope = ■.
Draw a ■ line through the points.
Pick a point. Use (0, 0).
Substitute into the inequality. $\quad 0 \le \frac{2}{5}(0) - 2$

Simplify. $\qquad\qquad\qquad\quad 0 \le 0 - 2$
$\qquad\qquad\qquad\qquad\quad 0 \le -2 \quad$ false

Shade the side of the line that does not contain (0, 0).

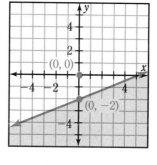

2. $y > x$

Graph $y = x$.
Use y-intercept = ■.
Use slope = ■.
Draw a ■ line through the points.
Pick a point. Use (0, 1).
Substitute into the inequality. $\quad 1 > 0 \quad$ true
Shade the side of the line that contains (0, 1).

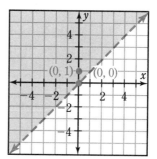

Practice

Graph the solution of each inequality.

1. $y > 2x + 1$ **2.** $y < 3x$ **3.** $y \le \frac{-2}{3}x + 3$

4. $y > -3x + 4$ **5.** $y \ge \frac{1}{2}x - 2$ **6.** $y < -x$

Do It Together!

7. Explain to a partner how to graph the inequality in number **3** in **Practice**.

8. Write an inequality. Write y on one side. Ask a partner to graph the inequality. Check the work.

7.7 Calculator: Checking Solutions

The graph of an inequality contains all solutions. Some ordered pairs in the solution contain decimals. You can use a calculator to check these ordered pairs.

EXAMPLE 1   Is $(1.5, 2.5)$ a solution of $y < 2x + 1$?

$$y < 2x + 1$$

Substitute 1.5 for *x* and 2.5 for *y*. $2.5 < 2 \bullet 1.5 + 1$

Use your calculator to simplify the right side.   **DISPLAY**

Enter 2 by pressing:	☐2	₂
Multiply by 1.5 by pressing:	☐× ☐1 ☐. ☐5 ☐=	₃
Add 1 by pressing:	☐+ ☐1 ☐=	₄

$2.5 < 4$ is true. $(1.5, 2.5)$ is a solution of $y < 2x + 1$.

EXAMPLE 2   Is $(2.4, 1.2)$ a solution of $y > 3x - 2$?

$$y > 3x - 2$$

Substitute 2.4 for *x* and 1.2 for *y*. $1.2 > 3 \bullet 2.4 - 2$

Use your calculator to simplify the right side.   **DISPLAY**

Enter 3 by pressing:	☐3	₃
Multiply by 2.4 by pressing:	☐× ☐2 ☐. ☐4 ☐=	7.2
Subtract 2 by pressing:	☐− ☐2 ☐=	5.2

$1.2 > 5.2$ is false. $(2.4, 1.2)$ is not a solution of $y > 3x - 2$.

EXAMPLE 3   Is $(3.9, .65)$ a solution of $y < \dfrac{x}{6}$?

$$y < \frac{x}{6}$$

Substitute 3.9 for *x* and .65 for *y*. $.65 < \dfrac{3.9}{6}$

Use your calculator to simplify the right side.   **DISPLAY**

Enter 3.9 by pressing:	☐3 ☐. ☐9	3.9
Divide by 6 by pressing:	☐÷ ☐6 ☐=	0.65

$.65 < .65$ is false. $(3.9, .65)$ is not a solution of $y < \dfrac{x}{6}$.

Practice

Tell whether each ordered pair is a solution of the inequality.

1. $(1.1, 1.8); y < 2x + 5$

2. $(2.1, 1.6); y \geq 3x - 1$

3. $(1.3, 7.2); y \leq 4x + 2$

4. $(2.6, 1.4); y > \dfrac{x}{2} - 4$

5. $(1.7, 2.8); y > 2x + 2$

6. $(3.5, 5.1); y < 5x - 2$

7. $(2.3, 1.9); y < \dfrac{x}{5} - 5$

8. $(3.9, 4.1); y \leq 3x - 8$

MATH CONNECTION

Restaurant Managers

Do you like to cook and serve good food? Can you plan meals and shopping lists? Do you like people? If so, you might enjoy a career as a restaurant manager.

Restaurant managers run a business. They make sure customers get good food and service. There must be enough food, clean napkins, plates, and silverware. The right numbers of servers, cooks, and helpers are needed too.

To keep track, managers need to be good at math. They estimate the number of customers. They plan how much food to buy. Imagine you work for a fine restaurant. The chef has made a new fish recipe. The fish must be very fresh. You need to buy just enough for the customers who will want it. If you buy too much, it may be wasted. You can use an inequality to help decide how much to buy.

A manager keeps a restaurant from losing money. If the service and food are poor, customers will stop coming. If too much food is ordered, it will be wasted. Good food and service mean more customers and more money!

7.8 Problem Solving: Using Inequalities

You can use inequalities to solve many problems. It is helpful to know other words for the inequality symbols.

$$\geq$$ $$\leq$$

at least   at most
no less than   no greater than

To begin, pick variables for the numbers you do not know. Then, use symbols for the other words.

The number of students is at least 200.

don't know $\geq$ 200
n $\geq$ 200

EXAMPLE 1 Coach Roberts needs to buy baseballs for the team. Each baseball costs $5.00. How many baseballs can he buy if he wants to spend at most $45.00?

Write the inequality.   baseballs   each $5   at most $45

Choose a variable.   don't know $\bullet$ 5 $\leq$ 45

Use b for baseballs.

Check: Use 7.
5b < 45
5(7) < 45
35 < 45   true

Solve the inequality.

$$5b \leq 45$$
$$\frac{5b}{5} \leq \frac{45}{5}$$
$$b \leq 9$$

Coach Roberts can buy no more than 9 baseballs.

EXAMPLE 2 Anthony has $20.00. How much more money does he need to earn to have at least $50.00 in all?

Write the inequality.   has $20   needs   at least $50

Choose a variable   20 + don't know $\geq$ 50

Use m for money.

Check: Use 31.
$20 + m \geq 50$
$20 + 31 \geq 50$
$51 \geq 50$ true

Solve the inequality.

$$20 + m \geq 50$$
$$20 - 20 + m \geq 50 - 20$$
$$m \geq 30$$

Anthony needs to earn at least $30.00 more.

1. To go on vacation this summer, the 3 members of the Garner family must save more than $1,500. How much must each member save?

   Choose a variable and write the inequality. Use *d* for dollars.

   $d \bullet 3 \; \blacksquare \; 1{,}500$

   $3d \; \blacksquare \; 1{,}500$

   Solve the inequality.

   $\dfrac{3d}{3} \; \blacksquare \; \dfrac{1{,}500}{3}$

   $d > \blacksquare$

   Each member must save more than $\blacksquare$.

2. A caterer wants to make at least $2,000 at an event with 50 people. How much should the caterer charge per person?

   Choose a variable and write the inequality. Use *m* for money.

   $m \bullet 50 \; \blacksquare \; 2{,}000$

   $50m \; \blacksquare \; 2{,}000$

   Solve the inequality.

   $\dfrac{50m}{50} \; \blacksquare \; \dfrac{2{,}000}{50}$

   $m \geq \blacksquare$

   The caterer should charge at least $\blacksquare$ per person.

Practice

Write an inequality for each problem. Then, solve the inequality.

1. Maria wants to buy tickets to a concert. How many $12 tickets can she buy if she wants to spend less than $48.00?

2. Chris decides to wash cars to earn money for a ski trip. He charges $20.00 per car. How many cars will he have to wash to earn at least $300.00?

3. Jason has to write a report that is at least 15 pages long. He has written 7 pages already. How many more pages will he need to write?

Do It Together!

4. Explain to a partner how you solve the inequality in number **2** in **Practice.**

5. Write a problem that can be solved with an inequality. Ask a partner to solve.

7.9 Application: Using Solutions

The shaded area of a graph shows all the solutions of an inequality. The shaded area also contains the answers to problems.

EXAMPLE 1   Malik has $10.00 to buy milk and bread for the week. Milk costs $2.00 a gallon. Bread costs $1.00 a loaf. Can he buy 3 gallons of milk and 1 loaf of bread?

The inequality shows how much he can buy. Use _m_ for the number of gallons of milk. Use _b_ for the number of loaves of bread.

$$2m + 1b \leq 10$$

The shaded area of the graph shows the ordered pairs of (milk, bread) that make the inequality true.

Use the ordered pair (3, 1) to show 3 gallons of milk and 1 loaf of bread.

Locate (3, 1) on the graph.

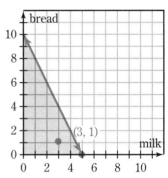

(3, 1) is in the shaded area. Malik can buy 3 gallons of milk and 1 loaf of bread.

EXAMPLE 2   Jaye wants a workout that will burn at least 300 calories. Jogging burns 12 calories a minute. Swimming burns 6 calories a minute. Is 10 minutes of jogging and 20 minutes of swimming enough exercise?

The inequality shows how much of each exercise she needs.

Use _j_ for jogging and _s_ for swimming.

$$12j + 6s \geq 300$$

The shaded area of the graph shows the ordered pairs of (jog, swim) that make the inequality true.

Use (10, 20) to show 10 minutes of jogging and 20 minutes of swimming.

Locate (10, 20) on the graph

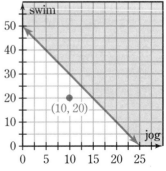

(10, 20) is not in the shaded area. That is not enough exercise.

The hockey team needs at least 20 more points to make the playoffs. The team gets 2 points for a win and 1 point for a tie. Use the ordered pair (wins, ties) to show the amount of each.

$$2w + 1t \geq 20$$

Use the graph of the solution of the inequality to answer the questions.

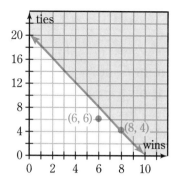

1. Will the team make the playoffs with 6 wins and 6 ties?

Use (■, ■) to show the wins and ties.

Locate the point on the graph.

(6, 6) ■ in the shaded area.

The team ■ make the playoffs.

2. Will the team make the playoffs with 8 wins and 4 ties?

Use (■, ■) to show the wins and ties.

Locate the point on the graph.

(8, 4) is in the shaded area.

The team ■ make the playoffs.

Practice

Liu has less than $3.00 in coins. All of the coins are nickels or dimes. The ordered pair (nickels, dimes) tells the number she has of each. Use the graph of the inequality to answer the questions. $.05n + .10d < 3.00$

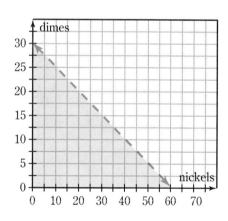

1. Could Liu have 10 nickels and 20 dimes?

2. Could Liu have 20 nickels and 25 dimes?

3. Could Liu have 10 nickels and 25 dimes?

Do It Together!

4. Explain to a partner how you solve number **1** in **Practice.**

5. Choose new numbers of nickels and dimes. Ask a partner if Liu could have that number of coins. Check the work.

Chapter 7 Summary

- You can graph the solution of an inequality containing one variable on a number line.
- You can solve an inequality with two variables by adding or subtracting the same number from both sides.
- You can solve an inequality by multiplying or dividing both sides by the same number.
- Multiplying or dividing both sides of an inequality by a negative number changes the inequality.
- You can solve inequalities that contain more than one operation by undoing each operation. Undo addition or subtraction. Then, undo multiplication or division.
- You can use coordinate planes to graph the solution of inequalities with two variables.
- The points on a dotted line are not solutions of an inequality. Points on a solid line are solutions.
- A calculator can be used to check the solutions of inequalities.
- You can solve problems by writing and using graphs of inequalities.

Reviewing Vocabulary

Fill in each blank with the correct word.

graph of a solution
inequality
≤
≥

1. Use the symbol ? to show "greater than or equal to" or "at least."

2. The ? is the set of points on a number line or coordinate plane that shows the solutions of an equation or inequality.

3. A statement that shows "greater than," "greater than or equal to," "less than," or "less than or equal to" is a(n) ? .

4. Use the symbol ? to show "less than or equal to" or "no greater than."

Chapter Quiz

Solve each inequality. Then, graph the solution on a number line.

1. $x > 4$

2. $b \leq -7$

3. $y \geq 6$

4. $b + 2 \leq 6$

5. $x - 1 > 5$

6. $\frac{x}{3} < 4$

7. $-5b \geq 10$

8. $2g - 2 > 6$

9. $-6m + 2 \leq 14$

Tell whether each point is a solution of $y \leq 3x - 1$.

10. $(2, 3)$

11. $(-1, 2)$

12. $(2, 5)$

Graph the solution of each inequality.

13. $y < -3x + 4$

14. $y > \frac{2}{3}x - 2$

15. $y \geq x - 3$

16. $y \leq 2x + 1$

17. $y < \frac{1}{2}x + 2$

18. $y > -x$

Write the inequality. Then, solve it.

19. Tina has put 15 of her old CDs in a storage crate. How many more CDs can she store in the crate if it can hold no more than 23 CDs?

Use the graph of the inequality to answer the question.

20. Bob is sending postcards and letters. He has $10.00 to spend on stamps. Stamps for letters cost $.32 each. Stamps for postcards cost $.20 each. The ordered pair (letters, postcards) tells how many of each. The inequality gives the ordered pairs that have a total cost less than or equal to $10.00.

Can he send 15 letters and 25 postcards?

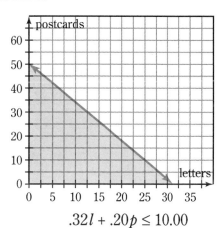

$.32l + .20p \leq 10.00$

Chapter 8

Systems of Linear Equations and Inequalities

An airport is a complicated system of planes, passengers, luggage, and employees. The control tower keeps track of the planes. Tower information is combined with all the other departments to keep the airport running smoothly.

Chapter Learning Objectives

- Identify a system of linear equations.
- Solve a system of linear equations.
- Identify a system of linear inequalities.
- Solve a system of linear inequalities.
- Use a calculator to check the solution of a system of linear equations.
- Solve problems using systems of linear equations.
- Apply concepts and skills to find minimum and maximum values.

Words to Know

system of linear equations two or more linear equations with the same variables

eliminating a variable removing one variable in a system of equations

system of linear inequalities two or more linear inequalities with the same variables

maximum largest number in a group

minimum smallest number in a group

In this chapter, you will learn the meaning of a solution of a system of linear equations. Then, you will learn how to graph systems of linear equations. You will also find the solution to systems of linear equations using substitution, addition or subtraction, and multiplication. You will learn how to find solutions of systems of linear inequalities by graphing. You will use your calculator to check solutions of systems of linear equations. You will also use systems of linear equations to solve problems. Finally, you will apply systems of equations to find the smallest and largest values for a solution of a problem.

8.1 Systems of Equations

Two linear equations with the same variables are a **system of linear equations.** The graphs below show systems of equations.

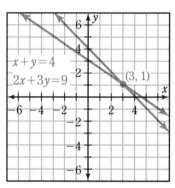

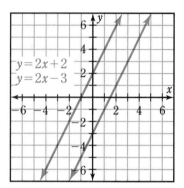

(3, 1) is a point on the graph of $x+y=4$ and $2x+3y=9$.

1 solution   no solution

The solution of the system $x+y=4$ and $2x+3y=9$ is shown by the point where the two lines cross or intersect. The ordered pair for this point make both equations true. (3, 1) is the solution of the system.

Check that (3, 1) is the solution by substituting into each equation.

$$x+y=4$$
$$3+1=4$$
$$4=4 \quad \text{true}$$

$$2x+3y=9$$
$$2(3)+3(1)=9$$
$$6+3=9$$
$$9=9 \quad \text{true}$$

EXAMPLE 1

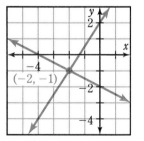

Tell whether $(-2,-1)$ is the solution of the system.

$$2y-3x=4$$
$$x+2y=-4$$

Substitute −2 for x and −1 for y.

$$2y-3x=4$$
$$2(-1)-3(-2)=4$$
$$-2+6=4$$
$$4=4 \quad \text{true}$$

$$x+2y=-4$$
$$-2+2(-1)=-4$$
$$-2-2=-4$$
$$-4=-4 \quad \text{true}$$

$(-2,-1)$ is the solution of the system.

EXAMPLE 2

Tell whether (2, 3) is the solution of the system.

$$x+y=5$$
$$x-y=1$$

Substitute 2 for x and 3 for y.

$$x+y=5$$
$$2+3=5$$
$$5=5 \quad \text{true}$$

$$x-y=1$$
$$2-3=1$$
$$-1=1 \quad \text{false}$$

(2, 3) is not the solution of the system.

Tell whether the ordered pair is the solution of the system.

1. $(-2, 0)$; $x = -2$
$-x + y = 2$

Substitute ■ for x and ■ for y.

$x = -2$ $-x + y = 2$
$■ = -2$ $-(■) + ■ = 2$
true $■ = 2$
                   true

$(-2, 0)$ ■ the solution of the system.

2. $(6, 1)$; $\frac{1}{2}x + y = 4$
$-2x + y = -6$

Substitute ■ for x and ■ for y.

$\frac{1}{2}x + y = 4$ $-2x + y = -6$
$\frac{1}{2}(■) + ■ = 4$ $-2(■) + ■ = -6$
$■ = 4$ $■ = -6$
true   false

$(6, 1)$ ■ the solution of the system.

Practice

Tell whether the ordered pair is the solution of the system.

1. $(1, 3)$; $x + y = 4$
$2x + y = 5$

2. $(2, -2)$; $y = 2$
$2x + y = 6$

3. $(6, 3)$; $x + y = 9$
$-2x + y = 0$

4. $(-1, -3)$; $3x + y = -6$
$2x - y = 1$

5. $(2, -1)$; $3x + 2y = 4$
$-x + 3y = -5$

6. $(4, 6)$; $2x - y = 2$
$4x + 3y = 24$

7. $(2, 0)$; $-2x + y = -4$
$\frac{1}{2}x + y = 1$

8. $(3, 1)$; $x + 6y = 15$
$-2x + 3y = -3$

Do It Together!

9. Explain to a partner how to tell if the ordered pair is the solution of the system in number **7** in **Practice.**

10. Work with a partner to tell if $(3, 6)$ is the solution of the system in number **3** in **Practice.** You check one equation and have your partner check the other.

8.2 Solving Systems by Graphing

You can find the solution of a system of equations by graphing. Graph each equation on the same set of axes. Then, find the point where the lines intersect.

EXAMPLE 1   Solve by graphing. $y = x + 2$
                                    $y = 2x + 4$

First, graph $y = x + 2$.   **Then, graph $y = 2x + 4$ on the same axes.**

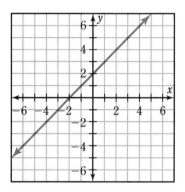 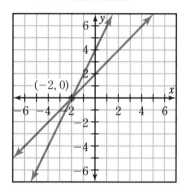

The lines intersect at $(-2, 0)$.
$(-2, 0)$ is the solution of the system.

EXAMPLE 2   Solve by graphing. $y = 3x + 4$
                                    $y = 3x - 5$

First, graph $y = 3x + 4$.   **Then, graph $y = 3x - 5$ on the same axes**

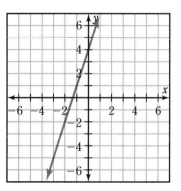 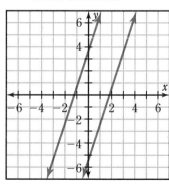

The lines do not intersect.
The system does not have a solution.

Graph each system of linear equations to find the solution. Then, check.

1. $y=-2$
   $y=3x+1$
   Graph $y=-2$.
   Then, graph
   $y=3x+1$ on the
   same axes.
   Find the
   intersection.

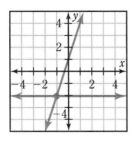

   (■, ■)   Check:
   ■ $=-2$ true
   ■ $=3($■$)+1$ true

2. $y=x-2$
   $y=-\frac{1}{2}x+4$
   Graph $y=x-2$.
   Then, graph
   $y=-\frac{1}{2}x+4$ on
   the same axes.
   Find the
   intersection.

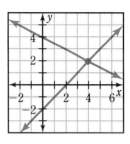

   (■, ■)   Check:
   ■ $=$■-2 true
   ■ $=-\frac{1}{2}($■$)+4$ true

Practice

Graph each system of linear equations to find the solution.

1. $y=x+1$
   $y=3x+3$

2. $y=x-2$
   $y=2x+2$

3. $y=-1$
   $y=2x-3$

4. $y=x-2$
   $y=x+4$

5. $y=-2x-3$
   $y=-2x+2$

6. $y=2$
   $y=x-4$

7. $y=x+5$
   $y=\frac{1}{2}x+2$

8. $y=x-5$
   $y=-\frac{1}{2}x+4$

9. $y=x+2$
   $y=-x$

Do It Together!

10. Explain to a partner how to graph to solve the system in number **2** in **Practice.**

11. Write the equation $y=x+2$. Then, write another equation. Have a partner graph the equations to find the solution of the system. Check the work.

8.3 Using Substitution

You can rewrite a system of equations with two variables as a system with one variable. This is called **eliminating a variable.** Then, you can solve for the other variable. You can do this by substituting an equivalent expression for one of the variables.

$$y=x+3 \quad \rightarrow \quad y \text{ and } x+3 \text{ and are equivalent.}$$
$$y=5 \quad\quad \rightarrow \quad y \text{ and } 5 \text{ are equivalent.}$$

So, substitute 5 for y, *or* substitute $x+3$ for y.

$$5=x+3 \text{ or } x+3=5 \rightarrow x=2 \text{ and } y=5$$

EXAMPLE 1 Solve. $y=x+4$
$y=3x$

$$y=x+4 \text{ and } y=3x$$

Substitute 3x for y. $\qquad\qquad\qquad 3x=x+4$

Solve for x. $\qquad\qquad\qquad\qquad\quad 2x=4$

$$x=2$$

Use $x=2$ to find y in either equation. $\qquad y=x+4$

Check: $\qquad\qquad\qquad\qquad\qquad\qquad\qquad y=2+4$
$y=x+4 \qquad y=3x$ $\qquad\qquad\qquad\qquad\qquad y=6$
$6=2+4 \qquad 6=3(2)$
$6=6$ true $\quad 6=6$ true $\qquad$ $(2, 6)$ is the solution of the system.

EXAMPLE 2 Solve. $y=-x-5$
$y=x+3$

$$y=-x-5 \text{ and } y=x+3$$

You could also substitute $\qquad$ Substitute x+3 for y. $\qquad\qquad x+3=-x-5$
$-x-5$ for y.
Solve for x. $\qquad\qquad\qquad\qquad\quad 2x=-8$

$$x=-4$$

Use $x=-4$ to find y in either equation. $\quad y=-x-5$

Check: $\qquad\qquad\qquad\qquad\qquad\qquad\qquad y=-(-4)-5$
$y=-x-5 \qquad\quad y=x+3$ $\qquad\qquad\qquad\qquad y=-1$
$-1=-(-4)-5 \quad -1=-4+3$
$-1=4-5 \qquad\quad -1=-1$ true $\qquad (-4,-1)$ is the solution of the system.
$-1=-1$ true

Solve each system of linear equations.

1. $y = -x - 3$
   $x = -2$

	$y = -x - 3$
	$x = -2$
Substitute ■ for *x*.	$y = -(■) - 3$
Solve for *y*.	$y = ■$
Solve for *x*.	$x = ■$
(■, ■)	
Check:	

$x = -2$ and $y = -x - 3$
             $■ = -(■) - 3$
$■ = -2$ true $■ = ■$ true
(■, ■) is the solution of the system.

2. $y = -x + 15$
   $y = 4x$

	$y = -x + 15$
	$y = 4x$
Substitute ■ for *y*.	$■ = -x + 15$
Solve for *x*.	$x = ■$
Substitute 3 for *x* to find *y* in either equation.	$y = -x + 15$ $y = -(■) + 15$
(■, ■)	$y = ■$
Check:	

$y = -x + 15$ and $y = 4x$
$■ = -(■) + 15$ $■ = 4(■)$
$■ = ■$ true $■ = ■$ true
(■, ■) is the solution of the system.

Practice

Solve each system of linear equations.

1. $y = x + 2$
   $y = 2x$

2. $y = -2x + 6$
   $y = x$

3. $y = -x - 5$
   $x = -3$

4. $y = x - 6$
   $y = -4$

5. $y = -x - 4$
   $y = x + 2$

6. $y = x - 3$
   $y = -x + 5$

Do It Together!

7. Explain to a partner how to find the solution in number **4** in **Practice.**

8. Write a system of equations. Make one equation $x = 3$. Write another equation that uses both *x* and *y*. Have a partner solve the system by substitution. Check the work.

8.4 Using Addition or Subtraction

Substitution is one way to eliminate a variable in a system of equations. You can also use addition or subtraction to eliminate one of the variables and solve the system. Use addition when the coefficients of one of the variables are opposites.

EXAMPLE 1   Solve. $-x+2y=8$
$3x-2y=4$

The coefficients of y are 2 and -2. $-x+2y=8$
Add the equations. $+3x-2y=4$
                                        $\overline{\qquad 2x+\ 0=12}$

Solve for x. $2x=12$

                                        $x=6$

Check:
$-x+2y=8$
$-6+2(7)=8$
$\qquad 8=8$ true

$3x-2y=4$
$3(6)-2(7)=4$
$\qquad 4=4$ true

Substitute 6 for x in either $-x+2y=8$
equation to solve for y. $-6+2y=8$
                               $2y=14$
                               $y=7$

(6, 7) is the solution of the system.

Use subtraction if one of the variables has the same coefficient in both equations.

EXAMPLE 2   Solve. $x-2y=-6$
$x+y=3$

$-(x+y=3)$ means
$-x-y=-3$.

The coefficients of x are the $x-2y=-6\ \rightarrow\ x-2y=-6$
same. Subtract the equations. $-(x+y=3)\ \rightarrow \underline{-x-\ y=-3}$
                                $\qquad\qquad\qquad 0-3y=-9$

Check:
$x-2y=-6$
$0-2(3)=-6$
$\qquad -6=-6$ true

$x+y=3$
$0+3=3$
$\qquad 3=3$ true

Solve for y. $-3y=-9$

                                $y=3$

Substitute 3 for y in either $x-2y=-6$
equation to solve for x. $x-2(3)=-6$
                               $x=0$

(0, 3) is the solution of the system.

Solve each system of equations.

1. $2x+y=-9$
$-2x-3y=3$

The coefficients of x are opposites.	$2x+\;\;y=-9$
	$+\;-2x-\;3y=3$
■ the equations.	$■x-■y=-6$
Solve for ■.	$■y=■$
	$y=■$

Substitute ■ for y.	$2x+y=-9$
	$2x+■=-9$
Solve for ■.	$2x=■$
	$x=■$
Check:	$2(■)+■=-9$
	$-2(■)-3(■)=3$

(■, ■) is the solution of the system.

2. $2x-y=1$
$x-y=3$

The coefficients of y are the same.	$2x-\;\;y=\;\;1$
	$(-x+\;\;y=-3)$
■ the equations.	$x+0y=■$
Solve for ■.	$x\;\;\;\;\;=■$
Substitute ■ for x.	$2x-\;\;y=\;\;1$
Solve for ■.	$2(■)-\;\;y=\;\;1$
	$-\;\;y=\;\;5$
	$y=■$
Check:	$2(■)-(■)=\;\;1$
	$■-(■)=\;\;3$

(■, ■) is the solution of the system.

Practice

Solve each system of equations.

1. $x+y=6$
$x-y=4$

2. $x-y=-3$
$x+y=9$

3. $2x+y=-5$
$2x-y=-3$

4. $2x+y=-6$
$3x+y=-10$

5. $4x-y=5$
$x-y=-7$

6. $3x+6y=48$
$-5x+6y=32$

Do It Together!

7. Explain to a partner how to use addition to find the solution of the system of equations in number **3** in **Practice.**

8. Ask a partner to explain what the solution to number **5** in **Practice** means.

8.5 Using Multiplication

Sometimes, you have to multiply to make the coefficients of one of the variables opposites. Then, you can eliminate a variable by adding.

EXAMPLE 1   Solve. $3x+y=2$
            $x+2y=4$

Make coefficients of
x opposites.

Multiply $x+2y=4$ by -3.
Add the equations.

$$3x + y=2 \rightarrow 3x + y = 2$$
$$-3(x+2y=4) \rightarrow \underline{-3x-6y=-12}$$
$$0-5y=-10$$

Solve for y.

$$-5y=-10$$
$$y=2$$

Check:
$3x+y=2$
$3(0)+2=2$
$2=2$ true

$x+2y=4$
$0+2(2)=4$
$4=4$ true

Substitute 2 for y in either
equation.

Solve for x.

$$x+2y=4$$
$$x+2(2)=4$$
$$x+4=4$$
$$x=0$$

$(0, 2)$ is the solution of the system.

EXAMPLE 2   Solve. $-x+2y=-4$
            $-2x+3y=-2$

Make coefficients of
x opposites.

Multiply $-x+2y=-4$
by -2.
Add the equations.

$$-2(-x+2y=-4) \rightarrow 2x-4y= 8$$
$$-2x +3y=-2 \rightarrow \underline{-2x+3y=-2}$$
$$0- y= 6$$

Solve for y.

$$-y=6$$
$$y=-6$$

Check:
$-x+2y=-4$
$-(-8)+2(-6)=-4$
$-4=-4$ true

$-2x+3y=-2$
$-2(-8)+3(-6)=-2$
$-2=-2$ true

Substitute -6 for y in
either equation.

Solve for x.

$$-x+2(-6)=-4$$
$$-x-12=-4$$
$$x=-8$$

$(-8,-6)$ is the solution of the system.

Solve each system of linear equations.

1. $2x - 3y = 5$ and $3x + y = 2$

    Make coefficients of y opposites.

    Multiply $3x + y = 2$ by 3.

    Add the equations.

    Solve for ■.

    Substitute ■ for x in either equation. Solve for ■.

$$2x - 3y = 5 \;\rightarrow\; 2x - 3y = 5$$
$$3(3x + y = 2) \rightarrow \underline{\;9x + ■\,y = ■\;}$$
$$11x + ■\,y = 11$$
$$x = ■$$
$$2x - 3y = 5 \;\rightarrow\; 2(■) - 3y = 5$$
$$y = ■$$

(■, ■) is the solution of the system.

2. $2x + 3y = -4$ and $x + y = -2$

    Make coefficients of x ■.

    Multiply $x + y = -2$ by ■.

    ■ the equations.

    Solve for ■.

    Substitute ■ for y in either equation. Solve for ■.

$$2x + 3y = -4 \;\rightarrow\; 2x + 3y = -4$$
$$-2(x + y = -2) \rightarrow \underline{\;■\,x - 2y = \;\;4\;}$$
$$0x + ■\,y = \;\;■$$
$$y = ■$$
$$x + y = -2 \;\rightarrow\; x + ■ = -2$$
$$x = -2$$

$(-2, ■)$ is the solution of the system.

Practice

Solve each system of linear equations.

1. $4x + y = 2$
   $x + 2y = 4$

2. $-x - 5y = -6$
   $3x + y = 4$

3. $-3x + y = 8$
   $x + y = -4$

4. $2x + 3y = 5$
   $-x + 2y = 1$

5. $-x + 2y = -6$
   $4x - 3y = 4$

6. $4x + y = -6$
   $3x - 2y = 1$

Do It Together!

7. Explain to a partner how to use multiplication to help find the solution in number **6** in **Practice.**

8. Take turns with a partner to solve the following system of equations. Check each other's work.

    $x + y = 3$
    $2x + y = 4$

8.6   Using More than One Equation

Sometimes, you have to multiply both equations. Choose a variable to eliminate. Then, multiply both equations so the coefficients of this variable are opposites.

EXAMPLE 1   Solve. $3x+2y=5$
              $2x+4y=6$

Choose a variable to eliminate: x

Multiply $3x+2y=5$ by 2. $2(3x+2y=5) \rightarrow \quad 6x+ \ 4y= \ \ 10$
Multiply $2x+4y=6$ by -3. $-3(2x+4y=6) \rightarrow \underline{-6x-12y=-18}$
Add the equations. $0x-8y = \ -8$

Solve for y. $-8y=-8$
                                $y=1$

Substitute 1 for y in $2x+4(1)=6$
$2x+4y=6$.

Solve for x. $2x+4=6$
                                $x=1$

(1, 1) is the solution of the system.

Check:
$3x+2y=5$
$3(1)+2(1)=5$
$3+2=5$
$5=5$ true

$2x+4y=6$
$2(1)+4(1)=6$
$2+4=6$
$6=6$ true

EXAMPLE 2   Solve. $3x+2y=8$
              $2x+4y=8$

Choose a variable to eliminate: y

Multiply $3x+2y=8$ by -2. $-2(3x+2y=8) \rightarrow -6x-4y=-16$
Multiply $2x+4y=8$ by 1. $1(2x+4y=8) \rightarrow \underline{\ \ 2x+4y=8}$
Add the equations. $-4x+0y=-8$

Solve for x. $-4x=-8$
                                $x=2$

Substitute 2 for x in $3(2)+2y=8$
$3x+2y=8$.

Solve for y $6+2y=8$
                                $y=1$

(2, 1) is the solution of the system.

Check:
$3x+2y=8$
$3(2)+2(1)=8$
$6+2=8$
$8=8$ true

$2x+4y=8$
$2(2)+4(1)=8$
$4+4=8$
$8=8$ true

Solve each system.

1. $3x - 4y = -6$
$-5x + 3y = -1$

**Choose a variable
to eliminate:** y

**Multiply
$3x - 4y = -6$ by 3.** $\blacksquare x - 12y = -18$

**Multiply
$-5x + 3y = -1$ by 4.** $\underline{\blacksquare x + 12y = -4}$

Add the equations. $-11x + 0y = \blacksquare$

Solve for $\blacksquare$. $-11x = -22$
$x = \blacksquare$

**Substitute $\blacksquare$ for x
in $3x - 4y = -6$** $3(2) - 4y = -6$

Solve for $\blacksquare$. $-4y = \blacksquare$
$y = \blacksquare$

$(\blacksquare, \blacksquare)$ is the solution of the
system.

2. $2x + 3y = -1$
$-5x + 2y = 12$

**Choose a variable
to eliminate:** x

**Multiply
$2x + 3y = -1$ by 5.** $10x + \blacksquare y = -5$

**Multiply
$-5x + 2y = 12$ by 2.** $\underline{-10x + \blacksquare y = 24}$

Add the equations. $0x + 19y = 19$

Solve for $\blacksquare$. $19y = 19$
$y = \blacksquare$

**Substitute $\blacksquare$ for y
in $2x + 3y = -1$.** $2x + 3(1) = -1$

Solve for $\blacksquare$. $2x = \blacksquare$
$x = \blacksquare$

$(\blacksquare, \blacksquare)$ is the solution of the
system.

Practice

Solve each system.

1. $3x + 2y = 10$
$4x + 3y = 12$

2. $4x + 3y = 3$
$3x - 5y = -5$

3. $5x + 3y = 2$
$3x + 2y = 3$

4. $5x - 3y = 7$
$2x + 4y = 8$

5. $2x + 3y = -1$
$5x - 2y = -12$

6. $3x + 2y = -6$
$4x - 7y = -8$

Do It Together!

7. Explain to a partner the steps to find the solution in number **3** in **Practice.**

8. Write $2x - 2y = 4$ and $3x + 3y = -6$ on your paper. Solve by eliminating one of the variables. Have a partner solve by eliminating the other variable.

8.7 Systems of Inequalities

You have learned that the solution of a linear inequality is an area of ordered pairs. The solution of a **system of linear inequalities** is the area of ordered pairs that makes both inequalities true.

$y \geq -x + 1$

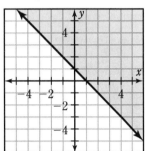

$y < 2x - 1$

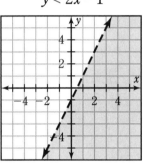

$y \geq -x + 1$
$y < 2x - 1$

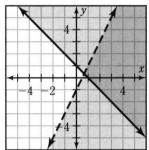

All points in the overlapping shaded area in the last graph are solutions of the system. The ordered pairs in this darker shaded area make both inequalities true.

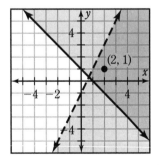

EXAMPLE 1

Tell whether (2, 1) is a solution of the system.

$$y \geq -x + 1$$
$$y < 2x - 1$$

Substitute 2 for x and 1 for y in each inequality.

$y \geq -x + 1$
$1 \geq -(2) + 1$
$1 \geq -2 + 1$
$1 \geq -1$ true

$y < 2x - 1$
$1 < 2(2) - 1$
$1 < 4 - 1$
$1 < 3$ true

(2, 1) is a solution.

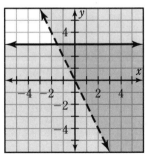

EXAMPLE 2

Tell whether (−1, 2) is a solution of the system.

$$y \leq 3$$
$$y > -2x$$

Substitute −1 for x and 2 for y in each inequality.

$y \leq 3$
$2 \leq 3$ true

$y > -2x$
$2 > -2(-1)$
$2 > 2$ false

(−1, 2) is not a solution.

Tell whether each ordered pair is a solution of the system.

1. $(3, 4)$; $\quad y > 3$
$\qquad\qquad y \le x + 1$

Substitute ■ for *x* and ■ for *y* in each inequality.

$y > 3$
$■ > 3 \quad$ true

$y \le x + 1$
$■ \le ■ + 1$
$■ \le ■ \quad$ true

$(3, 4)$ ■ a solution.

2. $(3, -1)$; $\quad y < 2x + 4$
$\qquad\qquad\quad y > 2x - 3$

Substitute ■ for *x* and ■ for *y* in each inequality.

$y < 2x + 4$
$■ < 2(■) + 4$
$■ < ■ \quad$ true

$y > 2x - 3$
$■ > 2(■) - 3$
$■ > ■ \quad$ false

$(3, -1)$ ■ a solution.

Practice

Tell whether each ordered pair is a solution of the system.

1. $(2, 0)$; $\quad y < x + 5$
$\qquad\qquad y \le x - 2$

2. $(-2, 3)$; $\quad y > x + 4$
$\qquad\qquad\quad y < 2x + 5$

3. $(1, 3)$; $\quad y > 2$
$\qquad\qquad y \le x + 3$

4. $(-2, -2)$; $\quad y < -2x + 3$
$\qquad\qquad\qquad y \le 2x + 3$

5. $(-1, 4)$; $\quad y > 2x - 6$
$\qquad\qquad\quad y < 2x + 5$

6. $(-1, -5)$; $\quad y < -4$
$\qquad\qquad\qquad y > x - 5$

Do It Together!

7. Explain to a partner how to tell whether the ordered pair is a solution in number **2** in **Practice.**

8. Work with a partner. Find a point that is a solution to number **5** in **Practice.** Check the work.

8.8   Finding a Solution by Graphing

You can graph the solution of a system of inequalities.
Graph each inequality on the same set of axes. The solution
of the system is the area where the solutions overlap.

EXAMPLE 1   Solve by graphing. $y < x + 2$
$$y > -2x - 1$$

Graph $y < x + 2$.

**Then, graph $y > -2x - 1$
on the same axes.**

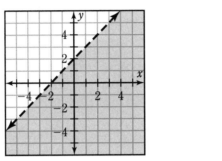

Use a dotted line for < or >.

Check: Pick a point in the solution: (2, 2).

$y < x + 2$ $y > -2x - 1$

$2 < 2 + 2$ $2 > -2(2) - 1$

$2 < 4$ true $2 > -5$ true

EXAMPLE 2   Solve by graphing. $y < 3$
$$y \geq x + 1$$

Use a solid line for ≥.

Graph $y < 3$.

**Then, graph $y \geq x + 1$
on the same axes.**

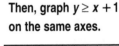

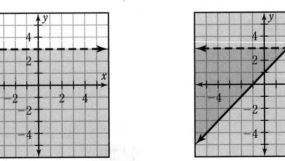

Check: Pick a point in the solution: (−4, 0).

$y < 3$ $y \geq x + 1$

$0 < 3$ true $0 \geq (-4) + 1$

                     $0 \geq -3$ true

Solve by graphing.

1. $y > 1$
$y \leq x + 2$
Graph $y > 1$.
Then, graph
$y \leq x + 2$.

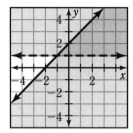

Check: Pick a point in the ■ area. Use (2, 2).

$y > 1$ $y \leq x + 2$
■ > 1 true   ■ $\leq$ ■ $+ 2$
                        $2 \leq$ ■   true

2. $y \geq 2x - 2$
$y > -2x + 1$
Graph $y \geq 2x - 2$.
Then, graph
$y > -2x + 1$.

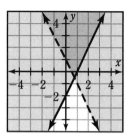

Check: Pick a point in the ■ area. Use (1, 2).

$y \geq 2x - 2$ $y > -2x + 1$
■ $\geq 2($■$) - 2$ ■ $> -2($■$) + 1$
■ $\geq$ ■ $- 2$ ■ $>$ ■ $+ 1$
■ $\geq$ ■   true   ■ $>$ ■   true

Practice

Solve by graphing.

1. $y < x + 1$
$y \leq -x - 3$

2. $y > x + 2$
$y < 2x + 1$

3. $y > 2$
$y \leq x + 2$

4. $y \leq 2x + 2$
$y < -\frac{2}{3}x + 4$

5. $y < 2x + 1$
$y > \frac{1}{2}x - 3$

6. $y < -2$
$y > x - 4$

7. $y \geq 1$
$y > -2x + 3$

8. $y \geq -2x - 1$
$y \leq 2x - 4$

9. $y < x$
$y \leq 0$

Do It Together!

10. Explain to a partner how to find all the solutions of the system by graphing in number **4** in **Practice.**

11. Write two inequalities in slope-intercept form. Have a partner find all the solutions of the system by graphing. Check the work.

8.9 Calculator: Checking Possible Solutions

You can use a calculator to check solutions of linear systems.

EXAMPLE 1   Tell if (1.3, .6) is the solution of the system.

$$x + 5y = 4.3$$
$$2x - y = 2$$

Check $x + 5y = 4.3$ first.

$$x + 5y = 4.3$$

Substitute 1.3 for x and .6 for y.

$$1.3 + 5(.6) = 4.3$$

Use your calculator to simplify.   **DISPLAY**

Multiply before adding or subtracting.

Enter 5 by pressing: `5`   `5`

Multiply by .6 by pressing: `×` `.` `6` `=`   `3`

Add 1.3 by pressing: `+` `1` `.` `3` `=`   `4.3`

$4.3 = 4.3$ true

Check $2x - y = 2$ next. $2x - y = 2$

Substitute 1.3 for x and .6 for y. $2(1.3) - .6 = 2$

Use your calculator to simplify.   **DISPLAY**

Enter 2 by pressing: `2`   `2`

Multiply by 1.3 by pressing: `×` `1` `.` `3` `=`   `2.6`

Subtract .6 by pressing: `−` `.` `6` `=`   `2`

$2 = 2$ true

(1.3, .6) is the solution of the system.

Practice

Tell whether each ordered pair is the solution of the system.

1. $(14, 21)$; $x+y=35$
                   $22x+y=329$

2. $(2,-4)$; $2x-1.5y=10$
                 $.3x-.05y=.8$

3. $(-2, 2)$; $6.2x+4.65y=-3.1$
                 $1.5x+6.2y=9.3$

4. $(12, 18)$; $x+y=30$
                  $6.9x+4.5y=14$

5. $(22, 28)$; $x+y=50$
                  $.15x+.24y=10.02$

6. $(15, 7.4)$; $2x-3y=9.4$
                  $5x-9y=12.4$

MATH CONNECTION

Air Traffic Controller

Air traffic controllers direct airplanes as they land and take off. These people work in the tall tower at the airport. From this tower, controllers make sure landings and takeoffs are safe. They also direct the airplanes on the runways.

    Air traffic controllers use systems of equations to make flight plans. They keep track of the speed, altitude, and location of many airplanes. They do this to make sure that two airplanes don't get in each other's way.

    Air traffic controllers decide which runway each airplane should use. They plan exactly when each airplane should land or take off. They also must decide how much time an airplane needs to land and move off the runway. To do this, they must know the weather and wind speed. Then they can direct another airplane to land or take off. This work is important if air traffic is to run smoothly.

8.10 Problem Solving: Using Systems

You can write a system of equations to describe a problem. Then, solve the system to solve the problem.

EXAMPLE 1 — The sum of two numbers is 12. The difference of the numbers is 14. Find both numbers.

Pick variables for the two numbers. Use *x* and *y* for the two numbers.

| The sum of two numbers is 12. | $x+y=12$ |
| The difference of the numbers is 14. | $x-y=14$ |

Solve the system.
Add the equations.

$$x+y=12$$
$$\underline{+x-y=14}$$
$$2x+0=26$$

Check:
$x+y=12$
$13+(-1)=12$
$12=12$ true
$x-y=14$
$13-(-1)=14$
$14=14$ true

Solve for *x*.

$$2x=26$$
$$x=13$$

Substitute 13 for *x* in $x+y=12$.

$$13+y=12$$

Solve for *y*.

$$y=-1$$

The numbers are 13 and -1.

EXAMPLE 2 — Five baseballs and 2 gloves cost $65.00. One baseball and 1 glove cost $25.00. How much does each cost?

Pick variables for what you don't know.

Use *b* for the price of a baseball.
Use *g* for the price of a glove.

5*b* is the cost of 5 baseballs.
2*g* is the cost of 2 gloves.

5 baseballs and 2 gloves cost $65.00.

$$5b+2g=65$$

1 baseball and 1 glove cost $25.00.

$$b+g=25$$

Solve the system.
Multiply $b+g=25$ by -2.
Add the equations.

$$5b+2g=65 \rightarrow 5b+2g=65$$
$$-2(b+g=25) \rightarrow \underline{-2b-2g=-50}$$
$$3b+0g=15$$

Check:
$5b+2g=65$
$5(5)+2(20)=65$
$25+40=65$
$65=65$ true

$b+g=25$
$5+20=25$
$25=25$ true

Solve for *b*.

$$3b=15$$
$$b=5$$

Substitute 5 for *b* in $b+g=25$.

$$5+g=25$$

Solve for *g*.

$$g=20$$

Baseballs cost $5.00 each. Gloves cost $20.00 each.

1. Four gardeners and their 4 assistants earn $60.00 total in an hour. When 5 gardeners and 2 assistants work, they also earn $60.00 total in an hour. Write a system of equations to describe how much the gardeners and assistants earn.

   Use g for the amount a gardener makes in an hour.
   Use a for the amount an assistant makes in an hour.

Write how much they make total.	$4g \blacksquare 4a \blacksquare 60$
Write how much they make total.	$5g \blacksquare 2a \blacksquare 60$
Write the equations as a system.	$4g + 4a = 60$
	$5g + 2a = 60$

2. Use the system to find the amount a gardener makes in an hour.

   Write the system.
   $$4g + 4a = 60$$
   Make the coefficients of a opposites.
   $$5g + 2a = 60$$

   Multiply $5g + 2a = 60$ by -2. $\qquad -2(5g + 2a = 60) \rightarrow$
   $$\begin{aligned} 4g + 4a &= 60 \\ \blacksquare g - \blacksquare a &= -120 \\ \hline \blacksquare g + 0a &= -60 \end{aligned}$$
   Add the equations.
   Solve for g.
   $$-6g = -60$$
   $$g = \blacksquare$$

   A gardener makes $\$\blacksquare$ an hour.

Practice

Write a system to describe each problem. Then, solve the system.

1. The sum of two numbers is 4. Their difference is 2. Find the numbers.

2. Twice a number plus another number is 4. Their sum is 2. Find the numbers.

3. Three pounds of tomatoes and 2 pounds of broccoli cost $9.00. One pound of tomatoes and 2 pounds of broccoli cost $7.00. How much does each cost?

Do It Together!

4. Explain to a partner how to write the equations in number **2** in **Practice.**

5. Work with a partner. Use your answer to number **2** in **Try These** to find the amount an assistant makes in an hour. Check each other's work.

8.11 Application: Maximum and Minimum

You can use variable equations to describe problems. You can also describe the values for these variables with inequalities. Then, you can find a **maximum** or a **minimum** value for the solution of the equation.

A company makes books and disks. It wants to make at least 1,000 books and disks total. It costs $8.00 to make a book and $2.00 to make a disk. The company needs at most 700 books and 400 disks. How many of each should the company make to minimize the cost?

Use *b* for the number of books. Use *d* for the number of disks.

$$\text{Total Cost} = \text{Cost of Books} + \text{Cost of Disks}$$
$$\text{Total Cost} = \$8b + \$2d$$

EXAMPLE **1** Write the inequalities to describe the problem.

At most 700 books	$b \leq 700$
At most 400 disks	$d \leq 400$
Total must be at least 1,000	$b + d \geq 1,000$

The graphs of these inequalities form a triangle. The maximum and minimum costs will each be at one of the corners of this triangle. The pairs are (books, disks).

EXAMPLE **2** Use the graph of the inequalities to find the number of books and disks that will give the minimum cost.

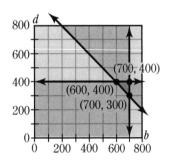

Find the ordered pairs at the triangle corner points.

(600, 400)
(700, 300)
(700, 400)

Write the cost equation.

$$\text{Total cost} = \$8b + \$2d$$

Substitute the ordered pairs into the cost equation.

$$\$5,600 = \$8(600) + \$2(400)$$
$$\$6,200 = \$8(700) + \$2(300)$$

Find the ordered pair that gives the smallest cost.

$$\$6,400 = \$8(700) + \$2(400)$$
(600, 400)

Making 600 books and 400 disks would give the minimum cost.

A food center has at most $36.00 to spend on cereal each week. The center needs at least 9 pounds of corn and at least 4 pounds of wheat. Corn costs $2.00 per pound, and wheat costs $3.00 per pound.

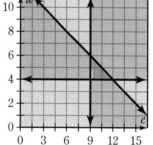

1. Write the inequalities for the number of pounds of corn, c, the number of pounds of wheat, w, and the total cost.

At least 9 pounds of corn $c\ \blacksquare\ 9$

At least 4 pounds of wheat $w\ \blacksquare\ 4$

Cost $= 2c + 3w$

$36 at most to spend on corn and wheat $2c + 3w\ \blacksquare\ 36$

2. Use the graph of the inequalities and the equation Total $= c + w$ to find the maximum number of pounds of each cereal the center can buy.

Find the pairs (corn, wheat) at the corner points. $(9,\ \blacksquare)\quad(\blacksquare,\ 4)\quad(9,\ \blacksquare)$

Substitute the ordered pairs into the equation Total $= c + w$.
$9 + \blacksquare \qquad \blacksquare + 4 \qquad 9 + \blacksquare$
$\blacksquare \qquad\qquad \blacksquare \qquad\qquad \blacksquare$

The center can buy $\blacksquare$ pounds of corn cereal and $\blacksquare$ pounds of wheat.

Practice

A deli owner orders at least 10 pounds of meat. She needs no more than 7 pounds of beef and 6 pounds of pork. The cost is $8.00 per pound of beef and $6.00 per pound of pork.

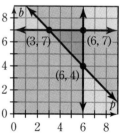

1. Write the inequalities for the pounds of beef, pounds of pork, and total number of pounds. Use b for beef and p for pork.

2. Find the minimum cost of ordering meat using the equation Cost $= 8b + 6p$. Use the ordered pairs (pork, beef).

Do It Together!

3. Explain to a partner how to find the minimum in number **2** in **Practice.**

4. Use the equation from number **2** in **Practice.** Write new inequalities for the amount of beef and pork to order. Have a partner solve the new system.

Chapter Review

Chapter 8 Summary

- You can graph a system of linear equations to find the solution. The solution of the system is the intersection of the two lines.
- The solution of a system of equations is the ordered pair that makes both equations true. Not all systems have a solution.
- You can use substitution to rewrite a system of equations with two variables as a system with one variable.
- You can solve a system of equations by adding the equations when the coefficients of one of the variables are opposites.
- You can multiply an equation by a number to make the coefficients of one of the variables opposites.
- Sometimes, you multiply both equations to make the coefficients of a variable opposites.
- The solution of a system of linear inequalities is an area of ordered pairs that make both equations true.
- You can find the solution of a system of inequalities by graphing.
- You can use a calculator to check whether points are solutions of systems.
- You can apply what you know about graphing inequalities to find the minimum and maximum value for a solution.

Reviewing Vocabulary

Fill in each blank with the correct word.

system of linear
  equations
eliminating a variable
system of linear
  inequalities
maximum
minimum

1. The _?_ is the smallest number of a group.
2. The largest number of a group is the _?_.
3. A(n) _?_ is two or more linear equations with the same variables.
4. _?_ is what you do when you remove one of the variables in a system.
5. Two or more linear inequalities is a _?_.

Chapter Quiz

Tell whether the ordered pair is the solution of the system.

1. (2, 0); $x+y=2$
$2x+y=4$

2. (−3, −1); $x+y=−4$
$−2x+y=5$

3. (2, −2); $y=2$
$2x+y=2$

4. (3, 0); $y>−x$
$y\leq x−1$

5. (−2, 6); $y\leq x+8$
$y>2x+4$

6. (0, 5); $y<x+7$
$y\leq x+5$

Graph each system to find its solution.

7. $y=x+2$
$y=2x+3$

8. $y=x−2$
$y=2x−1$

9. $y<x+4$
$y\leq x−6$

10. $y\geq x+1$
$y<2x+3$

Use substitution to find the solution of each system.

11. $y=x+2$
$y=3x$

12. $y=x$
$y=−3x+8$

13. $y=x+4$
$y=−x−6$

Find the solution of each system with addition, subtraction, or multiplication.

14. $x+y=8$
$x−y=4$

15. $−x+y=−3$
$x+y=11$

16. $x+2y=−6$
$x−2y=10$

17. $3x+2y=6$
$2x+y=6$

18. $x−4y=−2$
$3x+2y=8$

19. $2x−3y=4$
$4x+2y=−8$

20. The difference of two numbers is 3. Their sum is −5. Find the numbers.

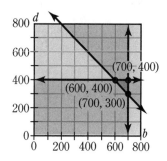

The book and disk company sells its books for a $3.00 profit and its disks for a $4.00 profit. The company needs at least 1,000 books and disks total and at most 700 books and 400 disks. Its profit is shown by the equation Profit $=3b+4d$.

21. Use the graph and the equation Profit $=3b+4d$ to find how many books and disks give the maximum income.

Chapter 9

More About Data and Data Analysis

Marketing departments of companies gather information about the interests, tastes, and hobbies of people. Companies then use the data to meet the needs of a diverse population.

Chapter Learning Objectives

- Find the mean, mode, and median.
- Make a frequency table.
- Make a stem-and-leaf plot.
- Make a scatter plot.
- Use a calculator to find the mean of large numbers.
- Solve problems by deciding whether to use the mean, mode, or median.
- Apply concepts and skills to finding quartiles.

Words to Know

data   information gathered from surveys or experiments

statistics   the study of collecting and organizing data

mean   sum of the data divided by the number of data; also
called average

mode   number or numbers that appear most often in a set of data

median   middle number when data are ordered from least to greatest

range   difference between minimum and maximum values in a set
of data

frequency table   chart that shows the number of times an item appears in
a set of data

stem-and-leaf plot   tool that uses place value to arrange and display data

scatter plot   graph that shows two sets of related data as ordered pairs

positive correlation   the data in two sets increase together

negative correlation   the data in one set increase while the data in the
second set decrease

quartiles   numbers in the middle of half of a set of data

In this chapter, you will learn how to find the mean,
mode, median, and range for sets of data. You will see
how to organize data using different charts and graphs.
Using a calculator to find the mean of some numbers is
another skill you will learn. Learning when to use
mean, median, or mode to describe data is an important
problem-solving skill presented in this chapter. You will
also apply your skills to finding quartiles.

9.1 Mean

People take surveys and do experiments to gather information. This information is called **data.** Often, data is shown as collections or sets of numbers. The study of data is called **statistics.**

Mean is sometimes called average.

Finding the **mean** is one way to describe data. You find the mean of a set of data by adding the numbers in the set. Then, divide the sum by the number of items in that set.

EXAMPLE 1   Find the mean of the set of data.   1, 2, 1, 4, 3, 1

Add the numbers. $1+2+1+4+3+1=12$

Count the number of items. 6 items

Divide the sum by 6. $12 \div 6 = 2$

The mean of the set of data is 2.

EXAMPLE 2   Kristin counted 24, 26, 19, 28, and 13 students in five college history classes. Find the mean number of students.

Add the number of students. $24+26+19+28+13=110$

Divide by the number of classes. $110 \div 5 = 22$

The mean number of students is 22.

EXAMPLE 3   A bank gives the daily balance of an account. For three days, the balance is $12.00, $9.00, and $6.00. Find the average daily balance, or mean, for these days.

Add the 3 balances. $12+9+6=27$

Divide by the number of days. $27 \div 3 = 9$

The average daily balance for the three days is $9.00.

1. Find the mean temperature for four days in Alaska. The temperatures were $2°$, $-5°$, $-10°$, and $-7°$.

   Add the temperatures. $2 + (-5) + (-10) + (-7) = -20$

   Divide by the number of days. $-20 \div ■ = -5$

   The mean temperature was ■°.

2. Juan made $2.00, $4.00, $4.00, $2.00, and $3.00 baby-sitting for five days. What was the mean amount he made?

   Add the amounts. $■ + ■ + ■ + ■ + ■ = ■$

   Divide by the number of days. $■ \div 5 = ■$

   The mean amount is $■.

Practice

Find the mean.

1. 25, 30, 35

2. 112, 114, 116, 118

3. 423, 523, 412, 446

4. $2, -4, -3, 10, -1, 8$

5. $-20, 30, -40$

6. 32, 42, 12, 8, 46

7. $-4, -8, -6, -2$

8. $2, $4, $3, $7, $2, $6

9. A scout troop records the amount of cookies its members sold each day for a week: 12, 15, 19, 18, 30, 54, and 62 boxes. What was the mean number of boxes they sold per day for the week?

Do It Together!

10. Explain to a partner how to find the mean in number **4** in **Practice**.

11. Write four dollar amounts. Ask a partner to find the mean.

9.2 Mode and Median

You have learned about the mean, one way to describe data. There are other ways to describe a set of data. The **mode** is the number or numbers that appear most often in a set of data.

EXAMPLE 1

Count the items to be sure you didn't forget any.

Find the mode of the set of data.   5, 4, 6, 5, 4, 6, 6

Order the numbers from least to greatest.   4, 4, 5, 5, 6, 6, 6

Find the number that appears most often.   4, 4, 5, 5, 6, 6, 6

The mode is 6.

A set of data can have more than one mode.

EXAMPLE 2

Find the mode of the set of data.   9, 5, −6, 9, −6, 10

Order the numbers from least to greatest.   −6, −6, 5, 9, 9, 10

Find the numbers that appear most often.   −6, −6, 5, 9, 9, 10

The modes are −6 and 9.

When you order a set of data from least to greatest, the middle number is the called the **median.**

EXAMPLE 3

Find the median of the set of data.   5, 4, 6, 5, 4, 6, 6

Order the numbers from least to greatest.   4, 4, 5, 5, 6, 6, 6

Find the middle number.   4, 4, 5, 5, 6, 6, 6

The median is 5.

When the number of items in a set of data is even, the median is the average of the two middle numbers.

EXAMPLE 4

Find the median of the set of data.   9, 5, −6, 9, −6, 10

Order the numbers from least to greatest.   −6, −6, 5, 9, 9, 10

To find the average of two numbers, add them, and then divide by 2.

There are 6 items in the set of data.   −6, −6, 5, 9, 9, 10

Find the average of the two middle numbers. $\dfrac{5+9}{2} = \dfrac{14}{2} = 7$

The median is 7.

1. Find the mode of the set of data. $1, -2, 1, 4, 4, 3, 1$

   Order the numbers from least to greatest. $-2, 1, 1, 1, 3, 4, 4$

   Find the number that appears most often.   ■ appears most often.

   The mode is ■.

2. Find the median of the set of data. $4, 12, 1, 4, 1, 8, 10, 8$

   Order the numbers from least to greatest.   ■, ■, ■, ■, ■, ■, ■, ■

   There are ■ items in the set of data. $4, ■$

   Find the average of the two middle numbers. $\dfrac{4+■}{2} = \dfrac{■}{2} = ■$

   The median is ■.

Practice

Find the mode.

1. $-3, 4, 9, -3, 8, 4, -3$

2. $24, 25, 26, 24, 22, 28, 30$

3. $16, 20, 32, 34, 16, 24, 34, 16$

4. $4, 6, 3, 4, 4, 9, 6, 6$

5. $-1, 6, 4, 0, 12, -1, 0$

6. $-100, -500, 300, 200, 0$

Find the median.

7. $-3, 4, 9, -3, 8, 4, -3$

8. $24, 25, 26, 24, 22, 28, 30$

9. $16, 20, 32, 34, 16, 24, 34, 16$

10. $4, 6, 3, 4, 4, 9, 6, 6$

11. $0, 0, 52, 1, 12$

12. $-450, 100, 500, -600, -500$

Do It Together!

13. Explain to a partner how to find the mode in number **3** in **Practice**.

14. Write a set of data that has seven numbers. Make some of the numbers the same. Have a partner find the median and mode.

9.3 Minimum, Maximum, and Range

Another way to describe data is to find the smallest value, called the minimum, and the largest value, called the maximum.

EXAMPLE 1   Find the minimum and maximum   15, 4, −1, 6, −5, 10
of the set of data.

Order the numbers from least to greatest.   −5, −1, 4, 6, 10, 15

Find the smallest value or minimum.   −5, −1, 4, 6, 10, 15

Find the largest value or maximum.   −5, −1, 4, 6, 10, 15

The minimum is −5. The maximum is 15.

The **range** is the difference between the minimum and maximum values. To find the range, subtract the minimum from the maximum.

EXAMPLE 2   Find the range of the set   −8, −12, −2, −20, −3, −7
of data.

Order the numbers from least   −20, −12, −8, −7, −3, −2
to greatest.

Find the minimum.   −20, −12, −8, −7, −3, −2

Find the maximum.   −20, −12, −8, −7, −3, −2

Subtract the minimum from the $-2 - (-20)$
maximum.

The range is 18. $-2 + 20 = 18$

EXAMPLE 3   Find the range of the set   −5, 8, −1, 3, 2, 2, 4, 5, 7
of data.

Order the numbers from least   −5, −1, 2, 2, 3, 4, 5, 7, 8
to greatest.

Find the minimum.   −5, −1, 2, 2, 3, 4, 5, 7, 8

Find the maximum.   −5, −1, 2, 2, 3, 4, 5, 7, 8

Subtract the minimum from the $8 - (-5)$
maximum.

The range is 13. $8 + 5 = 13$

1. Find the minimum and maximum of the set of data.   1, 9, 2, 3, 8

   Order the numbers from least to greatest.   1, 2, 3, 8, 9

   Find the smallest value or ■.   ■

   Find the largest value or ■.   ■

   The minimum is ■. The maximum is ■.

2. Find the range of the set of data.   3, −5, 9, −2, 12

   Order the numbers from least to greatest.   ■, ■, ■, ■, ■

   Find the ■.   ■

   Find the ■.   ■

   Subtract the ■ from the ■.   ■ − ■ = ■

   The range is ■.

Practice

Find the minimum, maximum, and range.

1. 2, 9, 0, 4, 12, 6, 4, 8, 3, 5

2. 23, 88, 36, 96, 41, 75, 21, 20, 68

3. −8, −2, −6, −7, −9, −5, −7

4. −10, −4, −20, −18, −5, −22, −35

5. 0, 2, −2, 1, −4, 3, −6

6. −54, 65, −21, 33, 48, −12, 85, 61

7. 59, 752, 411, 688, 325, 102

8. 1,005; 965; 1,548; 845; 1,656

Do It Together!

9. Explain to a partner how to find the range in number **2** in **Practice.**

10. Write a set of data that contains six numbers. Ask a partner to find the minimum, maximum, and range. Check the work.

9.4 Frequency Tables

A **frequency table** makes it easy to see how many times each item appears. You make a tally mark for each time an item in the set of data appears. Then, you count the tallies.

EXAMPLE 1

There are 22 students in a class. On their final exam, they received the following grades: B, A, C, A, B, B, C, A, B, A, A, C, C, B, A, A, B, C, B, C, A, B. Make a frequency table.

For each grade listed, find the correct row in the table and make a tally mark in the Tally column.

Write the total for each row in the Frequency column.

Mark	Tally	Frequency
A's	ЖТ III	8
B's	ЖТ III	8
C's	ЖТ I	6
		22

The sum of the frequencies should equal the number of items in the set of data.

Add the frequencies. Write the sum at the bottom of the frequency column.

Sometimes, you group data to show items in a group.

EXAMPLE 2

The ages of people at a restaurant are 21, 2, 18, 44, 6, 12, 10, 32, 15, 11, 16, 42, 19, and 50. Use the frequency table to show how many people of each age group are at the restaurant. Describe the results.

There are five age groups of 10 years each for ages 1 to 50.

For each age listed, make a tally mark in the Tally column next to the correct age group.

Write the total for each row in the Frequency column.

Add the frequencies. Write the sum at the bottom of the Frequency column.

Age group	Tally	Frequency
1–10	III	3
11–20	ЖТ I	6
21–30	I	1
31–40	I	1
41–50	III	3
		14

There are 14 people: 3 people between 1–10, 6 people between 11–20, 1 person between 21–30, 1 person between 31–40, and 3 people between 41–50.

1. Students surveyed said they spent the following amount of time studying each day: 1 h, 3 h, 2 h, 5 h, 7 h, 4 h, 3 h, 4 h, 1 h, and 6 h. Complete the frequency table

Time	Tally	Frequency
0–2 h	■	■
3–5 h	■	■
6–8 h	■	■
Total →		■

2. Look at the table. Which time range is the least common?

   The lowest frequency is ■.

   The least common time range is ■.

3. Look at the table. How many students study less than 6 hours?

   Identify the groups that study less than 6 hours.

   Add the frequencies.   ■ + ■ = ■

   ■ students study less than 6 hours.

Practice

1. Complete the frequency table for the following ages: 5, 2, 12, 23, 1, 13, 29, 8, 13, 5, 7, 22.

Time	Tally	Frequency
1–10	?	?
11–20	?	?
21–30	?	?
Total →		?

2. How many people were over 10 years of age?

3. What was the most common age range?

4. The baseball team is ordering shirts. Make a frequency table for the sizes: S, L, M, S, S, M, S, L, L, M, L, S, M, L, S. Describe the results.

Do It Together!

5. Explain to a partner how you complete the table in number **1** in **Practice.**

6. Write a question that can be answered with the table in number **4** in **Practice.** Have a partner answer the question. Check the work.

9.5 Stem-and-Leaf Plots

Like a frequency table, a **stem-and-leaf plot** is a way to display data. It uses place value. The leaves can represent the ones place. The stem can represent the tens place. With a stem-and-leaf plot, you can easily see the number of items in groups of data.

EXAMPLE 1   The ages of people at a restaurant are 21, 18, 44, 12, 10, 57, 11, 42, 19, and 50. Make a stem-and-leaf plot.

Order the data from least to greatest.   10, 11, 12, 18, 19, 21, 42, 44, 50, 57

Write the tens-place digits from least to greatest under Stem.

For each age, write the ones-place digit under Leaves next to the correct stem.

No people are in the 30s age group.

Stem	Leaves
1	0 1 2 8 9
2	1
3	
4	2 4
5	0 7

The age group between 10 and 19 years old has the most people.

The stem can be more than one digit. It may show both the tens and hundreds place.

EXAMPLE 2   The number of pennies in 10 piggy banks was 128, 104, 124, 113, 104, 108, 117, 121, 132, and 125. Make a stem-and-leaf plot. Describe the results.

Order the data from least to greatest.   104, 104, 108, 113, 117, 121, 124, 125, 128, 132

Write the hundreds- and tens-place digits from least to greatest under Stem.

Write the ones-place digits under Leaves next to the correct stems.

Stem	Leaves
10	4 4 8
11	3 7
12	1 4 5 8
13	2

The greatest number of piggy banks had between 120 and 129 pennies. The smallest number of piggy banks had between 130 and 139 pennies.

1. Make a stem-and-leaf plot for the set of data. 235, 241, 254, 236, 238, 247, 248

Order the data from least to greatest.

Write the hundreds- and tens-place digits from least to greatest under Stem.

Write the ones-place digit for each number next to the correct stem.

■, ■, ■, ■, ■, ■, ■

Stem	Leaves
23	■ ■ ■
24	■ ■ ■
■	■

2. Look at the stem-and-leaf plot. Describe the results.

The ■ group has five items.
The ■ group has one item.

Stem	Leaves
55	1
56	2 4 4 5 8
57	3 5
58	6 7 9

The smallest number of items appears in the ■ group.
The greatest number of items appears in the ■ group.

Practice

Make a stem-and-leaf plot for each set of data.

1. 23, 21, 31, 15, 28, 36, 14, 42, 21, 35, 48, 33

2. 147, 158, 167, 131, 141, 142, 168, 157, 130, 128

3. 748, 724, 735, 748, 758, 761, 749, 764, 720, 748

Do It Together!

4. Explain to a partner how you choose the stems in number **3** in **Practice.**

5. Write eight numbers between 10 and 40. Ask a partner to make a stem-and-leaf plot to display the numbers. Have your partner describe the data.

9.6 Scatter Plots

Sometimes, sets of data are in pairs. You can plot them as ordered pairs. This makes a graph called a **scatter plot.**

EXAMPLE 1

A zookeeper measures the length and weight of eight pythons. Use the data from the chart. Make a scatter plot.

Read each pair of data.

Plot each ordered pair on the scatter plot.

Length (feet)	Weight (pounds)
2	2
5	6
3	4
4	5
3	5
4	6
5	8
2	3

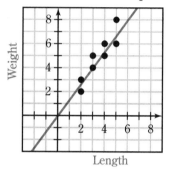

A line that goes up from the lower left has a positive slope.

Notice that the weight increases as the length increases. This is called **positive correlation.** A line drawn through the data has a positive slope.

A scatter plot can also show **negative correlation.** A line drawn through the data will have a negative slope.

EXAMPLE 2

Copy costs vary based on the number of copies you make. Use the table to make a scatter plot. Is the correlation positive or negative?

Read each pair of data.

Plot each ordered pair on the scatter plot.

Number of Copies	Cost per Copy
1	15
5	10
10	8
20	6
30	5
40	4

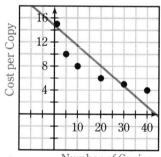

A line that goes down from the upper left has a negative slope.

The cost per copy decreases as the number of copies increases. This is a negative correlation.

1. Use the data from the chart. Make a scatter plot.

Hours (h)	Miles (mi)
1	60
3	175
2	130
3	150
1	30
4	200

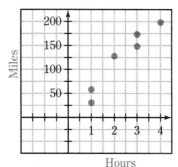

Read each ■ of data.

Plot each ordered pair on the ■.

2. Look at the scatter plot. Tell whether there is a positive or negative correlation.

   The miles increase as the hours ■.

   There is a ■ correlation.

Practice

Make a scatter plot for each set of data. Then, tell if the correlation is positive or negative.

1.

Number of Guests	Cost ($) per guest
1	$34
2	$22
3	$18
4	$16

2.

Height of Tree (ft)	Cost ($)
4	$10
6	$15
8	$30
10	$50
12	$100

Do It Together!

3. Explain to a partner how to find the correlation in number **2** in **Practice**.

4. Draw a scatter plot. Ask a partner to identify whether the scatter plot shows a positive or negative correlation.

9.7 Calculator: Finding the Mean

Some sets of data have large numbers. You can use a calculator to find the mean of sets of large numbers.

EXAMPLE 1   Find the mean of the set of data.   896; 943; 823; 992; 1,322

DISPLAY

To find the mean, add the data. Then, divide the sum by the number of data items.

		DISPLAY
Enter 896 by pressing:	`8` `9` `6`	896
Add 943 by pressing:	`+` `9` `4` `3`	943
Add 823 by pressing:	`+` `8` `2` `3`	823
Add 992 by pressing:	`+` `9` `9` `2`	992
Add 1,322 by pressing:	`+` `1` `3` `2` `2`	1322
Find the total by pressing:	`=`	4976

There are 5 items in the set of data.

Divide by 5 by pressing: `÷` `5` `=`   995.2

The mean is 995.2.

You can also use a calculator to find the mean of sets containing decimals.

EXAMPLE 2   Find the mean of the set of data.   1.202, 1.049, 1.726, 1.903

DISPLAY

		DISPLAY
Enter 1.202 by pressing:	`1` `.` `2` `0` `2`	1.202
Add 1.049 by pressing:	`+` `1` `.` `0` `4` `9`	1.049
Add 1.726 by pressing:	`+` `1` `.` `7` `2` `6`	1.726
Add 1.903 by pressing:	`+` `1` `.` `9` `0` `3`	1.903
Find the total by pressing:	`=`	5.88

There are 4 data items.

Divide by 4 by pressing: `÷` `4` `=`   1.47

The mean is 1.47.

Practice

Find the mean.

1. 327, 928, 778, 824

2. 3.246, 4.003, 3.192, 4.325

3. 901, 854, 972, 995

4. .075, .105, 1.244, .662

5. 654, 687, 610, 701, 722

6. 7.044, 7.035, 7.108, 7.184

7. 104, 118, 25, 103, 161

8. 1.004, .302, .651, .117, .018

MATH CONNECTION

Physician's Assistant

You may have been to a doctor's office or hospital at some time. If so, you might have been helped by a physician's assistant. Physician's assistants are a little like nurses. They both work closely with the doctor.

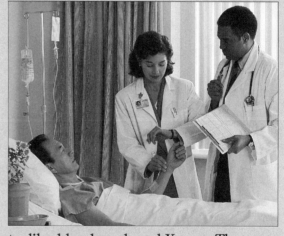

Assistants help doctors by doing basic tasks. This way, the doctors can spend more time on complex cases. Assistants give exams and check-ups. They can order special tests, like blood work and X-rays. They can also order medicines, with the doctor's okay.

Doctors and physician's assistants use many statistics in their jobs. They read medical charts. They use terms like *average cure rate* and *median age*. This helps them learn about an illness.

Assistants must speak clearly. They talk with patients about how they are feeling. They also pass on information to doctors about their patients. Assistants keep the patient's files in order and up-to-date, too.

If you like helping sick people, you might like to be a physician's assistant.

9.8 Problem Solving: The Best Description

You can use the mean, mode, or median to represent data. Sometimes, one or two of these better describe the data.

EXAMPLE 1

Which best describes the set of data: mean, mode, or median?   100; 130; 120; 100; 160; 140; 1,000

Write the data in order from least to greatest.   100; 100; 120; 130; 140; 160; 1,000

Add the numbers.   The sum is 1,750

Find the mean. $1,750 \div 7 = 250$

Find the mode.   100; 100; 120; 130; 140; 160; 1,000

Find the median.   100; 100; 120; 130; 140; 160; 1,000

The mean is 250. The median is 130. The mode is 100. The mean is higher than most of the numbers. The mode is too low. The median is the best description of the data.

EXAMPLE 2

A company president has four employees. The president earns $80.00 an hour. The employees each earn $10.00 an hour. Which is a good description of the typical wage: mean, mode, or median?

4 employees earn $10 each.

Write the wages in order from least to greatest.   10, 10, 10, 10, 80

Add the wages.   The sum is 120

Find the mean. $120 \div 5 = 24$

Find the mode.   10, 10, 10, 10, 80

Find the median.   10, 10, 10, 10, 80

The mean is $24.00. The median is $10.00. The mode is $10.00. The mean is much higher than most of the hourly wages. The median and mode are both better descriptions of the typical wage earned at the company.

Find the mean, mode, and median of each set of data. Then, tell which of the mean, mode, and median best describes the data.

1. 2, 3, 3, 5, 6, 35

Find the mean.   sum $= 54$
                  $54 \div 6 = 9$

Find the median. $(3 + 5) \div 2 = \blacksquare$

Find the mode. $\blacksquare$

The $\blacksquare$ is higher than most of the numbers. The $\blacksquare$ and $\blacksquare$ are better descriptions of the data.

2. 12, 12, 45, 46, 59, 70, 71

Find the mean.   sum $= \blacksquare$
                  $\blacksquare \div 7 = 45$

Find the median. $\blacksquare$

Find the mode. $\blacksquare$

The $\blacksquare$ is lower than most of the numbers. The $\blacksquare$ and $\blacksquare$ are better descriptions of the data.

Practice

Find the mean, mode, and median. Then, tell which is the best description for each set of data.

1. 60, 74, 3, 4, 3, 60

2. 38, 1, 34, 33, 34

3. A store was surveyed for the cost of tennis shoes. The prices of six different brands of shoes were $84.00, $15.00, $16.00, $80.00, $15.00, and $90.00.

4. You poured five bowls of cereal to find out the number of fruit flavored pieces you get in a bowl. The fruit flavored pieces numbered 3, 23, 20, 23, and 21.

Do It Together!

5. Explain to a partner how you choose the best descriptions of the data in number **2** in **Practice.**

6. Write five numbers. Work with a partner to find the mean, mode, and median. Decide which you think are good descriptions of the data.

9.9 Application: Quartiles

Sometimes, **quartiles** are used to describe test results and other information. To find a quartile, first find the median. Then, look at the data above and below the median.

$$\underbrace{10, 10, 12, 13, 13,}\; 14,\; \underbrace{15, 16, 16, 17, 17}$$

↑   ↑   ↑

1st   median   3rd
quartile   quartile

The first quartile is the middle number in the group less than the median. The third quartile is the middle number in the group greater than the median. The median is sometimes called the 2nd quartile.

EXAMPLE 1   Find the quartiles in the set of data.
52, 50, 57, 64, 66, 68, 65

Order the data from least to greatest.	50, 52, 57, 64, 65, 66, 68.
Find the median.	50, 52, 57, 64, 65, 66, 68
Find the first quartile.	50, 52, 57
Find the third quartile.	65, 66, 68

The quartiles are 52, 64, and 66.

EXAMPLE 2   Find the quartiles in the set of test scores.
80, 50, 52, 74, 75, 85, 70, 66, 63, 90, 99

Order the data from least to greatest.	50, 52, 63, 66, 70, 74, 75, 80, 85, 90, 99
Find the median.	50, 52, 63, 66, 70, 74, 75, 80, 85, 90, 99
Find the first quartile.	50, 52, 63, 66, 70
Find the third quartile.	75, 80, 85, 90, 99

The quartiles are 63, 74, and 85.

Find the quartiles in each set of data.

1. Number of family members: 9, 2, 3, 7, 3, 4, 6

Order the data from least to greatest.	2, 3, 3, 4, 6, 7, 9
Find the median.	2, 3, 3, ■, 6, 7, 9
Find the first quartile.	2, ■, 3
Find the third quartile.	6, ■, 9

The quartiles are ■, ■, and ■.

2. Daily bank balance: $35.00, $33.00, $25.00, $28.00, $29.00, $41.00, $27.00, $52.00, $23.00, $44.00, $53.00

Order the data from least to greatest.	23, 25, 27, 28, 29, 33, 35, 41, 44, 52, 53
Find the median.	23, 25, 27, 28, 29, ■, 35, 41, 44, 52, 53
Find the first quartile.	23, 25, ■, 28, 29
Find the third quartile.	35, 41, ■, 52, 53

The quartiles are ■, ■, and ■.

Practice

Find the quartiles in each set of data.

1. 97, 82, 94, 84, 87, 88, 91

2. 5, 7, 11, 8, 1, 9, 1, 6, 11, 2, 10

3. Miles driven each day: 4, 6, 8, 4, 5, 7, 9, 2, 3, 2, 9

4. Daily temperatures for the week: 62°, 52°, 42°, 31°, 53°, 48°, 37°

Do It Together!

5. Explain to a partner how you find the quartiles in number **1** in **Practice.**

6. Write a set of data containing seven numbers. Ask a partner to find the quartiles.

Chapter Review

Chapter 9 Summary

- You can describe sets of data using mean, mode, median, maximum, minimum, and range.
- You can organize sets of data using frequency tables and stem-and-leaf plots.
- You can organize paired sets of data using a scatter plot and describe the data as a positive or negative correlation.
- You can use a calculator to find the mean of large numbers or decimals.
- You can decide which of mean, mode, or median are the better descriptions of a set of data.
- You can find quartiles in a set of data.

Reviewing Vocabulary

Fill in each blank with the correct word.

data
statistics
mean
mode
median
range
frequency table
stem-and-leaf plot
scatter plot
positive correlation
negative correlation
quartile

1. The number that appears most often in a set of data is called the ? .
2. A chart that shows how many times an item appears in a set of data is called a ? .
3. To arrange data by looking at the tens place, use a ? .
4. Information that is gathered from surveys and experiments is called ? .
5. The number in the middle of half of a set of data is a ? .
6. The study of collecting and organizing data is called ? .
7. When two sets of data increase together, you have a ? .
8. The middle number in a set of data is called the ? .
9. A graph that shows two sets of data as ordered pairs is called a ? .
10. The difference between the maximum and minimum values is the ? .
11. When one set of data increases while the second set decreases, you have a ? .
12. If you divide the sum of the data by the number of items, you get the average or ? .

Chapter Quiz

Find the mean, mode, and median.

1. 6, 5, 5, 3, 6, 5, 12

2. 15, 8, 20, 10, 10, 10, 14, 12, 18

Find the minimum, maximum, and range.

3. 4, 64, 2, 32, 5, 14, 6, 7, 3, 22

4. 100, 88, 22, 43, 10, 75, 54, 23, 18

5. Make a frequency table for the set of data of shirt sizes: S, L, M, M, S, M, S, S, L, M, L, M, M, L, S. Describe the results.

6. Use the frequency table from number **5** to tell how many more medium shirts were ordered than large.

Make a stem-and-leaf plot for each set of data.

7. 10, 12, 15, 21, 24, 31, 32, 33

8. 72, 92, 74, 83, 73, 87, 95, 74, 99

For each scatter plot, tell whether the correlation is positive or negative.

9.

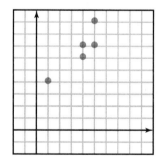

10.

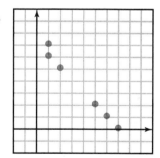

Find the mean, mode, and median of each set of data. Then, tell which of the mean, mode, and median best describes the data.

11. 2, 2, 2, 32, 37, 39

12. 94, 97, 1, 97, 99, 5, 97

Find the quartiles in each set of data.

13. 12, 14, 16, 19, 32, 35, 37

14. 58, 49, 43, 47, 43, 53, 55

Unit Three Review

Solve each inequality.

1. $x - 4 \geq -4$ **2.** $y - 3 < 2$ **3.** $-2a > 4$ **4.** $\frac{n}{3} + 2 \leq 5$

Write and solve the inequality.

5. Shawna makes $5 per hour at her job. Her car payment is $300 per month. At this rate, how many hours a month does Shawna work to make enough to pay the car payment?

Tell whether the ordered pair is the solution of the system.

6. $(1, -1);\ x - y = 2$
$4x + y = 3$

7. $(-1, 6);\ x = -1$
$y = 2x + 4$

8. $(-2, 1);\ y \geq x + 2$
$y < -3x + 1$

Graph each system to find its solution.

9. $y = 2x - 4$
$y = x + 1$

10. $y = -2$
$y = \frac{1}{2}x + 4$

11. $y \leq 3x + 1$
$y \leq -x + 5$

12. $y \geq x$
$y \leq 2x - 3$

Find the solution of the system.

13. $y = -2x$
$y = x + 6$

14. $-x + y = 7$
$x + y = -5$

15. $x + 4y = -6$
$x - 4y = 10$

16. $5x + 2y = 10$
$x - 4y = 2$

Find the number.

17. The sum of two numbers is 4. Their difference is 8.

Find the mean, median, mode, minimum, maximum, and range for each set of data.

18. 10, 2, 3, 7, 3, 4, 6

19. 28, 45, 23, 29, 41, 23, 35

Complete a frequency table.

20. Survey results asking people how many brothers and sisters they have:
1, 0, 2, 2, 3, 2, 0, 1, 1, 4, 1, 2, 1, 3, 2

Make a stem-and-leaf plot.

21. 34, 46, 32, 54, 45, 32, 43, 54

Unit Four

Chapter 10

Exponents and Functions

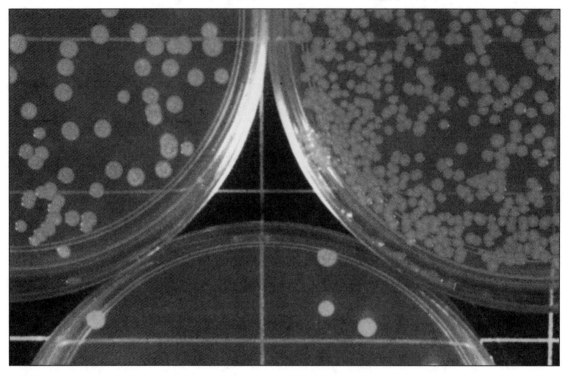

Some functions increase very quickly. Bacteria cells grow as a function of time. One cell could become millions in just a few hours. Scientists put samples of bacteria in dishes to study how fast they grow.

Chapter Learning Objectives

- Multiply and divide with exponents.
- Use zero and negative exponents.
- Find numbers named by scientific notation.
- Make a table of values to graph an exponential function.
- Find the value of powers using a calculator.
- Solve problems by drawing a tree diagram to count choices.
- Apply concepts and skills to finding compound interest.

Words to Know

exponent   the number that tells how many times the base is used as a factor

power   the product when the factors are the same; In $3^2 = 9$, 9 is the power

base   a factor; In 3^2, 3 is the base used as a factor two times

scientific notation   a number written as the product of two factors; The first is a number greater than 1 and less than 10 and the second is a power of 10

exponential functions   functions of the form $y = a \bullet b^x$, where b is a positive number not equal to 1

tree diagram   a way of showing choices so you can count them

compound interest   interest earned on your previous interest

In this chapter, you will review powers. Then, you will learn the rules for multiplying and dividing with exponents. You will also work with zero and negative exponents. You will learn how to write numbers in scientific notation. You will make tables of values for powers and then graph the functions. You will use your calculator to find values of powers. You will also solve counting problems using tree diagrams. You will apply your knowledge of exponential functions to calculate compound interest.

10.1 Finding Powers

You have already used exponents to write numbers.

$$\text{base} \rightarrow 4^2 = 4 \bullet 4 = 16 \leftarrow \textbf{power}$$

exponent ↓ (above the 2)

You have also written variables with exponents.

$$a^3 = aaa \rightarrow a \text{ is used as a factor } 3 \text{ times.}$$
$$a^2b^4 = aabbbb \rightarrow a \text{ is used as a factor } 2 \text{ times.}$$
$$b \text{ is used as a factor } 4 \text{ times.}$$

EXAMPLE 1   Use an exponent to rewrite *xxxx*.

$$x \bullet x \bullet x \bullet x$$

x is used as a factor 4 times.

$$x^4$$

$$xxxx = x^4$$

EXAMPLE 2   Rewrite a^5y without an exponent.

$$a^5y$$

y is the same as y^1.

a is used as a factor 5 times. *y* is used as a factor 1 time.

$$aaaaay$$

$$a^5y = aaaaay$$

EXAMPLE 3   Rewrite $-y^4$ without an exponent.

$$-y^4$$

$-y^4$ means $-(y^4)$.

y is used as a factor 4 times.

$$-yyyy$$

$$-y^4 = -yyyy$$

You can also find the value of a power.

EXAMPLE 4   Find the value of b^3 when *b* is -4.

b is used as a factor 3 times.

$$b^3$$

Substitute -4 for *b*.

$$bbb$$

The product of three negative numbers is negative.

Multiply.

$$(-4)(-4)(-4)$$

$$-64$$

$b^3 = -64$ when *b* is -4.

Use exponents to rewrite each product.

1. nnn

    n is used as a factor ■ times.   ■ • ■ • ■

    Write with an exponent. $n^{\blacksquare}$

2. xyy

    x is used as a factor ■ time. $x • \blacksquare • \blacksquare$

    y is used as a factor ■ times.

    Write with an exponent. $xy^{\blacksquare}$

Find the value of each power.

3. c^2 when c is -2

    c is used as a factor ■ times. c^2

    Substitute -2 for c. cc

    Multiply. $(-2)(\blacksquare)$

                    ■

4. a^4 when a is 3

    a is used as a factor ■ times. a^4

    Substitute 3 for a. $aaaa$

    Multiply.   ■ • ■ • ■ • ■

                    ■

Practice

Use exponents to rewrite each product.

1. ggg **2.** ppq **3.** $aabbb$ **4.** $hhhh$

5. rr **6.** $bccc$ **7.** $yyyyy$ **8.** $mmnn$

Find the value of each power.

9. a^3 when a is 4 **10.** x^3 when x is -1 **11.** $-y^5$ when y is 2

12. b^2 when b is -3 **13.** w^4 when w is 1 **14.** c^2 when c is 7

Do It Together!

15. Explain to a partner how to rewrite the expression in number **6** in **Practice.**

16. Pick a number between 1 and 5. Have a partner find x^3 when x is your number. Check the work.

10.2 Multiplying with Exponents

You can multiply powers when the bases are the same.
First, rewrite each power as the product of factors.
Then, see how many times each base is used as a factor.

EXAMPLE 1   Multiply. $a^2 \bullet a^3$

$a^2 \bullet a^3$

Write as factors. $aa \bullet aaa$

$aaaaa$

Rewrite with an exponent. a^5

$a^2 \bullet a^3 = a^5$

EXAMPLE 2   Multiply. $b^2 \bullet ab$

$b^2 \bullet ab$

The Commutative Property of Multiplication lets you rearrange the factors.

Write as factors. $bb \bullet ab$

Rearrange the factors. $abbb$

Rewrite with an exponent. ab^3

$b^2 \bullet ab = ab^3$

EXAMPLE 3   Multiply. $ab^2 \bullet a^2b^3$

$ab^2 \bullet a^2b^3$

Write as factors. $abb \bullet aabbb$

Rearrange the factors. $aaabbbbb$

Rewrite with exponents. a^3b^5

$ab^2 \bullet a^2b^3 = a^3b^5$

Multiply any coefficients first.

EXAMPLE 4   Multiply. $3x^2y \bullet 2x$

Multiply the coefficients. $3x^2y \bullet 2x$

Write as factors. $6xxy \bullet x$

Rearrange the factors. $6xxxy$

Rewrite the variables with an exponent. $6x^3y$

$3x^2y \bullet 2x = 6x^3y$

Multiply.

1. $b^4 \bullet 3b^2$

$$b^4 \bullet 3b^2$$

Write as factors. $bbbb \bullet 3\blacksquare$

Rearrange the factors. $3bbbbbb$

Rewrite with an exponent. $3b^\blacksquare$

$b^4 \bullet 3b^2 = \blacksquare$

2. $-2c^2d \bullet 5cd$

Multiply the coefficients. $-2c^2d \bullet 5cd$

$\blacksquare c^2dcd$

Write as factors. $\blacksquare ccdcd$

$\blacksquare$ the factors. $\blacksquare cccdd$

Rewrite the variables $\blacksquare c^\blacksquare d^\blacksquare$
with exponents.

$-2c^2d \bullet 5cd = \blacksquare$

Practice

Multiply.

1. $c^3 \bullet c$

2. $d^2 \bullet d^5$

3. $x^3 \bullet x^3$

4. $5a^3 \bullet 2ab^2$

5. $xy \bullet x$

6. $4c^2d \bullet 5c^2d$

7. $-3a \bullet -2b$

8. $5 \bullet 3t^2$

9. $x \bullet 2x$

10. $x^2y^2 \bullet x^2y$

11. $-3a^3d \bullet ad^2$

12. $2bc^4 \bullet 3b^2c^2$

13. $6b^4 \bullet 2ab^2$

14. $x^6y \bullet 3x^5y$

15. $-2h^3g^4 \bullet -4h^2g^2$

16. $7np^3 \bullet 3np$

17. $3y^2 \bullet -y$

18. $-4ab \bullet -6ab$

Do It Together!

19. Explain to a partner how to find the product in number **6** in **Practice.**

20. Write a power. Use n as the base and choose an exponent. Ask a partner to find the product of that power and n^3.

10.3   Rules for Multiplication

You have multiplied powers with the same base by rewriting as a product of factors.

$$a^3 \bullet a^2 = aaa \bullet aa = aaaaa = a^5$$

You can also multiply by adding the exponents.

$$a^3 \bullet a^2 = a^{3+2} = a^5$$

To multiply powers with the same base, add the exponents and keep the base.

EXAMPLE 1   Multiply. $x^5 \bullet x^7$

$$x^5 \bullet x^7$$

Add the exponents of x. $5 + 7 = 12$

Write the base with the sum of the exponents. x^{12}

$$x^5 \bullet x^7 = x^{12}$$

EXAMPLE 2   Multiply. $4b^2c^4 \bullet 3bc^2$

$$4b^2c^4 \bullet 3bc^2$$

Multiply the coefficients. $12b^2c^4 \bullet bc^2$

b is the same as b^1.   **Add the exponents of b.** $2 + 1 = 3$

Add the exponents of c. $4 + 2 = 6$

Write the bases with the sums of the exponents. $12b^3c^6$

$$4b^2c^4 \bullet 3bc^2 = 12b^3c^6$$

Sometimes, the base of a power is another power. Rewrite the product as factors. Then, add the exponents.

EXAMPLE 3   Multiply. $(a^3)^2$

$$(a^3)^2$$

Use a^3 as a factor 2 times. $a^3 \bullet a^3$

Add the exponents. $3 + 3 = 6$

Write the base with the sum of the exponents. a^6

$$(a^3)^2 = a^6$$

Multiply.

1. $2x^2y \cdot 5xy$

	$2x^2y \cdot 5xy$
Multiply the coefficients.	$\blacksquare x^2y \cdot xy$
Add the exponents of x.	$2 + 1 = \blacksquare$
Add the exponents of y.	$1 + \blacksquare = \blacksquare$
Write the bases with the sums of the exponents.	$10x^{\blacksquare}y^{\blacksquare}$

2. $(c^4)^3$

	$(c^4)^3$
c^4 is used as a factor $\blacksquare$ times.	$c^4 \cdot c^4 \cdot c^4$
Add the exponents.	$\blacksquare + \blacksquare + \blacksquare = 12$
Write the base with the sum of the exponents.	$(c^4)^3 = c^{\blacksquare}$

Practice

Multiply.

1. $x^4 \cdot x^6$

2. $a^2b \cdot a^3$

3. $w^2x^3 \cdot w^3x^3$

4. $x^7 \cdot x^3$

5. $b^6c^6 \cdot b^2c^6$

6. $5w^4x^5 \cdot x^2$

7. $a^2 \cdot 3a^2$

8. $2b^3 \cdot 4wb^4$

9. $5c^5q^3 \cdot 6cq$

10. $-6a^4b \cdot 2a^5b^6$

11. $(a^3)^3$

12. $(4c^2)^3$

13. $(d^5)^2$

14. $(x^6)^2$

15. $(y^4)^5$

16. $x^4y^5 \cdot -4$

17. $-8n^5 \cdot 4n^2p$

18. $-6x^5y \cdot 6xy^5$

Do It Together!

19. Explain to a partner how to find the product in number **4** in **Practice.**

20. Write a power using a and b as bases. Have a partner write another power using a and b as bases. Multiply the powers.

10.4 Division with Exponents

To divide two powers with the same base, write the division as a fraction. Then, remove common factors.

A number divided by itself equals 1.

$$a^4 \div a^2 = \frac{\cancel{a}\cancel{a}aa}{\cancel{a}\cancel{a}} = \frac{1aa}{1} = a^2$$

EXAMPLE 1   Divide. $a^5 \div a^2$

Write as a fraction.
$$\frac{a^5}{a^2}$$

Rewrite as factors. Remove common factors.
$$\frac{aaaaa}{aa} = \frac{\cancel{a}\cancel{a}aaa}{\cancel{a}\cancel{a}}$$

Simplify. aaa

Rewrite with an exponent. a^3

$$a^5 \div a^2 = a^3$$

EXAMPLE 2   Divide. $b^4c^3 \div b^2c^2$

Write as a fraction.
$$\frac{b^4c^3}{b^2c^2}$$

Rewrite as factors. Remove common factors.
$$\frac{bbbbccc}{bbcc} = \frac{\cancel{b}\cancel{b}bb\cancel{c}\cancel{c}c}{\cancel{b}\cancel{b}\cancel{c}\cancel{c}}$$

Simplify. bbc

Rewrite with an exponent. b^2c

$$b^4c^3 \div b^2 c^2 = b^2c$$

Be sure to divide the coefficients.

EXAMPLE 3   Divide. $10x^2y \div 5x$

Write as a fraction.
$$\frac{10x^2y}{5x}$$

$10 \div 5 = 2$

Divide the coefficients.
$$\frac{2x^2y}{x}$$

Rewrite as factors. Remove common factors.
$$\frac{2xxy}{x} = \frac{2\cancel{x}xy}{\cancel{x}}$$

Simplify. $2xy$

$$10x^2y \div 5x = 2xy$$

Divide.

1. $12w^3 \div 6w^2$

Write as a fraction.

$$\frac{12w^3}{6w^2}$$

Divide the coefficients.

$$\frac{\blacksquare w^3}{w^2}$$

Rewrite as factors.
Remove common factors.

$$\frac{\blacksquare www}{ww}$$

Simplify. $\blacksquare$

$12w^3 \div 6w^2 = \blacksquare$

2. $a^2b^4 \div ab^2$

Write as a fraction.

$$\frac{a^2b^4}{ab^2}$$

Rewrite as factors.
Remove common factors.

$$\frac{aabbbb}{abb}$$

Simplify.
Rewrite with exponents. $\blacksquare$

$ab^{\blacksquare}$

$a^2b^4 \div ab^2 = \blacksquare$

Practice

Divide.

1. $b^4 \div b^3$

2. $x^2y \div x$

3. $5c^2d^3 \div cd^2$

4. $15w^4 \div 3w$

5. $s^2t^8 \div st^3$

6. $14x^3y^4 \div 7x^2y$

7. $6n^2p \div np$

8. $12x^4y^5 \div -4x^3y^4$

9. $9x^2y \div y$

10. $8m^4n^2 \div 2mn^2$

11. $pq^4 \div pq^2$

12. $x^3y^4 \div x^2y$

13. $r^4k^3 \div r^3k^3$

14. $24xy^5 \div 4xy$

15. $ab^2c \div bc$

16. $-21x^4y^2 \div 3x^2$

17. $18x^6y^3 \div 3x^2y$

18. $4a^3b \div 4b$

Do It Together!

19. Explain to a partner how to find the quotient in number **4** in **Practice**.

20. Work with a partner to find the quotient of $15a^3b^5 \div 3a^2b^3$.

10.5 Rules for Division

You have divided two powers with the same base using properties of division and multiplication.

$$\frac{x^5}{x^3} = \frac{xxxxx}{xxx} = \frac{1 \bullet xx}{1} = x^2$$

You can also divide by subtracting the exponents.

$$x^5 \div x^3 = x^{5-3} = x^2$$

To divide powers with the same base, keep the base and subtract the exponent in the denominator from the exponent in the numerator.

EXAMPLE 1   Divide. $\dfrac{x^7}{x^2}$

$$\frac{x^7}{x^2}$$

Subtract the exponents of x. $7 - 2 = 5$

Write the base with the difference of exponents. x^5

$$\frac{x^7}{x^2} = x^5$$

EXAMPLE 2   Divide. $\dfrac{a^6 b^3}{a^2}$

$$\frac{a^6 b^3}{a^2}$$

Subtract the exponents of a. $6 - 2 = 4$

The exponent of b stays 3.

Write the bases with the difference of exponents. $a^4 b^3$

$$\frac{a^6 b^3}{a^2} = a^4 b^3$$

EXAMPLE 3   Divide. $\dfrac{12c^5}{3c^2}$

Divide the coefficients. $\dfrac{4c^5}{c^2}$

Subtract the exponents of the factors of c. $5 - 2 = 3$

Write the base with the difference of exponents. $4c^3$

$$\frac{12c^5}{3c^2} = 4c^3$$

Divide.

1. $\dfrac{8x^6}{2x^3}$

2. $\dfrac{g^6h^5}{g^2h^3}$

$$\dfrac{8x^6}{2x^3}$$

Divide the coefficients. $\quad\dfrac{4x^6}{x^3}$

Subtract the exponents of x. $\quad\blacksquare - \blacksquare = 3$

Write the base with the difference of exponents. $\quad 4x^{\blacksquare}$

$$\dfrac{8x^6}{2x^3} = \blacksquare$$

$$\dfrac{g^6h^5}{g^2h^3}$$

Subtract the exponents of g. $\quad 6 - \blacksquare = \blacksquare$

Subtract the exponents of h. $\quad \blacksquare - \blacksquare = \blacksquare$

Write the bases with the differences of exponents. $\quad g^{\blacksquare}h^{\blacksquare}$

$$\dfrac{g^6h^5}{g^2h^3} = \blacksquare$$

Practice

Divide.

1. $\dfrac{b^8}{b^6}$

2. $\dfrac{a^5}{a^4}$

3. $\dfrac{6r^7}{2r^3}$

4. $\dfrac{x^4y}{x^2}$

5. $\dfrac{c^5d^3}{cd}$

6. $\dfrac{w^5g}{w^2}$

7. $\dfrac{10m^4n^5}{2mn^2}$

8. $\dfrac{7b^6c^5}{b^2c}$

9. $\dfrac{x^7y^4}{x^2y}$

10. $\dfrac{b^2c^4}{bc^3}$

11. $\dfrac{18x^4y^3}{3x^2y}$

12. $\dfrac{a^2b^2c^6}{abc^3}$

Do It Together!

13. Explain to a partner how to find the quotient in number **7** in **Practice.**

14. Write a variable expression with a positive exponent. Write another expression with the same variable and a smaller positive exponent. Ask a partner to find the quotient. Check the work.

10.6 Zero As an Exponent

Zero can be an exponent. Use the rules for dividing to find the value of a power with an exponent of 0.

$$1 = \frac{a^3}{a^3} = a^3 \div a^3 = a^{3-3} = a^0$$

Any power with a zero exponent $= 1$.

EXAMPLE 1   Multiply. $a^2 \bullet a^0$

$a^2 \bullet a^0$

Write 1 for the power with a 0 exponent. $a^2 \bullet 1$

Simplify. a^2

$a^2 \bullet a^0 = a^2$

EXAMPLE 2   Divide. $\dfrac{c^3 d^5}{c^3 d^2}$

$\dfrac{c^3 d^5}{c^3 d^2}$

Subtract the exponents of c. $3 - 3 = 0$

Subtract the exponents of d. $5 - 2 = 3$

Write the bases with the exponents. $c^0 d^3$

Write 1 for the power with a 0 exponent. $1 \bullet d^3$

Simplify. d^3

$\dfrac{c^3 d^5}{c^3 d^2} = d^3$

EXAMPLE 3   Divide. $\dfrac{15 x^4 y^6}{x^4 y^6}$

$\dfrac{15 x^4 y^6}{x^4 y^6}$

Subtract the exponents of x. $4 - 4 = 0$

Subtract the exponents of y. $6 - 6 = 0$

Write the bases with the exponents. $15 x^0 y^0$

Write 1 for the powers with 0 exponents. $15 \bullet 1 \bullet 1$

Simplify. 15

$\dfrac{15 x^4 y^6}{x^4 y^6} = 15$

Divide.

1. $\dfrac{a^3b^5}{a^3b^3}$

$\dfrac{a^3b^5}{a^3b^3}$

Subtract the exponents of *a*.	$3-3=\blacksquare$
Subtract the exponents of *b*.	$5-3=\blacksquare$
Write the bases with the exponents.	$a^{\blacksquare}b^{\blacksquare}$
Write 1 for the power with a 0 exponent.	$1 \bullet b$
Simplify.	$b^{\blacksquare}$

$\dfrac{a^3b^5}{a^3b^3}=b^{\blacksquare}$

2. $\dfrac{xy^4}{y^4}$

$\dfrac{xy^4}{y^4}$

Subtract the exponents of *y*.	$4-4=\blacksquare$
Write the bases with the exponents.	$x^{\blacksquare}y^{\blacksquare}$
Write 1 for the power with a 0 exponent.	$\blacksquare \bullet \blacksquare$
Simplify.	$\blacksquare$

$\dfrac{xy^4}{y^4}=\blacksquare$

Practice

Multiply.

1. $b^0 \bullet b^6$

2. $x^4y \bullet x^2y^0$

3. $c^3de^0 \bullet c^0d^5e^0$

Divide.

4. $\dfrac{m^4}{m^4}$

5. $\dfrac{s^2t^5}{s^2t}$

6. $\dfrac{h^8g^3}{hg^3}$

7. $\dfrac{y^4z^5}{z^5}$

8. $\dfrac{b^2c^5}{b^2c^3}$

9. $\dfrac{x^2y^4z^6}{xy^4}$

10. $\dfrac{q^2r^8}{q^2r^8}$

11. $\dfrac{h^2j^5k^7}{h^2j^5k^7}$

12. $\dfrac{t^7u}{t^6u}$

Do It Together!

13. Explain to a partner how you find the product in number **3** in **Practice.**

14. Write a division or multiplication problem that uses a zero exponent. Have a partner solve your problem. Check the work.

10.7   Negative Exponents

An exponent can be negative. You can find the meaning of a negative exponent by using what you know about division and exponents.

$a^{-1} = \dfrac{1}{a}$

$$\dfrac{a^2}{a^3} = \dfrac{aa}{aaa} = \dfrac{1}{a} \text{ and } \dfrac{a^2}{a^3} = a^{2-3} = a^{-1}$$

A number with a negative exponent is the same as 1 divided by the number with a positive exponent.

EXAMPLE 1   Write with a positive exponent. a^{-6}

Write as a fraction with a positive exponent. $\dfrac{1}{a^6}$

$a^{-6} = \dfrac{1}{a^6}$

EXAMPLE 2   Divide. Then, write with a positive exponent. $\dfrac{b^4}{b^8}$

$\dfrac{b^4}{b^8}$

Subtract the exponents of b. $4 - 8 = -4$

Write the base with the exponent. b^{-4}

Write as a fraction with a positive exponent. $\dfrac{1}{b^4}$

$\dfrac{b^4}{b^8} = \dfrac{1}{b^4}$

EXAMPLE 3   Divide. Then, write with positive exponents. $\dfrac{x^2 y^6}{x^4 y^2}$

$\dfrac{x^2 y^6}{x^4 y^2}$

Subtract the exponents of x. $2 - 4 = -2$

Subtract the exponents of y. $6 - 2 = 4$

Write the bases with the exponents. $x^{-2} y^4$

Write with positive exponents. $\dfrac{1}{x^2} y^4$

Simplify. $\dfrac{y^4}{x^2}$

$\dfrac{x^2 y^6}{x^4 y^2} = \dfrac{y^4}{x^2}$

Multiply or divide.

1. $x^{-6}y^9 \bullet x^2y^{-6}$

$$x^{-6}y^9 \bullet x^2y^{-6}$$

Add the exponents of x.　$-6+2=\blacksquare$

Add the exponents of y.　$9+(-6)=\blacksquare$

Write the bases with the　$x^{\blacksquare}y^{\blacksquare}$
exponents.

Write using positive　$\blacksquare \bullet \blacksquare$
exponents.

Simplify.　$\dfrac{y^{\blacksquare}}{x^{\blacksquare}}$

$$x^{-6}y^9 \bullet x^2y^{-6} = \dfrac{y^{\blacksquare}}{x^{\blacksquare}}$$

2. $\dfrac{a^4b^5}{a^2b^8}$

$$\dfrac{a^4b^5}{a^2b^8}$$

Subtract the exponents of a.　$4-2=\blacksquare$

Subtract the exponents of b.　$5-8=\blacksquare$

Write the bases with the　$a^{\blacksquare}b^{\blacksquare}$
exponents.

Write using positive　$a^2 \bullet \blacksquare$
exponents.

Simplify.　$\blacksquare$

$$\dfrac{a^4b^5}{a^2b^8} = \blacksquare$$

Practice

Multiply.

1. $b^{-6} \bullet b^8$

2. $n^2 \bullet n^{-5}$

3. $c^5d^{-4} \bullet c^{-6}d^7$

4. $x^{-2}y \bullet x^2y^{-3}$

5. $q^{-1}r^5 \bullet q^{-2}r$

6. $w^{-7}z^2 \bullet w^3z^{-4}$

Divide.

7. $\dfrac{m^4}{m^9}$

8. $\dfrac{p^3}{p^8}$

9. $\dfrac{bc^5}{b^{-9}c}$

10. $\dfrac{y^{-2}z^4}{y^5z^4}$

11. $\dfrac{j^6k}{jk^3}$

12. $\dfrac{d^5e}{de^4}$

Do It Together!

13. Explain to a partner how you find the product in number **2** in **Practice.**

14. Write a division problem. Use a and b as bases. Have a partner find the answer. Check the work.

10.8 Scientific Notation

Scientific notation is used to name large numbers such as 324,000. A number in scientific notation has two factors.

$$3.24 \qquad \times \qquad 10^5$$

first factor   second factor

a number between 1 and 10   a power of 10

You can find the large number by multiplying.

$3.24 \times 10^5 = 3.24 \times 100{,}000 = 324000. = 324{,}000$

Move the decimal point one place for each zero in the power of ten. This is the same as the exponent in the second factor. Move to the right when the exponent is positive.

EXAMPLE 1   Find the number named by 9.2×10^3.

3 is the exponent in 10^3.

10^3 is equal to 1,000. $9.2 \times 1{,}000$

Move the decimal point 3 places to the right. $9200. = 9{,}200$

$9.2 \times 10^3 = 9{,}200$

EXAMPLE 2   Find the number named by 4.32×10^5.

10^5 is equal to 100,000. $4.32 \times 100{,}000$

Move the decimal point 5 places to the right. $432000. = 432{,}000$

$4.32 \times 10^5 = 432{,}000$

You can use a negative exponent to name a very small number. Move the decimal point one place to the left for each decimal place in the power of 10.

EXAMPLE 3   Find the number named by 3.8×10^{-4}.

10^{-4} is equal to .0001 $3.8 \times .0001$

Move the decimal point 4 places to the left. $.00038 = .00038$

$3.8 \times 10^{-4} = .00038$

Find each number named in scientific notation.

1. 9.08×10^{-5} **2.** 1.3×10^3

9.08×10^{-5} 1.3×10^3

10^{-5} is equal to ■. $9.08 \times .00001$ 10^3 is equal to ■. $1.3 \times$ ■

Move the decimal point $.0000908$ **Move the decimal point** $1300.$

■ places to the ■.   **■ places to the right.**

$9.08 \times 10^{-5} =$ ■ $1.3 \times 10^3 =$ ■

Practice

Find each number named in scientific notation.

1. 1.61×10^2 **2.** 8.4×10^3 **3.** 9.24×10^5

4. 5.29×10^4 **5.** 2.742×10^5 **6.** 3.9×10^2

7. 2.6×10^{-2} **8.** 1.04×10^{-3} **9.** 4.1×10^{-5}

10. 6.08×10^4 **11.** 4.7×10^{-6} **12.** 1.9×10^5

Find the number written in scientific notation in each sentence.

13. The distance from the earth to the sun is about 9.3×10^7 miles.

14. One atom of oxygen has a mass of 2.66×10^{-23} grams.

Do It Together!

15. Write a number in scientific notation. Ask a partner to find the number you named.

16. Pick a decimal number between 1 and 10. Ask a partner to find the product of your number and 10^4.

10.9   Exponential Functions

In some functions, the exponent is a variable. These are called **exponential functions.**

$$y = 2^x \leftarrow \text{exponent is a variable}$$

You can find ordered pairs for these functions by substituting values for the variable. Then, you can make a table of values.

EXAMPLE 1   Find four ordered pairs for $y = 2^x$.
Make a table of values.

$2^0 = 1$

Substitute 0 for x. Simplify 2^0.

Substitute 1 for x. Simplify 2^1.

Substitute 2 for x. Simplify 2^2.

Substitute 3 for x. Simplify 2^3.

x	2^x	y
0	2^0	1
1	2^1	2
2	2^2	4
3	2^3	8

$(0, 1)$, $(1, 2)$, $(2, 4)$, and $(3, 8)$ are four ordered pairs.

EXAMPLE 2   Find four ordered pairs for $y = 2 \cdot 3^x$.
Make a table of values.

Substitute 0 for x. Simplify $2 \cdot 3^0$.

Substitute 1 for x. Simplify $2 \cdot 3^1$.

Substitute 2 for x. Simplify $2 \cdot 3^2$.

Substitute 3 for x. Simplify $2 \cdot 3^3$.

x	$2 \cdot 3^x$	y
0	$2 \cdot 3^0$	2
1	$2 \cdot 3^1$	6
2	$2 \cdot 3^2$	18
3	$2 \cdot 3^3$	54

$(0, 2)$, $(1, 6)$, $(2, 18)$, and $(3, 54)$ are four ordered pairs.

EXAMPLE 3   Find four ordered pairs for $y = -4^x$.
Make a table of values.

-4^x means $-1 \cdot 4^x$.

Substitute 0 for x. Simplify $-1 \cdot 4^0$.

Substitute 1 for x. Simplify $-1 \cdot 4^1$.

Substitute 2 for x. Simplify $-1 \cdot 4^2$.

Substitute 3 for x. Simplify $-1 \cdot 4^3$.

x	$-1 \cdot 4^x$	y
0	$-1 \cdot 4^0$	-1
1	$-1 \cdot 4^1$	-4
2	$-1 \cdot 4^2$	-16
3	$-1 \cdot 4^3$	-64

$(0, -1)$, $(1, -4)$, $(2, -16)$, and $(3, -64)$ are four ordered pairs.

Find five ordered pairs for each function. Make a table of values.

1. $y = 5^x$

Substitute:	x	5^x	y
0 for x	0	$5^{\blacksquare}$	■
1 for x	1	$5^{\blacksquare}$	■
2 for x	2	$5^{\blacksquare}$	■
3 for x	3	$5^{\blacksquare}$	■
4 for x	■	$5^{\blacksquare}$	■

$(0, \blacksquare)$, $(1, \blacksquare)$, $(2, \blacksquare)$, $(3, \blacksquare)$, and $(\blacksquare, \blacksquare)$ are five ordered pairs for $y = 5^x$.

2. $y = 4 \bullet 2^x$

Substitute:	x	$4 \bullet 2^x$	y
0 for x	0	$4 \bullet 2^0$	■
1 for x	1	$4 \bullet 2^{\blacksquare}$	■
2 for x	2	$4 \bullet 2^{\blacksquare}$	■
3 for x	3	$4 \bullet 2^{\blacksquare}$	■
4 for x	■	$4 \bullet 2^{\blacksquare}$	■

$(0, \blacksquare)$, $(1, \blacksquare)$, $(2, \blacksquare)$, $(3, \blacksquare)$, and $(\blacksquare, \blacksquare)$ are five ordered pairs for $y = 4 \bullet 2^x$.

Practice

Find five ordered pairs for each function. Make a table of values.
Begin with $x = 0$.

1. $y = 4^x$ **2.** $y = 3^x$ **3.** $y = -2 \bullet 5^x$

Find four ordered pairs for each function. Make a table of values.
Begin with $x = 0$.

4. $y = 10^x$ **5.** $y = 8^x$ **6.** $y = 20^x$

Do It Together!

7. Explain to a partner how you find the ordered pairs in number **2** in **Practice**.

8. Write x^4 and 4^x. Ask a partner to find the base in each. Then, ask your partner to find the exponent in each. Finally, have your partner find the value of x^4 and 4^x when x is 3. Why are the values different?

10.10 Graphing Exponential Functions

You have written tables of ordered pairs from exponential functions. You can use these tables to graph the ordered pairs.

When you look at the tables, you can see that the value of y increases much faster than the value of x. You cannot connect the points with a straight line. You connect them with a curved line.

EXAMPLE 1

x	3^x	y
0	3^0	1
1	3^1	3
2	3^2	9
3	3^3	27
4	3^4	81

Graph $y = 3^x$ using the five ordered pairs from the table.

Write each row as an ordered pair. (0, 1), (1, 3), (2, 9), (3, 27), (4, 81)

Graph the points on a coordinate plane.

Connect the points with a curve.

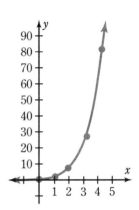

EXAMPLE 2

x	10^x	y
0	10^0	1
1	10^1	10
2	10^2	100
3	10^3	1,000
4	10^4	10,000

Graph $y = 10^x$ using the five ordered pairs from the table.

Write each row as an ordered pair. (0, 1), (1, 10), (2, 100), (3, 1,000), (4, 10,000)

Graph the points on a coordinate plane.

Connect the points with a curve.

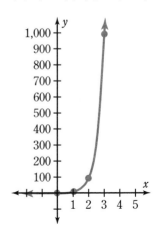

Graph each function using the five ordered pairs from the table.

1. Find five ordered pairs for $y = 4^x$.

x	4^x
0	1
1	4
2	16
3	64
4	256

Write each row as an ordered pair.

(0, 1)

(1, ■)

(2, ■)

(3, ■)

(4, ■)

Write five ordered pairs from the table.

2. Write five ordered pairs from the graph.

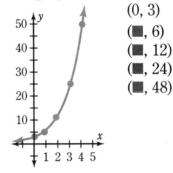

(0, 3)

(■, 6)

(■, 12)

(■, 24)

(■, 48)

Practice

Graph the five ordered pairs for each function from the table.

1.

x	2^x
0	1
1	2
2	4
3	8
4	16

2.

x	$5 \bullet 2^x$
0	5
1	10
2	20
3	40
4	80

3.

x	6^x
0	1
1	6
2	36
3	216
4	1,296

Do It Together!

4. Explain to a partner how you graph the ordered pairs in number **2** in **Practice.**

5. Write an exponential function. Pick a positive number for the base. Use x for the exponent. Have a partner find three values for your function.

10.11 Calculator: Finding Values of Powers

Sometimes, the base of a power is a decimal. You can use a calculator to evaluate a power with a decimal base.

EXAMPLE 1   Find the value. 1.5^3 DISPLAY

Enter 1.5 by pressing: `1` `.` `5` 1.5

Find the second power by pressing: `×` `1` `.` `5` `=` 2.25

$1.5^3 = 1.5 \cdot 1.5 \cdot 1.5$ Find the third power by pressing: `×` `1` `.` `5` `=` 3.375

$1.5^3 = 3.375$

When you find a power of a decimal, the number of decimal places gets larger each time you multiply. You can round your answer to two decimal places.

EXAMPLE 2   Find the value. 1.2^5 DISPLAY

Enter 1.2 by pressing: `1` `.` `2` 1.2

Find the second power by pressing: `×` `1` `.` `2` `=` 1.44

Find the third power by pressing: `×` `1` `.` `2` `=` 1.728

Find the fourth power by pressing: `×` `1` `.` `2` `=` 2.0736

$1.2^5 = 1.2 \cdot 1.2 \cdot 1.2 \cdot 1.2 \cdot 1.2$ Find the fifth power by pressing: `×` `1` `.` `2` `=` 2.48832

1.2^5 is about 2.49

EXAMPLE 3   Find the value. $.25^3$ DISPLAY

Enter .25 by pressing: `.` `2` `5` 0.25

Find the second power by pressing: `×` `.` `2` `5` `=` 0.0625

Find the third power by pressing: `×` `.` `2` `5` `=` 0.015625

$.25^3$ is about .016

Practice

Find the value of each power. Round your answer to two decimal places.

1. 7^4

2. $2 \bullet 4^3$

3. $9 \bullet 5^2$

4. $.1^5$

5. 9^4

6. 4^3

7. 1.8^2

8. $.6^5$

9. 3.8^5

10. 1.2^4

11. 2.9^3

12. 1.31^2

MATH CONNECTION

Chien Shiung-Wu

Chien Shiung-Wu was born in China in 1912. Her name in Chinese means strong hero. As a young girl, she loved solving puzzles. Her interest in puzzles and math led her to study physics.

Madame Wu, as she was known, moved to the United States in 1936. She received her Ph.D. in 1940.

Madame Wu worked in physics. She planned one project that changed science. Her work helped scientists better understand how nuclear particles react.

Madame Wu won many awards for her work. The National Medal of Science was one of the best awards. In the United States, this is the highest award in science you can receive.

Other work she did helped scientists find the cause of sickle-cell anemia. This blood disease causes people to become very weak. Much of her work has helped the whole world!

10.12 Problem Solving: Counting Choices

You can use a **tree diagram** to show choices.

EXAMPLE 1   In a class election, there are 3 candidates for president (Tia, Nelson, and Michael). There are 2 candidates for vice president (Darryl and Joanne). How many ways are there to choose a president and vice president?

Step 1	**Step 2**	**Step 3**
3 choices for president	2 choices for vice president	Make pairs.

Tia
- Darryl —— Tia and Darryl
- Joanne —— Tia and Joanne

Nelson
- Darryl —— Nelson and Darryl
- Joanne —— Nelson and Joanne

Michael
- Darryl —— Michael and Darryl
- Joanne —— Michael and Joanne

total of 6 choices

There are 6 ways to choose.

EXAMPLE 2   There are 3 roads that go from Acton to Belmont. There are 2 roads that go from Belmont to Canton. How many ways are there to go from Acton to Canton if you have to go through Belmont?

Step 1	**Step 2**	**Step 3**
There are 3 roads to Belmont.	There are 2 roads to Canton.	Count the branches.

Acton
- Belmont
  - Canton 1 — 1
  - Canton 2 — 2
- Belmont
  - Canton 3 — 3
  - Canton 4 — 4
- Belmont
  - Canton 5 — 5
  - Canton 6 — 6

total of 6 choices

There are 6 ways to go.

1. Draw a tree diagram to show all the choices for 1 hat and 1 pair of gloves if you have two hats (blue and tan) and three pairs of gloves (black, brown, and red).

2. Now do **Step 3.** List all the possible choices.

   ■ hat and Black gloves
   ■ hat and Brown gloves
   ■ hat and Red gloves

   ■ hat and ■ gloves
   ■ hat and ■ gloves
   ■ hat and ■ gloves

   You have ■ different choices.

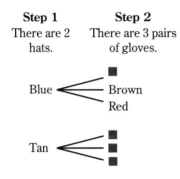

Step 1
There are 2 hats.

Step 2
There are 3 pairs of gloves.

Blue ──< ■ Brown Red

Tan ──< ■ ■ ■

Practice

Find the number of choices using a tree diagram.

1. You have three pairs of socks (red, blue, and white) and two pairs of sneakers (black and green). How many different combinations of socks and sneakers can you wear?

2. You have two hats (blue and green), and four jackets (black, grey, brown, and red). How many different combinations of hat and jacket can you wear?

Do It Together!

3. Explain to a partner how you draw the tree diagram in number **2** in **Practice.**

4. Write a new problem in which you have to choose two different items. Have a partner solve the problem.

10.13 Application: Compound Interest

When you save money in a bank, your money earns interest every month, or year, or other time period. After the first time period, the interest is added to your money for a new total. Then, interest is earned on this new total. So, you earn interest on the interest.

First Period $100.00 at 10% interest earn $10.00
Second Period $110.00 at 10% interest earn $11.00
Third Period $121.00 at 10% interest earn $12.10

This is called **compound interest.** You can use a formula to find your new total.

initial deposit   rate of interest
$$\downarrow \qquad \downarrow$$
$$\text{Total} = a(1+r)^x \leftarrow \text{number of periods}$$

Use a calculator to help you find the power.

EXAMPLE 1

Find the total after 2 years. The initial deposit is $100. The rate of interest is 5% a year. Use the formula $T = 100(1.05)^x$.

$5\% = .05 = .05$

$1 + .05 = 1.05$

$(1.05)^2 = 1.05 \cdot 1.05 = 1.1025$ **Simplify.**

Substitute 2 for x.

$$T = 100(1.05)^x$$
$$T = 100(1.05)^2$$
$$T = 100(1.1025)$$
$$T = 110.25$$

The total is $110.25 after 2 years.

EXAMPLE 2

Find the total after 3 years. The initial deposit is $20. The rate of interest is 10%. Use the formula $T = 20(1.1)^x$.

$$T = 20(1.1)^x$$

$(1.1)^3 = 1.1 \cdot 1.1 \cdot 1.1$ **Substitute 3 for x.** $T = 20(1.1)^3$

$(1.1)^3 = 1.331$ **Simplify.** $T = 20(1.331)$

$$T = 26.62$$

The total is $26.62 after 3 years.

Find the total after 2 years. Use the formula.

1. $T = 1,000(1.08)^x$

                                 $T = 1,000(1.08)^x$

Substitute 2 for x. $T = 1,000(1.08)^\blacksquare$

Simplify. $T = 1,000(\blacksquare)$

                                 $T = \blacksquare$

After 2 years, the total is $\blacksquare$.

2. $T = 500(1.15)^x$

                                   $T = 500(1.15)^x$

Substitute 2 for x. $T = 500(1.15)^\blacksquare$

Simplify. $T = 500(\blacksquare)$

                                 $T = \blacksquare$

After 2 years, the total is $\blacksquare$.

Practice

In each equation find the initial balance and the interest rate.

1. $T = 1,000(1 + .05)^x$ **2.** $T = 200(1 + .10)^x$ **3.** $T = 150(1 + .08)^x$

4. $T = 2,500(1 + .15)^x$ **5.** $T = 10(1 + .05)^x$ **6.** $T = 10,000(1 + .02)^x$

Find each total after the given number of periods.

7. 1 year
$T = 350(1.1)^x$

8. 3 years
$T = 400(1.05)^x$

9. 0 years
$T = 50,000(1.18)^x$

10. 3 years
$T = 10,000(1.16)^x$

11. 2 years
$T = 500(1.1)^x$

12. 1 year
$T = 2,550(1.07)^x$

Do It Together!

13. Explain to a partner how you find the total in number **8** in **Practice.**

14. Pick an initial deposit and an interest rate. Have a partner find the total after 3 years. Check the work.

Chapter 10 Summary

- You write a power using a base and an exponent.
- When the bases are the same, multiply powers by adding exponents.
- When the bases are the same, divide powers by subtracting exponents.
- A power with a zero exponent is equal to 1.
- You use negative exponents to indicate the power is a fraction.
- You can use scientific notation to write very small or very large numbers.
- You can write ordered pairs for a function with an exponent and graph the ordered pairs on a coordinate plane.
- Use a calculator to find the value of powers.
- Use a tree diagram to count choices.
- Use an exponential function to find compound interest.

Reviewing Vocabulary

Fill in each blank with the correct word.

exponent
power
base
scientific notation
exponential functions
tree diagram
compound interest

1. Interest the bank pays on your previous year's interest is called ?.

2. The product of multiplying when the factors are the same is called a(n) ?.

3. You use a(n) ? to see all the choices so you can count them.

4. In 5^3, the 5 is called the ?.

5. Functions of the form $y = a \bullet b^x$ are called ?.

6. In 5^3, the 3 is called a(n) ?.

7. In ?, numbers are written as the product of two factors. The first factor is between 1 and 10. The second factor is a power of 10.

Chapter Quiz

Use exponents to rewrite each product.

1. *www*

2. *stt*

3. *pppqqqq*

Find the value of each power.

4. b^5 when b is -1

5. a^3 when a is 3

6. n^2 when n is 6

Multiply. Write using positive exponents.

7. $-3x^6 \cdot 2x^5$

8. $6b^4c^5 \cdot b^6c^8$

9. $(w^2)^3$

10. $pn^4 \cdot 4n^3$

11. $x^{-3}y \cdot x^3y^{-5}$

12. $(a^0)^4$

Divide. Write using positive exponents.

13. $\dfrac{b^9}{b^7}$

14. $\dfrac{3x^6y}{x^4}$

15. $\dfrac{6c^8d^9}{2cd}$

16. $\dfrac{3b^8}{b^4}$

17. $\dfrac{c}{c^2}$

18. $\dfrac{y^{-3}z^5}{y^2z^6}$

Find each number named in scientific notation.

19. 1.3×10^2

20. 2.7×10^5

21. 1.03×10^{-4}

22. 2.32×10^6

23. 9.8×10^{-3}

24. 3.4×10^4

25. Find five ordered pairs for the function $y = 2^x$. Make a table. Graph the function on a coordinate plane.

26. Use a tree diagram to find how many different combinations of coat and boots you can wear if you have two coats (black and brown) and four pairs of boots (red, yellow, blue, and green).

27. Find the total savings after 2 years. Use the formula $T = 100(1.07)^x$.

Chapter 11

Quadratic Functions and Equations

Functions describe many things in the world around us. The height of a bouncing ball can be described using a quadratic function.

Chapter Learning Objectives

- Graph quadratic functions.
- Find minimum, maximum, and zeros of functions from their graphs.
- Find square roots.
- Find zeros of quadratic functions.
- Solve quadratic equations.
- Use a calculator to find square roots.
- Solve problems by writing quadratic equations.
- Apply concepts and skills to using the vertical motion formula.

Words to Know

quadratic function   an equation in the form $y = ax^2 + bx + c$

degree 2   describes an equation whose largest exponent is 2

minimum   the smallest possible value of y in a function

maximum   the largest possible value of y in a function

zeros   the values of x where a function crosses the x-axis

square   raise a number to the second power

square root   a number that when multiplied by itself gives the original number; The square root of 16 is 4; In symbols, $\sqrt{16} = 4$

quadratic equation   an equation with one variable that has degree 2

quadratic formula   formula to find the solutions of a quadratic equation in the form $ax^2 + bx + c = 0$

In this chapter, you will learn how to graph quadratic functions from tables and learn about the properties of these graphs. You will find the square roots of numbers and then use this skill to find special values of functions. You will also use the quadratic formula to solve quadratic equations. With your calculator, you will find square roots. You will write and use quadratic equations to solve problems. You will use the vertical motion formula to apply your knowledge of quadratic equations.

11.1 Quadratic Functions

This equation is an example of a **quadratic function.**

$$y = x^2 + 3x + 5 \quad \text{The largest exponent is } 2.$$

A quadratic function has **degree 2.**

Quadratic functions	**Not quadratic functions**
$y = x^2$	$y = x^3$
$y = 3 + x^2$	$y = x^2 + x^3$
$y = x^2 + x + 2$	$y = x + 2$

The equations below show the standard form of a quadratic function.

$$y = ax^2 + bx + c$$
$$\downarrow \quad \downarrow \quad \downarrow$$
$$y = 1x^2 + 3x + 2$$

In $y = x^2 + 3x + 2$, $a = 1$, $b = 3$, and $c = 2$. The coefficient of x^2 is 1. The coefficient of x is 3. The constant is 2.

EXAMPLE 1

The coefficient of x^2 is 1.

Find a, b, and c for the quadratic function. $y = x^2 + 4x + 2$

Write in standard form. $\qquad y = 1x^2 + 4x + 2$

Find a. It is the coefficient of x^2. $\qquad a = 1$

Find b. It is the coefficient of x. $\qquad b = 4$

Find c. It is the constant. $\qquad c = 2$

In $y = x^2 + 4x + 2$, $a = 1$, $b = 4$, and $c = 2$.

If a function is not in standard form, you can reorder the terms. First write the x^2 term, then the x term. Write the constant term last. If a term is missing, you can write it as zero.

EXAMPLE 2

Find a, b, and c for the quadratic function. $y = 8x - 3x^2$

Write in standard form. $\qquad y = -3x^2 + 8x + 0$

Find a. It is the coefficient of x^2. $\qquad a = -3$

Find b. It is the coefficient of x. $\qquad b = 8$

Find c. Write the constant. $\qquad c = 0$

In $y = 8x - 3x^2$, $a = -3$, $b = 8$, and $c = 0$.

Find a, b, and c for each quadratic function.

1. $y = 5x^2 + 8$

Write in standard form.	$y = 5x^2 + 0x + 8$
Find a.	$a = \blacksquare$
Find b.	$b = \blacksquare$
Find c.	$c = \blacksquare$

In $y = 5x^2 + 8$, $a = \blacksquare$, $b = \blacksquare$, and $c = \blacksquare$.

2. $y = 6x^2 + 3 - x$

Write in standard form.	$y = \blacksquare - \blacksquare + \blacksquare$
Find a.	$a = \blacksquare$
Find b.	$b = \blacksquare$
Find c.	$c = \blacksquare$

In $y = 6x^2 + 3 - x$, $a = \blacksquare$, $b = \blacksquare$, and $c = \blacksquare$.

Practice

Find a, b, and c for each quadratic function.

1. $y = 2x^2 + 3x + 5$

2. $y = 6x^2 + x - 5$

3. $y = x^2 + x + 1$

4. $y = -x^2 + x$

5. $y = 7x^2 + 6 + x$

6. $y = 9x^2 - 8 + 2x$

7. $y = 8 + 3x^2 + 7x$

8. $y = 9 - 5x - 2x^2$

9. $y = 5x^2 - 4$

10. $y = 6x + 3 + x^2$

11. $y = 2x^2 + 8x - 1$

12. $y = 2 + 3x - 4x^2$

13. $y = 4 - 3x^2$

14. $y = -x^2 - 6x$

15. $y = x^2 - 4 - 6x$

Do It Together!

16. Explain to a partner how to find a, b, and c for the quadratic function in number **4** in **Practice.**

17. Write a quadratic function. Ask a partner to find a, b, and c for your quadratic function. Check the work.

11.2 Graphs of Quadratic Functions

You can make a table of values for a quadratic function.
Then, you can graph the ordered pairs to see the
graph of the quadratic function.

The graph of a quadratic function is not a straight line.
You should connect the points with a curved line.

EXAMPLE 1

Make a table of values.
Then, graph. $y = -x^2$

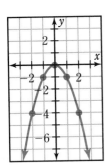

Substitute 2 for **x**. Simplify.

Substitute 1 for **x**. Simplify.

Substitute 0 for **x**. Simplify.

Substitute −1 for **x**. Simplify.

Substitute −2 for **x**. Simplify.

x	$-x^2$	y
2	$-(2)^2$	−4
1	$-(1)^2$	−1
0	$-(0)^2$	0
−1	$-(-1)^2$	−1
−2	$-(-2)^2$	−4

Graph the points on a coordinate plane.

Connect the points with a curved line.

Sometimes, you need to graph many points before you
can see the shape of the curve.

EXAMPLE 2

Make a table of values.
Then, graph. $y = x^2 + 4x + 1$

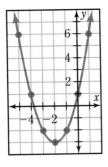

Substitute 1 for **x**. Simplify

Substitute 0 for **x**. Simplify.

Substitute −1 for **x**. Simplify.

Substitute −2 for **x**. Simplify.

Substitute −3 for **x**. Simplify.

Substitute −4 for **x**. Simplify.

Substitute −5 for **x**. Simplify.

x	$x^2 + 4x + 1$	y
1	$(1)^2 + 4(1) + 1$	6
0	$(0)^2 + 4(0) + 1$	1
−1	$(-1)^2 + 4(-1) + 1$	−2
−2	$(-2)^2 + 4(-2) + 1$	−3
−3	$(-3)^2 + 4(-3) + 1$	−2
−4	$(-4)^2 + 4(-4) + 1$	1
−5	$(-5)^2 + 4(-5) + 1$	6

Graph the points on a coordinate plane.

Connect the points with a curved line.

1. Make a table of values for the function.
$y = x^2 + 2x$

2. Find the ordered pairs.

	x	$x^2 + 2x$	y
Substitute 2 for *x*. Simplify.	2	$(2)^2 + 2(2)$	■
Substitute 1 for *x*. Simplify.	1	$(■)^2 + 2(■)$	3
Substitute 0 for *x*. Simplify.	0	$(0)^2 + 2(0)$	■
Substitute −1 for *x*. Simplify.	−1	$(■)^2 + 2(■)$	−1
Substitute −2 for *x*. Simplify.	−2	$(■)^2 + 2(■)$	■
Substitute −3 for *x*. Simplify.	−3	$(-3)^2 + 2(-3)$	■
Substitute −4 for *x*. Simplify.	−4	$(-4)^2 + 2(-4)$	■

Practice

Make a table of values for each function. Then, graph.

Use $x = 2, 1, 0, -1, -2$.

1. $y = 4x^2$ **2.** $y = -x^2 + 3$ **3.** $y = x^2 + 4$

Use $x = 2, 1, 0, -1, -2, -3, -4$.

4. $y = x^2 + 2x + 3$ **5.** $y = 2x^2 + 4x$ **6.** $y = -x^2 - 4x$

Do It Together!

7. Explain to a partner how to graph the function in number **2** in **Practice.**

8. Write a quadratic function in standard form. Use $a = 1$. Have a partner make a table of values for your function. Graph the function.

11.3 Properties of Graphs

The graphs of quadratic equations have some special features. The coefficient of x^2 tells you whether the graph opens upward or downward.

$y = 2x^2 + 2$

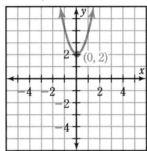

$y = -2x^2 + 2$

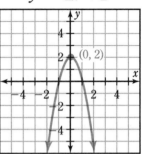

a is the coefficient of x^2.

If *a* is positive, the graph opens upward. It has a **minimum** or low point.

The minimum of $y = 2x^2 + 2$ is at $(0, 2)$.

If *a* is negative, the graph opens downward. It has a **maximum** or high point.

The maximum of $y = -2x^2 + 2$ is at $(0, 2)$.

EXAMPLE 1   Does the graph of $y = -5x^2 + 7$ open upward or downward? Tell whether it has a minimum or maximum.

$$y = -5x^2 + 7$$

Find the value of *a*. $a = -5$

Find the direction.   *a* is negative → graph opens downward

The graph opens downward and has a maximum.

EXAMPLE 2   Does the graph of $y = 2x^2 - x + 3$ open upward or downward? Tell whether it has a minimum or maximum.

$$y = 2x^2 - x + 3$$

Find the value of *a*. $a = 2$

Find the direction.   *a* is positive → graph opens upward

The graph opens upward and has a minimum.

Does the graph of each equation open upward or downward?
Tell whether it has a minimum or maximum.

1. $y = 4x^2 + 2x$

$$y = 4x^2 + 2x$$

Find the value of a. $a = \blacksquare$

Find the direction. The graph opens $\blacksquare$.

Tell whether the graph has a minimum or maximum. The graph has a $\blacksquare$.

2. $y = -2x^2 + 4x + 2$

$$y = -2x^2 + 4x + 2$$

Find the value of $\blacksquare$. $\blacksquare = \blacksquare$.

Find the direction. The graph opens $\blacksquare$.

Tell whether the graph has a minimum or maximum. The graph has a $\blacksquare$.

Practice

Does the graph of each equation open upward or downward?
Tell whether it has a minimum or maximum.

1. $y = -4x^2$

2. $y = 5x^2$

3. $y = -x^2$

4. $y = -3x^2 + 3x$

5. $y = -4x^2 - 2$

6. $y = 2x^2 + 9$

7. $y = x^2 - x + 12$

8. $y = -2x^2 + 2x - 1$

9. $y = 3x^2 - 6x + 7$

10. $y = 4 - 3x^2$

11. $y = 3x - 5 + x^2$

12. $y = 2x^2 - 4x - 8$

Do It Together!

13. Explain to a partner how to tell whether the graph for the equation in number **6** in **Practice** opens upward or downward.

14. Write a quadratic function in standard form. Ask a partner whether the function has a minimum or maximum.

11.4 Zeros

The **zeros** of a quadratic function are the values of x where the graph crosses or touches the x-axis. A quadratic function can have two zeros, one zero, or no zeros. You can find the zeros by looking at where the graph crosses the x-axis.

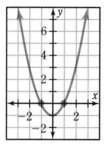

Crosses x-axis
twice

Two zeros

Crosses x-axis
once

One zero

Does not cross
x-axis

No zeros

EXAMPLE 1

The x-axis is the horizontal axis.

Find the zeros from the graph.

Find the ordered pairs where the graph crosses the x-axis. $\quad (-2, 0), (2, 0)$

Find the x-values of the ordered pairs. $\quad -2$ and 2

The zeros are 2 and -2.

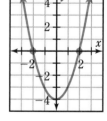

EXAMPLE 2

Find the zeros from the graph.

Find the ordered pair where the graph crosses the x-axis. $\quad (1, 0)$

Find the x-value of the ordered pair. $\quad 1$

The zero is 1.

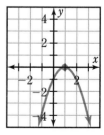

Find the zeros of each quadratic function from its graph.

1. $y = -x^2 + 4$

Find the points
where the graph
crosses the *x*-axis.

(■, ■) and (■, ■)

Find the *x*-values of
the ordered pairs.

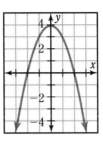

2. $y = x^2 + x + 2$

The line does not
cross the *x*-axis.

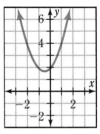

The zeros are ■ and ■.

The function has no zeros.

Practice

Find the zeros of each quadratic function from its graph.

1. $y = x^2 + 2x + 1$

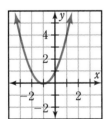

2. $y = x^2 - 1$

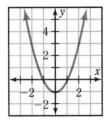

3. $y = x^2 - 6x + 9$

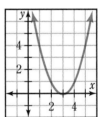

Do It Together!

4. Explain to a partner how to find the zeros in number **2**
in **Practice.**

5. Draw the graph of a quadratic function that has two zeros.
Ask a partner to find the zeros.

11.5 Square Roots

To **square** a number is to multiply it by itself.

$$5^2 = 5 \bullet 5 = 25 \quad \text{and} \quad (-5)^2 = -5 \bullet -5 = 25$$

To find a **square root** of a number, you find one of two equal factors of a number. You will use square roots to find values of quadratic functions.

All positive numbers have two square roots. One is positive, and one is negative. The symbol ± means "positive or negative." For example, ±2 means +2 or −2.

$\pm\sqrt{25} \rightarrow$ the positive or negative square root of $25 = \pm 5$

$\sqrt{25} \rightarrow$ the positive square root of $25 = 5$

$-\sqrt{25} \rightarrow$ the negative square root of $25 = -5$

Negative numbers do not have a square root. You cannot find the square root of a negative number.

EXAMPLE 1   Find the square roots of 16.

Write 16 as a product of two equal factors. $4 \bullet 4 \text{ or} -4 \bullet -4$

The square roots of 16 are 4 and −4.

EXAMPLE 2   Find the value of $\sqrt{144}$.

Write 144 as a product of two $12 \bullet 12$
equal positive factors.

$\sqrt{144} = 12$

EXAMPLE 3   Find the value of $-\sqrt{100}$.

Write 100 as a product of two $-10 \bullet -10$
equal negative factors.

$-\sqrt{100} = -10$

EXAMPLE 4   Find $\pm\sqrt{400}$.

Write 400 as a product of two equal factors. $20 \bullet 20 \text{ or}$
                                                      $-20 \bullet -20$

$\pm\sqrt{400} = \pm 20$

1. Find the square roots of 9.

   Write 9 as a product of two equal factors.
   $3 \bullet \blacksquare$ or
   $\blacksquare \bullet \blacksquare$

   The square roots of 9 are ■ and ■.

2. Find $\pm\sqrt{36}$.

   Write 36 as a product of two equal factors.
   $\blacksquare \bullet 6$ or
   $\blacksquare \bullet \blacksquare$

   $\pm\sqrt{36} = \blacksquare$ or ■

3. Find $-\sqrt{49}$.

   Write 49 as a product of two equal negative factors.
   $\blacksquare \bullet \blacksquare$

   $-\sqrt{49} = \blacksquare$

4. Find $\sqrt{0}$.

   Write 0 as a product of two equal factors.
   $\blacksquare \bullet \blacksquare$

   $\sqrt{0} = \blacksquare$

Practice

Find the square roots of each number.

1. 64
2. 81
3. 100
4. 36
5. 1
6. 169

Find the value of each square root.

7. $\sqrt{121}$
8. $\pm\sqrt{16}$
9. $-\sqrt{9}$
10. $\sqrt{4}$
11. $\pm\sqrt{81}$
12. $-\sqrt{144}$
13. $-\sqrt{169}$
14. $\sqrt{196}$
15. $\pm\sqrt{225}$
16. $\pm\sqrt{256}$
17. $\sqrt{625}$
18. $\sqrt{400}$

Do It Together!

19. Explain to a partner how to find the square roots in number **6** in **Practice.**

20. Think of a number from 1 to 10. Write the square of the number. Have a partner find the square roots of your square.

11.6   Solving Quadratic Equations

To find the zeros of a quadratic function, look for values of x that make $y=0$. To do this, substitute 0 for y in the function. The result is called a **quadratic equation.**

Quadratic function		**Quadratic equation**
$y=ax^2+bx+c$	$\rightarrow$	$0=ax^2+bx+c$
$y=x^2-36$	$\rightarrow$	$0=x^2-36$

Sometimes, you can write a quadratic equation so the x^2 term is on one side and a constant is on the other side. Then, you can use square roots to find the solutions of the quadratic equation. You solve the equation by finding the square roots of the constant.

$$0=x^2-36$$
$$36=x^2$$
$$\pm\sqrt{36}=x$$
$$\pm6=x \quad \rightarrow \quad \text{The solutions are 6 and} -6.$$

Check: 6 and −6.

$0=(6)^2-36 \qquad 0=(-6)^2-36$
$0=36-36 \qquad 0=36-36$
$0=0$ true $\qquad 0=0$ true

EXAMPLE 1   Solve. $x^2-9=40$

Get the x^2 term alone.	$x^2-9=40$
Add 9 to both sides.	$x^2-9+9=40+9$
Simplify.	$x^2=49$
Find the square root of both sides.	$x=\pm\sqrt{49}$
	$x=7$ or $x=-7$

Check: 7 and −7.
$(7)^2-9=40$
$49-9=40$
$40=40$ true

$(-7)^2-9=40$
$49-9=40$
$40=40$ true

The solutions are 7 and −7.

EXAMPLE 2   Solve. $2x^2=18$.

Get the x^2 term alone.	$2x^2=18$
Divide both sides by 2.	$\dfrac{2x^2}{2}=\dfrac{18}{2}$
Simplify.	$x^2=9$
Find the square root of both sides.	$x=\pm\sqrt{9}$
	$x=3$ or $x=-3$

Check: 3 and −3.
$2(3)^2=18$
$2(9)=18$
$18=18$ true

$2(-3)^2=18$
$2(9)=18$
$18=18$ true

The solutions are 3 and −3.

Solve each equation.

1. $x^2 + 20 = 84$

$$x^2 + 20 = 84$$

Subtract ■ from $x^2 + 20 - ■ = 84 - ■$
both sides.

Simplify. $x^2 = ■$

Find the square $x = \pm\sqrt{64}$
root of both $x = 8$ or $x = ■$
sides.

The solutions are ■ and ■.

Check:
$8^2 + 20 = ■ + 20 = 84$ true
$(■)^2 + 20 = ■ + 20 = 84$ true

2. $3x^2 = 48$

$$3x^2 = 48$$

Divide both sides $\dfrac{3x^2}{■} = \dfrac{48}{■}$
by ■.

Simplify. $x^2 = ■$

Find the square $x = \pm\sqrt{■}$
root of both $x = ■$ or $x = ■$
sides.

The solutions are ■ and ■.

Check:
$3 \cdot ■^2 = 3 \cdot ■ = 48$ true
$3 \cdot ■^2 = 3 \cdot ■ = 48$ true

Practice

Solve each equation.

1. $x^2 = 100$

2. $x^2 = 169$

3. $x^2 = 121$

4. $x^2 + 10 = 35$

5. $x^2 - 60 = 4$

6. $x^2 - 11 = 70$

7. $3x^2 = 12$

8. $5x^2 = 45$

9. $10x^2 = 10$

Do It Together!

10. Explain to a partner how to solve the equation in number **4** in **Practice.**

11. Find the square of a number. Write a quadratic equation with the square equal to x^2. Ask a partner to solve the equation. Check the work.

11.7 Zeros and The Quadratic Formula

Sometimes, you cannot find the zeros of a quadratic function easily. To find the zeros of $y = ax^2 + bx + c$, substitute 0 for y and solve for x. When a quadratic equation is in standard form, you can use the **quadratic formula** to solve this equation.

The solutions of $0 = ax^2 + bx + c$ are $x = \dfrac{-b \pm \sqrt{b^2 - 4ac}}{2a}$

So, $x = \dfrac{-b + \sqrt{b^2 - 4ac}}{2a}$ or $x = \dfrac{-b - \sqrt{b^2 - 4ac}}{2a}$.

A quadratic equation has one, two, or no solutions.

EXAMPLE 1

$a = 1, b = -7, c = 12$

Find the zeros of the function. $y = x^2 - 7x + 12$

Substitute 0 for *y*. Use the quadratic formula. $0 = 1x^2 - 7x + 12$

Substitute 1 for *a*, −7 for *b*, and 12 for *c*. $x = \dfrac{-(-7) \pm \sqrt{(-7)^2 - 4(1)(12)}}{2(1)}$

Simplify. Square and multiply first. Then, subtract. $x = \dfrac{7 \pm \sqrt{49 - 48}}{2}$ $x = \dfrac{7 \pm \sqrt{1}}{2}$

Find the square root. Add or subtract. $x = \dfrac{7 \pm 1}{2} \rightarrow x = \dfrac{8}{2}$ or $\dfrac{6}{2}$

Simplify. $x = 4$ or $x = 3$

The zeros of $y = x^2 - 7x + 12$ are 4 and 3.

EXAMPLE 2

$a = 1, b = -5, c = 9$

Find the zeros of the function. $y = x^2 - 5x + 9$

Substitute 0 for *y*. Use the quadratic formula. $0 = x^2 - 5x + 9$

Substitute 1 for *a*, −5 for *b*, and 9 for *c*. $x = \dfrac{-(-5) \pm \sqrt{(-5)^2 - 4(1)(9)}}{2(1)}$

Simplify. Square and multiply first. Then, subtract. $x = \dfrac{5 \pm \sqrt{25 - 36}}{2}$

You cannot find the square root of −11. $x = \dfrac{5 - \sqrt{-11}}{2}$

The function $y = x^2 - 5x + 9$ has no zeros.

1. Write the quadratic formula.

$$\blacksquare = \frac{-\blacksquare \pm \sqrt{\blacksquare^2 - 4\,\blacksquare\,\blacksquare}}{2\,\blacksquare}$$

2. Use the quadratic formula to find $y = x^2 + 4x + 4$.

Substitute 0 for *y*. $0 = x^2 + 4x + 4$

Find *a*, *b*, and *c*. $a = \blacksquare,\ b = \blacksquare,\ c = \blacksquare$

Substitute 1 for *a*, 4 for *b*, and 4 for *c*. $x = \dfrac{-\blacksquare \pm \sqrt{\blacksquare^2 - 4(\blacksquare)(\blacksquare)}}{2(1)}$

Square and multiply. Then, subtract. $x = \dfrac{-4 \pm \sqrt{16 - \blacksquare}}{2}$

Simplify. $x = \dfrac{-4 - \blacksquare}{2}$

$x = \blacksquare$

The zero of $y = x^2 + 4x + 4$ is $\blacksquare$.

Practice

Find the zeros of each function using the quadratic formula.

1. $y = x^2 - 2x + 1$ **2.** $y = x^2 - 3x + 2$ **3.** $y = x^2 - 5x + 6$

4. $y = x^2 - x - 6$ **5.** $y = x^2 + 2x + 1$ **6.** $y = x^2 - 3x - 4$

7. $y = x^2 + 6x + 8$ **8.** $y = x^2 + 8x + 15$ **9.** $y = x^2 - 2x + 15$

10. $y = x^2 - 6x + 5$ **11.** $y = x^2 + 7x + 12$ **12.** $y = x^2 + 9x + 20$

Do It Together!

13. Work with a partner to compare your answers to number **8** and number **9** in **Practice.** What is different about the answers? What is the same?

14. Work with a partner to find the zeros of the function $y = x^2 - x - 30$.

11.8 Calculator: Finding Square Roots

Most numbers do not have square roots that are easy to find. Some calculators have a square root key. If your calculator has a key that looks like √, then you can use it to find the square roots of numbers you do not know. Your calculator will only show you the positive square root. You have to remember to find the negative square root.

EXAMPLE 1 Find the square roots of .0081.   **DISPLAY**

Enter .0081 by pressing: `.` `0` `0` `8` `1`   `.0081`

Find the square root by pressing: `√`   `.09`

Find the other square root.   −.09

The square roots of .0081 are .09 and −.09.

EXAMPLE 2 Find the square roots of 2,025.   **DISPLAY**

Enter 2,025 by pressing: `2` `0` `2` `5`   `2025`

Find the square root by pressing: `√`   `45`

Find the other square root.   −45

The square roots of 2,025 are 45 and −45.

You cannot find the exact square root of most numbers. Their square roots have decimals that go on forever. You can round the square roots to two decimal places.

EXAMPLE 3 Find the square roots of 48.   **DISPLAY**

Enter 48 by pressing: `4` `8`   `48`

Find the square root by pressing: `√`   `6.9282032`

Round to two decimal places.   6.93

Find the other square root.   −6.93

The square roots of 48 are about 6.93 and −6.93.

Practice

Find the square roots of each number.

1. .0009

2. 2

3. 72

4. 150

5. .004

6. .16

7. 3,600

8. 9,000

9. 9,801

10. .025

11. 1.21

12. 160

MATH CONNECTION

Comets

A comet is a frozen ball of dust, water, and gases. A comet flies through space in an orbit. As it nears our sun, the frozen gases melt. This forms the tail. The tail can be up to 10 million kilometers long.

Edmund Halley was a famous astronomer. He studied things in space like moons, planets, and comets. In 1705, he saw a comet and studied it. Back then, no one knew how comets moved. Halley said that they traveled around the sun. He predicted that his comet would return again in 75 years. He was right! This is the famous Halley's Comet. The last time it was seen was 1985. It will not be seen again until 2061.

A comet's orbit is in the shape of a quadratic function. Astronomers use quadratic equations to predict when comets can be seen from Earth. Most comets can only be seen with a telescope. Some comets, like Halley's, can be seen without a telescope.

Many people look at the stars as a hobby. They have discovered some of our comets. You can tell it's a comet by its long white tail. If you live in a place with few street lights, you might discover the next comet yourself!

11.9 Problem Solving: Writing and Using Quadratic Equations

You can write quadratic equations to describe some geometry problems. Sometimes, you do not use both solutions.

EXAMPLE 1 A landscaper needs a garden with an area of 64 square feet. He wants the area of the garden to be a square. How long should the landscaper make the sides of the square?

Write the formula for the area of a square. $A = s^2$

The landscaper wants an area of 64 square feet. So, substitute 64 for A. $64 = s^2$

Solve for s. $\pm\sqrt{64} = s$

Length cannot be negative. Use the positive square root. $8 = s \text{ or } -8 = s$
$8 = s$

To make a square garden with an area of 64 square feet, the landscaper should make the sides 8 feet.

EXAMPLE 2 A coach is planning a field with an area of 75 square feet. She wants the field to be a rectangle. She also wants the length to be 3 times the width. Find the width.

Write an equation for length. length is 3 times width
$$l = 3w$$

Write the area formula. $A = lw$

Substitute 75 for A and 3w for l. $75 = 3ww$

$75 \div 3 = 25$

Solve for w^2. Divide by 3. $75 = 3w^2$

Solve for w. $25 = w^2$
$$\pm\sqrt{25} = w$$

Width cannot be negative. Use the positive square root. $5 = w \text{ or } -5 = w$
$5 = w$

The width is 5 feet. The length $= 3 \times 5 = 15$ feet.

Solve each problem by using a quadratic equation.

1. An architect wants to design a room so that the length is twice the width. She needs the area to be 800 square feet. How long should each side be?

Write an equation for the length.   length is twice the width
$$l = \blacksquare$$

Write the formula for the area of a rectangle. $A = lw$

Substitute ■ for *A* and 2*w* for *l*. $\blacksquare = 2w^2$

Solve for ■. Divide by ■. $\dfrac{\blacksquare}{2} = \dfrac{2w^2}{2} \rightarrow \blacksquare = w^2$

Solve for *w*. Use the ■ square root. $\blacksquare = w$

Find *l*. Use *l* = 2*w*. $l = 2(\blacksquare) \rightarrow l = \blacksquare$

The width of the room is ■ feet and the length is ■ feet.

2. A decorator has 121 square tiles to cover a square area. How many tiles should he put along each side?

Write the formula for the area of a square. $A = s^2$

The decorator has 121 squares to cover the area. Use ■ for area. $121 = s^2$

Solve for *s*. Use the ■ square root. $\blacksquare = s$

There should be ■ tiles along each side.

Practice

Solve each problem by using a quadratic equation.

1. The area of a square is 144 square yards. Find the length of a side.

2. The area of a rectangle is 144 square yards. The length is 4 times the width. Find the length and width of the rectangle.

Do It Together!

3. Work with a partner to find the width of a rectangle. The length of the rectangle is twice its width. The area is 72 square meters.

4. Pick a number and square it. Multiply the squared number by 3. Use that number for *A* in the equation $A = 3w^2$. Ask a partner to solve for *w*.

11.10 Application: Vertical Motion Formula

When an object is dropped, the height of the object is a quadratic function of time. The vertical motion formula describes the height of the object at any time.

$$h = -16t^2 + vt + s$$

h is the height in feet. v is the starting speed.
t is the time in seconds. s is the starting height.

When an object falls or is dropped, the starting speed is 0.

EXAMPLE 1   A rock falls off a cliff 1,600 feet high. At what time is the height of the rock 1,200 feet?

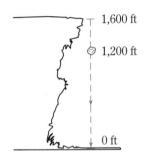

1,600 ft

1,200 ft

0 ft

The height is 1,200.
Starting speed is 0, height is 1,600.
Substitute the values you know into the formula. Simplify.

$$h = -16t^2 + vt + s$$
$$h = 1,200, \ v = 0, \ s = 1,600$$
$$1,200 = -16t^2 + 0t + 1,600$$

Solve for t. Subtract 1,600 from both sides.

$$1,200 = -16t^2 + 1,600$$

Divide both sides by −16.

$$-400 = -16t^2$$

Take the positive square root.

$$25 = t^2$$
$$5 = t$$

The rock is at 1,200 feet after 5 seconds.

EXAMPLE 2   At what time does the rock hit the ground?

The height is 0 on the ground.
Starting speed is 0, height is 1,600.

$$h = -16t^2 + vt + s$$
$$h = 0, \ v = 0, \ s = 1,600$$

Substitute the values you know into the formula. Simplify.

$$0 = -16t^2 + 0t + 1,600$$

Solve for t. Subtract 1,600 from both sides.

$$0 = -16t^2 + 1,600$$

Divide both sides by −16.

$$-1,600 = -16t^2$$

Take the positive square root.

$$100 = t^2$$
$$10 = t$$

The rock hits the ground after 10 seconds.

Solve each problem using the vertical motion formula.

1. A skydiver falls out of a plane at a height of 11,400 feet. Her parachute opens at 5,000 feet above ground. At what time does her parachute open?

Find *h*, *v*, and *s*. Substitute into the formula. Simplify. $\blacksquare = -16t^2 + vt + s;\ h = 5{,}000,\ v = 0,\ s = 11{,}400$

Solve for *t*: $\blacksquare = -16t^2 + 11{,}400$

Subtract ■ from both sides. $\blacksquare = -16t^2$

Divide both sides by ■. $\blacksquare = t^2 \qquad \blacksquare = t$

Use the positive square root. The parachute opens after ■ seconds.

2. You drop a ball off a cliff 400 feet high. How much time will it take for the ball to hit the ground?

Find *h*, *v*, and *s*. Substitute into the formula. Simplify. $0 = -16t^2 + vt + \blacksquare;\ h = \blacksquare,\ v = 0,\ s = \blacksquare$

Solve for *t*: $0 = -16t^2 + \blacksquare$

Subtract ■ from both sides. $\blacksquare = -16t^2$

Divide both sides by ■. $\blacksquare = t^2 \qquad \blacksquare = t$

Use the positive square root. The ball will hit the ground after 5 seconds.

Practice

Solve each problem using the vertical motion formula.

1. A shovel drops down a mine shaft 5,000 feet deep. How much time will it take for the shovel to reach 3,400 feet above the bottom of the shaft?

2. A plant falls from a building 256 feet high. When does the plant hit the ground?

Do It Together!

3. Explain to a partner how to solve the problem in number **1** in **Practice.**

4. Work with a partner and use the number given in **2** in **Practice.** Find at what time the plant reaches a height of 112 feet.

Chapter Review

Chapter 11 Summary

- The standard form of a quadratic function is $y = ax^2 + bx + c$.
- You can graph a quadratic function from a table of values.
- You can tell the direction of a graph and tell whether it has a maximum or a minimum by looking at the coefficient of the x^2 term.
- You can look at the graph to find the zeros of a quadratic function.
- All positive numbers have two square roots. One is positive, and the other is negative. You can use square roots to solve equations.
- You can use the quadratic formula to find the zeros of quadratic functions.
- You can use a calculator to find the square roots of numbers.
- You can write quadratic equations to solve problems.
- You can find the height of a falling object with the vertical motion formula.

Reviewing Vocabulary

Fill in each blank with the correct word.

quadratic function
degree 2
minimum
maximum
zeros
square
square root
quadratic equation
quadratic formula

1. A number that when multiplied by itself gives another number is called a _?_ of the other number.
2. A function of the form $y = ax^2 + bx + c$ is called a _?_.
3. The values of x where a quadratic function crosses the x-axis are called _?_.
4. _?_ describes an equation whose largest exponent is 2.
5. The largest value of y in a quadratic equation is called a _?_.
6. An equation with one variable and degree 2 is called a _?_.
7. The smallest value of y in a quadratic equation is called a _?_.
8. The formula for the solutions of a quadratic equation is called the _?_.
9. To _?_ a number is to raise it to the second power.

Chapter Quiz

Find a, b, and c for each quadratic function.

1. $y = 6x^2 + 8x + 9$ **2.** $y = x + 6x^2 - 8$

Make a table of values for each function. Then, graph. Use $x = 2, 1, 0, -1, -2, -3$.

3. $y = 2x^2$ **4.** $y = x^2 + 2x$ **5.** $y = x^2 + 1$

Tell whether the graph opens upward or downward. Tell whether it has a minimum or maximum.

6. $y = -x^2$ **7.** $y = -4x^2 - 2$ **8.** $y = 2x^2$

Find the zeros of each quadratic function from its graph.

9. $y = 3x^2$ 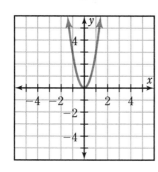   **10.** $y = x^2 - 9$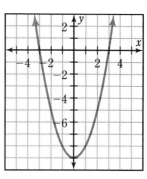

Find each value.

11. square roots of 81   **12.** $\sqrt{100}$ **13.** $-\sqrt{16}$

Solve each equation. Use the quadratic formula if necessary.

14. $x^2 = 9$ **15.** $x^2 + 3 = 28$ **16.** $0 = x^2 - 9x + 18$

17. The area of a rectangle is 180 square meters. The length is 5 times the width. Find the length and width of the rectangle.

Solve using the vertical motion formula: $h = -16t^2 + vt + s$.

18. A pebble falls off a cliff 784 feet high. At what time does it hit the ground?

Chapter 12

Polynomials and Factoring

Quadratic expressions and polynomials are an important part of engineering and construction. Arches and other curved structures are based on quadratic formulas.

Chapter Learning Objectives

- Add, subtract, and multiply polynomials.
- Factor polynomials.
- Solve equations by factoring.
- Use a calculator to check solutions of quadratic equations.
- Solve problems using either factoring or the quadratic formula.
- Apply concepts and skills to using formulas.

Words to Know

polynomial a term or the sum or difference of terms

monomial an expression with one term; a number, a variable, or the product of a number and a variable

binomial a polynomial with two terms

trinomial a polynomial with three terms

factors numbers or variables being multiplied

factor to write an expression as the product of its factors

greatest common factor (GCF) the largest common factor of two or more terms

Zero Product Property if the product of two numbers is 0, then one of the numbers must be 0

In this chapter, you will learn about polynomials, monomials, binomials, and trinomials. In these lessons, you learn how to add, subtract, and multiply polynomials. Then, you will learn how to factor binomials and trinomials. You will use the Zero Product Property and factoring to solve equations. You will use your calculator to check possible solutions of equations. You will solve problems by choosing between factoring or using the quadratic formula. Finally, you will use formulas to solve problems.

12.1 Polynomials

There are special names for some expressions. You can call an expression a **polynomial.** A polynomial is one term or the sum or difference of terms. A **monomial** is a polynomial with one term. A **binomial** has two terms. A **trinomial** has three terms.

A term is a number, a variable, or the product of a number and a variable.

Expression	Number of Terms	Polynomial Name
$-2x$	1	monomial
$3x + 4$	2	binomial
$5x^2 - x + 3$	3	trinomial

EXAMPLE 1   Name the type of polynomial and the constant.
$2x^2 + 3x + 7$

The constant is the number alone.

$$2x^2 + 3x + 7$$
$$\uparrow \quad \uparrow \quad \uparrow$$

Count the terms.

Name the polynomial.   3 terms

$2x^2 + 3x + 7$ is a trinomial. The constant is 7.

EXAMPLE 2   Name the type of polynomial and the constant.
$3x^2 - 8$

$$3x^2 - 8$$
$$\uparrow \quad \uparrow$$

Count the terms.

Name the polynomial.   2 terms

$3x^2 - 8$ is a binomial. The constant is -8.

If you do not see a constant, the constant is 0.

EXAMPLE 3   Name the type of polynomial and the constant.
$3x^2$

$$3x^2$$
$$\uparrow$$

Count the terms.

Name the polynomial.   1 term

$3x^2$ is a monomial. The constant is 0.

Name the type of polynomial and the constant.

1. $6x^2 + 6xy - 3$

$$6x^2 + 6xy - 3$$
$$\uparrow \quad \uparrow \quad \uparrow$$

Count the terms.   ■ terms

Name the constant.   ■

$6x^2 + 6xy - 3$ is a ■.
The constant is ■.

2. $-5n + m$

$$-5n + m$$
$$\uparrow \quad \uparrow$$

Count the terms.   ■ terms

Name the constant.   ■

$-5n + m$ is a ■.
The constant is ■.

Practice

Name the type of polynomial and the constant.

1. $3x^2 + 3x$

2. -5

3. $2x + 6$

4. $-4pq - 3q$

5. $y^2 + 4y - 2$

6. $5k^2 + 3k + 4$

7. $-x^2 + 3xy - 5$

8. 3

9. $-9xy$

10. $-2a^2 - 5b - 6$

11. $3y^2 + y$

12. $5k^2 - 3k - 6$

13. $y^2 - 7y$

14. $w + 5$

15. $x^3 + 2x^2y - 4$

16. $5b^2$

17. $-4 + 3x$

18. $a^2 - 5 - 2a$

Do It Together!

19. Explain to a partner how to name the type of polynomial in number **7** in **Practice.**

20. Write a polynomial with one, two, or three terms. Have a partner count the terms and name the type of polynomial. Check the work.

12.2 Adding Polynomials

To add like terms you add the coefficients. To add polynomials, add like terms from both polynomials.

EXAMPLE 1

x^2 means $1x^2$.
x means $1x$.

Add. $2x^2 + 2x + 2$ and $x^2 + x + 4$

Write the polynomials.	$2x^2 + 2x + 2$
Line up like terms.	$1x^2 + 1x + 4$
Add the coefficients of like terms.	$3x^2 + 3x + 6$

$$(2x^2 + 2x + 2) + (x^2 + x + 4) = 3x^2 + 3x + 6$$

EXAMPLE 2

Add. $3x^2 + 2x - 8$ and $-4x^2 - 2x + 10$

Write the polynomials.	$3x^2 + 2x - 8$
Line up like terms.	$-4x^2 - 2x + 10$
Add the coefficients of like terms.	$-1x^2 + 0x + 2$
Simplify.	$-x^2 + 2$

$$(3x^2 + 2x - 8) + (-4x^2 - 2x + 10) = -x^2 + 2$$

Be sure to line up like terms when some terms are missing.

EXAMPLE 3

Add. $w^2 + 2w - 6$ and $3w^3 + 3$

Write the polynomials.	$w^2 + 2w - 6$
Line up like terms.	$3w^3 + 3$
Add the coefficients of like terms.	$3w^3 + w^2 + 2w - 3$

$$(w^2 + 2w - 6) + (3w^3 + 3) = 3w^3 + w^2 + 2w - 3$$

EXAMPLE 4

$3p^2 + (-3p^2) = 0p^2 = 0$

Add. $3p^2 - 1$ and $-3p^2 - 2p - 4$

Write the polynomials.	$3p^2 - 1$
Line up like terms.	$-3p^2 - 2p - 4$
Add the coefficients of like terms.	$-2p - 5$

$$(3p^2 - 1) + (-3p^2 - 2p - 4) = -2p - 5$$

Add.

1. $a^2 + 2a - 4$ and $-4a^2 + 3a - 6$

Write the
polynomials. $a^2 + 2a - 4$
Line up like terms. $-4a^2 + 3a - 6$
                                    _____
Add the ■ of like $■a^2 + ■a - ■$
terms.

$(a^2 + 2a - 4) + (-4a^2 + 3a - 6) = ■$

2. $-3x - y$ and $2x + 4y + 3$

Write the
polynomials. $-3x - y$
Line up like terms. $2x + 4y + 3$
                                    _____
Add the ■ of like $■x + ■y + ■$
terms.

$(-3x - y) + (2x + 4y + 3) = ■$

Practice

Add the polynomials.

1. $3x^2 + 3x + 1$ and $x^2 + x + 5$

2. $k^2 + k + 2$ and $2k^2 + 3k + 1$

3. $4s - 3t$ and $2s + 5t$

4. $-4a - 2b$ and $3a + 4b$

5. $c^2 + 3c - 3$ and $-3c^2 + 3c - 2$

6. $2x^3 + 4x - 5$ and $-5x^2 + 3x + 1$

7. $x^2 + 3x - 5$ and $4x + 2$

8. $2w^2 + w - 4$ and $3w - 1$

9. $2n^3 - 2$ and $-2n^2 - 3n - 3$

10. $4z^2 - 3$ and $-2z^2 - 5z - 6$

11. $8r - 3$ and $-r^3 + r + 3$

12. y^2 and $-y^2 + 3y$

Do It Together!

13. Explain to a partner how to add the polynomials in number **6** in **Practice.**

14. Write two polynomials with no more than three terms each. Have a partner add the polynomials. Check the work.

12.3 Subtracting Polynomials

You have added polynomials by adding the coefficients of like terms. To subtract a polynomial, you add the opposite of the polynomial.

$-2x^2 - 1x + 2$ is the opposite of $2x^2 + x - 2$.

$$4x^2 + 2x + 5 \qquad\qquad 4x^2 + 2x + 5$$
$$\underline{-(2x^2 + x - 2)} \quad \rightarrow \quad \underline{-2x^2 - 1x + 2}$$
$$\qquad\qquad\qquad\qquad\qquad 2x^2 + x + 7$$

EXAMPLE 1   Subtract $x^2 + x + 2$ from $3x^2 + 3x + 4$.

Find the opposite of $x^2 + x + 2$. $-(x^2 + x + 2) \rightarrow -x^2 - x - 2$

Add the opposite to $3x^2 + 3x + 4$. $3x^2 + 3x + 4$

Add the coefficients of like terms. $\underline{-1x^2 - 1x - 2}$

$$\qquad\qquad\qquad\qquad\qquad 2x^2 + 2x + 2$$

$$(3x^2 + 3x + 4) - (x^2 + x + 2) = 2x^2 + 2x + 2$$

EXAMPLE 2   Subtract $-s^2 - 3s + 2$ from $5s^2 + 4s - 3$.

Find the opposite of $-s^2 - 3s + 2$. $-(-s^2 - 3s + 2) \rightarrow +s^2 + 3s - 2$

Add the opposite to $5s^2 + 4s - 3$. $5s^2 + 4s - 3$

Add the coefficients of like terms. $\underline{+1s^2 + 3s - 2}$

$$\qquad\qquad\qquad\qquad\qquad 6s^2 + 7s - 5$$

$$(5s^2 + 4s - 3) - (-s^2 - 3s + 2) = 6s^2 + 7s - 5$$

EXAMPLE 3   Subtract $5y^3 + 2$ from $3y^2 + 2y - 4$.

Find the opposite of $5y^3 + 2$. $-(5y^3 + 2) \rightarrow -5y^3 - 2$

Add the opposite to $3y^2 + 2y - 4$. $3y^2 + 2y - 4$

Add the coefficients of like terms. $\underline{-5y^3 \qquad\qquad\qquad -2}$

$$\qquad\qquad\qquad\qquad\qquad -5y^3 + 3y^2 + 2y - 6$$

$$(3y^2 + 2y - 4) - (5y^3 + 2) = -5y^3 + 3y^2 + 2y - 6$$

Subtract.

1. x^2+3x-5 from $-3x^2+2x-7$

Find the ▦ of
x^2+3x-5. $-x^2-3x+5$

Add the opposite. $-3x^2+\ 2x-7$

Add the coefficients $\underline{-x^2-\ 3x+5}$

of like terms. $▦x^2-▦x-▦$

$(-3x^2+2x-7)-(x^2+3x-5)=▦$

2. $-4p-2q+3$ from $2p+5q$

Find the opposite of $4p▦2q▦3$
$-4p-2q+3$.

Add the opposite. $2p+\ 5q$

Add the coefficients $\underline{4p+\ 2q-3}$

of ▦ terms. $▦p+▦q-3$

$(2p+5q)-(-4p-2q+3)=▦$

Practice

Subtract the polynomials.

1. $4k^2+2k+3$ from k^2+k+6

2. y^2+y+3 from $3y^2+4y+2$

3. $5m-n$ from $3m+6n$

4. $-2a-3b$ from $3a+b$

5. w^2+2w-4 from $-2w^2+4w-6$

6. $3r^2+2r-7$ from $-4r^3+2r+4$

7. z^3+4z-1 from $5z^2+3$

8. $3x^2+x-3$ from $4x-2$

9. $3h^2-2$ from $3h^2-4h-1$

10. $5s^2-2s$ from $-3s^2-4s-5$

11. y^2+y+2 from y^2

12. $-b^2-b-2$ from $3b+2$

13. $3x^3-1$ from $3x^3-x+1$

14. $-2y^2+3y$ from y^2

Do It Together!

15. Explain to a partner how to subtract the polynomials in number **8** in **Practice.**

16. Write a subtraction problem using two polynomials with no more than three terms each. Have a partner subtract the first polynomial from the second. Check the work.

12.4 Multiplying by a Monomial

You have used the Distributive Property to multiply a binomial by a number. You also can use the Distributive Property to multiply a binomial by a monomial.

$$2x(3x+2)$$
$$2x(3x)+2x(2)$$
$$6x^2+4x$$

EXAMPLE 1 Simplify. $w(4w+3)$

$$w(4w+3)$$

$w \bullet w = w^2$

Use the Distributive Property. $w(4w)+w(3)$

Multiply. $4w^2+3w$

$$w(4w+3)=4w^2+3w$$

EXAMPLE 2 Simplify. $-4x(-2x+5)$

$$-4x(-2x+5)$$

$-4x(-2x)=(-4)(-2)x \bullet x=8x^2$ **Use the Distributive Property.** $-4x(-2x)-4x(5)$

Multiply. $8x^2-20x$

$$-4x(-2x+5)=8x^2-20x$$

You also use the Distributive Property to multiply a trinomial by a monomial.

EXAMPLE 3 Simplify. $3k(k^2-2k+4)$

$$3k(k^2-2k+4)$$

Use the Distributive Property. $3k(k^2)+3k(-2k)+3k(4)$

Multiply. $3k^3-6k^2+12k$

$$3k(k^2-2k+4)=3k^3-6k^2+12k$$

Simplify.

1. $-2a(a-3)$

$-2a(a-3)$

Use the Distributive Property.
Multiply.

$-2a(a-3) = \blacksquare$

$-2a(a)-2a(-3)$
$\blacksquare + \blacksquare$

2. $3x(x^2-2x+1)$

Use the $\blacksquare$ Property.
Multiply.

$3x(x^2-2x+1) = \blacksquare$

$3x(x^2-2x+1)$
$(\blacksquare)(x^2)+(\blacksquare)(-2x)+(\blacksquare)(1)$
$\blacksquare - \blacksquare + \blacksquare$

Practice

Simplify.

1. $3b(2b+4)$

2. $2x(x^2+3x+5)$

3. $y(3y^2+y)$

4. $4w(w^2-2w-5)$

5. $-2s(s-3)$

6. $k(k^2+2k+2)$

7. $-4x^2(x-5)$

8. $-a(2a+3)$

9. $p(p^2-4p+1)$

10. $-2x(x^2+x+6)$

Do It Together!

11. Explain to a partner how to use the Distributive Property in number **4** in **Practice.**

12. Write $(2x+4)$, and then write a monomial. Have a partner multiply the binomial by the monomial. Check the work.

12.5 More Multiplication

You have used the Distributive Property to multiply a monomial by a binomial or a trinomial. You also can use the Distributive Property to multiply a binomial by a binomial.

$$(x+2)(x+3)$$
$$x(x+3)+2(x+3)$$
$$x^2+\underbrace{3x+2x}+6$$
$$x^2+5x+6$$

Multiply each term in the second set of parentheses by each term in the first set of parentheses. Then, simplify.

EXAMPLE 1   Multiply. $(n+4)(n+5)$

$$(n+4)(n+5)$$

$n \bullet 5 = 5n$

Multiply each term of $(n+5)$ by n and 4. $n(n+5)+4(n+5)$

Combine like terms. $n^2+\underbrace{5n+4n}+20$

$$n^2+9n+20$$

$$(n+4)(n+5)=n^2+9n+20$$

EXAMPLE 2   Multiply. $(y-3)(y-4)$

$$(y-3)(y-4)$$

$-3 \bullet -4 = 12$

Multiply each term of $(y-4)$ by y and -3. $y(y-4)-3(y-4)$

Combine like terms. $y^2\underbrace{-4y-3y}+12$

$$y^2-7y+12$$

$$(y-3)(y-4)=y^2-7y+12$$

EXAMPLE 3   Multiply. $(k+2)(k-2)$

$$(k+2)(k-2)$$

Multiply each term in $(k-2)$ by k and 2. $k(k-2)+2(k-2)$

Combine like terms. $k^2\underbrace{-2k+2k}-4$

$$k^2+0-4$$

$$k^2-4$$

$$(k+2)(k-2)=k^2-4$$

Multiply.

1. $(x+2)(x-5)$

Multiply each term in $(x-5)$ by x and 2.
Combine like terms.

$(x+2)(x-5)$
$x(x-5) + \blacksquare(x-5)$
$x^2 - \blacksquare x + 2x - \blacksquare$
$x^2 - \blacksquare x - \blacksquare$

$(x+2)(x-5) = \blacksquare$

2. $(a-3)(a+3)$

Multiply each term in $(a+3)$ by $\blacksquare$ and -3
Combine like terms.

$(a-3)(a+3)$
$\blacksquare(a+3) - \blacksquare(a+3)$
$a^2 + \blacksquare - 3a - 9$
$a^2 + \blacksquare - 9$

$(a-3)(a+3) = \blacksquare$

Practice

1. $(x+1)(x+2)$

2. $(x+3)(x+5)$

3. $(y+4)(y+2)$

4. $(x+3)(x-4)$

5. $(a+4)(a-2)$

6. $(y+4)(y-4)$

7. $(x-5)(x+5)$

8. $(x-3)(x+6)$

9. $(y+1)(y-1)$

10. $(x-1)(x+4)$

11. $(a-2)(a-2)$

12. $(y-2)(y+6)$

13. $(x+2)(x+5)$

14. $(a-4)(a+6)$

15. $(y+3)(y+3)$

Do It Together!

16. Explain to a partner how to do the multiplication in number **2** in **Practice.**

17. Write two binomials with the same variable. Have a partner multiply the binomials. Check the work.

12.6 Factors

Numbers or variables that you multiply are **factors** of the product.

$$2xy \leftarrow \text{product}$$
$$2 \bullet x \bullet y \leftarrow \text{factors}$$

2, x, and y are all factors of $2xy$. $2x$, $2y$, xy and $2xy$ are also factors. Each factor divides the product.

$$\frac{2xy}{2x} = y \qquad \frac{2xy}{2y} = x \qquad \frac{2xy}{xy} = 2 \qquad \frac{2xy}{2xy} = 1$$

EXAMPLE 1   Is 6 a factor of $12ab$?

Write the factors of 12ab. $2 \bullet 2 \bullet 3 \bullet a \bullet b$

Write the factors of 6. $2 \bullet 3$

Look for common factors.   All the factors of 6 are factors of $12ab$.

6 is a factor of $12ab$.

EXAMPLE 2   Is $4x^2y$ a factor of $8x^3y^2$?

Write the factors of 8x³y². $2 \bullet 2 \bullet 2 \bullet x \bullet x \bullet x \bullet y \bullet y$

Write the factors of 4x²y. $2 \bullet 2 \bullet x \bullet x \bullet \quad y$

Look for common factors.   All the factors of $4x^2y$ are factors of $8x^3y^2$.

$4x^2y$ is a factor of $8x^3y^2$.

EXAMPLE 3   Is $2p$ a factor of $7p^2q$?

Write the factors of 7p²q. $7 \bullet p \bullet p \bullet q$

Write the factors of 2p. $2 \bullet p$

Look for common factors.   2 is not a factor of $7p^2q$.

$2p$ is not a factor of $7p^2q$.

1. Is $5x^2$ a factor of $10x^2y$?

Write the factors of $10x^2y$.

Write the factors of $5x^2$.

Look for common factors.

$\blacksquare \bullet \blacksquare \bullet x \bullet x \bullet y$

$\blacksquare \bullet x \bullet x$

$\blacksquare$ the factors of $5x^2$ are factors of $10x^2y$.

$5x^2 \blacksquare$ a factor of $10x^2y$.

2. Is $6xy^2$ a factor of $12xy$?

Write the factors of $12xy$.

Write the factors of $6xy^2$.

Look for common factors.

$6xy^2 \blacksquare$ a factor of $12xy$.

$\blacksquare \bullet 2 \bullet \blacksquare \bullet \blacksquare \bullet y$

$\blacksquare \bullet \blacksquare \bullet x \bullet y \bullet \blacksquare$

$y^2 \blacksquare$ a factor of $12xy$.

Practice

Tell whether the first expression is a factor of the second expression.

1. 3 a factor of $6k^2$

2. 5 a factor of $5xy$

3. a a factor of $2b^2$

4. m a factor of $8mn$

5. $2x$ a factor of $2xy^2$

6. $3w$ a factor of $10w^2$

7. x^2 a factor of xy^2

8. $3s^2$ a factor of $9s^2t$

9. $8x$ a factor of $8x$

10. $2b$ a factor of $6ab^2$

11. xy a factor of $2y^2$

12. mn^2 a factor of $4mn^2$

Do It Together!

13. Explain to a partner how to tell whether $3s^2$ is a factor of $9s^2t$ in number **8** in **Practice.**

14. Write two monomials. Ask a partner to tell whether one of the monomials is a factor of the other.

12.7 Factoring by Finding the Greatest Common Factor

You **factor** when you write an expression as the product of its factors. To factor a binomial or trinomial, find the **greatest common factor (GCF)** of all of its terms. This is the largest factor of all the terms.

$$6x \quad + \quad 3x^2$$
$$3 \bullet 2 \bullet x + 3 \bullet x \bullet x$$

$3x$ is the greatest common factor. Divide each term by $3x$ to find the other factor.

$$\frac{3 \bullet 2 \bullet x}{3 \bullet x} + \frac{3 \bullet x \bullet x}{3 \bullet x} \rightarrow 2+x \text{ is the other factor.}$$

So, $6x + 3x^2 = 3x(2+x)$.

EXAMPLE 1

Factor by finding the GCF. $\quad 4y^3 - 2y^2 + y$

Find the GCF of all three terms.

$$4y^3 - 2y^2 + y$$

$$2 \bullet 2 \bullet y \bullet y \bullet y - 2 \bullet y \bullet y + y$$
y is the GCF.

To find the other factor, divide each term by the GCF.

$$\frac{4y^3}{y} - \frac{2y^2}{y} + \frac{y}{y} \rightarrow 4y^2 - 2y + 1$$

Check by multiplying:

$y(4y^2 - 2y + 1)$

$y \bullet 4y^2 - y \bullet 2y + y \bullet 1$

$4y^3 - 2y^2 + y$

Write the product of the factors.

$$y(4y^2 - 2y + 1)$$

$$4y^3 - 2y^2 + y = y(4y^2 - 2y + 1)$$

EXAMPLE 2

Factor by finding the GCF. $\quad 10x^2y - 15xy$

Find the GCF of both terms.

$$10x^2y - 15xy$$

$$5 \bullet 2 \bullet x \bullet x \bullet y - 5 \bullet 3 \bullet x \bullet y$$
$5xy$ is the GCF.

To find the other factor, divide each term by the GCF.

$$\frac{10x^2y}{5xy} - \frac{15xy}{5xy} \rightarrow 2x - 3$$

Check by multiplying:

$5xy(2x-3)$

$5xy \bullet 2x - 5xy \bullet 3$

$10x^2y - 15xy$

Write the product of the factors.

$$10x^2y - 15xy = 5xy(2x - 3)$$

Factor by finding the GCF.

1. $4x + 8y$

Find the GCF of both terms.

$4x + 8y$
$2 \bullet \blacksquare \bullet x + 2 \bullet \blacksquare \bullet \blacksquare \bullet y$

The GCF of $4x$ and $8y$ is $\blacksquare$.
Find the other factor. Divide each term by the GCF.

$\dfrac{4x}{\blacksquare} + \dfrac{8y}{\blacksquare} \rightarrow \blacksquare + 2y$

Write the product of the GCF and the other factor.
$4x + 8y = \blacksquare$

$\blacksquare(x + 2y)$

2. $6a^2b - 2ab$

Find the GCF of both terms.

$6a^2b - 2ab$
$2 \bullet \blacksquare \bullet a \bullet a \bullet b - 2 \bullet a \bullet b$

The GCF of $6a^2b$ and $2ab$ is $\blacksquare$.
Find the other factor. Divide each term by the GCF.

$\dfrac{6a^2b}{\blacksquare} - \dfrac{2ab}{\blacksquare} \rightarrow 3a - \blacksquare$

Write the product of the GCF and the other factor.
$6a^2b - 2ab = \blacksquare$

$2ab(\blacksquare - \blacksquare)$

Practice

Factor by finding the GCF.

1. $3x + 9y$

2. $10s + 5t$

3. $3k^2 + 8k$

4. $y^2 + 4y$

5. $a^3 + a^2 - a$

6. $y^3 - 3y$

7. $8x^2 - 4x^2y$

8. $12a^3 + 3a^2 + 6a$

9. $20m^2n - 5n$

Do It Together!

10. Explain to a partner how to factor the binomial in number **9** in **Practice.**

11. Multiply a monomial by a binomial. Have a partner factor the product. Check the work.

12.8 Factoring Trinomials

You can use what you know about multiplying binomials to factor some trinomials. In $x^2 + 5x + 6$, the middle term is $5x$. It is positive. The last term, 6, is also positive.

$$\overset{\text{sum of}}{\underset{\downarrow}{\text{2 and 3}}}$$

$$(x+2)(x+3) = x^2 + 3x + 2x + 6 = x^2 + 5x + 6$$

$$\underset{\substack{\uparrow \\ \text{product of} \\ \text{2 and 3}}}{}$$

EXAMPLE 1 Factor. $x^2 + 7x + 10$

$$x^2 + 7x + 10$$

Factor x^2. $(x \quad)(x \quad)$

Check by multiplying:
$(x+2)(x+5)$
$x(x+5) + 2(x+5)$
$(x^2 + 5x) + (2x + 10)$
$x^2 + 7x + 10$

Find two numbers with a product of 10. $1 \bullet 10$ or $2 \bullet 5$

Find the pair with a sum of 7. $2 + 5$

Complete the factors. $(x+2)(x+5)$

$$x^2 + 7x + 10 = (x+2)(x+5)$$

Sometimes, the middle term of the trinomial is negative and the last term is positive.

$$\overset{\text{sum of}}{\underset{\downarrow}{-5 \text{ and } -6}}$$

$$(x-6)(x-5) = x^2 - 5x - 6x + 30 = x^2 - 11x + 30$$

$$\underset{\substack{\uparrow \\ \text{product of} \\ -5 \text{ and } -6}}{}$$

EXAMPLE 2 Factor. $y^2 - 9y + 20$

$$y^2 - 9y + 20$$

Factor y^2. $(y \quad)(y \quad)$

Check by multiplying.
$(y-4)(y-5)$
$y(y-5) - 4(y-5)$
$y^2 - 5y - 4y + 20$
$y^2 - 9y + 20$

Find two numbers with a product of 20. $1 \bullet 20, 2 \bullet 10,$ or $4 \bullet 5$

Use one pair to make a sum of −9. $-4 + -5$

Complete the factors. $(y-4)(y-5)$

$$y^2 - 9y + 20 = (y-4)(y-5)$$

Factor each trinomial.

1. $y^2 + 7y + 12$

Factor y^2. $(y \quad)(y \quad)$

Find two numbers with
a product of 12. $1 \bullet 12; 2 \bullet \blacksquare; 3 \bullet \blacksquare$

Find the pair with a sum of $\blacksquare$. $3 + \blacksquare$

Complete the factors. $(y + \blacksquare)(y + \blacksquare)$

$y^2 + 7y + 12 = \blacksquare$

2. $a^2 - 10a + 16$

Factor a^2. $(\blacksquare \quad)(\blacksquare \quad)$

Find two numbers with a product 16. $1 \bullet 16; 2 \bullet \blacksquare; \blacksquare \bullet \blacksquare$

Use a pair to make a sum of $\blacksquare$. $\blacksquare + \blacksquare$

Complete the factors. $(a - \blacksquare)(a - \blacksquare)$

$a^2 - 10a + 16 = \blacksquare$

Practice

Factor each trinomial.

1. $x^2 + 5x + 4$ **2.** $n^2 + 6n + 8$ **3.** $c^2 + 4c + 4$

4. $y^2 + 9y + 20$ **5.** $a^2 - 4a + 3$ **6.** $y^2 - 5y + 6$

7. $x^2 - 7x + 12$ **8.** $a^2 - 9a + 14$ **9.** $x^2 + 11x + 30$

Do It Together!

10. Explain to a partner how to factor the trinomial in number **4** in **Practice.**

11. Write two binomials. Begin with $(x + \quad)(x + \quad)$. Multiply the binomials. Then, ask a partner to factor the product. Check the work.

12.9 More Factoring Trinomials

You have factored trinomials with a positive last term. Sometimes the last term of a trinomial is negative. Look at the product of binomials to help you factor.

$$\overset{\substack{\text{sum of} \\ -7 \text{ and } 1 \\ \downarrow}}{(x-7)(x+1)} = x^2 + 1x - 7x - 7 = \underset{\substack{\uparrow \\ \text{product of} \\ -7 \text{ and } 1}}{x^2 - 6x - 7}$$

When the last term is negative, the binomial factors are a sum and a difference.

EXAMPLE 1   Factor. $y^2 + y - 12$

$$y^2 + 1y - 12$$

Factor y^2. $(y\ \ )(y\ \ )$

Find two numbers with a product of 12. $1 \cdot 12,\ 2 \cdot 6,\ \text{or } 3 \cdot 4$

Find the pair with a difference of 1. $4 - 3 = 1$

Use the pair to make a sum of 1. $+4 - 3 = 1$

Complete the factors. $(y+4)(y-3)$

$$y^2 + y - 12 = (y+4)(y-3)$$

Check:
$(y+4)(y-3)$
$y(y+4) - 3(y+4)$
$y^2 + 4y - 3y - 12$
$y^2 + y - 12$

EXAMPLE 2   Factor. $x^2 - 2x - 15$

$$x^2 - 2x - 15$$

Factor x^2. $(x\ \ )(x\ \ )$

Find two numbers with a product of 15. $1 \cdot 15 \text{ or } 3 \cdot 5$

Find the pair with a difference of 2. $5 - 3 = 2$

Use the pair to make a sum of −2. $-5 + 3 = -2$

Complete the factors. $(x-5)(x+3)$

$$x^2 - 2x - 15 = (x-5)(x+3)$$

Check:
$(x-5)(x+3)$
$x(x-5) + 3(x-5)$
$x^2 - 5x + 3x - 15$
$x^2 - 2x - 15$

Factor each trinomial.

1. $x^2 + 3x - 18$

Factor x^2.

Find two numbers with a product of 18.

Find the pair with a difference of ■.

Use the pair to make a sum of 3.

Complete the factors.

$x^2 + 3x - 18 = ■$

$x^2 + 3x - 18$
$(x \quad)(x \quad)$
$1 \cdot 18; 2 \cdot ■; 3 \cdot ■$
$6 - 3 = ■$
$+6 - 3 = ■$
$(x + ■)(x - ■)$

2. $a^2 - 8a - 20$

Factor a^2.

Find two numbers with a product of 20.

Find the pair with a difference of ■.

Use the pair to make a sum of ■.

Complete the factors.

$a^2 - 8a - 20 = ■$

$a^2 - 8a - 20$
$(■ \quad)(■ \quad)$
$1 \cdot 20; 2 \cdot ■; 4 \cdot ■$
$■ - 2 = ■$
$-10 + 2 = ■$
$(a - ■)(a + ■)$

Practice

Factor each trinomial.

1. $x^2 + 4x - 5$

2. $h^2 + 9h - 10$

3. $y^2 - 5y - 6$

4. $w^2 + w - 6$

5. $a^2 + 2a - 8$

6. $y^2 - 3y - 10$

7. $x^2 - 6x - 16$

8. $a^2 + 2a - 24$

9. $k^2 + 4k - 12$

Do It Together!

10. Explain to a partner how to factor the trinomial in number **8** in **Practice.**

11. Write two binomials. Begin with $(x - \quad)(x + \quad)$. Use any two numbers for the second terms. Multiply the binomials. Then, ask a partner to factor the product. Check the work.

12.10 Factoring the Difference of Two Squares

Multiplication can show you a way to factor a binomial that is the difference of two squares.

$$\underset{\substack{\uparrow \\ \text{product of the sum and} \\ \text{difference of } x \text{ and } 4}}{(x+4)} \underset{\substack{\uparrow}}{(x-4)} = x^2 + 4x - 4x - 16 = x^2 \overset{\substack{\text{difference of} \\ (x)^2 \text{ and } (4)^2 \\ \downarrow}}{-} 16$$

EXAMPLE 1   Factor. $a^2 - 9$

Find the two squares. $a^2 = (a)^2,\ 9 = (3)^2$

**Write the product of the sum
and difference of a and 3.** $(a+3)(a-3)$

$a^2 - 9 = (a+3)(a-3)$

EXAMPLE 2   Factor. $x^2 - 1$

$$x^2 - 1$$

Find the two squares. $x^2 = (x)^2,\ 1^2 = (1)^2$

**Write the product of the sum
and difference of x and 1.** $(x-1)(x+1)$

$x^2 - 1 = (x+1)(x-1)$

Sometimes the square of the variable term and the square of the number term are in a different order. Keep this order when you factor.

EXAMPLE 3   Factor. $25 - n^2$

$$25 - n^2$$

Find the two squares. $25 = (5)^2,\ n^2 = (n)^2$

**Write the product of the sum
and difference of 5 and n.** $(5+n)(5-n)$

$25 - n^2 = (5+n)(5-n)$

Factor.

1. $x^2 - 36$

$x^2 - 36$
$x^2 = (x)^2$
$36 = \blacksquare^2$

Find the two
squares.

Write the product of
the sum and difference
of x and 6.

$(x + \blacksquare)(x - \blacksquare)$

$x^2 - 36 = \blacksquare$.

2. $100 - y^2$

$100 - y^2$
$100 = \blacksquare^2$
$y^2 = (y)^2$

Find the two
squares.

Write the product of
the sum and difference
of 10 and y

$(\blacksquare + y)(\blacksquare - y)$

$100 - y^2 = \blacksquare$.

Practice

Factor as the product of two binomials.

1. $x^2 - 64$

2. $n^2 - 4$

3. $49 - c^2$

4. $y^2 - 1$

5. $a^2 - 81$

6. $144 - k^2$

7. $x^2 - 400$

8. $a^2 - 121$

9. $b^2 - 169$

10. $n^2 - 225$

11. $625 - x^2$

12. $c^2 - 256$

Do It Together!

13. Explain to a partner how to factor number **4** in **Practice.**

14. Write a positive number. Find its square. Use the square to write the difference of two squares. Ask a partner to factor as the product of two binomials. Check the work.

12.11 Using the Zero Product Property

If the product of two factors is 0, then at least one factor must be 0. This is called the **Zero Product Property.**

$$x \bullet y = 0$$

means $x = 0$ or $y = 0$

You can use this property to find the solutions of quadratic equations that equal 0.

$$(x - 2)(x + 4) = 0$$

means $x - 2 = 0$ or $x + 4 = 0$

So, to solve $(x - 2)(x + 4) = 0$, solve:

$x - 2 = 0$ and	$x + 4 = 0$
$x - 2 + 2 = 0 + 2$	$x + 4 - 4 = 0 - 4$
$x = 2$	$x = -4$
Solution: 2	Solution: -4

EXAMPLE 1   Solve. Then, check. $(x - 6)(x + 5) = 0$

Let each factor equal 0. $x - 6 = 0$ or $x + 5 = 0$

Check: 6 and -5

$(6 - 6)(6 + 5) = 0$
$0(11) = 0$
$0 = 0$ true

Solve $x - 6 = 0$.

$x - 6 = 0$

$x = 6$

$(-5 - 6)(-5 + 5) = 0$
$(-11)0 = 0$
$0 = 0$ true

Solve $x + 5 = 0$.

$x + 5 = 0$

$x = -5$

The solutions of $(x - 6)(x + 5) = 0$ are 6 and -5.

EXAMPLE 2   Solve. Then, check. $x(2x - 8) = 0$

Let each factor equal 0. $x = 0$ or $2x - 8 = 0$

Solve $x = 0$. $x = 0$

Check:
$0(2 \bullet 0 - 8) = 0$
$0(-8) = 0$
$0 = 0$ true

Solve $2x - 8 = 0$.

$2x - 8 = 0$

$2x = 8$

$\dfrac{2x}{2} = \dfrac{8}{2}$

$4(2 \bullet 4 - 8) = 0$
$4(8 - 8) = 0$
$4(0) = 0$
$0 = 0$ true

$x = 4$

The solutions of $x(2x - 8) = 0$ are 0 and 4.

Solve. Then, check.

1. $3y(y-5)=0$

$$3y(y-5)=0$$
$$3y=0 \text{ or } \blacksquare=0$$

Let each factor equal ■.

Solve $3y=0$. $\qquad 3y=\blacksquare$
$$y=\blacksquare$$

Solve $y-5=0$. $\qquad y-5=0$
$$y=\blacksquare$$

The solutions of $3y(y-5)=0$ are ■ and ■.

Check: 0	Check: 5
$3y(y-5)=0$	$3y(y-5)=0$
$3\blacksquare(\blacksquare-5)=0$	$3\,\blacksquare(\blacksquare-5)=0$
$\blacksquare(-5)=0$	$15(\blacksquare)=0$
true $0=0$	true $0=0$

2. $(x+2)(3x+9)=0$

$$(x+2)(3x+9)=0$$
$$\blacksquare=0 \text{ or } \blacksquare=0$$

Let each factor equal ■.

Solve $x+2=0$. $\qquad x+2=0$
$$x=\blacksquare$$

Solve $3x+9=0$. $\qquad 3x+9=0$
$$3x=\blacksquare$$
$$x=\blacksquare$$

The solutions of $(x+2)(3x+9)=0$ are ■ and ■.

Check: −2	Check: −3
$(x+2)(3x+9)=0$	$(x+2)(3x+9)=0$
$(\blacksquare+2)(3\blacksquare+9)=0$	$(\blacksquare+2)(3\blacksquare+9)=0$
$\blacksquare(\blacksquare+9)=0$	$\blacksquare(\blacksquare+9)=0$
true $0=0$	true $0=0$

Practice

Solve. Then, check.

1. $x(x+3)=0$

2. $z(z-6)=0$

3. $2y(y-7)=0$

4. $4x(x+1)=0$

5. $(y+2)(y-2)=0$

6. $(a-4)(a+4)=0$

7. $(z+4)(4z+8)=0$

8. $(3y+6)(y+5)=0$

9. $(3x-12)(x-5)=0$

Do It Together!

10. Explain to a partner how to solve the equation in number **7** in **Practice.**

11. Write an equation with the product of two binomials equal to zero. Ask a partner to solve the equation. Check the work.

12.12 Solving Equations by Factoring

The equations you have solved were already factored on one side. The other side was 0. Sometimes, one side of the equation is a binomial or trinomial and the other side is 0. Factor the binomial or trinomial. Then, solve.

EXAMPLE 1   Solve. $y^2 - 16 = 0$

Factor the difference of two squares. $y^2 - 16 = 0$

$$(y+4)(y-4) = 0$$

Check: −4 and 4

$(-4)^2 - 16 = 0$

$16 - 16 = 0$

$0 = 0$ true

Let each factor equal 0. $y+4 = 0$ or $y-4 = 0$

Solve $y+4 = 0$. $y+4 = 0$

$$y = -4$$

$(4)^2 - 16 = 0$

$16 - 16 = 0$

$0 = 0$ true

Solve $y-4 = 0$. $y-4 = 0$

$$y = 4$$

The solutions of $y^2 - 16 = 0$ are −4 and 4.

EXAMPLE 2   Solve. $v^2 - 5v - 14 = 0$

Factor the trinomial. $v^2 - 5v - 14 = 0$

$$(v+2)(v-7) = 0$$

Check: −2 and 7

$(-2)^2 - 5(-2) - 14 = 0$

$4 + 10 - 14 = 0$

$14 - 14 = 0$

$0 = 0$ true

Let each factor equal 0. $v+2 = 0$ or $v-7 = 0$

Solve $v+2 = 0$. $v+2 = 0$

$$v = -2$$

$(7)^2 - 5(7) - 14 = 0$

$49 - 35 - 14 = 0$

$14 - 14 = 0$

$0 = 0$ true

Solve $v-7 = 0$. $v-7 = 0$

$$v = 7$$

Solutions of $v^2 - 5v - 14 = 0$ are −2 and 7.

EXAMPLE 3   Solve. $0 = x^2 + 4x + 4$

Factor the trinomial. $0 = x^2 + 4x + 4$

Both factors are the same. $0 = (x+2)(x+2)$

Check: $x = -2$

$0 = (-2)^2 + 4(-2) + 4$

$0 = 4 - 8 + 4$

$0 = -4 + 4$

$0 = 0$ true

Let either factor equal 0. $0 = x+2$

$$-2 = x$$

The solution of $0 = x^2 + 4x + 4$ is −2.

Solve.

1. $y^2 + 4y = 0$

$$y^2 + 4y = 0$$

Factor the binomial. $y(y + \blacksquare)$

Let each factor equal 0. $y = 0$ or $y + \blacksquare = 0$

Solve $y = \blacksquare$. $y = \blacksquare$

Solve $y + 4 = 0$. $y + \blacksquare = 0$

$$y = \blacksquare$$

The solutions of $y^2 + 4y = 0$ are $\blacksquare$ and $\blacksquare$.

2. $x^2 - 10x + 25 = 0$

$$x^2 - 10x + 25 = 0$$

Factor the trinomial. $(x - \blacksquare)(x - \blacksquare)$

$$x - \blacksquare = 0$$

The factors are the same. Let one factor equal 0. $x = \blacksquare$

The solution of $x^2 - 10x + 25 = 0$ is $\blacksquare$.

Practice

Solve.

1. $y^2 + 2y + 1 = 0$

2. $x^2 + 7x + 10 = 0$

3. $y^2 - 8y + 16 = 0$

4. $x^2 - 9x + 18 = 0$

5. $a^2 - 49 = 0$

6. $y^2 + 6y - 7 = 0$

7. $y^2 + 2y - 15 = 0$

8. $v^2 - 25 = 0$

9. $a^2 - 5a - 36 = 0$

10. $x^2 - 10x + 16 = 0$

11. $n^2 + 3n - 28 = 0$

12. $y^2 + 19y + 48 = 0$

Do It Together!

13. Explain to a partner how to solve the equation in number **3** in **Practice.**

14. Write two binomials and multiply them. Use the product to write an equation equal to 0. Ask a partner to solve your equation. Check the work.

12.13 Calculator: Checking Solutions

You can use your calculator to check solutions of equations that have a binomial or trinomial on one side and 0 on the other.

EXAMPLE 1 Tell whether 3.1 is a solution of $x^2 + 2.5x - 17.36 = 0$.

Substitute 3.1 for x. $\qquad (3.1)^2 + 2.5(3.1) - 17.36 = 0$

Use your calculator to simplify each term. $\qquad$ DISPLAY

		DISPLAY
Find (3.1)². Enter 3.1 by pressing:	`3` `.` `1`	3.1
$(3.1)^2 = 9.61$ Multiply by 3.1 by pressing:	`×` `3` `.` `1` `=`	9.61
Find 2.5(3.1). Enter 2.5 by pressing:	`2` `.` `5`	2.5
$(2.5)(3.1) = 7.75$ Multiply by 3.1 by pressing:	`×` `3` `.` `1` `=`	7.75

Add the 3 terms.

		DISPLAY
Enter 9.61 by pressing:	`9` `.` `6` `1`	9.61
Add 7.75 by pressing:	`+` `7` `.` `7` `5`	17.36
Subtract 17.36 by pressing:	`−` `1` `7` `.` `3` `6` `=`	0

3.1 is a solution of $x^2 + 2.5x - 17.36 = 0$.

EXAMPLE 2 Tell whether 2.5 is a solution of $2x^2 - 12.5 = 0$.

Substitute 2.5 for x. $\qquad 2(2.5)^2 - 12.5$

Use your calculator to simplify the first term. $\qquad$ DISPLAY

		DISPLAY
Find (2.5)². Enter 2.5 by pressing:	`2` `.` `5`	2.5
$(2.5)^2 = 6.25$ Multiply by 2.5 by pressing:	`×` `2` `.` `5` `=`	6.25
Multiply 6.25 by 2 by pressing:	`×` `2` `=`	12.5
$2(2.5)^2 = 12.5$ Subtract the two terms.	$12.5 - 12.5 = 0$	

2.5 is a solution of $2x^2 - 12.5 = 0$.

Practice

Tell whether the number is a solution of the trinomial.

1. $.08; v^2 - 2.08v + .16 = 0$

2. $4.2; x^2 + 5.1x + 3.78 = 0$

3. $1.6; a^2 - 4.2a + 4.16 = 0$

4. $.15; x^2 + .85x - .15 = 0$

5. $.9; x^2 + 56.1x - 51.3 = 0$

6. $7.9; y^2 + 9.83y - .693 = 0$

Muhammad ibn Musa Al-Khwarizmi

Muhammad ibn Musa Al-Khwarizmi is a very famous mathematician. He wrote about algebra. He lived during the 800s in Baghdad. People at that time went there to learn math and astronomy.

Al-Khwarizmi wrote two important books on arithmetic and algebra. The title of one book is *Hisab al-jabr w' al-muqa-bilah*. This means "the science of putting together and taking apart." We get the word algebra from the word al-jabr.

Some of his books were copied into Latin. This helped people in Europe study his work centuries later. The word *algebra* came to mean the science of equations.

We also get the word *algorithm* from Al-Khwarizmi. A Latin translator called him Algoritmi. This became the word *algorithm*. Algorithm means a rule for solving a problem. One example is the Order of Operations.

12.14 Problem Solving: Choosing the Best Method

You have learned two ways to solve quadratic equations. You can use factoring, or you can use the quadratic formula. For both methods, the equation must be written in standard form.

To solve $ax^2 + bx + c = 0$, factor the polynomial. Or, use the quadratic formula:

$$x = \frac{-b \pm \sqrt{b^2 - 4ac}}{2a}$$

You can choose the method you find easier. You do not have to use the same method all the time

EXAMPLE 1   Solve. $3x^2 - 6x = 0$

Look for common factors in the terms of the polynomial.	$3x^2 - 6x = 0$
Factor out 3x.	$3x(x - 2) = 0$
Let each factor equal 0.	$3x = 0$ or $x - 2 = 0$
Solve 3x = 0.	$3x = 0 \rightarrow x = 0$
Solve x − 2 = 0.	$x - 2 = 0 \rightarrow x = 2$

The solutions of $3x^2 - 6x = 0$ are 2 and 0.

EXAMPLE 2   Solve. $2x^2 + 9x + 4$

There are no common factors. $2x^2 + 9x + 4$

$\dfrac{-b \pm \sqrt{b^2 - 4ac}}{2a}$

Use the quadratic formula.

$$x = \frac{-9 \pm \sqrt{(9)^2 - 4(2)(4)}}{2(2)}$$

$$x = \frac{-9 \pm \sqrt{81 - 32}}{4}$$

$$x = \frac{-9 \pm 7}{4} = \frac{-2}{4} \text{ or } \frac{-16}{4}$$

$$x = -\frac{1}{2} \text{ or } -4$$

The solutions of $2x^2 + 9x + 4$ are $-\dfrac{1}{2}$ and -4.

Solve each equation. Use factoring or the quadratic formula.

1. $x^2 + 5x + 6 = 0$

    There are no common factors. $x^2 + 5x + 6 = 0$

    Try to factor as the product of two binomials. $(x + 2)(x + \blacksquare) = 0$

    $2 \cdot \blacksquare = 6$ and $2 + \blacksquare = \blacksquare$

    Let each factor equal $\blacksquare$. $x + 2 = 0$ or $x + \blacksquare = 0$

    Solve each equation. $x = -2$ or $x = \blacksquare$

    The solutions of $x^2 + 5x + 6 = 0$ are -2 and $\blacksquare$.

2. $x^2 - 19x - 120 = 0$

    There are no common factors. $x^2 - 19x - 120 = 0$

    Don't know two numbers whose product is $\blacksquare$ and whose difference is $\blacksquare$.

    Use the quadratic formula. $x = \dfrac{19 \pm \sqrt{(-19)^2 - 4(1)(-120)}}{2(1)}$

$$x = \frac{19 \pm \sqrt{361 + 480}}{2}$$

$$x = \frac{19 \pm 29}{2} = \frac{48}{2} \text{ or } \frac{-10}{2}$$

$$x = \blacksquare \text{ or } \blacksquare$$

Practice

Solve each equation. Use factoring or the quadratic formula.
Tell which method you used.

1. $x^2 + 15x - 54 = 0$ **2.** $2x^2 - 8x = 0$ **3.** $x^2 - 19x + 48 = 0$

4. $2x^2 + 2x - 4 = 0$ **5.** $3x^2 - 45x = 0$ **6.** $x^2 + 1x - 72 = 0$

Do It Together!

7. Explain to a partner how to choose which method to use to solve number **4** in **Practice.**

8. Work with a partner to solve $0 = x^2 + 8x - 65$. First, try to solve by factoring. Then, use the quadratic formula.

12.15 Application: Using a Formula

Formulas can help you solve problems. You can use what you know about exponents to use formulas with degree 2.

You can use a formula to find the height of an object thrown upward if you know the amount of time in the air. The formula is $h = 40t - 5t^2$, where h means height in meters and t means time.

EXAMPLE 1   At what height is a ball 4 seconds after it is thrown up in the air?

Write the formula.	$h = 40t - 5t^2$
Substitute 4 for t.	$h = 40(4) - 5(4)^2$
Multiply.	$h = 160 - 80$
Subtract.	$h = 80$

$-5(4)^2 = -5 \cdot 4 \cdot 4$

The ball is 80 meters high 4 seconds after it is thrown up in the air.

You can use a formula to find the number of diagonals in a polygon. The formula is $d = \frac{s^2 - 3s}{2}$. Here, d means diagonals and s means sides.

EXAMPLE 2   Find the number of diagonals in a polygon with 6 sides.

Write the formula.	$d = \dfrac{s^2 - 3s}{2}$
Substitute 6 for s.	$d = \dfrac{6^2 - 3(6)}{2}$
Multiply.	$d = \dfrac{36 - 18}{2}$
Subtract.	$d = \dfrac{18}{2}$
Divide.	$d = 9$

A polygon with 6 sides has 9 diagonals.

Meteorologists find formulas that can be used to predict the average monthly high temperature in some cities. Such a formula is $t = -m^2 + 19m + 19$. The variable t stands for the temperature in degrees Fahrenheit. The variable m stands for the month of the year.

1. Find the average monthly high temperature for February.

$$t = -m^2 + 19m + 19$$

Substitute 2 for m.
$$t = -(2)^2 + 19\blacksquare + 19$$

Multiply.
$$t = \blacksquare + \blacksquare + \blacksquare$$

Add.
$$t = \blacksquare$$

The average monthly high temperature is $\blacksquare°$F.

2. Find the average monthly high temperature for May.

$$t = -m^2 + 19m + 19$$

Substitute 5 for m.
$$t = -\blacksquare^2 + 19\blacksquare + 19$$

Multiply.
$$t = \blacksquare + \blacksquare + \blacksquare$$

Add.
$$t = \blacksquare$$

The average monthly high temperature is $\blacksquare°$F.

Practice

Use the formulas in this lesson to answer each question.

1. Find the height of a ball 2 seconds after it has been thrown.

2. Find the height of a ball 7 seconds after it has been thrown.

3. Find the average monthly high temperature for January from the formula.

4. Find the number of diagonals in a polygon with 8 sides.

5. Find the number of diagonals in a polygon with 9 sides.

Do It Together!

6. Explain to a partner how to use the formula to solve number **1** in **Practice.**

7. Choose a number between 3 and 7. Have a partner find the number of diagonals for a polygon with that number of sides. Check the work.

Chapter Review

Chapter 12 Summary

- You can name a monomial, binomial, or trinomial by counting the terms.
- To add polynomials, line up the like terms and add their coefficients.
- To subtract polynomials, add the opposite of the polynomial.
- Use the Distributive Property to multiply a binomial by a monomial.
- Use the Distributive Property to multiply two binomials. Multiply each term in one binomial by each term in the other binomial.
- The factors of a monomial are the numbers or variables that divide the monomial.
- You can factor some polynomials by finding the greatest common factor of the terms.
- You can factor some trinomials as the product of two binomials. Factor the first term. Then, find two numbers that have a sum or difference equal to the middle term and a product equal to the last term.
- Solve quadratic equations by factoring and by letting each factor equal zero.
- You can use your calculator to check solutions of equations.
- You can use factoring or the quadratic formula to solve problems that have a quadratic equation.
- Formulas can help you solve problems.

Reviewing Vocabulary

Fill in each blank with the correct word.

polynomial
monomial
binomial
trinomial
factors
GCF
Zero Product
   Property
factor

1. A polynomial with three terms is called a _?_.
2. The _?_ means that if the product of two numbers is zero, then one of the numbers must be zero.
3. An expression with one term is called a _?_.
4. A _?_ is a polynomial with two terms.
5. A monomial or the sum or difference of monomials is called a _?_.
6. _?_ are numbers or variables being multiplied.
7. The largest common factor of two or more terms is the _?_.
8. You _?_ an expression when you rewrite it as a product.

Chapter Quiz

Name the type of polynomial.

1. $-10xy$

2. $-3x^2 - xy - 8y^2$

3. $-4a + b$

Combine each pair of polynomials.

4. Add $x^2 + 5x - 8$ and $2x + 6$.

5. Subtract $4x^2 - 8$ from $3x^2 + 4x + 1$.

Multiply.

6. $x(3x + 2)$

7. $-2x(x^2 + x)$

8. $x(x^2 + 3y + 4)$

9. $(y + 3)(y + 9)$

10. $(a - 2)(a - 8)$

11. $(x - 5)(x + 7)$

Tell whether the first expression is a factor of the second expression.

12. Is xy a factor of $5x^2$?

13. Is $2xy$ a factor of $8xy^2$?

Factor by finding the greatest common factor.

14. $a^2 + 4ab$

15. $2k^3 + 4k$

16. $10x^2y - 5xy$

Factor as the product of two binomials.

17. $x^2 + 9x + 8$

18. $x^2 + 8x - 9$

19. $y^2 - y - 12$

20. $y^2 - 12y + 20$

21. $x^2 - 25$

22. $n^2 + 8n + 16$

Solve each equation. Use factoring or the quadratic formula.

23. $6x(x + 4) = 0$

24. $(3a - 12)(a + 5) = 0$

25. $x^2 + 6x + 5 = 0$

26. $x^2 - 49 = 0$

27. $2x^2 - 16x = 0$

28. $x^2 - 18x + 80 = 0$

29. Use the formula $h = 40t - 5t^2$ to find the height in meters of a ball 5 seconds after it is thrown.

Unit Four Review

Simplify each expression.

1. x^5 when x is 2

2. k^2 when k is -6

3. $-\sqrt{64}$

4. $a^2 \bullet a^3$

5. $2x^3y^2 \bullet 4xy^2$

6. $(w^2)^3$

7. $s^0t^{-1} \bullet ts^3$

8. $\dfrac{r^5}{r^2}$

9. $\dfrac{6mn^2}{3m^2n}$

10. $4(x^2+x+8)$

11. $-b(b+3)$

12. $(a+1)(a+3)$

13. $(y-2)(y+8)$

14. $(k-4)(k-4)$

15. $(y-1)(y+1)$

Find each number named in scientific notation.

16. $4.8 \bullet 10^3$

17. $2.85 \bullet 10^5$

18. $1.3 \bullet 10^{-3}$

19. $9.8 \bullet 10^{-5}$

Make a table of values for each function. Use the values of x below. Then, graph.

20. $y=2^x$
$x=0, 1, 2, 3, 4, 5$

21. $y=-x^2$
$x=-2, -1, 0, 1, 2$

22. $y=x^2-5$
$x=-2, -1, 0, 1, 2$

Identify the direction of each graph. Tell whether it has a maximum or a minimum.

23. $y=x^2$

24. $y=4x^2-2$

25. $y=-3x^2$

Factor.

26. $4n^2+6n$

27. a^2-6a+9

28. x^2-4

Solve.

29. $x^2=100$

30. $k^2-10=39$

31. $x(3x+9)=0$

32. $0=(b+8)(b-2)$

33. $a^2+4a+3=0$

34. $x^2+x-12=0$

35. A ball falls off a building 400 feet high. Use the formula $h=-16t^2+vt+s$ to find how much time it will take for the ball to hit the ground. s is the starting height. v is the starting speed, $v=0$.

Chapter 13

Radicals and Geometry

Ancient peoples used right triangles to measure distances and heights. Today, surveyors use right triangles and radical equations to find the heights and distances of things such as buildings, hills, and roads.

Chapter Learning Objectives

- Simplify radicals.
- Solve radical equations.
- Identify the sides and angles of a right triangle.
- Use the Pythagorean Theorem.
- Use a calculator to check equations.
- Solve problems by identifying right triangles.
- Apply concepts and skills to find distance in the coordinate plane.

Words to Know

radical   square root written as a number under a radical sign

irrational number   numbers with decimals that do not end and do not repeat

radical equation   an equation that has a variable under a radical sign

right triangle   a triangle with one right angle and two acute angles

hypotenuse   the side across from the right angle of a right triangle

Pythagorean Theorem   a formula for finding the length of a side of a right triangle when you know the lengths of the other sides; $a^2 + b^2 = c^2$

45°–45°–90° triangle   a right triangle whose acute angles both measure 45°

30°–60°–90° triangle   a right triangle whose acute angles measure 30° and 60°

Pythagorean triple   three positive whole numbers that satisfy the Pythagorean Theorem; The numbers can be the measures of the sides of a right triangle

Distance Formula   a way to find the distance between two points using the Pythagorean Theorem

---

In this chapter, you will add, subtract, multiply, and divide radicals. Then, you will solve equations with radicals. You will learn to recognize right triangles. Then you will learn the Pythagorean Theorem to find the lengths of sides of a right triangle. You will check solutions to radical equations with a calculator. You will use radicals again when you use the Pythagorean Theorem to find the distance between two points.

13.1 Radicals and the Number Line

You have learned about squares and square roots. Square roots are also known as **radicals.**

$\sqrt{3}$ is a radical number.

$\sqrt{}$ is the radical sign. In $\sqrt{3}$, 3 is the radicand.

Radicals can be the square roots of perfect squares, or they can be **irrational numbers.**

4 is a perfect square. Its square root is $\sqrt{4} = 2$.

9 is a perfect square. Its square root is $\sqrt{9} = 3$.

If the radicand is not a perfect square, the radical is an irrational number. The decimal form of an irrational number does not repeat and does not end.

$$\sqrt{2} = 1.414\ldots \qquad \sqrt{3} = 1.732\ldots \qquad \sqrt{5} = 2.236\ldots$$

All the numbers shown on the number line are radicals. Notice that $\sqrt{2}$ is between the radicals of two perfect squares, $\sqrt{1}$ and $\sqrt{4}$.

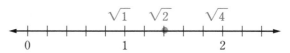

EXAMPLE 1 $\sqrt{7}$ is between what two whole numbers?

Find the closest perfect square less than 7.	4
Find its square root.	$\sqrt{4} = 2$
Find the closest perfect square greater than 7.	9
Find its square root.	$\sqrt{9} = 3$

$\sqrt{7}$ is between 2 and 3.

EXAMPLE 2 $\sqrt{3}$ is between what two whole numbers?

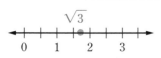

Find the closest perfect square less than 3.	1
Find its square root.	$\sqrt{1} = 1$
Find the closest perfect square greater than 3.	4
Find its square root.	$\sqrt{4} = 2$

$\sqrt{3}$ is between 1 and 2.

1. $\sqrt{6}$ is between what two whole numbers?

Find the closest perfect square less than 6.	4
Find its square root.	$\sqrt{4} = \blacksquare$
Find the closest perfect square $\blacksquare$ than 6.	$\blacksquare$
Find its square root.	$\sqrt{\blacksquare} = \blacksquare$

   $\sqrt{6}$ is between $\blacksquare$ and $\blacksquare$.

2. $\sqrt{11}$ is between what two whole numbers?

Find the closest perfect square $\blacksquare$ than 11.	$\blacksquare$
Find its square root.	$\sqrt{\blacksquare} = \blacksquare$
Find the closest perfect square greater than 11.	16
Find its square root.	$\sqrt{16} = \blacksquare$

   $\sqrt{11}$ is between $\blacksquare$ and $\blacksquare$.

Practice

Locate each square root between two whole numbers.

1. $\sqrt{5}$ is between what two whole numbers?

2. $\sqrt{14}$ is between what two whole numbers?

3. $\sqrt{19}$ is between what two whole numbers?

4. $\sqrt{10}$ is between what two whole numbers?

5. $\sqrt{8}$ is between what two whole numbers?

6. $\sqrt{17}$ is between what two whole numbers?

7. $\sqrt{13}$ is between what two whole numbers?

8. $\sqrt{26}$ is between what two whole numbers?

Do It Together!

9. Explain to a partner how to locate the radical between two whole numbers in number **6** in **Practice.**

10. Write a radical whose radicand is not a perfect square. Ask a partner to locate the square root between two whole numbers.

13.2 Simplifying Radicals

You have found the square roots of perfect squares.
You can simplify radicals that are not perfect squares.
Write the radicand as a product of a perfect square and
another factor. The perfect square should be the
largest one you can find. Then, find the square root of
the perfect square.

$$\sqrt{8} = \sqrt{4 \bullet 2} = \sqrt{4} \bullet \sqrt{2} = 2 \bullet \sqrt{2} = 2\sqrt{2}$$

EXAMPLE 1 Simplify. $\sqrt{12}$

$12 = 1 \bullet 12$

$12 = 2 \bullet 6$

$12 = 3 \bullet 4$

Write 12 as the product of a perfect square and another factor. Use 4 • 3.

Simplify.

Take the square root of the perfect square.

$\sqrt{12}$

$\sqrt{4 \bullet 3}$

$\sqrt{4} \bullet \sqrt{3}$

$2 \bullet \sqrt{3}$

$2\sqrt{3}$

$$\sqrt{12} = 2\sqrt{3}$$

EXAMPLE 2 Simplify. $\sqrt{27}$

$27 = 1 \bullet 27$

$27 = 3 \bullet 9$

Write 27 as the product of a perfect square and another factor. Use 9 • 3.

Simplify.

Take the square root of the perfect square.

$\sqrt{27}$

$\sqrt{9 \bullet 3}$

$\sqrt{9} \bullet \sqrt{3}$

$3 \bullet \sqrt{3}$

$3\sqrt{3}$

$$\sqrt{27} = 3\sqrt{3}$$

EXAMPLE 3 Simplify. $\sqrt{48}$

$48 = 1 \bullet 48$ $48 = 4 \bullet 12$

$48 = 2 \bullet 24$ $48 = 6 \bullet 8$

$48 = 3 \bullet 16$

Write 48 as the product of a perfect square and another factor. Use 16 • 3.

Simplify.

Take the square root of the perfect square.

$\sqrt{48}$

$\sqrt{16 \bullet 3}$

$\sqrt{16} \bullet \sqrt{3}$

$4 \bullet \sqrt{3}$

$4\sqrt{3}$

$$\sqrt{48} = 4\sqrt{3}$$

Simplify.

1. $\sqrt{20}$

**Write 20 as a product of
a perfect square.**
Simplify.

$$\sqrt{20}$$
$$\sqrt{4 \cdot 5}$$
$$\sqrt{4} \cdot \sqrt{\blacksquare}$$
$$\blacksquare \cdot \sqrt{\blacksquare}$$
$$\blacksquare\sqrt{\blacksquare}$$

$$\sqrt{20} = \blacksquare\sqrt{\blacksquare}$$

2. $\sqrt{18}$

**Write 18 as a product of
a perfect square.**
Simplify.

$$\sqrt{18}$$
$$\sqrt{\blacksquare \cdot 2}$$
$$\sqrt{\blacksquare} \cdot \sqrt{\blacksquare}$$
$$\blacksquare \cdot \sqrt{\blacksquare}$$
$$\blacksquare\sqrt{\blacksquare}$$

$$18 = \blacksquare\sqrt{\blacksquare}$$

Practice

Simplify.

1. $\sqrt{24}$　　　　　　**2.** $\sqrt{40}$　　　　　　**3.** $\sqrt{28}$

4. $\sqrt{50}$　　　　　　**5.** $\sqrt{60}$　　　　　　**6.** $\sqrt{54}$

7. $\sqrt{44}$　　　　　　**8.** $\sqrt{72}$　　　　　　**9.** $\sqrt{52}$

10. $\sqrt{63}$　　　　　**11.** $\sqrt{80}$　　　　　**12.** $\sqrt{75}$

13. $\sqrt{90}$　　　　　**14.** $\sqrt{56}$　　　　　**15.** $\sqrt{96}$

Do It Together!

16. Explain to a partner how to simplify the radical in number **2**
in **Practice.**

17. Choose a perfect square and multiply it by 5. Use the product
to write a radical. Ask a partner to simplify the radical.
Check the work.

13.3 Adding and Subtracting Radicals

You add and subtract to simplify radicals the same way you combine like terms.

Like radicals	Unlike radicals
$2\sqrt{3}$ and $4\sqrt{3}$	$\sqrt{3}$ and $\sqrt{5}$
$\sqrt{2}$ and $3\sqrt{2}$	$7\sqrt{2}$ and $2\sqrt{7}$

To add or subtract like radicals, add or subtract the numbers in front of the radicals.

$$2\sqrt{3} + 4\sqrt{3} = (2+4)\sqrt{3} = 6\sqrt{3}$$

EXAMPLE 1 Simplify. $2\sqrt{5} + 3\sqrt{5}$

Add the numbers in front of the like radicals. $2\sqrt{5} + 3\sqrt{5}$

$$5\sqrt{5}$$

$$2\sqrt{5} + 3\sqrt{5} = 5\sqrt{5}$$

A sum or difference may have unlike radicals. First, group like radicals together. Then, add or subtract the like radicals.

EXAMPLE 2 Simplify. $3\sqrt{3} - 4\sqrt{2} + \sqrt{3} + 7\sqrt{2}$

$\sqrt{3} = 1\sqrt{3}$

Group like radicals. $3\sqrt{3} - 4\sqrt{2} + \sqrt{3} + 7\sqrt{2}$

Add the numbers in front of the like radicals. $3\sqrt{3} + 1\sqrt{3} - 4\sqrt{2} + 7\sqrt{2}$
$4\sqrt{3} + 3\sqrt{2}$

$$3\sqrt{3} - 4\sqrt{2} + \sqrt{3} + 7\sqrt{2} = 4\sqrt{3} + 3\sqrt{2}$$

Sometimes, you need to simplify a radical before you can add or subtract.

EXAMPLE 3 Simplify. $\sqrt{8} - \sqrt{5} + 4\sqrt{2}$

Simplify $\sqrt{8}$. $\sqrt{8} - \sqrt{5} + 4\sqrt{2}$

$\sqrt{8} = \sqrt{4} \cdot \sqrt{2} = 2\sqrt{2}$

Group like radicals. $2\sqrt{2} - \sqrt{5} + 4\sqrt{2}$

Add the numbers in front of like radicals. $2\sqrt{2} + 4\sqrt{2} - \sqrt{5}$
$6\sqrt{2} - \sqrt{5}$

$$\sqrt{8} - \sqrt{5} + 4\sqrt{2} = 6\sqrt{2} - \sqrt{5}$$

Simplify.

1. $5\sqrt{6} + 3\sqrt{7} - 2\sqrt{6} + \sqrt{7}$

    Group like radicals.

    Add.

$5\sqrt{6} + 3\sqrt{7} - 2\sqrt{6} + \sqrt{7}$
$5\sqrt{6} - \blacksquare + 3\sqrt{7} + \blacksquare$
$\blacksquare + 4\sqrt{7}$

$5\sqrt{6} + 3\sqrt{7} - 2\sqrt{6} + \sqrt{7} = \blacksquare$

2. $\sqrt{12} - \sqrt{2} + 4\sqrt{3}$

    Simplify $\sqrt{12}$.

    Group like radicals.

    Add.

$\sqrt{12} - \sqrt{2} + 4\sqrt{3}$
$\blacksquare - \sqrt{2} + 4\sqrt{3}$
$\blacksquare + 4\sqrt{3} - \sqrt{2}$
$\blacksquare - \blacksquare$

$\sqrt{12} - \sqrt{2} + 4\sqrt{3} = \blacksquare$

Practice

Simplify.

1. $7\sqrt{2} + 3\sqrt{2}$

2. $5\sqrt{3} - 2\sqrt{3}$

3. $2\sqrt{5} - \sqrt{6} + 4\sqrt{5} + 9\sqrt{6}$

4. $\sqrt{7} + 2\sqrt{7} - 2\sqrt{7}$

5. $5\sqrt{2} - 2\sqrt{2} + 3\sqrt{6}$

6. $\sqrt{11} + 2\sqrt{11} + 6\sqrt{11}$

7. $\sqrt{8} - \sqrt{2}$

8. $7\sqrt{13} + 3\sqrt{7} - 5\sqrt{13} - 4\sqrt{7}$

9. $\sqrt{20} + \sqrt{5} + 3\sqrt{5}$

10. $\sqrt{18} + \sqrt{2} - \sqrt{3}$

11. $\sqrt{7} + \sqrt{24} - \sqrt{6}$

12. $4\sqrt{13} - \sqrt{2} + \sqrt{18}$

Do It Together!

13. Explain to a partner how to simplify number **11** in **Practice.**

14. Write an expression with like and unlike radicals. Ask a partner to simplify it. Check the work.

13.4 Multiplying and Dividing Radicals

You can multiply radicals by first multiplying the numbers outside the radicals. Then, multiply the radicands. Be sure to simplify the radical if needed.

EXAMPLE 1 Simplify. $5\sqrt{2} \cdot 3\sqrt{6}$

$$5\sqrt{2} \cdot 3\sqrt{6}$$

Multiply the numbers outside the radicals, and multiply the radicands. $15 \cdot \sqrt{12}$

Simplify the radical. $15 \cdot \sqrt{4} \cdot \sqrt{3}$

Multiply. $15 \cdot 2\sqrt{3}$

$$30\sqrt{3}$$

$$5\sqrt{2} \cdot 3\sqrt{6} = 30\sqrt{3}$$

To divide radicals, divide the numbers in front of the radicals. Then, divide the radicands.

EXAMPLE 2 Simplify. $\dfrac{18\sqrt{10}}{3\sqrt{2}}$

Divide the numbers outside the radicals, and divide the radicands. $\dfrac{18}{3} \cdot \dfrac{\sqrt{10}}{\sqrt{2}}$

$$6 \cdot \sqrt{5}$$

$$\dfrac{18\sqrt{10}}{3\sqrt{2}} = 6\sqrt{5}$$

Sometimes, you cannot divide the radicals. Do not leave a radical in the denominator. To simplify, multiply the numerator and denominator by the radical in the denominator.

EXAMPLE 3 Simplify. $\dfrac{\sqrt{2}}{\sqrt{3}}$

Multiply the numerator and denominator by $\sqrt{3}$. Then, simplify. $\dfrac{\sqrt{2}}{\sqrt{3}} \cdot \dfrac{\sqrt{3}}{\sqrt{3}}$

$$\dfrac{\sqrt{6}}{\sqrt{9}} = \dfrac{\sqrt{6}}{3}$$

$$\dfrac{\sqrt{2}}{\sqrt{3}} = \dfrac{\sqrt{6}}{3}$$

Simplify.

1. $2\sqrt{15} \cdot 4\sqrt{3}$

$$2\sqrt{15} \cdot 4\sqrt{3}$$

Multiply. $(2 \cdot 4) \cdot (\blacksquare \cdot \blacksquare)$

Simplify the radical. $8 \cdot \sqrt{\blacksquare}$
$8 \cdot \sqrt{9} \cdot \sqrt{\blacksquare}$

Multiply. $8 \cdot \blacksquare \cdot \sqrt{\blacksquare}$
$\blacksquare \cdot \sqrt{\blacksquare}$

$$2\sqrt{15} \cdot 4\sqrt{3} = \blacksquare$$

2. $\dfrac{\sqrt{3}}{\sqrt{48}}$

$$\dfrac{\sqrt{3}}{\sqrt{48}}$$

Cannot divide. So, simplify the radical.

$$\dfrac{\sqrt{3}}{\sqrt{16} \cdot \sqrt{3}}$$

Divide. $\dfrac{1}{\blacksquare}$

Simplify. $\dfrac{1}{\blacksquare}$

$$\dfrac{\sqrt{3}}{\sqrt{48}} = \blacksquare$$

Practice

Simplify.

1. $3\sqrt{5} \cdot \sqrt{18}$

2. $\dfrac{\sqrt{14}}{\sqrt{21}}$

3. $\dfrac{10\sqrt{2}}{\sqrt{8}}$

4. $\sqrt{6} \cdot 4\sqrt{2}$

5. $\sqrt{12} \cdot \sqrt{18}$

6. $\dfrac{2\sqrt{45}}{6}$

7. $\sqrt{3} \cdot 3\sqrt{21}$

8. $\dfrac{4\sqrt{12}}{2\sqrt{3}}$

9. $2\sqrt{10} \cdot 3\sqrt{2}$

10. $2\sqrt{7} \cdot \sqrt{14}$

11. $\dfrac{2\sqrt{75}}{5\sqrt{3}}$

12. $\dfrac{2}{\sqrt{27}}$

Do It Together!

13. Choose one of the division problems in **Practice.** Ask a partner to explain how to solve the problem.

14. Write a multiplication problem with radicals. Ask a partner to simplify. Check the work.

13.5 Radical Equations

An equation that contains a variable in the radical is called a **radical equation.** To solve a radical equation, get the radical alone on one side. Square both sides of the equation. Then, solve the equation. Check your solution.

EXAMPLE 1 Solve. $2\sqrt{y} = 8$

$$2\sqrt{y} = 8$$

Get the radical alone. Divide both sides by 2. $\dfrac{2\sqrt{y}}{2} = \dfrac{8}{2}$

Simplify. $\sqrt{y} = 4$

Square both sides. $(\sqrt{y})^2 = 4^2$

$$y = 16$$

Check: $2\sqrt{y} = 8$
$2\sqrt{16} = 8$
$2 \cdot 4 = 8$
$8 = 8$ true

The solution of $2\sqrt{y} = 8$ is 16.

EXAMPLE 2 Solve. $\sqrt{5b} + 3 = 8$

$$\sqrt{5b} + 3 = 8$$

Get the radical alone. Subtract 3 from both sides. $\sqrt{5b} + 3 - 3 = 8 - 3$

$$\sqrt{5b} = 5$$

Square both sides. $(\sqrt{5b})^2 = 5^2$

Solve for b. $5b = 25$

$$b = 5$$

Check: $\sqrt{5b} + 3 = 8$
$\sqrt{5 \cdot 5} + 3 = 8$
$\sqrt{25} + 3 = 8$
$5 + 3 = 8$
$8 = 8$ true

The solution of $\sqrt{5b} + 3 = 8$ is 5.

EXAMPLE 3 Solve. $\sqrt{2m - 1} = 7$

$$\sqrt{2m - 1} = 7$$

Square both sides. $(\sqrt{2m - 1})^2 = 7^2$

Solve for m. $2m - 1 = 49$

$$2m = 50$$

$$m = 25$$

Check: $\sqrt{2m - 1} = 7$
$\sqrt{2 \cdot 25 - 1} = 7$
$\sqrt{50 - 1} = 7$
$\sqrt{49} = 7$
$7 = 7$ true

The solution of $\sqrt{2m - 1} = 7$ is 25.

Solve.

1. $3\sqrt{2n} = 12$

$3\sqrt{2n} = 12$

Get the radical alone:
Divide both sides by 3. $\dfrac{3\sqrt{2n}}{3} = \dfrac{12}{3}$

$\blacksquare = 4$

Square both sides. $(\sqrt{2n})^2 = 4^2$

Solve for n. $\blacksquare = 16$

$\dfrac{2n}{\blacksquare} = \dfrac{16}{\blacksquare}$

$n = \blacksquare$

$\blacksquare$ is the solution of
$3\sqrt{2n} = 12$.

2. $\sqrt{5t+1} = 4$

$\sqrt{5t+1} = 4$

Square both sides. $(\sqrt{5t+1})^2 = 4^2$

$\blacksquare = 16$

Solve for t. $5t + 1 - \blacksquare = 16 - \blacksquare$

$5t = 15$

$\dfrac{5t}{\blacksquare} = \dfrac{15}{\blacksquare}$

$t = \blacksquare$

$\blacksquare$ is the solution of
$\sqrt{5t+1} = 4$.

Practice

Solve.

1. $3\sqrt{x} = 6$

2. $5\sqrt{n} + 1 = 6$

3. $3\sqrt{3x} = 9$

4. $\sqrt{b} = 3$

5. $\sqrt{n+2} = 2$

6. $\sqrt{4x} = 8$

7. $\sqrt{2p-6} = 4$

8. $\sqrt{6a} - 2 = 4$

9. $\sqrt{6k+4} = 4$

10. $\sqrt{3y} = 3$

11. $\sqrt{9x} = 6$

12. $\sqrt{2a} + 5 = 13$

13. $\sqrt{3w+4} = 5$

14. $6\sqrt{3a} = 18$

15. $\sqrt{3t} = 6$

Do It Together!

16. Explain to a partner how to solve number **7** in **Practice.**

17. Choose a number between 5 and 10. Substitute the number for r in this equation: $\sqrt{x} = r$. Ask a partner to solve the equation.

13.6   Parts of Right Triangles

A right angle measures 90°. **Right triangles** have one right angle. The other two angles in a right triangle measure less than 90°. Angles that measure less than 90° are acute angles. The sum of the measures of all three angles in any triangle is 180°.

The sides of right triangles have special names.

The side opposite the right angle is the **hypotenuse.** The hypotenuse is always the longest side. The sides opposite the acute angles are the legs. The legs form the right angle.

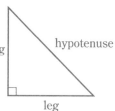

EXAMPLE 1   Name the hypotenuse and the legs.

Find the right angle. The hypotenuse is the side opposite.

The other sides are the legs.

The hypotenuse is *c*. The legs are *a* and *b*.

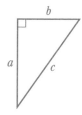

EXAMPLE 2   Name the longest side.

The hypotenuse is always the longest side.

Find the right angle. The hypotenuse is the side opposite.

The longest side is *p*.

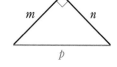

EXAMPLE 3   Which two sides form the right angle?

Find the right angle.

Name the sides that form the right angle.

Sides *p* and *q* form the right angle.

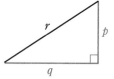

1. Name the legs and the hypotenuse.

   Find the right angle. The hypotenuse is the side opposite.

   The other sides are the legs.

   The hypotenuse is ■. The legs are ■ and ■.

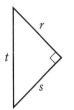

2. Which two sides form the right angle?

   Find the right angle.

   Name the sides that form the right angle.

   Sides ■ and ■ form the right angle.

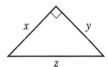

Practice

Name the hypotenuse and the legs of each triangle.

1.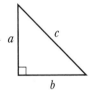

2.

3.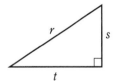

4.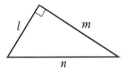

5.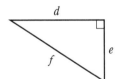

6.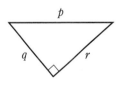

Do It Together!

7. Explain to a partner how to name the sides in number **3** in **Practice.**

8. Draw a right triangle and label the sides with letters. Have a partner name the legs and the hypotenuse of your triangle.

13.7   The Pythagorean Theorem

You have identified the sides of a right triangle. When you know the lengths of two sides of a right triangle, you can find the length of the third. Use the formula known as the **Pythagorean Theorem** to find the length of the third side.

$$a^2 + b^2 = c^2$$
$$\downarrow \qquad \downarrow \qquad \qquad \downarrow$$
$$\text{leg}^2 + \text{leg}^2 = \text{hypotenuse}^2$$

EXAMPLE 1 | Find c.

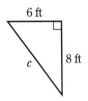

Write the Pythagorean Theorem.	$a^2 + b^2 = c^2$
Find a and b.	a is 6, b is 8
Substitute 6 for a and 8 for b.	$6^2 + 8^2 = c^2$
Simplify.	$36 + 64 = c^2$
	$100 = c^2$

Length is positive, so you do not need to find the negative square root.

Take the square root of both sides.	$\sqrt{100} = \sqrt{c^2}$
Simplify.	$10 = c$

c is 10 feet long.

EXAMPLE 2 | Find a.

Write the Pythagorean Theorem.	$a^2 + b^2 = c^2$
Find c and b.	c is 7, b is 5
Substitute 5 for b and 7 for c.	$a^2 + 5^2 = 7^2$
Simplify.	$a^2 + 25 = 49$
Subtract 25 from both sides.	$a^2 + 25 - 25 = 49 - 25$
	$a^2 = 24$

$\sqrt{24} = \sqrt{4} \cdot \sqrt{6} = 2\sqrt{6}$

Take the square root of both sides.	$\sqrt{a^2} = \sqrt{24}$
Simplify.	$a = 2\sqrt{6}$

a is $2\sqrt{6}$ inches long.

Find the length of each missing side.

1.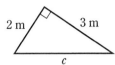

Write the Pythagorean Theorem. $a^2 + b^2 = c^2$

Substitute 2 for *a* and ■ for *b*. $2^2 + ■^2 = c^2$

Simplify. $4 + ■ = c^2$

$$13 = c^2$$

Take the square root of both sides. $\sqrt{13} = \sqrt{c^2}$

Simplify as much as possible. $\sqrt{13} = ■$

c is ■ meters long.

2.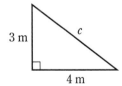

Write the Pythagorean Theorem.   ■

Substitute ■ for *a* and ■ for *c*. $9^2 + b^2 = ■^2$

Simplify. $■ + b^2 = 225$

Subtract ■ from both sides. $■ + b^2 - ■ = 225 - ■$

$$b^2 = 144$$

Take the ■ of both sides. $\sqrt{b^2} = \sqrt{144}$

Simplify. $■ = ■$

b is ■ yards long.

Practice

Find the length of each missing side.

1.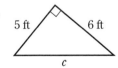

2.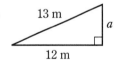

3.

Do It Together!

4. Explain to a partner how to find the length of the missing side in number **2** in **Practice.**

5. Draw a right triangle. Give lengths of two of the sides. Have a partner find the third side.

13.8 Special Right Triangles: 45°–45°–90°

A right triangle with two equal acute angles is a
45°–45°–90° right triangle. If you know one side
of this triangle, you can find the other two sides using
a shortcut.

The lengths of the legs are equal.

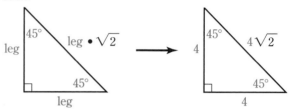

$$\text{leg} = \text{leg}$$
$$\text{hypotenuse} = \text{leg} \cdot \sqrt{2}$$

EXAMPLE 1

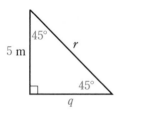

Find the lengths of the missing sides.

Write an equation for the side you know. $\text{leg} = 5$

Write the equation for the hypotenuse. $\text{hypotenuse} = \text{leg}\sqrt{2}$

Substitute 5 for leg. $\text{hypotenuse} = 5\sqrt{2}$

$q = 5$ meters and $r = 5\sqrt{2}$ meters.

EXAMPLE 2

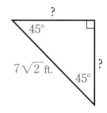

Find the lengths of the legs.

Write an equation for the side you know. $\text{hypotenuse} = \text{leg}\sqrt{2}$

Substitute $7\sqrt{2}$ for hypotenuse. $7\sqrt{2} = \text{leg}\sqrt{2}$

Solve for leg. $\dfrac{7\sqrt{2}}{\sqrt{2}} = \dfrac{\text{leg}\sqrt{2}}{\sqrt{2}}$

$$7 = \text{leg}$$

The legs are 7 feet each.

EXAMPLE 3

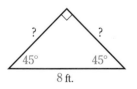

Find the lengths of the legs.

Write the equation for the side you know. $\text{hypotenuse} = \text{leg}\sqrt{2}$

Substitute 8 for hypotenuse. $8 = \text{leg}\sqrt{2}$

Solve for leg. $\dfrac{8}{\sqrt{2}} = \dfrac{\text{leg}\sqrt{2}}{\sqrt{2}}$

Simplify. Multiply numerator
and denominator by $\sqrt{2}$. $\dfrac{8}{\sqrt{2}} \cdot \dfrac{\sqrt{2}}{\sqrt{2}} = \text{leg}$

$$4\sqrt{2} = \text{leg}$$

The legs are $4\sqrt{2}$ feet each.

Find the lengths of the missing sides.

1.

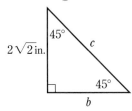

Write the equation for the side you know.

$$\text{leg} = \blacksquare$$

Write the equation for the hypotenuse.

$$\text{hypotenuse} = \text{leg}\sqrt{2}$$

Substitute $2\sqrt{2}$ for $\blacksquare$.

$$\text{hypotenuse} = \blacksquare$$

$b = \blacksquare$ inches and $c = \blacksquare$ inches.

2.

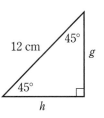

Write the equation for the side you know.

$$\blacksquare = \text{leg}\sqrt{2}$$

Substitute $\blacksquare$ for hypotenuse.

$$\blacksquare = \text{leg}\sqrt{2}$$

Divide both sides by $\blacksquare$.

$$\frac{\blacksquare}{\blacksquare} = \frac{\text{leg}\sqrt{2}}{\blacksquare}$$

Simplify.

$$\blacksquare = \text{leg}$$

The lengths of the legs are $\blacksquare$.

$g = \blacksquare$ centimeters and $h = \blacksquare$ centimeters.

Practice

Find the lengths of the missing sides.

1.

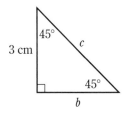

2.

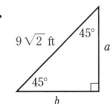

3.

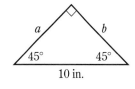

Do It Together!

4. Explain to a partner how to find the legs in number **3** in **Practice.**

5. Draw a 45°–45°–90° right triangle like the ones in **Practice.** Label the length of one leg. Ask a partner to find the measurements of the other two sides.

13.9 Special Right Triangles: 30°–60°–90°

You can also use a shortcut for a **30°–60°–90° right triangle.**

The short leg is opposite the 30° angle. The long leg is opposite the 60° angle.

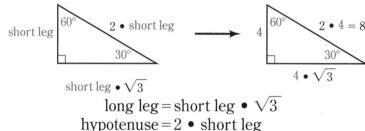

$$\text{long leg} = \text{short leg} \bullet \sqrt{3}$$
$$\text{hypotenuse} = 2 \bullet \text{short leg}$$

EXAMPLE 1   Find the lengths of the sides.

Write an equation for the side you know. $\text{long leg} = \text{short leg}\sqrt{3}$

Substitute 5 for short leg. $\text{long leg} = 5\sqrt{3}$

Write the equation for the hypotenuse. $\text{hypotenuse} = 2 \bullet \text{short leg}$

Substitute 5 for short leg. $\text{hypotenuse} = 2 \bullet 5$

Simplify. $\text{hypotenuse} = 10$

$m = 5\sqrt{3}$ feet and $n = 10$ feet

EXAMPLE 2   Find the lengths of the sides.

Write an equation for the side you know. $\text{long leg} = \text{short leg}\sqrt{3}$

Substitute 6 for the long leg. $6 = \text{short leg}\sqrt{3}$

Solve for the short leg: divide both sides by $\sqrt{3}$. $\dfrac{6}{\sqrt{3}} = \dfrac{\text{short leg}\sqrt{3}}{\sqrt{3}}$

Simplify. $2\sqrt{3} = \text{short leg}$

The hypotenuse is 2 times the short leg. $\text{hypotenuse} = 2 \bullet 2\sqrt{3}$

$$\text{hypotenuse} = 4\sqrt{3}$$

The missing sides are $a = 2\sqrt{3}$ feet and $c = 4\sqrt{3}$ feet.

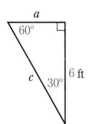

Find the missing sides.

1. Find the length of the short leg.

   Find the side you know. hypotenuse = ■

   Write the equation for the short leg. hypotenuse = 2 • short leg

   Divide by ■. ■ = short leg

   The length of the short leg is ■ meters.

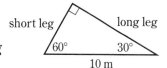

2. Find the length of the long leg.

   Write equation for the long leg. long leg = ■$\sqrt{3}$

   Substitute ■ for short leg. long leg = ■$\sqrt{3}$

   The length of the long leg is ■ meters.

Practice

Find the missing sides.

1.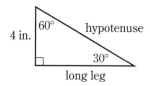

2.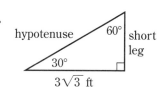

3.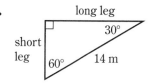

4.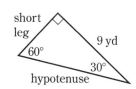

5.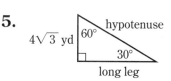

6.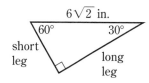

Do It Together!

7. Explain to a partner how to find the long leg in number **3** in **Practice**.

8. Draw a 30°–60°–90° right triangle like the ones in **Practice**. Label the hypotenuse with a measurement between 10 and 20. Ask a partner to find the lengths of the two legs.

13.10 Calculator: Checking Solutions

You can use your calculator to check solutions to radical equations. Most radicals are irrational numbers. Your calculator cannot find an exact value of an irrational number. The calculator display is very close to the exact value. Round the number to two decimal places before you check your solutions.

EXAMPLE 1 Tell whether 4.47 is a solution of the equation $x = \sqrt{20}$.

Substitute 4.47 for x. $4.47 = \sqrt{20}$

Use your calculator to simplify.   DISPLAY

Enter 20 by pressing: [2][0]   20

Find the square root by pressing: [√]   4.472135

4.47 is a solution of $x = \sqrt{20}$.

EXAMPLE 2 Tell whether 9.01 is a solution of $\sqrt{3x} = 5.2$.

Substitute 9.01 for x. $\sqrt{3 \bullet 9.01} = 5.2$

Use your calculator to simplify.   DISPLAY

Simplify the radicand first.   **Enter 3 by pressing:**   [3]   3

Multiply by 9.01 by pressing: [×][9][.][0][1][=]   27.03

Round to 2 decimal places: **Find the square root by pressing:**   [√]   5.19903
5.19903 → 5.20

5.19903 is close to 5.2.

9.01 is a solution of $\sqrt{3x} = 5.2$.

EXAMPLE 3 Tell whether 20 is a solution of $\sqrt{x} + 12 = 18.93$.

Substitute 20 for x. $\sqrt{20} + 12 = 18.93$

Use your calculator to simplify.   DISPLAY

Enter 20 by pressing: [2][0]   20

Find the square root before   **Find the square root by pressing:**   [√]   4.47213
adding.

Add 12 by pressing: [+][1][2][=]   16.47213

16.47 is not close to 18.93.

20 is not a solution of $\sqrt{x} + 12 = 18.93$.

Practice

Tell whether the number is a solution of the equation.

1. $.39;\ \sqrt{50x} = 4.42$

2. $62.8;\ \sqrt{x - 7.2} = 7.46$

3. $96;\ \sqrt{x} + 18 = 27.8$

4. $5.4;\ \sqrt{3.6x} = 10.41$

5. $2.1;\ \sqrt{x + 3.82} = 2.43$

6. $43;\ \sqrt{x} - 2.84 = 1.65$

MATH CONNECTION

Building with Blueprints

Skyscrapers, bridges, tunnels, and houses all have something in common. They were all planned first! Large structures are complicated to build. Before a builder can start, an architect or engineer must make a plan.

Plans for buildings are called blueprints. They show every part, such as walls, floors, doors, and windows. All the measurements for each part are there too. Builders use the plans to make and put together the parts. Both the builders and planners need to know math. Geometric formulas like the Pythagorean Theorem can help them plan and measure the parts.

Architects don't just think about the builders. They think about the purpose of the structure when it's done. Will the inside need elevators or stairs? Does it need heating and cooling systems? What safety features are needed? Will people be comfortable? Will it look nice from the outside? The blueprints will have the answers to all of these questions.

13.11 Problem Solving: Pythagorean Triples

Special groups of three positive whole numbers are called **Pythagorean triples.** When these three numbers are substituted into the Pythagorean Theorem, you get a true equation. These numbers can be the measures of the sides of a right triangle.

$$\text{Pythagorean Theorem} \quad a^2 + b^2 = c^2$$
$$\downarrow \quad \downarrow \quad \downarrow$$
$$3^2 + 4^2 = 5^2$$
$$9 + 16 = 25$$
$$25 \quad = 25 \quad \text{true}$$

The numbers 3, 4, and 5 make a Pythagorean triple. So, a triangle with sides of 3 in., 4 in., and 5 in. is a right triangle.

EXAMPLE 1   Tell whether a triangle with sides 9 in., 12 in., and 15 in. is a right triangle.

The hypotenuse is the longest side of a right triangle. So, substitute the largest number of the triple for c.

Write the Pythagorean Theorem.	$a^2 + b^2 = c^2$
Substitute 9 for a, 12 for b, and 15 for c.	$9^2 + 12^2 = 15^2$
Simplify.	$81 + 144 = 225$
	$225 \quad = 225 \quad \text{true}$

The group 9, 12, and 15 is a Pythagorean triple. A triangle with sides 9 in., 12 in., and 15 in. is a right triangle.

EXAMPLE 2   Tell whether a triangle with sides 4 cm, 10 cm, and 12 cm is a right triangle.

Write the Pythagorean Theorem.	$a^2 + b^2 = c^2$
Substitute 4 for a, 10 for b, and 12 for c.	$4^2 + 10^2 = 12^2$
Simplify.	$16 + 100 = 144$
	$116 \quad = 144 \quad \text{false}$

A triangle with the sides 4 cm, 10 cm, and 12 cm is not a right triangle. 4, 10, 12 is not a Pythagorean triple.

Tell whether the three numbers are measures of the sides of a right triangle.

1. 5, 12, 13

Write the Pythagorean $a^2 + b^2 = c^2$
Theorem.

Substitute ■ **for** a, $■^2 + ■^2 = 13^2$
■ **for** b, **and 13 for** c.

Simplify.   ■ + ■ = ■

   ■ = ■

The numbers 5, 12, and 13 ■ measures of the sides of a right triangle.

2. 50, 120, 130

Write the ■. $a^2 + b^2 = c^2$

Substitute ■ **for** a, $■^2 + ■^2 = ■^2$
■ **for** b, **and** ■ **for** c.

Simplify. $2{,}500 +$ ■ = ■

   ■ = ■

The numbers 50, 120, and 130 ■ measures of the sides of a right triangle.

Practice

Tell whether the three lengths are measures of the sides of a right triangle.

1. 6 ft, 8 ft, 10 ft

2. 10 cm, 24 cm, 26 cm

3. 4 m, 8 m, 10 m

4. 30 yd, 40 yd, 50 yd

5. 10 in., 20 in., 35 in.

6. 15 mm, 20 mm, 25 mm

7. 15 ft, 36 ft, 39 ft

8. 12 m, 16 m, 20 m

9. 6 cm, 8 cm, 12 cm

10. 21 in., 28 in., 35 in.

Do It Together!

11. Explain to a partner how to tell whether the lengths in number **6** in **Practice** are the sides of a right triangle.

12. Work with a partner to find another set of three positive whole numbers that is a Pythagorean triple. Use the Pythagorean Theorem to check your work.

13.12 Application: Finding Distance

You can use the Pythagorean Theorem to find the distance between any two points. Draw the two points on the coordinate plane. The line between them is the hypotenuse of a right triangle. When you use the Pythagorean Theorem this way, it is called the **Distance Formula.** Label the hypotenuse d for distance.

The line between (1, 2) and (4, 2) is $4 - 1 = 3$ units long.

The line between (1, 6) and (1, 2) is $6 - 2 = 4$ units long.

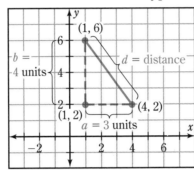

$$a^2 + b^2 = d^2$$
$$3^2 + 4^2 = d^2$$
$$9 + 16 = d^2$$
$$25 = d^2$$
$$5 = d$$

EXAMPLE 1

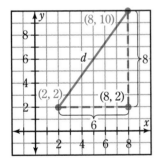

Find the distance between points (8, 10) and (2, 2).

Graph the points. Draw a right triangle.

Substitute 6 and 8 for a and b.

$$a^2 + b^2 = d^2$$
$$6^2 + 8^2 = d^2$$

Solve for d.

$$36 + 64 = d^2$$
$$100 = d^2 \rightarrow 10 = d$$

The distance between (8, 10) and (2, 2) is 10 units.

EXAMPLE 2

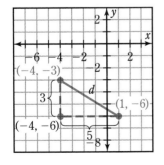

Find the distance between points $(-4, -3)$ and $(1, -6)$.

Graph the points. Draw a right triangle.

Substitute the 5 and 3 for a and b.

$$a^2 + b^2 = d^2$$
$$5^2 + 3^2 = d^2$$

Solve for d.

$$25 + 9 = d^2$$
$$34 = d^2 \rightarrow \sqrt{34} = d$$

The distance between $(-4, -3)$ and $(1, -6)$ is $\sqrt{34}$ units.

1. Find the distance between $(-4, 5)$ and $(0, 3)$.

   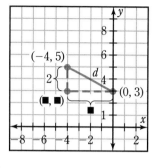

   Graph the points.

   Draw a right triangle.

   Find the legs of the triangle. ■, 2

   Substitute the legs into the Pythagorean Theorem.

   $$a^2 + b^2 = d^2$$
   $$■^2 + ■^2 = d^2$$

   Solve for d.

   $$■ = d^2$$
   $$■ = d$$

   The distance between $(-4, 5)$ and $(0, 3)$ is ■ units.

2. Find the distance between $(-3, 7)$ and $(2, 3)$.

   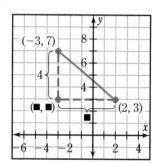

   Graph the points.

   Draw a right triangle.

   Find the legs of the triangle. ■, 4

   Substitute the legs into the Pythagorean Theorem.

   $$a^2 + b^2 = d^2$$
   $$■^2 + ■^2 = d^2$$

   Solve for d.

   $$■ = d^2$$
   $$■ = d$$

   The distance between $(-3, 7)$ and $(2, 3)$ is ■ units.

Practice

Graph each pair of points. Then, find the distance between the points.

1. $(4, 2)$ and $(-3, 4)$

2. $(-3, -3)$ and $(3, 5)$

3. $(1, 4)$ and $(5, -4)$

4. $(8, 3)$ and $(5, 7)$

Do It Together!

5. Explain to a partner how to find the distance between the points in number **3** in **Practice.**

6. Draw two points on a coordinate plane. Have a partner find the distance between the two points. Check the work.

Chapter Review

Chapter 13 Summary

- You can simplify a radical by rewriting it as a product of a perfect square and another factor.
- To add or subtract radicals, group numbers with the same radical and add or subtract the numbers in front of the radical.
- To multiply or divide radicals, multiply or divide the numbers outside the radicals and then multiply or divide the radicands.
- To solve radical equations, get the radical alone on one side of the equation.
- Use the Pythagorean Theorem to find the length of a missing side of a right triangle.
- Recognize 45°– 45°– 90° or 30°– 60°– 90° triangles.
- You can use your calculator to check solutions of radical equations.
- If you substitute three numbers into the equation $a^2 + b^2 = c^2$ and get a true equation, the three numbers can be the sides of a right triangle.
- Use the Pythagorean Theorem to find the distance between two points.

Reviewing Vocabulary

Fill in each blank with the correct word.

radicals

irrational numbers

radical equation

right triangle

hypotenuse

Pythagorean
  Theorem

45°– 45°– 90° triangle

30°– 60°– 90° triangle

Pythagorean triples

Distance Formula

1. A(n) _?_ has acute angles measuring 30° and 60°.
2. In a right triangle, the _?_ is across from the right angle.
3. A(n) _?_ equation contains a variable under a radical.
4. The _?_ is used to find a missing side of a right triangle.
5. Square roots written with a radical sign are called _?_.
6. A(n) _?_ has two acute angles measuring 45°.
7. Groups of three whole numbers that satisfy the Pythagorean Theorem are called _?_.
8. Numbers whose decimal form does not end and does not repeat are called _?_.
9. A triangle that has a 90° angle is called a(n) _?_.
10. The _?_ uses the Pythagorean Theorem to find the distance between two points.

Chapter Quiz

Between what two whole numbers is each radical?

1. $\sqrt{6}$ **2.** $\sqrt{85}$ **3.** $\sqrt{38}$

Simplify.

4. $\sqrt{20}$ **5.** $\sqrt{27}$ **6.** $5\sqrt{7} - 4\sqrt{2} + 3\sqrt{7}$

7. $4\sqrt{2} \cdot 9\sqrt{5}$ **8.** $\dfrac{3\sqrt{20}}{2}$ **9.** $\dfrac{12\sqrt{18}}{3\sqrt{9}}$

10. $3\sqrt{6} \cdot \sqrt{24}$ **11.** $\sqrt{48} + \sqrt{27}$ **12.** $\dfrac{5\sqrt{3}}{\sqrt{2}}$

Solve.

13. $2\sqrt{x} = 8$ **14.** $\sqrt{a} + 2 = 7$ **15.** $\sqrt{4x} = 3$

16. $4\sqrt{n+2} = 20$ **17.** $\sqrt{5x} - 2 = 8$ **18.** $\sqrt{2y+3} = 5$

Find the length of each missing side.

19.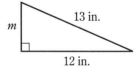

20.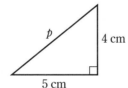

21.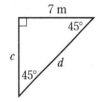

22.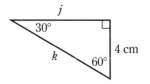

23.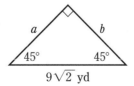

24.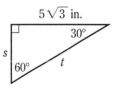

25. Tell whether a triangle with sides 27 m, 36 m, and 54 m is a right triangle.

26. Graph the points $(6, -5)$ and $(-6, 4)$. Then, find the distance between the two points.

Chapter 14

Rational Expressions and Equations

The current flowing through an electric circuit follows a pattern that uses fractions. Electricians need to evaluate rational expressions to figure out how many appliances can be put on one circuit.

Chapter Learning Objectives

- Evaluate rational expressions.
- Add, subtract, multiply, and divide rational expressions.
- Solve rational equations.
- Solve proportions by finding the cross products.
- Use a calculator to check solutions to a proportion.
- Use proportions to solve problems.
- Apply concepts and skills to using inverse variation.

Words to Know

rational number a number that can be written as a fraction

rational expression the quotient of two variable expressions; can be written as a fraction

undefined when a rational expression has zero as the denominator; has no value

least common multiple (LCM) the smallest positive common multiple of two or more numbers or polynomials

least common denominator (LCD) the LCM of two denominators

rational equation an equation that contains rational expressions

proportion a statement that two ratios are equal

cross products the products of numbers or expressions diagonally across from each other in a proportion

inverse variation a rational equation in the form $y = \frac{k}{x}$ where k is a positive constant

---

In this chapter, you will learn how to evaluate and simplify rational expressions. You will learn how to find the least common multiple of two polynomials. You will also add, subtract, multiply, and divide rational expressions. You will learn how to solve proportions with rational expressions. You will use your calculator to check possible solutions of proportions. You will learn to use proportions to solve problems. Finally, you will use rational equations with inverse variation to solve real-life problems.

14.1 Rational Numbers and Expressions

$2x$ means $\frac{2x}{1}$.

A **rational number** is any number that can be written as a fraction. A **rational expression** is a variable expression that can be written as a fraction. It is the quotient of the numerator and the denominator.

Rational numbers	Rational expressions
$3 \quad \frac{1}{4} \quad .79 \quad 2\frac{1}{2}$	$2x \quad \frac{x}{5} \quad \frac{2y}{5x^2-4}$

You evaluate rational expressions the same way you evaluate variable expressions. Substitute a value for the variable.

EXAMPLE 1 Evaluate $\dfrac{2x}{x+6}$ when x is 4.

$$\frac{2x}{x+6}$$

Substitute 4 for x.

$$\frac{2 \cdot 4}{4+6}$$

Simplify.

$$\frac{8}{10}$$

Write the fraction in lowest terms.

$$\frac{4}{5}$$

The value of $\dfrac{2x}{x+6}$ is $\dfrac{4}{5}$ when x is 4.

EXAMPLE 2 Evaluate $\dfrac{11}{2x^2-2}$ when x is -3.

$$\frac{11}{2x^2-2}$$

Substitute -3 for x.

$$\frac{11}{2(-3)^2-2}$$

Simplify.

$$\frac{11}{16}$$

The value of $\dfrac{11}{2x^2-2}$ is $\dfrac{11}{16}$ when x is -3.

EXAMPLE 3 Evaluate $\dfrac{x-y}{y+2x}$ when x is 3 and y is -2.

$$\frac{x-y}{y+2x}$$

Substitute 3 for x and -2 for y.

$$\frac{3-(-2)}{-2+2(3)}$$

Simplify.

$$\frac{5}{4}$$

The value of $\dfrac{x-y}{y+2x}$ is $\dfrac{5}{4}$ when x is 3 and y is -2.

Evaluate each expression.

1. $\dfrac{x+3}{x^2-2}$ when x is 4

Substitute ■ for x.

Simplify.

**Write the fraction
in lowest terms.** ■

The value of $\dfrac{x+3}{x^2-2}$ is ■ when
x is 4.

2. $\dfrac{2a}{3a+2b}$ when a is 4 and b is -4

**Substitute ■ for a and
■ for b.**

Simplify.

**Write the fraction
in lowest terms.** ■

The value of $\dfrac{2a}{3a+2b}$ is ■ when
a is 4 and b is -4.

Practice

Evaluate each expression.

1. $\dfrac{6}{y+3}$ when y is 9

2. $\dfrac{z-5}{8}$ when z is 21

3. $\dfrac{x}{x+7}$ when x is 4

4. $\dfrac{2k}{k-2}$ when k is 6

5. $\dfrac{2x}{3x+4}$ when x is 5

6. $\dfrac{y+1}{2y^2-3}$ when y is -2

7. $\dfrac{2+m}{6q}$ when m is 4 and q is -1

8. $\dfrac{4}{a+b}$ when a is 3 and b is 5

9. $\dfrac{4x}{3x+2y}$ when x is 3 and y is -4

10. $\dfrac{x-4}{y^2+5y+6}$ when x is 8 and y is -4

Do It Together!

11. Explain to a partner how to find the value of the rational expression in
number **9** in **Practice.**

12. Pick three integers between -4 and 4 for x. Ask a partner to evaluate $\dfrac{2x}{x^2+2}$
for each of the integers. Check the work.

14.2 Zero in the Denominator

Some values of the variable make the denominator 0. You cannot divide by 0. So, the rational expression is **undefined** when the denominator is 0. You can find the values that make this happen. Let the denominator equal 0. Then, solve this equation.

EXAMPLE 1   Find the value that makes $\dfrac{7}{a+5}$ undefined.

Let the denominator equal 0. $a+5=0$

Solve for *a*. $a=-5$

Solution: **−5**

$\dfrac{7}{a+5}$ is undefined when *a* is -5.

Sometimes, the denominator has two factors. Remember, let each factor equal 0 to solve this equation.

EXAMPLE 2   Find the values that make $\dfrac{x+3}{2x(x-2)}$ undefined.

Let the denominator equal 0. $2x(x-2)=0$

The denominator has two factors. $2x=0$ or $x-2=0$
Let each factor equal 0.

Solve each factor for *x*. $x=0$ or $x=2$

Solution: **0 or 2**

$\dfrac{x+3}{2x(x-2)}$ is undefined when *x* is 0 or 2.

Sometimes, you need to factor the denominator.

EXAMPLE 3   Find the values that make $\dfrac{y+4}{y^2+3y+2}$ undefined.

Find two numbers that have a sum of 3 and a product of 2: $1+2=3; 1\cdot 2=2.$

Let the denominator equal 0. $y^2+3y+2=0$

Factor. $(y+1)(y+2)=0$

Let each factor equal 0. $y+1=0$ or $y+2=0$

Solve each factor for *y*. $y=-1$ or $y=-2$

Solution: **−1 or −2**

$\dfrac{y+4}{y^2+3y+2}$ is undefined when *y* is -1 or -2.

Find the value or values that make each rational expression undefined.

1. $\dfrac{a^2-2}{2a-6}$

Let the ■ equal 0.   ■$=0$

Solve for ■. $2a=$ ■

             $a=$ ■

$\dfrac{a^2-2}{2a-6}$ is undefined when a is ■.

2. $\dfrac{y+1}{3y^2-12y}$

Let the ■ equal 0. $3y^2-12y=0$

Factor. $3y(y-4)=0$

Let each factor   ■$=0$ or   ■$=0$
equal 0.

Solve for ■. $y=$ ■   or $y=$ ■

$\dfrac{y+1}{3y^2-12y}$ is undefined when y is ■ or ■.

Practice

Find the value or values that make each rational expression undefined.

1. $\dfrac{8}{y+6}$

2. $\dfrac{2x}{x-3}$

3. $\dfrac{5(a+3)}{4a}$

4. $\dfrac{2y(y-4)}{3y+12}$

5. $\dfrac{x^2+3}{x(x+5)}$

6. $\dfrac{4}{5p(p-7)}$

7. $\dfrac{9}{y^2+5y}$

8. $\dfrac{4v}{v^2-6v+8}$

Do It Together!

9. Explain to a partner how to find the values that make number **5** in **Practice** undefined.

10. Write a rational expression with two factors in the denominator. Have a partner find the values that make the expression undefined. Check the work.

14.3 Simplifying Rational Expressions

To simplify rational expressions, factor the numerator and denominator. Then, divide the numerator and denominator by their common factors.

EXAMPLE 1

$9 = 3 \cdot 3$

$12 = 2 \cdot 2 \cdot 3$

Simplify. $\dfrac{9}{12}$

Factor 9 and 12.

$$\frac{3 \cdot 3}{2 \cdot 2 \cdot 3}$$

Divide numerator and denominator by the common factors.

$$\frac{3 \cdot \overset{1}{\cancel{3}}}{2 \cdot 2 \cdot \underset{1}{\cancel{3}}}$$

Simplify.

$$\frac{9}{12} = \frac{3}{4}$$

$$\frac{3}{4}$$

EXAMPLE 2

$4x^2 = 2 \cdot 2 \cdot x \cdot x$

$6x = 2 \cdot 3 \cdot x$

Simplify. $\dfrac{4x^2}{6x}$

Factor $4x^2$ and $6x$.

$$\frac{2 \cdot 2 \cdot x \cdot x}{3 \cdot 2 \cdot x}$$

Divide the numerator and denominator by the common factors.

$$\frac{2 \cdot \overset{1}{\cancel{2}} \cdot \overset{1}{\cancel{x}} \cdot x}{3 \cdot \underset{1}{\cancel{2}} \cdot \underset{1}{\cancel{x}}}$$

$$\frac{2x}{3}$$

Simplify.

$$\frac{4x^2}{6x} = \frac{2x}{3}$$

Sometimes, you need to factor polynomials before you can divide by common factors.

EXAMPLE 3

Find two numbers that have a sum of 5 and a product of 4: $1 + 4 = 5; 1 \cdot 4 = 4.$

Simplify. $\dfrac{2y+2}{y^2+5y+4}$

Factor the numerator and the denominator.

$$\frac{2(y+1)}{(y+1)(y+4)}$$

Divide the numerator and denominator by $(y+1)$.

$$\frac{2\overset{1}{\cancel{(y+1)}}}{\underset{1}{\cancel{(y+1)}}(y+4)}$$

$$\frac{2}{y+4}$$

Simplify.

$$\frac{2y+2}{y^2+5y+4} = \frac{2}{y+4}$$

Simplify each rational expression.

1. $\dfrac{10}{15}$

Factor 10 and 15. $\qquad \dfrac{2 \bullet 5}{\blacksquare \bullet \blacksquare}$

Divide by $\blacksquare$. $\qquad \dfrac{2 \bullet \cancel{5}}{\blacksquare \bullet \cancel{5}}$

Simplify. $\qquad \dfrac{\blacksquare}{\blacksquare}$

$\dfrac{10}{15} = \blacksquare$

2. $\dfrac{2a}{2a^2 - 4a}$

Factor the denominator. $\qquad \dfrac{2a}{\blacksquare(a-2)}$

Divide by the common factors. $\qquad \dfrac{\cancel{2a}}{\cancel{\blacksquare}(a-2)}$

Simplify. $\qquad \dfrac{1}{\blacksquare}$

$\dfrac{2a}{2a^2 - 4a} = \blacksquare$

Practice

Simplify each rational expression.

1. $\dfrac{4}{16}$

2. $\dfrac{8}{24}$

3. $\dfrac{14}{20}$

4. $\dfrac{6b^2}{9b}$

5. $\dfrac{2y}{8y^2}$

6. $\dfrac{3y^3}{18y^2}$

7. $\dfrac{(a-1)(a+2)}{a(a+2)}$

8. $\dfrac{3x(x-3)}{(x-3)(x+3)}$

9. $\dfrac{(p+5)(p-5)}{(p-5)(p-5)}$

10. $\dfrac{3y}{3y^2-6y}$

11. $\dfrac{2x+4}{5x^2+10x}$

12. $\dfrac{2m^2-8m}{4m}$

13. $\dfrac{a+1}{a^2+3a+2}$

14. $\dfrac{4y+8}{y^2+7y+10}$

15. $\dfrac{x^2-5x+6}{2x-4}$

Do It Together!

16. Explain to a partner how to simplify number **8** in **Practice.**

17. Ask a partner to simplify $\dfrac{4x}{2x^2+x}$. Check the work.

14.4 Finding the Least Common Multiple

The **least common multiple (LCM)** is the smallest non-zero multiple two or more numbers have in common.

Multiples of 4 → 0, 4, 8, 12, 16
Multiples of 6 → 0, 6, 12, 18, 24
The LCM of 4 and 6 is 12.

EXAMPLE 1   Find the LCM of 6 and 8.

Find multiples of 6.	0, 6, 12, 18, 24, 30
Find multiples of 8.	0, 8, 16, 24, 32, 40

The LCM of 6 and 8 is 24.

To find the LCM of variable expressions, first find the LCM of the coefficients. Then, use the higher power of each variable.

EXAMPLE 2   Find the LCM of x^3y and xy^2.

The LCM of 1 and 1 is 1.

Find the larger power of x.	x^3
Find the larger power of y.	y^2

The LCM of x^3y and xy^2 is x^3y^2.

EXAMPLE 3   Find the LCM of $3a^2$ and $6ab$.

3: 0, 3, 6, 9, 12

6: 0, 6, 12, 18, 24

Find the LCM of 3 and 6.	6
Find the larger power of a.	a^2
Find the larger power of b.	b

The LCM of $3a^2$ and $6ab$ is $6a^2b$.

The LCM of two polynomials with no common factors is the product of the two polynomials.

EXAMPLE 4   Find the LCM of $x-6$ and $x+5$.

$x-6$ and $x+5$ have no common factors. So, use their product.	$(x-6)(x+5)$

The LCM of $x-6$ and $x+5$ is $(x-6)(x+5)$.

Find the LCM of each pair of polynomials.

1. $4x^2y$ and $10xy$

$4x^2y$ and $10xy$

Find the LCM of 4 and 10. ■
Find the larger power of *x*. ■
Find the larger power of *y*. ■
The LCM of $4x^2y$ and $10xy$ is ■.

2. a and $a+1$

a and $a+1$

a and *a*+1 have no
common factors.
The LCM of a and $a+1$ is ■.

Practice

Find the LCM of each pair of numbers or polynomials.

1. 4 and 6

2. 5 and 15

3. x^2 and x

4. $3a$ and $6a^2$

5. $2x^2$ and $2xy$

6. b^2 and a

7. x and $x+6$

8. $a-5$ and $3a$

9. $6x^2$ and $9x$

10. $5ab$ and $6b^2$

11. $x-1$ and $x+1$

12. $z-3$ and $z+5$

Do It Together!

13. Explain to a partner how to find the LCM in number **9** in **Practice.**

14. Write two variable expressions. Ask a partner to find the LCM.

14.5 Addition and Subtraction

You add or subtract like fractions by adding the numerators and using the same denominator. To add or subtract fractions with unlike denominators, first find a common denominator. Use the LCM as the **least common denominator (LCD).**

LCM means least common multiple.

EXAMPLE 1   Add. $\dfrac{2}{3}+\dfrac{3}{4}$

The LCM of 3 and 4 is 12.

Use 12 for the LCD.

$$\dfrac{2}{3}+\dfrac{3}{4}$$

Rewrite each fraction with 12 as the denominator.

$$\dfrac{2\bullet 4}{3\bullet 4}+\dfrac{3\bullet 3}{4\bullet 3}$$

Add the numerators.

$$\dfrac{8+9}{12}$$

Simplify.

$$\dfrac{17}{12}$$

$$\dfrac{2}{3}+\dfrac{3}{4}=\dfrac{17}{12}$$

EXAMPLE 2   Add. $\dfrac{3x}{5}+\dfrac{x}{15}$

Use 15 for the LCD.

$$\dfrac{3x}{5}+\dfrac{x}{15}$$

Rewrite each fraction with 15 as the denominator.

$$\dfrac{3x\bullet 3}{5\bullet 3}+\dfrac{x\bullet 1}{15\bullet 1}$$

Add the numerators.

$$\dfrac{9x+x}{15}$$

Simplify.

$$\dfrac{10x}{15}=\dfrac{2x}{3}$$

$$\dfrac{3x}{5}+\dfrac{x}{15}=\dfrac{2x}{3}$$

The denominator may contain variables.

EXAMPLE 3   Subtract. $\dfrac{5}{4a^2}-\dfrac{3}{8a}$

The LCM of $4a^2$ and $8a$ is $8a^2$.

Use $8a^2$ for the LCD.

$$\dfrac{5}{4a^2}-\dfrac{3}{8a}$$

Rewrite each fraction with $8a^2$ as the denominator.

$$\dfrac{5\bullet 2}{4a^2\bullet 2}-\dfrac{3\bullet a}{8a\bullet a}$$

Subtract the numerators.

$$\dfrac{10-3a}{8a^2}$$

$$\dfrac{5}{4a^2}-\dfrac{3}{8a}=\dfrac{10-3a}{8a^2}$$

Add or subtract.

1. $\dfrac{1}{3x}+\dfrac{4}{3x}$

> The denominators are the same.
>
> Add the numerators.
>
> $\dfrac{1}{3x}+\dfrac{4}{3x}=\blacksquare$

$\dfrac{1}{3x}+\dfrac{4}{3x}$

$\dfrac{\blacksquare}{3x}$

2. $\dfrac{4x}{y^2}-\dfrac{3x}{y}$

> Use $\blacksquare$ as the LCD.
>
> Rewrite each fraction with $\blacksquare$ as the denominator.
>
> Subtract the numerators.

$\dfrac{4x}{y^2}-\dfrac{3x}{y}$

$\dfrac{4x\bullet 1}{y^2\bullet 1}-\dfrac{3x\bullet\blacksquare}{y\bullet\blacksquare}$

$\dfrac{4x}{y^2}-\dfrac{3x}{y}=\blacksquare$

Practice

Add or subtract.

1. $\dfrac{1}{2}+\dfrac{2}{5}$

2. $\dfrac{2}{3}-\dfrac{5}{12}$

3. $\dfrac{5}{6}-\dfrac{1}{8}$

4. $\dfrac{2}{9}+\dfrac{5}{6}$

5. $\dfrac{2a}{7}+\dfrac{a}{14}$

6. $\dfrac{3y}{5}-\dfrac{7y}{20}$

7. $\dfrac{b}{10}+\dfrac{5b}{15}$

8. $\dfrac{3m}{4}-\dfrac{m}{2}$

9. $\dfrac{4}{x}-\dfrac{6}{y}$

10. $\dfrac{5}{ab}+\dfrac{3}{b}$

11. $\dfrac{2}{m}+\dfrac{7}{p}$

12. $\dfrac{1}{r}-\dfrac{8}{dr}$

13. $\dfrac{2}{xy^2}+\dfrac{8}{x^2y}$

14. $\dfrac{x}{6}-\dfrac{1}{3x}$

15. $\dfrac{5a}{b^2}-\dfrac{6a}{b}$

16. $\dfrac{3x}{y}-\dfrac{2x}{y^2}$

Do It Together!

17. Explain to a partner how to subtract the rational expressions in number **14** in **Practice.**

18. Ask a partner to add $\dfrac{4x}{y}+\dfrac{2x^2}{y^2}$. Check the work.

14.6 More Addition and Subtraction

Sometimes, the denominator has more than one term. After you multiply by the LCD, you can use the Distributive Property to help simplify the problem.

EXAMPLE 1   Add. $\dfrac{5}{x} + \dfrac{3}{x+2}$

The LCD of x and $x+2$ is $x(x+2)$.

$$\frac{5}{x} + \frac{3}{x+2}$$

Write equivalent fractions with $x(x+2)$ as the denominator

$$\frac{5(x+2)}{x(x+2)} + \frac{3x}{x(x+2)}$$

Use the Distributive Property to simplify $5(x+2)$.

$$\frac{5x+10}{x(x+2)} + \frac{3x}{x(x+2)}$$

Add the numerators.

$$\frac{5x+10+3x}{x(x+2)}$$

$$\frac{8x+10}{x(x+2)}$$

$$\frac{5}{x} + \frac{3}{x+2} = \frac{8x+10}{x(x+2)}$$

EXAMPLE 2   Subtract. $\dfrac{2}{a+3} - \dfrac{5}{a+5}$

The LCD of $a+3$ and $a+5$ is $(a+3)(a+5)$.

$$\frac{2}{a+3} - \frac{5}{a+5}$$

Write equivalent fractions with $(a+3)(a+5)$ as the denominator.

$$\frac{2(a+5)}{(a+3)(a+5)} - \frac{5(a+3)}{(a+3)(a+5)}$$

Use the Distributive Property to simplify $2(a+5)$ and $5(a+3)$.

$$\frac{2a+10}{(a+3)(a+5)} - \frac{5a+15}{(a+3)(a+5)}$$

$-(5a+15) = -5a-15$ Subtract the numerators.

$$\frac{2a+10-(5a+15)}{(a+3)(a+5)}$$

$$\frac{2a+10-5a-15}{(a+3)(a+5)}$$

$$\frac{-3a-5}{(a+3)(a+5)}$$

$$\frac{2}{a+3} - \frac{5}{a+5} = \frac{-3a-5}{(a+3)(a+5)}$$

Add or subtract.

1. $\dfrac{x}{4} - \dfrac{4}{x}$

The LCD of 4 and x is ■.

$\dfrac{x}{4} - \dfrac{4}{x}$

Write equivalent fractions with ■ as the denominator.

$\dfrac{x■}{4■} - \dfrac{4■}{x■} \rightarrow \dfrac{x^2}{4x} - \dfrac{■}{4x}$

Subtract the numerators.

$\dfrac{x^2 - ■}{4x}$

$\dfrac{x}{4} - \dfrac{4}{x} = ■$

2. $\dfrac{4}{x+3} + \dfrac{6}{x-3}$

The LCD of $x+3$ and $x-3$ is $(x+3)(x-3)$.

$\dfrac{4}{x+3} + \dfrac{6}{x-3}$

Write equivalent fractions with $(x+3)(x-3)$ as the denominator.

$\dfrac{4(x-3)}{(x+3)(x-3)} + \dfrac{6(x+3)}{(x+3)(x-3)}$

Use the Distributive Property to simplify $4(x-3)$ and $6(x+3)$.

$\dfrac{■-■}{(x+3)(x-3)} + \dfrac{■+■}{(x+3)(x-3)}$

Add the numerators.

$\dfrac{■-12+■+18}{(x+3)(x-3)} = \dfrac{10x+■}{(x+3)(x-3)}$

$\dfrac{4}{x+3} + \dfrac{6}{x-3} = ■$

Practice

Add or subtract.

1. $\dfrac{6}{y} + \dfrac{2}{y+3}$

2. $\dfrac{2}{2x} + \dfrac{7}{x+5}$

3. $\dfrac{4}{y+1} + \dfrac{3}{y+3}$

4. $\dfrac{3}{a-2} + \dfrac{6}{a+4}$

5. $\dfrac{2a}{a+2} + \dfrac{5}{a-2}$

6. $\dfrac{3x}{x-4} + \dfrac{4}{x+4}$

7. $\dfrac{5}{x-3} - \dfrac{6}{x}$

8. $\dfrac{8}{a-5} - \dfrac{3}{a}$

Do It Together!

9. Explain to a partner how to add the expressions in number **3** in **Practice**.

10. Ask a partner to subtract $\dfrac{4}{y+1} - \dfrac{3}{y-1}$. Check the work.

14.7 Multiplication and Division

You multiply rational expressions the same way you multiply fractions with numbers. Multiply the numerators, and multiply the denominators.

EXAMPLE 1   Multiply. $\dfrac{2}{5} \cdot \dfrac{5}{6}$

Multiply numerators and multiply denominators. $\qquad\qquad \dfrac{2 \cdot 5}{5 \cdot 6}$

Divide by common factors. $\qquad\qquad \dfrac{2 \cdot \cancel{5}}{\cancel{5} \cdot \cancel{6}}_{3}$

Simplify. $\qquad\qquad\qquad\qquad \dfrac{1}{3}$

$$\frac{2}{5} \cdot \frac{5}{6} = \frac{1}{3}$$

EXAMPLE 2   Multiply. $\dfrac{3x}{4} \cdot \dfrac{2}{x}$

Multiply numerators and multiply denominators. $\qquad\qquad \dfrac{3x \cdot 2}{4 \cdot x}$

Divide by common factors. $\qquad\qquad \dfrac{3\cancel{x} \cdot \cancel{2}}{{}_{2}\cancel{4} \cdot \cancel{x}}$

Simplify. $\qquad\qquad\qquad\qquad \dfrac{3}{2}$

$$\frac{3x}{4} \cdot \frac{2}{x} = \frac{3}{2}$$

To divide by a fraction, you multiply by its reciprocal. You divide rational expressions the same way.

EXAMPLE 3   Divide. $\dfrac{3x}{y} \div \dfrac{9}{y}$

Multiply by the reciprocal. $\qquad\qquad \dfrac{3x}{y} \cdot \dfrac{y}{9}$

Multiply numerators and multiply denominators. $\qquad\qquad \dfrac{3x \cdot y}{y \cdot 9}$

Divide by common factors. $\qquad\qquad \dfrac{\cancel{3}x\cancel{y}}{{}_{3}\cancel{9}\cancel{y}}$

Simplify. $\qquad\qquad\qquad\qquad \dfrac{x}{3}$

$$\frac{3x}{y} \div \frac{9}{y} = \frac{x}{3}$$

Multiply or divide.

1. $\dfrac{6}{3a} \cdot \dfrac{2a}{5a}$

$\dfrac{6}{3a} \cdot \dfrac{2a}{5a}$

Multiply numerators and multiply denominators.

$\dfrac{6 \cdot 2a}{3a \cdot 5a}$

Divide by common factors.

$\dfrac{\overset{2}{\cancel{6}} \cdot 2\cancel{a}}{\cancel{3a} \cdot 5a}$

Simplify.

$\dfrac{6}{3a} \cdot \dfrac{2a}{5a} = \blacksquare$

2. $\dfrac{x}{y} \div \dfrac{3x^2}{4}$

Multiply by the ■.

Multiply numerators and multiply denominators.

Divide by common factors.

Simplify.

$\dfrac{x}{y} \div \dfrac{3x^2}{4} = \blacksquare$

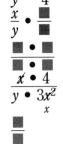

$\dfrac{x}{y} \div \dfrac{3x^2}{4}$

$\dfrac{x}{y} \cdot \dfrac{\blacksquare}{\blacksquare}$

$\dfrac{\blacksquare \cdot \blacksquare}{\blacksquare \cdot \blacksquare}$

$\dfrac{\cancel{x} \cdot 4}{y \cdot 3\overset{x}{\cancel{x^2}}}$

$\dfrac{\blacksquare}{\blacksquare}$

Practice

Multiply or divide.

1. $\dfrac{2}{7} \cdot \dfrac{7}{8}$

2. $\dfrac{1}{3} \cdot \dfrac{9}{10}$

3. $\dfrac{6}{7} \cdot \dfrac{14}{15}$

4. $\dfrac{2}{3} \div \dfrac{4}{9}$

5. $\dfrac{5}{8} \div \dfrac{3}{4}$

6. $\dfrac{7}{10} \div \dfrac{14}{25}$

7. $\dfrac{2y}{5} \cdot \dfrac{3y}{8}$

8. $\dfrac{4}{5x} \cdot \dfrac{1}{5x}$

9. $\dfrac{3m}{4} \cdot \dfrac{8m}{9}$

10. $\dfrac{7}{3x} \cdot \dfrac{3x}{2x}$

11. $\dfrac{8a}{3a} \cdot \dfrac{a}{6a^2}$

12. $\dfrac{5p^2}{2p} \cdot \dfrac{6}{10p}$

13. $\dfrac{a^2}{10} \div \dfrac{4a}{5}$

14. $\dfrac{x}{3} \div \dfrac{5x^2}{10}$

15. $\dfrac{7}{y^2} \div \dfrac{8y}{2y^2}$

16. $\dfrac{4y}{x} \div \dfrac{8}{x}$

Do It Together!

17. Explain to a partner how to multiply the rational expressions in number **11** in **Practice.**

18. Write two rational expressions. Have a partner divide the rational expressions. Check the work.

14.8 More Multiplication and Division

Sometimes, you can factor polynomials before multiplying and dividing. Then, multiply numerators and multiply denominators.

$$\frac{2x+4}{x-2} \cdot \frac{3x-6}{x+2} \rightarrow \frac{2(x+2)}{x-2} \cdot \frac{3(x-2)}{x+2} \rightarrow \frac{2(x+2) \cdot 3(x-2)}{(x-2)(x+2)} = \frac{6}{1} = 6$$

EXAMPLE 1 Divide. $\dfrac{3m}{3m+6} \div \dfrac{9m}{m+2}$

$$\frac{3m}{3m+6} \div \frac{9m}{m+2}$$

Multiply by the reciprocal.

$$\frac{3m}{3m+6} \cdot \frac{m+2}{9m}$$

Factor the denominator.

$$\frac{3m}{3(m+2)} \cdot \frac{m+2}{9m}$$

Multiply.

$$\frac{3m \cdot (m+2)}{3(m+2) \cdot 9m}$$

Divide by common factors.

$$\frac{3\cancel{m} \cdot \cancel{(m+2)}}{\cancel{3}\cancel{(m+2)} \cdot 9\cancel{m}}$$

Simplify.

$$\frac{1}{9}$$

$$\frac{3m}{3m+6} \div \frac{9m}{m+2} = \frac{1}{9}$$

EXAMPLE 2 Multiply. $\dfrac{4x+4}{x^2+3x+2} \cdot \dfrac{x+2}{3x}$

$$\frac{4x+4}{x^2+3x+2} \cdot \frac{x+2}{3x}$$

Factor the numerator and denominator.

$$\frac{4(x+1)}{(x+1)(x+2)} \cdot \frac{x+2}{3x}$$

Multiply.

$$\frac{4(x+1)(x+2)}{(x+1)(x+2)3x}$$

Divide by common factors.

$$\frac{4\cancel{(x+1)}\cancel{(x+2)}}{\cancel{(x+1)}\cancel{(x+2)}3x}$$

Simplify.

$$\frac{4}{3x}$$

$$\frac{4x+4}{x^2+3x+2} \cdot \frac{x+2}{3x} = \frac{4}{3x}$$

Multiply or divide.

1. $\dfrac{8}{4a-8} \cdot \dfrac{a-2}{9a}$

$\dfrac{8}{4a-8} \cdot \dfrac{a-2}{9a}$

Factor. $\dfrac{8}{4(\blacksquare-2)} \cdot \dfrac{a-2}{9a}$

Multiply. Divide by common factors. $\dfrac{8 \bullet (a-2)}{4(\blacksquare-2) \bullet 9a}$

Simplify. $\dfrac{\blacksquare}{\blacksquare}$

$\dfrac{8}{4a-8} \cdot \dfrac{a-2}{9a} = \blacksquare$

2. $\dfrac{5x+10}{x} \div \dfrac{x^2+5x+6}{5}$

$\dfrac{5x+10}{x} \div \dfrac{x^2+5x+6}{5}$

Multiply by the ■. $\dfrac{5x+10}{x} \cdot \dfrac{\blacksquare}{\blacksquare}$

Factor. $\dfrac{5(x+\blacksquare)}{x} \cdot \dfrac{5}{(x+\blacksquare)(x+3)}$

Multiply. Divide by common factors. $\dfrac{5(x+\blacksquare) \bullet 5}{x(x+\blacksquare)(x+3)}$

Simplify. $\dfrac{\blacksquare}{\blacksquare}$

$\dfrac{5x+10}{x} \div \dfrac{x^2+5x+6}{5} = \blacksquare$

Practice

Multiply or divide.

1. $\dfrac{3y+6}{5} \cdot \dfrac{4y}{y+2}$

2. $\dfrac{y}{6y+8} \cdot \dfrac{3y+4}{3y}$

3. $\dfrac{6}{5x-10} \cdot \dfrac{x-2}{7x}$

4. $\dfrac{10a}{a-3} \cdot \dfrac{4a-12}{2}$

5. $\dfrac{6b+18}{b} \div \dfrac{b+3}{b}$

6. $\dfrac{2x+4}{x} \div \dfrac{3x+6}{2}$

7. $\dfrac{5y}{5y+15} \div \dfrac{15y}{y+3}$

8. $\dfrac{12}{m+6} \div \dfrac{9m}{2m+12}$

9. $\dfrac{3}{x^2+4x+3} \cdot \dfrac{x+3}{5}$

Do It Together!

10. Explain to a partner how to divide the rational expressions in number **5** in **Practice.**

11. Write a rational expression with $x+1$ as the numerator and another rational expression with $2x+2$ as the denominator. Have a partner multiply the rational expressions. Check the work.

14.9 Solving Rational Equations

A **rational equation** contains rational expressions. To solve a rational equation, you change it to one you know how to solve. To do this, you multiply both sides of the equation by the least common denominator of all the denominators in the equation. Then, solve the remaining equation.

EXAMPLE 1 Solve. $\frac{x}{3}+\frac{x}{2}=10$

The LCD of 3 and 2 is 6.

$$\frac{x}{3}+\frac{x}{2}=10$$

Multiply each term by 6.

$$(6)\frac{x}{3}+(6)\frac{x}{2}=(6)10$$

Simplify.

$$2x+3x=60$$

Solve for x.

$$5x=60$$

$$x=12$$

Check:
$$\frac{x}{3}+\frac{x}{2}=10$$
$$\frac{12}{3}+\frac{12}{2}=10$$
$$4+6=10$$
$$10=10 \quad \text{true}$$

The solution of $\frac{x}{3}+\frac{x}{2}=10$ is 12.

EXAMPLE 2 Solve. $\frac{2}{n}+\frac{1}{3}=\frac{4}{n}$

The LCD for *n* and 3 is 3*n*.

$$\frac{2}{n}+\frac{1}{3}=\frac{4}{n}$$

Multiply each term by 3n.

$$(3n)\frac{2}{n}+(3n)\frac{1}{3}=(3n)\frac{4}{n}$$

Simplify.

$$6+n=12$$

Solve for n.

$$n=6$$

Check:
$$\frac{2}{n}+\frac{1}{3}=\frac{4}{n}$$
$$\frac{2}{6}+\frac{1}{3}=\frac{4}{6}$$
$$\frac{2}{6}+\frac{2}{6}=\frac{4}{6}$$
$$\frac{4}{6}=\frac{4}{6} \quad \text{true}$$

The solution of $\frac{2}{n}+\frac{1}{3}=\frac{4}{n}$ is 6.

EXAMPLE 3 Solve. $\frac{4}{x}+\frac{3}{2x}=\frac{11}{6}$

The LCD for *x*, 2*x*, and 6 is 6*x*.

$$\frac{4}{x}+\frac{3}{2x}=\frac{11}{6}$$

Multiply each term by 6x.

$$(6x)\frac{4}{x}+(6x)\frac{3}{2x}=(6x)\frac{11}{6}$$

Simplify.

$$24+9=11x$$

Add.

$$33=11x$$

Solve for x.

$$3=x$$

Check:
$$\frac{4}{x}+\frac{3}{2x}=\frac{11}{6}$$
$$\frac{4}{3}+\frac{3}{2\cdot 3}=\frac{11}{6}$$
$$\frac{4}{3}+\frac{3}{6}=\frac{11}{6}$$
$$\frac{8}{6}+\frac{3}{6}=\frac{11}{6}$$
$$\frac{11}{6}=\frac{11}{6} \quad \text{true}$$

The solution of $\frac{4}{x}+\frac{3}{2x}=\frac{11}{6}$ is 3.

Solve.

1. $\dfrac{1}{3} - \dfrac{2}{3a} = \dfrac{1}{a}$

The LCD is ■.

$\dfrac{1}{3} - \dfrac{2}{3a} = \dfrac{1}{a}$

Multiply each term by ■.

$■\dfrac{1}{3} - ■\dfrac{2}{3a} = ■\dfrac{1}{a}$

Simplify.

$■ - 2 = ■$

Solve for a.

$a = ■$

The solution of $\dfrac{1}{3} - \dfrac{2}{3a} = \dfrac{1}{a}$ is ■.

2. $\dfrac{3y}{5} - \dfrac{3}{2} = \dfrac{7y}{10}$

The LCD is ■.

$\dfrac{3y}{5} - \dfrac{3}{2} = \dfrac{7y}{10}$

Multiply each term by ■.

$■\dfrac{3y}{5} - ■\dfrac{3}{2} = ■\dfrac{7y}{10}$

Simplify.

$■y - 15 = ■y$

Solve for y.

$y = ■$

The solution of $\dfrac{3y}{5} - \dfrac{3}{2} = \dfrac{7y}{10}$ is ■.

Practice

Solve each rational equation.

1. $\dfrac{y}{3} + \dfrac{y}{6} = 1$

2. $\dfrac{b}{4} - \dfrac{b}{5} = 2$

3. $\dfrac{m}{3} - \dfrac{m}{4} = 3$

4. $\dfrac{4}{x} + \dfrac{2}{3} = \dfrac{8}{x}$

5. $\dfrac{1}{4} + \dfrac{3}{n} = \dfrac{4}{n}$

6. $\dfrac{3}{p} - \dfrac{1}{p} = \dfrac{1}{5}$

7. $\dfrac{1}{5} - \dfrac{2}{5n} = \dfrac{1}{n}$

8. $\dfrac{2}{7} - \dfrac{4}{7a} = \dfrac{2}{a}$

9. $\dfrac{1}{8b} + \dfrac{3}{8} = \dfrac{2}{b}$

10. $\dfrac{2x}{5} - \dfrac{5}{2} = \dfrac{3x}{10}$

11. $\dfrac{6}{3} - \dfrac{3v}{5} = \dfrac{6v}{15}$

12. $\dfrac{2y}{3} + \dfrac{5}{2} = \dfrac{7y}{6}$

13. $\dfrac{4}{n} + \dfrac{6}{4n} = \dfrac{11}{8}$

14. $\dfrac{1}{2x} + \dfrac{5}{6} = \dfrac{9}{3x}$

15. $\dfrac{1}{z} - \dfrac{3}{8} = \dfrac{1}{4z}$

Do It Together!

16. Explain to a partner how to solve the rational equation in number **10** in **Practice.**

17. Write a rational equation. Ask a partner to solve your equation. Check the work.

14.10 Solving Proportions

A **proportion** states that two ratios are equal. In a proportion, the **cross products** are equal.

$$\frac{5}{x} \diagdown\!\!\!\!\!\diagup \frac{4}{8}$$

You can solve a proportion by finding the cross products. The cross products are $5 \cdot 8$ and $x \cdot 4$. Then, solve the equation.

$$5 \cdot 8 = x \cdot 4$$

$$40 = 4x$$

$$10 = x$$

EXAMPLE 1 Solve. $\dfrac{2}{n+1} = \dfrac{4}{n}$

Find the cross products. $\qquad 2 \cdot n = 4(n+1)$

Simplify. $\qquad 2n = 4n + 4$

Solve for n. $\qquad -2n = 4$

$\qquad n = -2$

The solution of $\dfrac{2}{n+1} = \dfrac{4}{n}$ is -2.

Sometimes, the cross products are quadratic expressions. You can solve the equation by factoring or by using the quadratic formula.

EXAMPLE 2 Solve. $\dfrac{y}{y+1} = \dfrac{10}{y+7}$

Find the cross products. $\qquad y(y+7) = 10(y+1)$

Simplify. $\qquad y^2 + 7y = 10y + 10$

The equation is quadratic. Get all $\quad y^2 - 3y - 10 = 0$
terms on one side.

Factor. $\qquad (y-5)(y+2) = 0$

Let each factor equal 0. $\qquad y-5=0 \quad y+2=0$

Solve for y. $\qquad y=5 \qquad y=-2$

The solutions of $\dfrac{y}{y+1} = \dfrac{10}{y+7}$ are 5 or -2.

376   Chapter Fourteen

Solve.

1. $\dfrac{b-2}{b+3}=\dfrac{3}{8}$

$$\dfrac{b-2}{b+3}=\dfrac{3}{8}$$

Find the cross $\blacksquare(b-2)=\blacksquare(b+3)$
products.

Simplify. $8b-\blacksquare=3b+\blacksquare$

Get the variables $5b-16=9$
on one side.

Solve for *b*.

$$5b=\blacksquare$$
$$b=\blacksquare$$

The solution of $\dfrac{b-2}{b+3}=\dfrac{3}{8}$ is $\blacksquare$.

2. $\dfrac{7}{y-4}=\dfrac{5}{y-2}$

$$\dfrac{7}{y-4}=\dfrac{5}{y-2}$$

Find the $\blacksquare$. $7(y-\blacksquare)=5(y-\blacksquare)$

Simplify. $7y-\blacksquare=5y-\blacksquare$

Get the variables $\blacksquare y-14=-20$
on one side.

Solve for *y*.

$$\blacksquare=-6$$
$$y=\blacksquare$$

The solution of $\dfrac{7}{y-4}=\dfrac{5}{y-2}$ is $\blacksquare$.

Practice

Solve.

1. $\dfrac{6}{x}=\dfrac{4}{8}$

2. $\dfrac{6}{3}=\dfrac{x}{5}$

3. $\dfrac{3}{n+1}=\dfrac{6}{n}$

4. $\dfrac{x}{5}=\dfrac{x-2}{15}$

5. $\dfrac{y-3}{y+1}=\dfrac{6}{8}$

6. $\dfrac{1}{5}=\dfrac{a-2}{a-6}$

7. $\dfrac{3}{x-4}=\dfrac{6}{x-6}$

8. $\dfrac{y-1}{2}=\dfrac{y+2}{3}$

9. $\dfrac{n}{5n+6}=\dfrac{1}{n}$

Do It Together!

10. Explain to a partner how to solve the rational equation in number **9** in **Practice.**

11. Write an equation with a proportion. Have a partner solve the equation. Check the work.

14.11   Calculator: Checking Solutions

Some proportions have large numbers or decimals. You can tell whether a proportion is true by finding the cross products. You can also check a solution of a proportion.

EXAMPLE 1   Tell whether the proportion is true. $\dfrac{.29}{1.45} = \dfrac{2.61}{13.05}$

Find the cross products. $.29 \bullet 13.05 = 2.61 \bullet 1.45$

DISPLAY

Simplify the left side.

Enter .29 by pressing: `.` `2` `9`   .29

Multiply by 13.05 by pressing: `×` `1` `3` `.` `0` `5` `=`   3.7845

DISPLAY

Simplify the right side.

Enter 2.61 by pressing: `2` `.` `6` `1`   2.61

Multiply by 1.45 by pressing: `×` `1` `.` `4` `5` `=`   3.7845

Compare the results. $3.7845 = 3.7845$

$\dfrac{.29}{1.45} = \dfrac{2.61}{13.05}$ is a true proportion.

EXAMPLE 2   Tell whether 12 is a solution of $\dfrac{35}{7u + 56} = \dfrac{7}{28}$.

Substitute 12 for u. $\dfrac{35}{7(12) + 56} = \dfrac{7}{28}$

DISPLAY

Simplify the denominator first.

Enter 7 by pressing: `7`   7

Multiply by 12 by pressing: `×` `1` `2` `=`   84

Add 56 by pressing: `+` `5` `6` `=`   140

Then, divide the numerator by the denominator.

Enter 35 by pressing: `3` `5`   35

Divide by 140 by pressing: `÷` `1` `4` `0` `=`   .25

Simplify the right side.   **DISPLAY**

Enter 7 by pressing: `7`   7

Divide by 28 by pressing: `÷` `2` `8` `=`   .25

Compare the results. $.25 = .25$ true

12 is a solution of $\dfrac{35}{7u + 56} = \dfrac{7}{28}$.

Practice

Check the solution of each proportion.

1. $6; \dfrac{11x}{11x + 66} = \dfrac{33}{11x}$

2. $4; \dfrac{15.3}{3.4} = \dfrac{30.6}{1.7y}$

3. $6; \dfrac{15x}{75x + 90} = \dfrac{15}{15x}$

4. $2; \dfrac{3.12}{.52x + 1.04} = \dfrac{.52x + .52}{.52}$

5. $537.2; \dfrac{x}{31.6} = \dfrac{68}{4}$

6. $-2; \dfrac{20x}{20x + 20} = \dfrac{200}{20x + 140}$

7. $9; \dfrac{.7x - 4.9}{.7x + 1.4} = \dfrac{.7}{2.8}$

8. $-3; \dfrac{56}{8x - 32} = \dfrac{40}{8x - 16}$

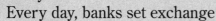

MATH CONNECTION

Currency Exchange

Perhaps you plan to travel to a foreign country. To pay your expenses while you travel, you may need that country's money. You can change United States dollars into the money of that country. This is called currency exchange. Currency is a form of money.

Every day, banks set exchange rates. The exchange rate tells you the amounts of each currency that are equal. For example, in May, you might exchange $100 for 63 British pounds. Exchange rates change with time. In September, you might only get 61 British pounds for $100.

The words strong and weak describe changes in currency exchange. Sometimes the dollar is strong compared to the British pound. That means you can exchange dollars for more pounds than usual. If the dollar is weak, that means you get fewer pounds for your dollar.

14.12 Problem Solving: Using Proportions

Proportions are helpful in solving many types of problems, such as problems involving scale or percents.

EXAMPLE 1

On a map, 5 centimeters stands for 9 miles. On this scale, how many centimeters stand for 36 miles?

Set up a proportion.	$\dfrac{5 \text{ cm}}{9 \text{ mi}} = \dfrac{x \text{ cm}}{36 \text{ mi}}$
Cross multiply.	$5 \bullet 36 = 9x$
Simplify.	$180 = 9x$
Solve for x.	$20 = x$

20 centimeters stands for 36 miles on the map.

EXAMPLE 2

At Hill High School, 2 out of 5 students leave campus for lunch. Each day, 600 students leave campus for lunch. What is the total number of students at the school?

2 out of 5 means that in a group of 5 students, 2 leave for lunch.

Set up a proportion.	$\dfrac{2 \text{ leave}}{5 \text{ total}} = \dfrac{600 \text{ leave}}{x \text{ total}}$
Find the cross products.	$2x = 5 \bullet 600$
Simplify.	$2x = 3,000$
Solve for x.	$x = 1,500$

There are 1,500 students at Hill High School.

EXAMPLE 3

Mr. Tatum can drive 3 miles on the highway in 4 minutes. At this rate, how many minutes will it take him to drive 9 miles?

$\dfrac{3 \text{ miles}}{4 \text{ min}} = \dfrac{9 \text{ miles}}{m \text{ min}}$

Set up a proportion.	$\dfrac{3}{4} = \dfrac{9}{m}$
Find the cross products.	$3m = 4 \bullet 9$
Simplify.	$3m = 36$
Solve for m.	$m = 12$

It will take Mr. Tatum 12 minutes to drive 9 miles.

1. Only 1 out of 4 of Terry's tomato plants survived a drought. Terry started with a total of 20 plants. How many survived the drought?

Set up a proportion.	$\dfrac{\blacksquare \text{ survived}}{4 \text{ total}} = \dfrac{x \text{ survived}}{\blacksquare \text{ total}}$
Find the cross products.	$\blacksquare \bullet \blacksquare = \blacksquare x$
Simplify.	$\blacksquare = \blacksquare x$
Solve for x.	$\blacksquare = x$

■ of Terry's tomato plants survived.

2. A scuba diver can get 12 feet under water in 8 seconds. Find how many seconds it will take to get 36 feet under water.

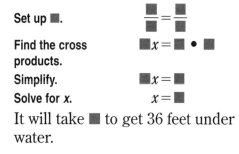

Set up ■.	$\dfrac{\blacksquare}{\blacksquare} = \dfrac{\blacksquare}{\blacksquare}$
Find the cross products.	$\blacksquare x = \blacksquare \bullet \blacksquare$
Simplify.	$\blacksquare x = \blacksquare$
Solve for x.	$x = \blacksquare$

It will take ■ to get 36 feet under water.

Practice

Use a proportion to solve each problem.

1. A map scale uses 8 cm to represent 28 miles. How many miles would 2 cm represent on the map?

2. At Park High School, 3 out of 4 seniors have part-time jobs. There are 75 seniors with part-time jobs. Find the total number of seniors.

3. Sandy has band practice 3 out of 5 school days each week. Find the number of days she has band practice in 40 school days.

4. A scuba diver can get 6 yards under water in 30 seconds. Find how many yards the diver can go under water in 10 seconds at the same rate.

Do It Together!

5. Explain to a partner how you solve number **4** in **Practice.**

6. Write a proportion to show how many days a week you exercise. Ask a partner to find out how many days you exercise in 28 days. Check the work.

14.13 Application: Inverse Variation

You can solve problems where the value of one variable increases as the other decreases. This is called **inverse variation.** Inverse variation is a rational equation in the form $y = \frac{k}{x}$. k is a positive constant.

In the table below, the variable x represents the number of people painting a house, and y represents the number of days it takes.

People	x	1	2	4	8	16
Days	y	16	8	4	2	1

The equation $y = \frac{16}{x}$ shows how the number of days is related to the number of people.

EXAMPLE 1   How many days will it take for 32 people to paint the house?

$$y = \frac{16}{x}$$

$\dfrac{16 \div 16}{32 \div 16} = \dfrac{1}{2}$ **Substitute 32 for x.** $y = \dfrac{16}{32}$

Simplify. $y = \dfrac{1}{2}$

It will take $\frac{1}{2}$ of a day if 32 people are painting the house.

You can use $y = \frac{60}{x}$ to find the time it takes to make a trip 60 miles long. x represents the rate (mph), and y represents the time (h).

EXAMPLE 2   How long will the trip take if you travel 30 mph?

$$y = \frac{60}{x}$$

Substitute 30 for x. $y = \dfrac{60}{30}$

Simplify. $y = 2$

The trip will take 2 hours if you travel 30 mph.

Use $y = \frac{24}{x}$ to find the width of a rectangle with area of 24 cm^2.
x represents the length, and y represents the width.

1. What is the width of the rectangle if the length is 8 cm?

$$y = \frac{24}{x}$$

Substitute ■ for x. $y = \frac{24}{\blacksquare}$

Simplify. $y = \blacksquare$

The width of the rectangle is ■ if the length is 8 cm.

2. What is the width of the rectangle if the length is 12 cm?

$$y = \frac{24}{x}$$

Substitute ■ for x. $y = \frac{24}{\blacksquare}$

Simplify. $y = \blacksquare$

The width of the rectangle is ■ if the length is 12 cm.

Practice

Use $t = \frac{90}{r}$ to solve each problem. r is the rate (mph), and t is the time (hours) for a 90 mile trip.

1. How long will the trip take if you travel 10 mph?

2. How long will the trip take if you travel 50 mph?

Use $h = \frac{48}{b}$ to solve each problem. b represents the base of a triangle of area 24, and h represents the height.

3. What is the height of the triangle if the base is 6 centimeters?

4. What is the height of the triangle if the base is 12 centimeters?

Do It Together!

5. Explain to a partner how to find the height of the triangle in number **4** in **Practice.**

6. Write a problem that can be solved using the inverse variation in **Try These.** Ask a partner to solve the problem. Check the work.

Chapter 14 Summary

- You evaluate rational expressions by substituting values for variables.
- A rational expression is undefined when the denominator is zero.
- You simplify rational expressions by factoring. Then, divide by common factors.
- Find the LCM of two polynomials by listing the multiples.
- You find the LCD to add or subtract rational expressions.
- Sometimes, you factor the denominator before you add or subtract.
- You multiply numerators and denominators to multiply rational expressions. You multiply by the reciprocal to divide rational expressions.
- Sometimes, you factor polynomials before you multiply or divide rational expressions.
- You multiply each term in a rational equation by the LCD to get rid of the denominator. Then, you solve the equation.
- You solve proportions with rational expressions by cross multiplying.
- You can use your calculator to check solutions to proportions.
- You can use proportions to solve different kinds of problems.
- Inverse variation is a rational equation you can use to solve problems.

Reviewing Vocabulary

Fill in each blank with the correct word.

rational number

rational expression

undefined

least common
multiple (LCM)

least common
denominator (LCD)

rational equation

proportion

cross products

inverse variation

1. The smallest positive common multiple of two or more numbers or polynomials is called the _?_.
2. A(n) _?_ is an equation that contains rational expressions.
3. A rational equation in the form $y = \frac{k}{x}$ is a(n) _?_.
4. A(n) _?_ is a number that can be written as a fraction.
5. A rational expression is _?_ when the denominator is zero.
6. A statement that two ratios are equal is called a(n) _?_.
7. A(n) _?_ is an expression that can be written as a fraction.
8. The _?_ is the LCM of two denominators.
9. The _?_ are the products of numbers or expressions diagonally across from each other in a proportion.

Chapter Quiz

Evaluate each expression.

1. $\dfrac{y+3}{y^2-1}$ when y is -2

2. $\dfrac{a^2-3}{a+4}$ when a is 4

Find the values that make the rational expression undefined.

Simplify each rational expression.

3. $\dfrac{3y+2}{4y(y-5)}$

4. $\dfrac{b-5}{(b+5)(b+6)}$

5. $\dfrac{(x-5)(x+3)}{x(x+3)}$

6. $\dfrac{2x-10}{x^2-10x+25}$

Find the least common multiple for each pair of expressions.

7. $4xy$ and $12y$

8. $2ab^2$ and $4ab$

9. $x-3$ and $4x$

Add, subtract, multiply, or divide.

10. $\dfrac{2}{7}+\dfrac{1}{2}$

11. $\dfrac{4}{xy}+\dfrac{7}{y}$

12. $\dfrac{y}{9}+\dfrac{5}{y}$

13. $\dfrac{x}{8}-\dfrac{3}{4x}$

14. $\dfrac{a-2}{6}\cdot\dfrac{2}{3a-6}$

15. $\dfrac{5x-15}{x}\cdot\dfrac{x^2}{5}$

16. $\dfrac{4x-12}{x^2}\div\dfrac{4}{x}$

17. $\dfrac{3x-9}{x^2-9}\cdot\dfrac{6x+18}{x}$

Solve.

18. $\dfrac{1}{2}+\dfrac{5}{n}=\dfrac{6}{n}$

19. $\dfrac{1}{6}-\dfrac{2}{6n}=\dfrac{1}{n}$

20. $\dfrac{3}{9}-\dfrac{5}{3a}=2$

21. $\dfrac{6}{n+1}=\dfrac{9}{n}$

22. $\dfrac{x}{6}=\dfrac{x-2}{18}$

23. $\dfrac{y+1}{y-3}=\dfrac{4}{3}$

Use a proportion to solve the problem.

24. A map shows that 3 centimeters represents 5 miles. Find how many centimeters represent 25 miles.

Use $y=\dfrac{18}{x}$ to solve the problem. y is the number of days it takes to fix a sidewalk, and x is the number of people fixing the sidewalk.

25. How many days will it take for 3 people to fix the sidewalk?

Chapter 15
Topics from Probability

People use probability to predict the outcome of simple games or the weather. Scientists also use probability in genetics to create new varieties of plants called hybrids.

Chapter Learning Objectives

- Find the number of permutations.
- Find the number of combinations.
- Find the probability of an event.
- Find the probability of compound events.
- Use a calculator to find the number of permutations and combinations.
- Solve problems using empirical probability.
- Apply concepts and skills to making a prediction.

Words to Know

permutations   ways of putting a group of objects in order; There are six permutations for three letters: ABC, ACB, BAC, BCA, CAB, CBA

combination   a group of objects in which order does not matter; In counting combinations, ABC is the same as CAB

at random   each outcome is equally likely to happen

outcomes   the results of an activity, experiment, or game

event   an outcome or group of outcomes that you are looking for

probability   value from 0 to 1 that tells how likely an event is to happen

complementary events   events that are opposites; If winning is the event, then losing is the complementary event

independent events   events whose outcomes do not affect each other

compound event   two or more independent events happening together

dependent events   events for which the outcome of one affects the outcome of the other

empirical probability   probability based on what has already happened

---

In this chapter, you will multiply choices to find the total number of choices. You will also count permutations and combinations. You will find the probability of an event. You will also learn about complementary events. Then, you will find the probability of independent events and dependent events. You will use a calculator to find the number of permutations and combinations. You will also find probability from experience. Finally, you will use probability to make predictions.

15.1 Counting

You can draw a tree diagram to show choices. The diagram below shows the different choices for sandwiches when you have two kinds of bread and three kinds of filling.

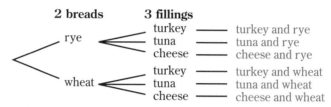

You can also multiply to find the total number of choices.

choice		choice		total choices
bread		filling		sandwich
↓		↓		↓
2	×	3	=	6

EXAMPLE 1 Denis can take one of three language classes and one of four science classes. How many ways can he choose a language class and a science class?

Find the number of languages. 3 choices

Find the number of science classes. 4 choices

Multiply. $3 \times 4 = 12$

There are 12 ways Denis can choose a language and a science class.

EXAMPLE 2 You can either bike or drive from A to C. There are 4 roads from A to B. There are 3 roads from B to C. How many ways can you ride from A to C through B?

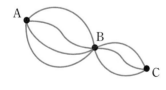

Find the number of vehicles. 2 choices

Find the number of roads from A to B. 4 choices

Find the number of roads from B to C. 3 choices

Multiply. $2 \times 4 \times 3 = 24$

There are 24 possible ways to go from A to C through B.

Find the total number of choices.

1. Karl has 5 pairs of pants and 6 shirts. How many choices does Karl have for a pair of pants and a shirt?

Find the number of pants. ■

Find the number of shirts. 6

Multiply. ■ × ■ = ■

Karl has ■ choices.

2. Liv has pens with red, blue, green, and purple ink. She has yellow, blue, and white paper. How many combinations of ink and paper does Liv have?

Find the number of inks. ■

Find the number of colors of paper. ■

Multiply. ■ × ■ = ■

Liv has ■ choices.

Practice

Find the total number of choices.

1. Stephanie has 8 T-shirts and 2 pairs of jeans. How many choices does she have to pick a T-shirt and a pair of jeans?

2. There are 6 scenic routes to the top of a mountain. At the top, there are 4 restaurants. How many choices are there for route and restaurant?

3. Dru can either go to school early for tutoring or go at the regular time. To get to school, he can take the bus, the subway, or his bicycle. Before he starts class, he gets either hot chocolate or orange juice. How many choices does he have for his morning routine?

Do It Together!

4. Explain to a partner how to find the choices in number **2** in **Practice.**

5. Write a problem that has choices for different things. Ask a friend to count the total number of choices. Check the work.

15.2　Permutations

You can arrange a group of objects in different ways. These are called **permutations.**

　ABC　　BAC　　CAB　　ACB　　BCA　　CBA

You can also count the number of arrangements using multiplication. There are 3 letters and 3 choices for the first position. For each position, there is one less letter to choose from than for the last position.

1st position		2nd position		3rd position	
3 letters		2 letters left		1 letter left	
3	×	2	×	1	= 6

There are 6 ways to arrange the letters A, B, and C.

EXAMPLE 1

How many different ways can 5 students stand in line?

There are 5 positions.　　　　1st　2nd　3rd　4th　5th

Count the number of choices　　5　　4　　3　　2　　1
for each position.

Multiply.　　　　　　　$5 \times 4 \times 3 \times 2 \times 1 = 120$

There are 120 ways 5 students can stand in line.

EXAMPLE 2

There are 15 students in a class. How many ways can you pick a president, vice president, and secretary?

There are 3 positions.　　　　　　P　　VP　　S

Count the number of choices.　　　15　　14　　13

Multiply.　　　　　　$15 \times 14 \times 13 = 2{,}730$

There are 2,730 ways to elect the 3 officers.

EXAMPLE 3

There are 10 runners in a race. How many ways can the runners finish first, second, and third?

There are 3 positions.　　　　　　1st　　2nd　　3rd

Count the number of choices.　　　　10　　9　　　8

Multiply.　　　　　　$10 \times 9 \times 8 = 720$

There are 720 ways for 10 runners to finish first, second, and third.

Find each number of permutations.

1. How many ways can you award first place and second place in a contest with 10 entries?

There are 2 positions.	1st	2nd
Count the number of choices.	10	9
Multiply.	■×■	
	■	

First and second place can be awarded ■ ways.

2. How many ways can you arrange the letters E, F, G, and H?

There are ■ positions. E F G H

Count the number of choices. ■ 3 ■ 1

Multiply. ■×3×■×1

■

E, F, G, and H can be arranged ■ ways.

Practice

Find each number of permutations.

1. How many ways can 3 people stand in a line?

2. How many ways can you arrange the letters M, N, O, P, Q?

3. There are 6 people on a committee. How many ways are there to elect a chairperson and recorder?

4. A competition has 5 finalists. They can win first, second, and third place. In how many ways can the finalists win?

Do It Together!

5. Explain to a partner how to find the number of permutations in number **3** in **Practice.**

6. Write a question that asks how many ways there are to arrange a group of objects. Be sure to include the number of objects and what the objects are. Ask a partner to answer the question.

15.3 Combinations

Here are the different ways you can choose two pieces of fruit from an Apple, Orange, Banana, and Plum:

A and O is the same as O and A.

A and O	O̶ a̶n̶d̶ A̶	B̶ a̶n̶d̶ A̶	P̶ a̶n̶d̶ A̶
A and B	O and B	B̶ a̶n̶d̶ O̶	P̶ a̶n̶d̶ O̶
A and P	O and P	B and P	P̶ a̶n̶d̶ B̶

In a **combination,** the order does not matter. There are 6 combinations of 2 pieces of fruit chosen from 4 different fruits. You can also use a formula to find the number of combinations.

Number of combinations of 2 objects from 4:

$$\frac{\text{number of arrangements of 2 objects from 4}}{\text{number of arrangements of 2 objects}}$$

$$\text{Number of fruit combinations} = \frac{4 \bullet 3}{2 \bullet 1} = \frac{\overset{2}{\cancel{4}} \bullet 3}{2 \bullet 1} = \frac{6}{1} = 6$$

EXAMPLE 1 How many ways are there to choose 3 different pizza toppings if there are 12 to choose from?

Find the number of arrangements of 3 objects chosen from 12. $12 \bullet 11 \bullet 10$

Find the number of arrangements of 3 objects. $3 \bullet 2 \bullet 1$

Divide. $\frac{12 \bullet 11 \bullet 10}{3 \bullet 2 \bullet 1} = 220$

There are 220 combinations of 3 pizza toppings.

EXAMPLE 2 How many ways can a teacher choose 5 volunteers from a class of 12?

Find the number of arrangements of 5 objects chosen from 12. $12 \bullet 11 \bullet 10 \bullet 9 \bullet 8$

Find the number of arrangements of 5 objects. $5 \bullet 4 \bullet 3 \bullet 2 \bullet 1$

Divide. $\frac{12 \bullet 11 \bullet 10 \bullet 9 \bullet 8}{5 \bullet 4 \bullet 3 \bullet 2 \bullet 1} = 792$

The teacher can choose 5 helpers in 792 different ways.

Find each number of combinations.

1. How many ways can you choose 3 photos from 6?

Find the number of arrangements of 3 photos chosen from 6.

$$6 \times 5 \times 4$$

Find the number of arrangements of 3 photos.

$$■ \times ■ \times ■$$

Divide

$$\frac{■ \times ■ \times ■}{■ \times ■ \times ■} = ■$$

You can choose 3 photos ■ different ways.

2. How many ways can you choose 2 ice cream flavors from 7?

Find the number of arrangements of 2 flavors chosen from 7.

$$■ \times ■$$

Find the number of arrangements of 2 flavors.

$$2 \times 1$$

Divide.

$$\frac{■ \times ■}{■ \times ■} = ■$$

There are ■ different ways to choose 2 flavors.

Practice

Find each number of combinations.

1. How many ways can you choose 3 flowers from an arrangement of 5?

2. How many ways can a student choose 2 exam questions from a group of 8?

3. How many ways can you choose 3 CDs from a collection of 10?

4. How many ways can 8 friends choose 3 to ride in a cab?

5. How many ways can you choose 1 sandwich from 6?

Do It Together!

6. Explain to a partner how to find the number of combinations in number **2** in **Practice.**

7. Write a problem that you can solve using combinations. Be sure to include the number of objects in the group and the number you want to choose. Ask a partner to solve the problem. Check the work.

15.4 Probability

When you toss a coin, two things can happen. It can land on heads. Or, it can land on tails. The coin has an equally likely chance of landing on heads or tails. So, the coin lands **at random**.

The results—heads or tails—are called the **outcomes** of a coin toss.

EXAMPLE 1

How many possible outcomes are there for the spinner?

List the possible outcomes. $\underbrace{R, R, Y, 1, 2, 3}_{6}$

Count the outcomes.

There are 6 possible outcomes for the spinner.

An outcome or a group of outcomes is called an **event.** **Probability** is the chance that an event will happen. When you find the probability that a coin lands on heads, heads is the event.

You can find the probability by dividing.

Probability of an event $= \dfrac{\text{number of outcomes in the event}}{\text{total number of outcomes}}$

There is a short way to show probability. P(event) means the probability of an event. In the coin toss, P(heads) means the probability that the coin lands on heads. So, $P(\text{heads}) = \frac{1}{2}$.

A probability of 1 means the event will always happen. A probability of 0 means the event is impossible.

EXAMPLE 2

A cube is numbered 0–5. What is the chance that the cube lands on a number less than 6?

List and count the possible outcomes. $0, 1, 2, 3, 4, 5 \rightarrow 6$

Count the numbers less than 6. $0, 1, 2, 3, 4, 5 \rightarrow 6$

Divide. $\frac{6}{6} = 1$

The probability that the cube lands on a number less than 6 is 1.

A number cube is marked with the numbers 1–6. Find each probability.

1. P(a number less than 5)

List and count the possible outcomes. $1, 2, 3, 4, 5, 6 \rightarrow 6$

Count the number of numbers less than 5.

Divide. $\dfrac{4}{\blacksquare}$

P(a number less than 5) $= \blacksquare$

2. P(even)

List and count the possible outcomes. $\blacksquare$

Count the number of even numbers. $2, 4, 6 \rightarrow \blacksquare$

Divide $\dfrac{3}{\blacksquare}$

P(even) $= \blacksquare$

Practice

A spinner is divided into 5 equal regions, numbered 1 through 5. An arrow is spun and lands on one of the regions. Find each probability.

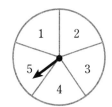

1. P(3)

2. P(odd number)

3. P(a number greater than 2)

A marble is drawn at random from a jar that contains 5 marbles. There are 2 white and 3 green marbles. Find each probability.

4. P(green)   **5.** P(white)   **6.** P(yellow)

Do It Together!

7. Explain to a partner how to find the probability in number **2** in **Practice**.

8. Write a list of 6 numbers. Ask a partner to find the probability that a number picked is divisible by 5.

15.5 Complementary Events

5 outcomes: A, B, C, 1, 2

3 letters: A, B, C

2 numbers: 1, 2

Use the jar to find the probabilities.

$P(\text{letter}) = \frac{3}{5}$ There are 3 letters.

$P(not \text{ a letter}) = \frac{2}{5}$ There are 2 that are *not* letters.

Add the probabilities. $\frac{3}{5} + \frac{2}{5} = \frac{5}{5} = 1$

When you add the probability that an event happens and the probability that the event does *not* happen, the sum is always 1. These are called **complementary events.**

$$P(\text{event}) + P(not \text{ the event}) = 1$$

To find the probability an event does *not* happen, you can subtract from 1.

$$P(not \text{ the event}) = 1 - P(\text{event})$$

EXAMPLE 1   Find the probability the spinner does *not* land on 8.

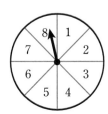

Find P(8). $\frac{1}{8}$

Write the formula. $P(not\ 8) = 1 - P(8)$

Substitute $\frac{1}{8}$ for P(8). $P(not\ 8) = 1 - \frac{1}{8}$

$$P(not\ 8) = \frac{8}{8} - \frac{1}{8}$$

$$P(not\ 8) = \frac{7}{8}$$

The probability the spinner does *not* land on 8 is $\frac{7}{8}$.

EXAMPLE 2   The probability that it will rain this weekend is $\frac{3}{4}$. What is the probability that it will not rain?

Find P(rain). $\frac{3}{4}$

Write the formula. $P(not \text{ rain}) = 1 - P(\text{rain})$

Substitute $\frac{3}{4}$ for P(rain). $P(not \text{ rain}) = 1 - \frac{3}{4}$

$$P(not \text{ rain}) = \frac{4}{4} - \frac{3}{4}$$

$$P(not \text{ rain}) = \frac{1}{4}$$

The probability that it will *not* rain is $\frac{1}{4}$.

Find each probability.

1. The probability that Leslie makes a free throw is $\frac{4}{5}$. What is the probability that she misses a free throw?

Find P(makes free throw). $\frac{4}{5}$

Write the formula. $P(\text{miss}) = 1 - \blacksquare$

Substitute ■ for P(makes free throw). $P(\text{miss}) = \frac{\blacksquare}{\blacksquare} - \frac{4}{5}$

Simplify. $P(\text{miss}) = \frac{\blacksquare}{\blacksquare}$

$P(\text{miss}) = \blacksquare$

2. The probability Lily guesses wrong on a multiple choice question is $\frac{2}{3}$. Find the probability that she guesses correctly.

Find P(wrong). $\frac{\blacksquare}{\blacksquare}$

Write the formula. $\blacksquare = 1 - P(\text{wrong})$

Substitute ■ for P(wrong). $\blacksquare = 1 - \frac{\blacksquare}{\blacksquare}$

Simplify. $\blacksquare = \frac{\blacksquare}{\blacksquare}$

$P(\text{correct}) = \blacksquare$

Practice

Pick a letter at random from the word PROBABILITY. Find each probability.

1. $P(not$ a B$)$ **2.** $P(not$ a vowel$)$ **3.** $P(not$ a Q$)$

Find each probability.

4. The probability that Jasmine gets a hit at bat is $\frac{2}{5}$. What is the probability that she does not get a hit?

5. A jar contains 3 blue and 2 orange marbles. Pick a marble at random. What is the probability that you do not pick a blue marble?

6. The probability that Liberty wins is $\frac{9}{10}$. What is the probability that the team loses?

Do It Together!

7. Explain to a partner how to find the probability in number **4** in **Practice.**

8. Describe an event and include its probability. Ask a partner to find the probability that the event does *not* happen.

15.6 Compound Events

You know how to find the probability of tossing a coin and having it land heads up. If you toss the coin again, the result of the first toss does not affect this toss. The two coin tosses are **independent events.**

A **compound event** is two or more independent events that happen together. To find the probability of a compound event, find the probability of each event and multiply.

$$\frac{\text{Probability of}}{\text{First Event}} \times \frac{\text{Probability of}}{\text{Second Event}} = \frac{\text{Probability of}}{\text{Compound Event}}$$

EXAMPLE 1   Lana flips a coin twice. What is the probability it will land heads then tails?

Find P(heads). $\frac{1}{2}$

Find P(tails). $\frac{1}{2}$

Multiply P(heads) and P(tails). $\frac{1}{2} \times \frac{1}{2} = \frac{1}{4}$

The probability of tossing heads then tails is $\frac{1}{4}$.

A compound event can have more than two events.

EXAMPLE 2   Spin the spinner, pick a letter from the cards, and then spin the spinner again. Find the probability that the spinner lands on an even number, you pick the letter G, and the spinner lands on 5.

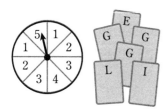

Find P(even). $\frac{3}{8}$

Find P(G). $\frac{3}{6}$

Find P(5). $\frac{1}{8}$

Multiply P(even), P(G), and P(tails). $\frac{3}{8} \times \frac{3}{6} \times \frac{1}{8} = \frac{9}{384}$

The probability of getting an even number, a G, and then a 5 is $\frac{9}{384}$.

Use the jar and the spinner to find each probability.

1. picking a green marble from the jar and spinning a 5

Find *P*(green marble). $\dfrac{3}{\blacksquare}$

Find *P*(5). $\dfrac{1}{\blacksquare}$

Multiply. $\blacksquare \times \blacksquare = \blacksquare$

The probability of picking a green marble and then spinning 5 is ■.

2. picking a black marble and spinning an odd number

Find *P*(black marble). $\dfrac{2}{\blacksquare}$

Find *P*(odd). $\dfrac{3}{\blacksquare}$

Multiply. $\blacksquare \times \blacksquare = \blacksquare$

The probability of getting a black marble and then an odd number is ■.

Practice

Use the jar, the spinner, the cards, and the coin above to find each probability.

1. You pick a black marble from the jar and an F from the cards.

2. You spin an even number and the coin lands on heads.

3. You pick a green marble from the jar and pick an R from the cards.

4. You pick a vowel from the cards, a green marble from the jar, and spin 7.

Do It Together!

5. Explain to a partner how to find the probability in **2** in **Practice.**

6. Write a problem with two independent events. Ask a partner to find the probability of the compound event.

15.7 Dependent Events

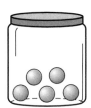

Sometimes an event can affect a second event. These are called **dependent events.**

A jar contains 3 grey marbles and 2 green marbles. Find the probability that you pick a grey marble, keep it, and then pick another grey marble. To do this, find each probability separately. Then, multiply. Find the probability that you pick a grey the first time. There are 3 greys out of 5 marbles. So, $P(\text{grey}) = \frac{3}{5}$.

When you pick the second marble, one grey marble is gone. There are only 2 grey marbles left and 4 left in all. So, $P(\text{another grey})$ is $\frac{2}{4}$.

The probability of picking a grey and then another grey:
$$\frac{3}{5} \times \frac{2}{4} = \frac{6}{20}$$

EXAMPLE 1

April has a bag of marbles. There are 3 blue and 4 yellow. She picks one, and then picks another. What is the probability that she picks a blue and then a yellow?

Find the probability of picking a blue. $\frac{3}{7}$

After the first pick, 1 blue is gone. So, there are only 6 marbles left.

Find the probability of then picking a yellow. $\frac{4}{6}$

Multiply. $\frac{3}{7} \times \frac{4}{6} = \frac{12}{42}$

The probability is $\frac{12}{42}$ that she picks a blue and then a yellow.

EXAMPLE 2

Find the probability that you pick an A, keep it, and then pick a vowel from the word ALPHABET.

Find the probability of picking an A. $\frac{2}{8}$

After you pick an A, there are only 7 letters left. Two letters are vowels.

Find the probability of picking a vowel. $\frac{2}{7}$

Multiply. $\frac{2}{8} \times \frac{2}{7} = \frac{4}{56}$

The probability of picking an A and then a vowel is $\frac{4}{56}$.

A bag contains 5 red marbles and 1 green marble. Without looking, you pick a marble, keep it, and then pick another.

1. Find the probability both marbles are red.

Find the probability that ■
the first is red.

Find how many are left. ■ red, 5 total

Find the probability that ■
the second is red.

Multiply. ■ × ■ = ■

The probability of red, red is ■.

2. Find the probability both marbles are green.

Find the probability ■
that the first is green.

Find how many are left. ■ green, ■ total

Find the probability ■
that the second is green.

Multiply. ■ × ■ = ■

The probability of green, green is ■.

Practice

A bag contains 2 green marbles and 3 yellow marbles. You pick a marble, keep it, and then pick another.

1. Find the probability both marbles are green.

2. Find the probability both marbles are yellow.

3. Find the probability the first marble is green and the second is yellow.

4. Find the probability the first marble is yellow and the second is green.

Do It Together!

5. Explain to a partner how to find the probability in number **3** in **Practice.**

6. Listen while a partner explains how to find the probability in number **4** in **Practice.**

15.8 Calculator: Permutations and Combinations

Permutations and combinations often contain large numbers. You can use a calculator to find these permutations and combinations.

EXAMPLE 1   How many ways can you award first, second, and third place from 20 entries?

	1st 2nd 3rd
There are 3 places.	
Multiply the number of choices for each.	$20 \bullet 19 \bullet 18$

Use your calculator to simplify.   DISPLAY

		DISPLAY
Enter 20 by pressing:	2 0	20
Multiply by 19 by pressing:	× 1 9	19
Multiply by 18 by pressing:	× 1 8 =	6840

First, second, and third places can be awarded 6,840 ways.

EXAMPLE 2   How many ways can a teacher choose 4 volunteers from 18 students?

Find the number of arrangements of 4 volunteers chosen from 18.	$18 \bullet 17 \bullet 16 \bullet 15$
Find the number of arrangements of 4 volunteers.	$4 \bullet 3 \bullet 2 \bullet 1$
Divide.	$\dfrac{18 \bullet 17 \bullet 16 \bullet 15}{4 \bullet 3 \bullet 2 \bullet 1}$

Use your calculator to simplify.   DISPLAY

		DISPLAY
Enter 18 by pressing:	1 8	18
Multiply by 17 by pressing:	× 1 7	17
Multiply by 16 by pressing:	× 1 6	16
Multiply by 15 by pressing:	× 1 5 =	73440
Multiply 4 • 3 • 2 • 1 by pressing	4 × 3 × 2 =	24
Divide 73,440 by 24 by pressing:	7 3 4 4 0	73440
	÷ 2 4 =	3060

Multiplying by 1 does not change a number.

A teacher can choose 4 volunteers 3,060 ways.

Practice

Find each number of permutations or combinations.

1. How many different ways can 9 students stand in a line?

2. How many ways can 20 runners finish first and second?

3. How many ways can 22 entries win first, second, third, and fourth place?

4. How many ways can a teacher pick 3 volunteers from a class of 20?

5. How many ways can you choose 4 photos from 25?

6. How many ways can you pick 2 flavors of ice cream from 22?

MATH CONNECTION

Weather Forecasting

What do you think "20% chance of rain" means? It doesn't really mean there are 20 out of 100 chances for rain today. Probability and predicting are only part of weather forecasting. It is really much more complex.

Meteorologists are people who study and predict weather. They use computers to model the weather. To predict rainfall, they input data such as temperature, wind speed, and humidity.

The computer model gives a forecast. It tells where and when it might rain. It also shows how much it might rain.

The National Weather Service uses many different computer models. Some model snowfall amounts. Some show strengths of thunderstorms. Others track the paths of hurricanes. Local forecasters use this data to tell the weather in their areas.

So what does "20% chance of rain" mean? It means that there's a 20% chance it might rain in your area. This is a low chance for rain. What if it said 80% chance of rain? This is a much higher chance. Now you know how to tell when to bring an umbrella!

15.9 Problem Solving: Another Kind of Probability

You have already found the probability of an event by counting the number of possible outcomes. You found this probability based on what could happen. You can also find probability based on what has already happened. This is called **empirical probability.**

You can find this new kind of probability in almost the same way. Probabilities of this kind are usually given as a percent.

EXAMPLE 1 A factory makes CD cases. In 50 cases, 3 were defective. Find the probability a case is defective.

Find the number of defective cases.   3

Find the total number of cases.   50

Find P(defective). $\dfrac{\text{number of defective cases}}{\text{total number of cases}} = \dfrac{3}{50}$

To change a fraction to a percent, divide the numerator by the denominator.

$50\overline{)3} = .06$

Write the fraction as a percent. $\dfrac{3}{50} = .06 = 6\%$

The probability a case is defective is 6%.

EXAMPLE 2 Sean scored a goal in 6 of his last 15 games. Find the probability he scores a goal.

Find the number of games he scored.   6

Find the total number of games.   15

Find P(scores). $\dfrac{\text{number of games he scored}}{\text{total number of games}} = \dfrac{6}{15}$

Write the fraction as a percent. $\dfrac{6}{15} = .40 = 40\%$

The probability Sean scores is 40%.

1. Maria scored on 5 of her last 8 free throws. Find the probability she makes a free throw.

   Find the number of free throws she made. ■

   Find the total number of free throws. 8

   Find P(makes free throw).

   $$\frac{\text{number of free throws made}}{\text{total number of free throws}} = \frac{■}{■}$$

   Write the fraction as a percent.

   $$\frac{■}{■} = ■ = 62.5\%$$

   The probability Maria will make a free throw is ■.

2. A telephone survey asked 50 people what they had for breakfast. 15 people said they had cereal. Find the probability a person had cereal for breakfast.

   Find the number of people who had cereal. ■

   Find the total number of people asked. ■

   Find P(cereal).

   $$\frac{\text{number of people who had cereal}}{\text{total number of people asked}} = \frac{■}{■}$$

   Write the fraction as a percent.

   $$\frac{■}{■} = ■ = ■\%$$

   The probability a person had cereal is ■.

Practice

1. A reporter asks 25 people if they read the newspaper. 23 people answer "yes." What is the probability a person reads the paper?

2. A small light bulb factory made 1,200 cases of light bulbs. 24 cases had a defective light bulb. Find the probability that a case contains a defective light bulb.

Do It Together!

3. Explain to a partner how to find the probability in number **1** in **Practice.**

4. Write a probability question that can be answered using what has already happened. Have a partner answer the question.

15.10 Application: Predicting Outcomes

You can use probability to predict outcomes. When you know the probability of an event, you can find how many times it may happen in the future by multiplying.

EXAMPLE 1

The probability that a tulip bulb will open is 80%. How many bulbs would you expect to open out of 200 bulbs?

Find 80% of 200.

Write the percent as a decimal. .8

Multiply. $.8 \bullet 200 = 160$

You would expect 160 bulbs to open.

EXAMPLE 2

Mo plays baseball. He gets a hit 34% of the time he is at bat. How many hits would you expect in 450 at bats?

Find 34% of 450.

Write the percent as a decimal. .34

Multiply. $.34 \bullet 450 = 153$

You would expect Mo to get a hit 153 times in 450 at bats.

The number you find is only a guess. The answer will not always be a whole number.

EXAMPLE 3

The probability of a defective CD case is 3%. How many defective cases would you expect in a group of 50 cases?

Find 3% of 50.

Write the percent as a decimal. .03

Multiply. $.03 \bullet 50 = 1.5$

You would expect 1.5 defective CD cases in 50.

1. 10% of popcorn kernels do not pop. Out of 450 kernels, how many would you expect to not pop?

   Find 10% of 450.

   Write the percent as a decimal. ■

   Multiply. ■ • 450 = ■

   You would expect ■ kernels not to pop.

2. John plays soccer. He makes 40% of his goal shots. If he takes 6 shots, how many goals does he expect to make?

   Find 40% of ■.

   Write the percent as a decimal. ■

   Multiply. ■ • ■ = ■

   He expects to make ■ goals.

Practice

1. 40% of the people in a survey exercise at least once a week. How many people in 30 do you expect exercise at least once a week?

2. In the winter, it snows on 25% of the days. On how many days would you expect it to snow in 40 days?

3. In a spark plug factory, 2% of the spark plugs are defective. How many defective spark plugs would you expect to find if you tested 500?

4. Chris plays tennis. She only misses her serve 8% of the time. In 30 serves, how many does she expect to miss?

5. Dawn dives for oysters. She finds a pearl in 5% of her oysters. How many pearls should she expect if she finds 20 oysters?

Do It Together!

6. Explain to a partner how to find the number of snowy days in **2** in **Practice.**

7. Make up a percentage for how many days a week you exercise. Ask a partner to find how many times you expect to exercise in 100 days. Check the work.

Chapter Review

Chapter 15 Summary

- You can find the total number of choices by multiplying the number of each different choice.
- You multiply to find permutations and combinations.
- To find the probability of an event, divide the number of ways the event can occur by the total number of possible outcomes.
- A probability of 0 means the event will never happen. A probability of 1 means it will always happen.
- The probability of a complementary event is the probability of the event subtracted from 1.
- When finding the probability of independent and dependent events, first find the probability each event will happen. Then, multiply the probabilities.
- A calculator is helpful when multiplying to find permutations and combinations.
- You can find empirical probability based on what has happened.
- Use probability to tell how many times you expect an event to happen.

Reviewing Vocabulary

permutations
combination
at random
outcomes
event
probability
complementary
  events
independent events
compound event
dependent events
empirical probability

1. _?_ are ways of arranging a group of objects in order.
2. _?_ are opposite events.
3. _?_ tells you how likely something is to happen.
4. A(n) _?_ is a group of objects in which the order they are chosen does not matter.
5. If the outcome of one event affects the outcome of a second event, the two events are _?_.
6. If the outcome of one event does not affect the outcome of a second event, the two events are _?_.
7. A(n) _?_ is an outcome or a group of outcomes.
8. Results of an activity, experiment, or game are called _?_.
9. A(n) _?_ is two or more independent events that happen together.
10. Probability that is based on what has happened is called _?_.
11. When the outcomes are equally likely to happen, the outcomes happen _?_.

Chapter Quiz

Find the total number of choices.

1. Karl has 4 pairs of pants and 7 shirts. How many choices does he have for 1 pair of pants and 1 shirt?

Find each number of permutations.

2. How many ways can 4 people stand in a line?

3. Eight runners compete for first and second prizes in a race. How many possible ways can the runners win prizes?

Find each number of combinations.

4. How many ways can you choose 2 pizza toppings from 10?

5. How many ways can a teacher choose 3 volunteers from 12 students?

A number cube is marked with numbers 1–6. Find each probability for one roll.

6. $P(2)$ **7.** $P(\text{odd})$ **8.** $P(6)$

9. $P(\textit{not } 6)$ **10.** $P(\textit{not } \text{odd})$ **11.** $P(\textit{not } 7)$

Find each probability.

12. Pick a letter at random from the word MATH and then from the word ALGEBRA. What is the probability you pick an A and then another A?

13. A bag has 4 blue marbles and 3 white marbles. You pick one at random, keep it, and then pick another. What is the probability you pick a blue and then a white marble?

14. A newspaper samples 400 residents and finds 300 like the new park. What is the probability a person will like the new park?

Find the expected outcome.

15. During August, it rains on 70% of the days. How many days would you expect it to rain in 10 days?

Unit Five Review

Simplify each expression.

1. $\sqrt{32}$

2. $4\sqrt{7} + 2\sqrt{5} - 2\sqrt{7}$

3. $\sqrt{24} + \sqrt{6}$

4. $8\sqrt{14} \cdot \sqrt{2}$

5. $\dfrac{4\sqrt{10}}{2}$

6. $\dfrac{9(x^2-1)}{3x^2-3x}$

7. $\dfrac{4}{a} - \dfrac{2}{3a^2}$

8. $\dfrac{6}{7n} + \dfrac{1}{3n^2}$

9. $\dfrac{2}{x} \div \dfrac{4}{5}$

Solve.

10. $6\sqrt{m} = 24$

11. $\sqrt{5x} - 1 = 4$

12. $\dfrac{4}{n+10} = \dfrac{-1}{n}$

Find the length of the missing side.

13.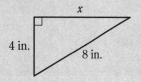

14.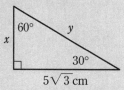

15.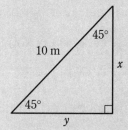

Plot each pair of points on coordinate axes. Then, use the Pythagorean Theorem to find the distance.

16. (1, 8) and (−2, 4)

17. (1, 3) and (−5, 0)

Find the number.

18. How many ways can you choose 2 volunteers from 100 people?

A spinner is marked with numbers 1–8. Find each probability.

19. $P(3)$

20. $P(\text{odd})$

21. $P(\textit{not } 7)$

Max has a bag with 3 red marbles and 4 blue marbles. Find the probability.

22. He picks a marble, keeps it, then picks another marble. What is the probability both marbles are blue?

Chapter One Additional Practice

Graph on a number line.

1. 4   **2.** ⁻6   **3.** 0

Compare. Use > or <.

4. ⁻9 and ⁻3   **5.** 1 and ⁻6   **6.** 0 and 4

Find the absolute value of each integer.

7. $|8|$ **8.** $|⁻13|$ **9.** $|⁺20|$

Find the opposite of each integer.

10. 14   **11.** ⁻4   **12.** ⁺9

Simplify.

13. ⁻5 + 8   **14.** 7 − 9   **15.** ⁻5 + 10

16. ⁻3 − 10   **17.** $(-3)(-7)$ **18.** $(6)(⁻2)$

19. ⁻20 ÷ ⁻4   **20.** ⁻15 ÷ 5   **21.** $(⁻5)^2$

Guess, test, and revise to solve the problem.

22. A restaurant manager ordered twice as many paper napkins as cloth napkins. He ordered 210 napkins in all. How many of each did he order?

Use the graph of Alex's savings to answer the question.

23. In which month did Alex have the most money in savings?

Six Months of Savings

Chapter Two Additional Practice

Simplify.

1. $17 - 16 \div 4$

2. $3 \bullet (12 - 4) \div 4$

3. $10 - 2(5 + 2)$

4. $6 + 3 \bullet 12$

5. $6 + 2 \bullet 5 - 6$

6. $-16 + 3 \bullet 0 \div 42$

Evaluate each variable expression.

7. $2a - 6$ when a is 1

8. $t \div 12$ when t is 36

9. $7(c - 4)$ when c is 4

10. $-5b$ when b is -6

Find the values of the expressions and tell whether the expressions are equivalent.

11. -12 and $2x$ when x is -6

12. 6×6 and $4(16 - 6)$

Name the property shown.

13. $32 + 0 = 32$

14. $12 \bullet 1 = 12$

15. $(x \bullet 5) \bullet 7 = x \bullet (5 \bullet 7)$

16. $10 + y = y + 10$

Simplify each expression.

17. $5x + 3x$

18. $2ab + 3ab - 7ab$

19. $16(1 - a)$

20. $12x - 4y + 3x$

21. $6c + 4 - 3 + c$

22. $3 + 7a - 6 + 6a$

23. $3(x + 4)$

24. $10(n - 3)$

25. $-(a + 7)$

26. $-(5 - x)$

27. $15x + 5(x - 4)$

28. $5 - (x + 8)$

Write a variable equation for the sentence.

29. Jeime's age is 4 more years than Megan's.

Use the formula $P = 2l + 2w$ to find the perimeter of each rectangle.

30. $l = 3$ cm and $w = 7$ cm

31. $l = 30$ ft and $w = 3$ ft

Chapter Three Additional Practice

Tell whether the number is the solution of the equation.

1. $5; 6x+20=50$

2. $-3; 16=3y+6$

3. $0; 4=12-8a$

4. $2; 3w-7=-1$

Solve. Then, check the solution.

5. $k+3=17$

6. $-2=6+d$

7. $8=b-1$

8. $w-15=5$

9. $\frac{x}{4}=-3$

10. $10=\frac{p}{2}$

11. $8n=24$

12. $-28=4s$

13. $2=3a-7$

14. $1+\frac{y}{5}=1$

15. $12=-2(q+5)$

16. $6(t-1)=18$

17. $-c+8=3c$

18. $7x=4+3x$

19. $-(n+4)=12$

20. $12a=-4a-16$

Find the number.

21. What is 45% of 80?

22. 5% of 20 is what number?

Find the discount or the sale price.

23. A $20 book is on sale for 15% off. Find the sale price.

24. Find the discount on a $10 t-shirt. It is 20% off.

Chapter Four Additional Practice

Use graph paper. Draw coordinate axes. Graph and label each point.

1. A at $(-3, 4)$ **2.** B at $(4, 0)$ **3.** C at $(6, -2)$

4. Write the ordered pairs. Graph.

Time (s)	Height (m)
1	3
2	7
3	12

5. Copy and complete the table.

x	$12 - 2x$	y
-1	$12 - 2(-1)$	?
0	?	?
1	?	?
2	?	?

Tell whether each group of ordered pairs is a function.

6. $(-1, 3)$, $(0, 3)$, $(1, 3)$, $(2, 7)$

7. $(-1, 0)$, $(0, 0)$, $(0, 6)$, $(2, 9)$

8.

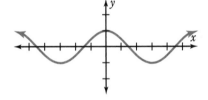

9.

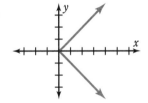

Find the value of each function.

10. $f(4)$ when $f(x) = 8 + x$

11. $f(-2)$ when $f(x) = 3x + 12$

Use the table or $d = 55t + 20$.

12. What is the distance when the time is 3 hours?

Time	Distance
1 hour	75 miles
2 hours	130 miles
3 hours	185 miles

Use the bar graph to answer the question.

13. In which year were there the fewest employees?

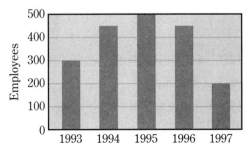

Chapter Five Additional Practice

Tell whether each ordered pair is a solution of the equation.

1. $(1, 16)$; $y = 11 + 3x$ **2.** $(5, -19)$; $y = 1 - 4x$ **3.** $(14, -5)$; $y = 2 - \dfrac{x}{2}$

Make a table of values for each equation. Then, graph the equation.

4. $y = 2x + 10$ **5.** $y = 9 - x$ **6.** $2y = y + \dfrac{x}{-2}$

Find the slope of each line that contains the pair of points.

7. $(12, 4)$ and $(11, 1)$ **8.** $(5, 9)$ and $(6, 9)$ **9.** $(-1, -5)$ and $(-1, -15)$

Tell whether the lines containing each pair of points are parallel or perpendicular.

10. $(4, 13)$ $(-4, 0)$ and $(16, 0)$ $(3, 8)$ **11.** $(-4, 8)$ $(2, -10)$ and $(6, 2)$ $(4, 8)$

Find the *x*-intercept and *y*-intercept of each line.

12. $y = 8x - 24$ **13.** $y = x - 14$ **14.** $y = -9x + 18$

Graph each line.

15. *y*-intercept: -5; slope: 4   **16.** $(3, 3)$; slope: $\dfrac{1}{4}$

Write each equation in slope-intercept form.

17. $6x + y = 12$ **18.** $5x - 5y = -20$ **19.** $28x - 7y = 14$

Find the slope to solve the problem.

20. At 6:00 A.M. Shane passes the 4 mile mark of a race course. At 7:00 A.M. he passes the 11 mile mark. If Shane continues at the same rate, where will he be at 9:00 A.M.?

The price of renting a video varies directly with the number of days. It costs $6.00 to rent a video for 2 days.

21. Find *k* in the equation for the price of renting a video. Use $P = kd$.

Chapter Six Additional Practice

Write the equation of the line described.

1. with slope $=1$ and y-intercept $=7$

2. with slope $=\frac{1}{2}$ and y-intercept $=-4$

3. with slope $=-1$ and y-intercept $=-3$

4. through $(-5, 4)$ and with slope $=0$

5. through $(1, 9)$ and with slope $=4$

6. through $(2, 3)$ and $(4, 1)$

7. with y-intercept $=6$ and parallel to $y=x-2$

8. through $(1, 3)$ and perpendicular to $y=\frac{-1}{2}x-1$

Write the equation of each line.

9.
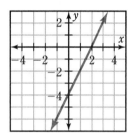

10.
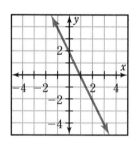

11.
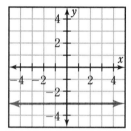

Find the pattern. Then, write the equation.

12.

Pints	Gallons
2	16
3	24
4	32

13.

x	y
2	4
3	5
4	6

Use the formula $l=\frac{2}{25}g+75$ to answer the question. Use l for length and g for mass.

14. What is the length of a spring when the mass is 500 grams?

Chapter Seven Additional Practice

Solve each inequality. Then, graph on a number line.

1. $m < 1$

2. $x \leq 2$

3. $c > -8$

4. $d - 1 < -6$

5. $y + 5 \geq 5$

6. $\dfrac{m}{-2} > -3$

7. $4a < 16$

8. $-4y - 8 > 12$

9. $\dfrac{n}{-5} - 1 \geq 0$

Tell whether each point is a solution of $y > -2x + 2$.

10. $(-3, 4)$

11. $(2, 1)$

12. $(1, 0)$

Graph the solution of each inequality on a coordinate plane.

13. $y \geq -3x - 3$

14. $y < \dfrac{3}{4}x - 1$

15. $y > 2x - 2$

16. $y \leq x + 4$

17. $y < \dfrac{1}{2}x + 1$

18. $y > x$

Write and solve the inequality.

19. Marcus is selling some of his old books to a used bookstore. How many $2 books does he need to sell to make at least $30.00?

Solve by looking at the graph.

20. Rachel has $20.00 to spend on dried fruit. Apricots are $5.00 per pound, and raisins are $2.00 per pound. The ordered pair (apricots, raisins) tells how many pounds of each. The inequality gives the ordered pairs that have a total less than or equal to $20.00. Can Rachel buy 3 pounds of apricots and 3 pounds of raisins?

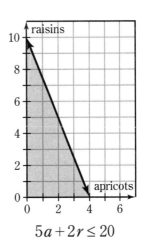

$$5a + 2r \leq 20$$

Chapter Eight Additional Practice

Tell whether the ordered pair is a solution of the system.

1. $(4, 4)$; $x+y=8$
$\quad\quad\quad\quad 2x+y=1$

2. $(-1, 5)$; $y > x+4$
$\quad\quad\quad\quad y < 4x+8$

3. $(-1, -4)$; $y > -5$
$\quad\quad\quad\quad\quad y \le x+2$

Graph each system to find its solution.

4. $y=x+4$
$\quad y=2x+6$

5. $y=6$
$\quad y=2x-6$

6. $y \le x+1$
$\quad y \le x-7$

7. $y \ge x+2$
$\quad y \le 2x+6$

Use substitution to find the solution of each system.

8. $y=x+8$
$\quad y=5x$

9. $y=x$
$\quad y=-4x+10$

10. $y=x+5$
$\quad\; y=-x-5$

Find the solution of each system with addition, subtraction, or multiplication.

11. $x+y=9$
$\quad\;\; x-y=5$

12. $-x+y=-5$
$\quad\quad\; x+y=-9$

13. $x+3y=-6$
$\quad\;\; x-3y=12$

14. $2x-3y=-7$
$\quad\;\; x+4y=2$

15. $5x-y=4$
$\quad\;\; 3x-2y=-6$

16. $2x+3y=-8$
$\quad\;\; 6x+2y=4$

17. Mr. Jones went to a bank to change a $100 bill. He received 6 bills total. All of the bills were $10 bills or $20 bills. How many did he receive of each?

The deli owner makes a profit of $2.00 on each pound of beef and $1.00 on each pound of pork. She orders at least 10 pounds total. She needs at most 7 pounds of beef and at most 6 pounds of pork. The graph shows these inequalities: $b \le 7$, $p \le 6$, and $b + p \ge 10$.

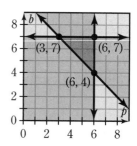

18. Find the maximum profit the deli can make. Use the graph of the inequalities and the equation Profit $= 2b + 1p$.

Chapter Nine Additional Practice

Find the mean, mode, and median.

1. 9, 6, 8, 8, 3, 5, 6, 9, 9

2. 80, 77, 75, 80, 91, 80, 52, 83, 75

Find the minimum, maximum, and range.

3. 10, 15, 9, 7, 11, 9, 2

4. 15, 20, 22, 10, 22, 10, 22, 12, 20

5. Make a frequency table for the set of data of class grades: A, B, B, C, F, C, A, C, B, B, A, B, A, F, B, A, B. Describe the data.

6. How many grades are above a C?

Make a stem-and-leaf plot for each set of data.

7. 40, 45, 49, 54, 54, 64, 65, 66

8. 80, 77, 75, 80, 91, 70, 62, 84, 75

For each scatter plot, tell whether the correlation is positive or negative.

9.
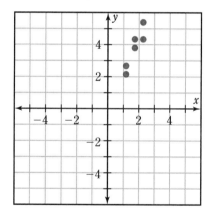

10.
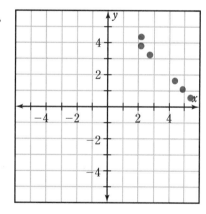

Find the mean, mode, and median of each set of data. Then, tell which of the mean, mode, and median best describes the data.

11. 2, 3, 3, 5, 42

12. 58, 2, 62, 90, 78, 2, 114

Find the quartiles in each set of data.

13. 11, 13, 15, 17, 19, 21, 23

14. 48, 55, 35, 36, 29, 49, 25

Chapter 10 Additional Practice

Use exponents to rewrite each power.

1. $xxxx$

2. $abbb$

3. $2mmnnn$

Find the value of each power.

4. $(-2)^3$

5. w^3 when w is 4

6. w^2 when w is 10

Multiply. Write using positive exponents.

7. $5x^2 \cdot 3x^3$

8. $b^4c^3 \cdot b^4c^3$

9. $(a^7)^2$

10. $4x^0 \cdot 2x^8$

11. $x^{-1}y \cdot x^6y^{-2}$

12. $(a^0)^5$

Divide. Write using positive exponents.

13. $\dfrac{b^{10}}{b^5}$

14. $\dfrac{x^8 y}{x^2}$

15. $\dfrac{8c^{12}d^2}{4cd}$

16. $\dfrac{b^{14}}{b^{14}}$

17. $\dfrac{3c^{-2}}{3c^2}$

18. $\dfrac{y^{-7}z^4}{y^3z}$

Find each number named in scientific notation.

19. 5×10^3

20. 1.1×10^4

21. 3.6×10^{-5}

22. 9.4×10^6

23. 9×10^{-2}

24. 4.09×10^5

25. Find five ordered pairs for the function $y = 3 \cdot 2^x$. Make a table. Graph the function on a coordinate plane.

26. Use a tree diagram to find how many different choices of shirt and shorts you can wear if you have three shirts (white, yellow, and red) and two pairs of shorts (green and blue).

27. Find the total after 3 years. Use the formula $T = 200(1.1)^x$.

Chapter Eleven Additional Practice

Find a, b, and c for each quadratic function.

1. $y = x^2 + 4x + 12$ **2.** $y = 3x - 5x^2 - 18$

Make a table of values for each function. Then, graph. Use $x = 2, 1, 0, -1, -2, -3$.

3. $y = x^2$ **4.** $y = x^2 + x$ **5.** $y = x^2 + 5$

Tell whether the graph opens upward or downward. Tell whether it has a minimum or a maximum.

6. $y = 3x^2$ **7.** $y = -7x^2 + 3$ **8.** $y = 6x^2$

Find the zeros of each quadratic function from its graph.

9. $y = \dfrac{x^2}{2} + 3$ **10.** $y = -x^2 + 2x + 3$

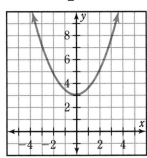 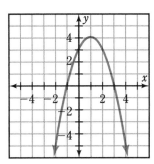

Find the value.

11. square roots of 49 **12.** $\sqrt{64}$ **13.** $-\sqrt{25}$

Solve each equation. Use the quadratic formula if necessary.

14. $x^2 = 36$ **15.** $x^2 + 10 = 59$ **16.** $0 = x^2 - 11x + 30$

17. The area of a rectangle is 400 square feet. The length is 4 times the width. Find the length and width.

Solve using the vertical motion formula: $h = -16t^2 + vt + s$.

18. A book falls off a building 500 feet high. At what time is the book 356 feet above the ground?

Chapter Twelve Additional Practice

Name the type of polynomial.

1. $2xy+8$

2. x^2-x-y^2

3. $-4y$

Combine each pair of polynomials.

4. Add y^2+5y-8 and $3y^2+2y+6$.

5. Subtract x^2-3 from $-2x^2+4x+4$.

Multiply.

6. $3(x^2+5x+6)$

7. $-2a(a-4)$

8. $2b(b^2-3b-10)$

9. $(x+5)(x+6)$

10. $(a-1)(a-9)$

11. $(y-2)(y+10)$

Tell whether the first expression is a factor of the second expression.

12. Is $3y$ a factor of $15y^2$?

13. Is $2x^2$ a factor of $6xy^2$?

Factor by finding the greatest common factor.

14. a^2+6a

15. $3n^3+12n$

16. $12x^2+6y$

Factor as the product of two binomials.

17. $y^2-11y+30$

18. $x^2+10x-11$

19. y^2-y-30

20. $x^2+14x+13$

21. x^2-81

22. $y^2+16y+64$

Solve each equation. Use factoring or the quadratic formula.

23. $x(2x+8)=0$

24. $(y-5)(y-8)=0$

25. $x^2+4x+3=0$

26. $x^2-4=0$

27. $x^2-4x=0$

28. $x^2+20x+75$

29. Use the formula $d=\dfrac{s^2-3s}{2}$ to find the number of diagonals in a polygon with 5 sides.

Chapter Thirteen Additional Practice

Between what two whole numbers is each radical.

1. $\sqrt{24}$

2. $\sqrt{40}$

3. $\sqrt{7}$

Simplify.

4. $\sqrt{18}$

5. $\sqrt{24}$

6. $9\sqrt{3} + 2\sqrt{6} - 7\sqrt{3}$

7. $3\sqrt{5} - 12\sqrt{5}$

8. $5\sqrt{2} + \sqrt{8}$

9. $4 \cdot 5\sqrt{6}$

10. $7\sqrt{3} \cdot 2\sqrt{10}$

11. $\dfrac{9\sqrt{12}}{6}$

12. $\dfrac{15\sqrt{8}}{3\sqrt{2}}$

Solve.

13. $8\sqrt{m-5} = 32$

14. $\sqrt{3y} + 2 = 8$

15. $\sqrt{10p-1} = 7$

Find the length of each missing side.

16.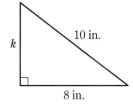

17.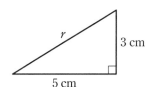

18.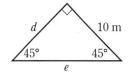

19.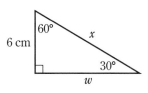

20.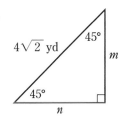

21.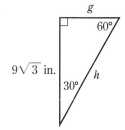

22. Tell whether a triangle with sides 18 m, 24 m, and 30 m is a right triangle.

23. Graph the points $(4, -3)$ and $(-2, 5)$. Then, find the distance between the two points.

Chapter Fourteen Additional Practice

Evaluate each expression.

1. $\dfrac{a^2-7}{a+6}$ when y is 4

2. $\dfrac{a^2-1}{a+1}$ when a is -5

Find the values that make the rational expression undefined.

Simplify each rational expression.

3. $\dfrac{2y+5}{y(y-7)}$

4. $\dfrac{b-2}{(b-8)(b+9)}$

5. $\dfrac{(x-5)(x+3)}{2x(x-5)}$

6. $\dfrac{8x(x-9)}{(x-9)(x+9)}$

Find the least common multiple for each pair of expressions.

7. $4y$ and $y+7$

8. $16a$ and $8a^2$

9. $x+9$ and $x-9$

Add, subtract, multiply, or divide.

10. $\dfrac{3}{4}+\dfrac{2}{5}$

11. $\dfrac{4}{y}-\dfrac{3}{2y^2}$

12. $\dfrac{2y}{8}+\dfrac{4}{y}$

13. $\dfrac{x}{9}-\dfrac{5}{3x}$

14. $\dfrac{3a}{4b}\cdot\dfrac{12b^2}{9a^2}$

15. $\dfrac{t^2}{16}\div\dfrac{t}{4}$

16. $\dfrac{4x-16}{3x}\div\dfrac{2x-8}{5x^2}$

17. $\dfrac{x^2+2x-63}{2x}\cdot\dfrac{3x^2}{x^2-81}$

Solve.

18. $\dfrac{5}{x}+\dfrac{3}{x}=\dfrac{4}{2}$

19. $\dfrac{1}{2}-\dfrac{3}{6n}=\dfrac{3}{n}$

20. $\dfrac{4}{12}-\dfrac{5}{3a}=2$

21. $\dfrac{3}{n+3}=\dfrac{6}{n}$

22. $\dfrac{a^2}{12}=\dfrac{a}{2}$

23. $\dfrac{4}{8}=\dfrac{y-1}{y+3}$

Use a proportion to solve the problem.

24. At Park High School, 2 out of 3 seniors will go to the prom. If 30 students go to the prom, how many seniors are there?

Use $y=\dfrac{100}{x}$ to solve the problem. x represents the rate (mph), and y represents time (hours) it takes to complete the trip.

25. How many hours will the trip take if you travel 50 mph?

Chapter Fifteen Additional Practice

Find the total number of choices.

1. An architect offers 5 door styles and 8 door knob styles. How many ways can you choose 1 door and 1 door knob?

Find each number of permutations.

2. How many ways can you arrange the letters MATH?

3. Fifteen students run for class office. How many ways can they be elected to the positions president, vice president, and treasurer?

Find each number of combinations.

4. How many ways can you choose 3 days from 7 days?

5. How many ways can a teacher choose 5 volunteers from 8 students?

A jar contains 1 yellow, 4 blue, and 3 white marbles. Pick one at random. Find each probability.

6. *P*(blue)   7. *P*(red)   8. *P*(*not* white)

Pick a letter at random from the word GEOMETRY. Find each probability.

9 *P*(E)   10. *P*(vowel)   11. *P*(*not* a vowel)

Find each probability.

12. Flip a coin 3 times. Find the probability that it lands heads, tails, heads.

13. A bag contains 4 red and 2 green marbles. You pick one, keep it, and then pick another. What is the probability that you pick two green marbles?

14. In an order of 500 lightbulbs, 3 are defective. What is the probability that a lightbulb is defective?

Find the expected outcome.

15. Eighty percent of adults read the newspaper each day. In a group of 200 adults, how many would you expect to read the newspaper?

Formulas from Geometry

Perimeter and Area

Perimeter

Rectangle
$P = 2l + 2w$

Square
$P = 4s$

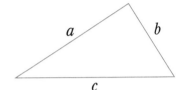

Triangle
$P = a + b + c$

Area

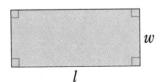

Rectangle
$A = lw$

Square
$A = s^2$

Volume

Box
$V = lwh$

Right Triangles

Right Triangle

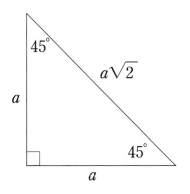

leg: b

hypotenuse: c

leg: a

Pythagorean Theorem

$$a^2 + b^2 = c^2$$

Special Right Triangles

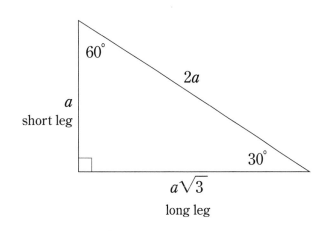

45°

$a\sqrt{2}$

a

45°

a

leg = leg
hypotenuse = leg • $\sqrt{2}$

60°

$2a$

a
short leg

30°

$a\sqrt{3}$
long leg

long leg = short leg • $\sqrt{3}$
hypotenuse = 2 • short leg

Squares

1-50

Number	Square
1	1
2	4
3	9
4	16
5	25
6	36
7	49
8	64
9	81
10	100
11	121
12	144
13	169
14	196
15	225
16	256
17	289
18	324
19	361
20	400
21	441
22	484
23	529
24	576
25	625

Number	Square
26	676
27	729
28	784
29	841
30	900
31	961
32	1,024
33	1,089
34	1,156
35	1,225
36	1,296
37	1,369
38	1,444
39	1,521
40	1,600
41	1,681
42	1,764
43	1,849
44	1,936
45	2,025
46	2,116
47	2,209
48	2,304
49	2,401
50	2,500

Squares
51-100

Number	Square		Number	Square
51	2,601		76	5,776
52	2,704		77	5,929
53	2,809		78	6,084
54	2,916		79	6,241
55	3,025		80	6,400
56	3,136		81	6,561
57	3,249		82	6,724
58	3,364		83	6,889
59	3,481		84	7,056
60	3,600		85	7,225
61	3,721		86	7,396
62	3,844		87	7,569
63	3,969		88	7,744
64	4,096		89	7,921
65	4,225		90	8,100
66	4,356		91	8,281
67	4,489		92	8,464
68	4,624		93	8,649
69	4,761		94	8,836
70	4,900		95	9,025
71	5,041		96	9,216
72	5,184		97	9,409
73	5,329		98	9,604
74	5,476		99	9,801
75	5,625		100	10,000

Squares Roots
1-50

Number	Square Root
1	1.000
2	1.414
3	1.732
4	2.000
5	2.236
6	2.449
7	2.646
8	2.828
9	3.000
10	3.162
11	3.317
12	3.464
13	3.606
14	3.742
15	3.873
16	4.000
17	4.123
18	4.243
19	4.359
20	4.472
21	4.583
22	4.690
23	4.796
24	4.899
25	5.000

Number	Square Root
26	5.099
27	5.196
28	5.292
29	5.385
30	5.477
31	5.568
32	5.657
33	5.745
34	5.831
35	5.916
36	6.000
37	6.083
38	6.164
39	6.245
40	6.325
41	6.403
42	6.481
43	6.557
44	6.633
45	6.708
46	6.782
47	6.856
48	6.928
49	7.000
50	7.071

Square Roots

51-100

Number	Square Root
51	7.141
52	7.211
53	7.280
54	7.348
55	7.416
56	7.483
57	7.550
58	7.616
59	7.681
60	7.746
61	7.810
62	7.874
63	7.937
64	8.000
65	8.062
66	8.124
67	8.185
68	8.246
69	8.307
70	8.367
71	8.426
72	8.485
73	8.544
74	8.602
75	8.660

Number	Square Root
76	8.718
77	8.775
78	8.832
79	8.888
80	8.944
81	9.000
82	9.055
83	9.110
84	9.165
85	9.220
86	9.274
87	9.327
88	9.381
89	9.434
90	9.487
91	9.539
92	9.592
93	9.644
94	9.695
95	9.747
96	9.798
97	9.849
98	9.899
99	9.950
100	10.000

Formulas from Algebra

The Coordinate Axes

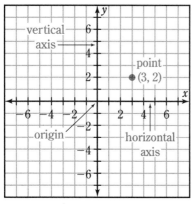

Ordered Pair (x, y)
Origin $(0, 0)$

$$\text{Slope} = \frac{\text{rise}}{\text{run}}$$

Slope-intercept Form of an Equation

$y = mx + b$

m is the slope. b is the y-intercept.

Direct Variation

$y = kx$, k is a positive number.

Inverse Variation

$y = \dfrac{k}{x}$, k is a positive number.

Quadratic Formula

$x = \dfrac{-b \pm \sqrt{b^2 - 4ac}}{2a}$ gives the values of x when $y = 0$ in the equation $y = ax^2 + bx + c$.

Probability

$P \,(\text{event}) = \dfrac{\text{number of ways an event can happen}}{\text{total number of outcomes}}$

GLOSSARY

absolute value the distance between 0 and a number on the number line

Addition Property of Opposites the sum of a number and its opposite is 0

Associative Property you can add or multiply more than two numbers in groups of two in any order

at random each outcome is equally likely to happen

bar graph a graph that uses bars to represent information

base a factor; In 3^2, 3 is the base used as a factor 2 times

binomial a polynomial with two terms

broken–line graph a graph made up of pieces of straight lines; used to display information

check substitute the solution for the variable

coefficient a number that multiplies a variable

combination a group of objects in which order does not matter; In counting combinations, ABC is the same as CAB

Commutative Property the order of two numbers does not matter when you add or multiply

complementary events events that are opposites; If winning is the event, then losing is the complementary event

compound event two or more independent events happening together

compound interest interest earned on your previous interest

constants numbers, or quantities, that do not change

coordinate axes perpendicular number lines

coordinate plane plane with two perpendicular number lines

cross products the products of numbers or expressions diagonally across from each other in a proportion

data information gathered from surveys or experiments

degree 2 describes an equation whose largest exponent is 2

dependent events events for which the outcome of one affects the outcome of the other

direct variation $y = kx$; k is a positive number; As one variable increases, the other increases

discount the amount you save when you buy an item on sale

Distance Formula a way to find the distance between two points using the Pythagorean Theorem

Distributive Property multiply a sum or difference by a number by multiplying each term of the sum or difference by the number

eliminating a variable removing one variable in a system of equations

empirical probability probability based on what has already happened

equation a statement that two expressions are equal

equivalent having the same value; equal

equivalent equations equations with the same solutions

evaluate find the value of an expression

event an outcome or group of outcomes that you are looking for

exponent the number that tells how many times the base is used as a factor

exponential functions functions of the form $y = a \bullet b^x$, where b is a positive number not equal to 1

expression a number, or a group of numbers written with operation signs

factor to write an expression as the product of its factors

factors numbers or variables being multiplied

frequency table chart that shows the number of times an item appears in a set of data

function a group of ordered pairs where no two ordered pairs have the same first number

function notation a way to write an equation to show it is a function

graph of a solution points on the number line or coordinate plane that show the solutions of an equation or inequality

graph of an ordered pair a dot that shows the location of an ordered pair

greatest common factor (GCF) the largest common factor of two or more terms

horizontal lines lines with slope = 0

hypotenuse the side across from the right angle of a right triangle

Identity Property adding 0, or multiplying by 1, does not change a number

independent events events whose outcomes do not affect each other

inequality a statement that shows "greater than," "greater than or equal to," "less than," or "less than or equal to"

$\geq$ the symbol for "is greater than or equal to" also means "at least" or "no less than"

$\leq$ the symbol for "is less than or equal to" also means "at most" or "no greater than"

integers the numbers … $-3, -2,$ $-1, 0, 1, 2, 3, …$

inverse operations operations that "undo" each other; Addition and subtraction are inverse operations, and multiplication and division are inverse operations

inverse variation a rational equation in the form $y = \dfrac{k}{x}$ where k is a positive constant

irrational number numbers with decimals that do not end and do not repeat

least common denominator (LCD) the LCM of two denominators

least common multiple (LCM) the smallest positive common multiple of two or more numbers or polynomials

like terms terms that have the same variables with the same exponents

linear equation an equation whose graph is a straight line

maximum　largest number in a group; the largest possible value of y in a function

mean　sum of the data divided by the number of data; also called average

median　middle number when data are ordered from least to greatest

minimum　smallest number in a group; the smallest possible value of y in a function

mode　number or numbers that appear most often in a set of data

monomial　an expression with one term; a number, a variable, or the product of a number and a variable

negative correlation　the data in one set increase while the data in the second set decrease

negative numbers　the numbers to the left of zero on the number line

opposites　numbers with the same absolute value on opposite sides of zero; One is negative and the other is positive; -3 and 3 are opposites

ordered pairs　two numbers in a special order; Ordered pairs give the locations of points

origin　the point where coordinate axes cross

outcomes　the results of an activity, experiment, or game

parallel lines　lines that have the same slope

permutations　ways of putting a group of objects in order; There are six permutations for three letters: ABC, ACB, BAC, BCA, CAB, CBA

perpendicular lines　two lines with slopes that are negative reciprocals

polynomial　a term or the sum or difference of terms

positive correlation　the data in two sets increase together

positive numbers　the numbers to the right of zero on the number line

power　the product when factors are the same; In $3^2 = 9$, 9 is the power

probability　value from 0 to 1 that tells how likely an event is to happen

properties of equality　adding, subtracting, multiplying, or dividing both sides of an equation by the same number gives an equivalent equation

proportion a statement that two ratios are equal

Pythagorean Theorem a formula for finding the length of a side of a right triangle when you know the lengths of the other sides; $a^2 + b^2 = c^2$

Pythagorean triple three positive whole numbers that satisfy the Pythagorean Theorem; The numbers can be the measures of the sides of a right triangle

quadratic equation an equation with one variable that has degree 2

quadratic formula formula to find the solutions of a quadratic equation in the form $ax^2 + bx + c = 0$

quadratic function an equation in the form $y = ax^2 + bx + c$

quartiles numbers in the middle of half of a set of data

radical square root written as a number under a radical sign

radical equation an equation that has a variable under a radical sign

range difference between minimum and maximum values in a set of data

rational equation an equation that contains rational expressions

rational expression the quotient of two variable expressions; can be written as a fraction

rational number a number that can be written as a fraction

revise change; to change a guess when you have more information

right triangle a triangle with one right angle and two acute angles

rise the change between two points on a line in an up-and-down direction

run the change between two points on a line in a left-to-right direction

sale price the regular price minus the discount

scatter plot graph that shows two sets of related data as ordered pairs

scientific notation a number written as the product of two factors; The first is a number greater than 1 and less than 10 and the second is a power of 10

simplify perform the operations; Find the value

slope   a measure of the steepness of a straight line; Tells how fast one variable changes compared with the other

slope-intercept form $y = mx + b$; m is the slope and b is the y-intercept

solution   a value of the variable that makes the equation true

solve   find the solution of an equation

square   raise a number to the second power

square root   a number that when multiplied by itself gives the original number; The square root of 16 is 4; In symbols, $\sqrt{16} = 4$

standard form $Ax + By = C$

statistics   the study of collecting and organizing data

stem-and-leaf plot   tool that uses place value to arrange and display data

substitute   replace a variable with a number or expression

system of linear equations   two or more linear equations with the same variables

system of linear inequalities   two or more linear inequalities with the same variables

terms   parts of an expression separated by a $+$ or $-$ sign

tree diagram   a way of showing choices so you can count them

30°– 60°– 90° triangle   a right triangle whose acute angles measure 30° and 60°

45°– 45°– 90° triangle   a right triangle whose acute angles both measure 45°

trinomial   a polynomial with three terms

undefined   when a rational expression has zero as the denominator; has no value

variable   a letter that represents a number

variable equation   an equation containing a variable

vertical line test   a test you use on a graph to tell if the graph is a function

vertical lines   lines with no slope

***x*-intercept**   the *x*-value of the ordered pair at the point where a line crosses the *x*-axis

***y*-intercept**   the *y*-value of the ordered pair at the point where a line crosses the *y*-axis

Zero Product Property   if the product of two numbers is 0, then one of the numbers must be 0

Zero Property of Multiplication   the product of any number and 0 is 0

zeros   the values of *x* where a function crosses the *x*-axis

Algebra 1
Selected Answers

Selected Answers

Unit One
Chapter 1 Numbers for Algebra
Page 5 Lesson 1.1

TRY THESE
1. left **2.** right **3.** < **4.** >

PRACTICE
1.

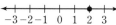
$$-3\ -2\ -1\quad 0\quad 1\quad 2\quad 3$$
3.
$$-10\ -9\ -8\ -7\ -6\ -5\ -4$$
5.
$$-1\quad 0\quad 1\quad 2\quad 3\quad 4\quad 5\quad 6\quad 7$$
7.
$$-7\ -6\ -5\ -4\ -3\ -2\ -1$$
9. > **11.** < **13.** > **15.** <

Page 7 Lesson 1.2

TRY THESE
1. 8 **2.** 12 **3.** 15 **4.** ⁻20

PRACTICE
1. 2 **3.** 3 **5.** 5 **7.** 1
9. 8 **11.** 9 **13.** 5
15. ⁻7 **17.** 22 **19.** 0

Page 9 Lesson 1.3

TRY THESE
1. 0 **2.** 1

PRACTICE
1. 3 **3.** ⁻9 **5.** ⁻6 **7.** ⁻6
9. 6 **11.** ⁻9 **13.** ⁻7 **15.** 6

Page 11 Lesson 1.4

TRY THESE
1. ⁻5 **2.** ⁻4

PRACTICE
1. 2 **3.** ⁻1 **5.** 13
7. 6 **9.** ⁻2 **11.** 9
13. ⁻23 **15.** 50

Page 13 Lesson 1.5

TRY THESE
1. 21 **2.** ⁻32 **3.** ⁻30 **4.** 0

PRACTICE
1. 15 **3.** 7 **5.** 18 **7.** ⁻45 **9.** 6 **11.** 18
13. ⁻28 **15.** 200

Page 15 Lesson 1.6

TRY THESE
1. 3 **2.** 0 **3.** ⁻4 **4.** ⁻6

PRACTICE
1. 5 **3.** ⁻1 **5.** 0 **7.** 4 **9.** 2 **11.** ⁻3
13. undefined **15.** ⁻6

Page 17 Lesson 1.7

TRY THESE
1. 6 **2.** ⁻20 **3.** ⁻20 **4.** ⁻6

PRACTICE
1. 15 **3.** 12 **5.** ⁻2 **7.** ⁻32
9. ⁻9 **11.** 0 **13.** 6
15. ⁻6 **17.** ⁻12

Page 19 Lesson 1.8

TRY THESE
1. −125 **2.** 81

PRACTICE
1. 36 **3.** 8 **5.** −169 **7.** −27,000
9. 6,561 **11.** 16 **13.** −27
15. −64 **17.** 64 **19.** 1

Page 21 Lesson 1.9

PRACTICE
1. −284 **3.** −24 **5.** 26 **7.** −1,633

Page 23 Lesson 1.10

TRY THESE
1. $28.00; $14.00 **2.** 8; 4

PRACTICE
1. $35.00 in July, $105.00 in August
3. 110 adult tickets, 130 student tickets

Page 25 Lesson 1.11

TRY THESE
1. March; 8   **2.** 14

PRACTICE
1. December   **3.** 7°

Chapter 2 Tools for Algebra
Page 31 Lesson 2.1

TRY THESE
1. 20   **2.** −1

PRACTICE
1. 7   **3.** 31   **5.** −1   **7.** 11
9. −3   **11.** −5   **13.** 31
15. 11   **17.** 5   **19.** 25   **21.** 0

Page 33 Lesson 2.2

TRY THESE
1. 18   **2.** 0

PRACTICE
1. 16   **3.** 20   **5.** 20   **7.** 2   **9.** −3   **11.** 2
13. 6   **15.** 10   **17.** 7   **19.** 7   **21.** 8

Page 35 Lesson 2.3

TRY THESE
1. $a \bullet b \bullet b$ **2.** $7 \bullet a \div 8 + 3$

PRACTICE
1. $\bullet$ **3.** $\bullet, -$ **5.** $\bullet, +$ **7.** $\bullet, \bullet$ **9.** $\bullet, \div$
11. $+, \bullet$ **13.** $\bullet, \div$ **15.** $\bullet, \bullet, +, \bullet$

Page 37 Lesson 2.4

TRY THESE
1. $4, y^3, -x$ **2.** 5; −10; 3   **3.** like   **4.** unlike

PRACTICE
1. $3n, 4p, 2$ **3.** $7a^3b^2c$ **5.** 1, −7   **7.** −2, 3
9. 1, 2, 1   **11.** like

Page 39 Lesson 2.5

TRY THESE
1. $6x$ **2.** $-2y$ **3.** $6a - 14$ **4.** $2c^2 + c$

PRACTICE
1. $10x^3$ **3.** $-11b$ **5.** $3a$ **7.** $3r + 3s$
9. $-4x + 2y^2$ **11.** $-4a + 3b$ **13.** $4t + 10$
15. $3x - 3x^2$

Page 41 Lesson 2.6

TRY THESE
1. −3   **2.** 16

PRACTICE
1. 8   **3.** −9   **5.** −12   **7.** 14   **9.** 9

Page 43 Lesson 2.7

TRY THESE
1. true   **2.** false

PRACTICE
1. 8=8; true   **3.** 5=5; true
5. 6=6; true   **7.** 7=6; false
9. 20=40; false   **11.** 10=12; false
13. 20=20; true

Page 45 Lesson 2.8

TRY THESE
1. Identity Property of Addition   **2.** 5

PRACTICE
1. Commutative   **3.** Addition Property of Opposites
5. Identity   **7.** Commutative; $3d$
9. adding opposites; $6m$
11. commutative; x
13. commutative; 3

Page 47 Lesson 2.9

TRY THESE
1. Identity Property of Multiplication
2. Zero Property of Multiplication
3. 5   **4.** b

PRACTICE
1. Commutative Property of Multiplication
3. Associative Property of Multiplication
5. Identity Property of Multiplication
7. commutative; $-8d$ **9.** associative; h
11. identity; 1

Page 49 Lesson 2.10

TRY THESE
1. $2r - 2$ **2.** $4a + 4c$

PRACTICE
1. $14 - 7y$ **3.** $-24 + 2k$ **5.** $-15 + 5x$
7. $4a - 28$ **9.** $-18 + 6d$ **11.** $6 - 4n$
13. $2x + 2k$ **15.** $10w + 20$

Page 51 Lesson 2.11

TRY THESE

1. $4x-7$ **2.** $5m+11n$

PRACTICE

1. $2a+2$ **3.** $-r-2$ **5.** $6y-58$ **7.** $7b-4$
9. $4t+6$ **11.** $11p$ **13.** $3m$ **15.** $3x-8$
17. $-3p+8$ **19.** $5-m$ **21.** $5y-2x$

Page 53 Lesson 2.12

PRACTICE

1. 214 **3.** 7.7 **5.** 31 **7.** 6.75

Page 55 Lesson 2.13

TRY THESE

1. $2 \cdot j$ **2.** $a+b+c$

PRACTICE

1. $A=lw$ **3.** $t=y-5$

Page 57 Lesson 2.14

TRY THESE

1. 74 ft **2.** 336 yd^2

PRACTICE

1. 47 m **3.** 72 in.^{2} **5.** 16 yd^2 **7.** 12 cm^3

Chapter 3 Solving Equations
Page 63 Lesson 3.1

TRY THESE

1. is not **2.** is

PRACTICE

1. yes **3.** yes **5.** yes **7.** yes **9.** yes
11. no **13.** no **15.** yes **17.** yes
19. no **21.** no

Page 65 Lesson 3.2

TRY THESE

1. -4 **2.** 14

PRACTICE

1. $10-7=3; 3=3$
3. $7=12+(-5); 7=7$
5. $(2)(6)=12; 12=12$
7. $(-2)(10)-3=-23; -20-3=-23; -23=-23$
9. $8+6(0)=8; 8+0=8; 8=8$
11. $-3(-2)+1=7; 6+1=7; 7=7$

Page 67 Lesson 3.3

TRY THESE

1. $-$ **2.** 3

PRACTICE

1. 5 **3.** $\bullet$ **5.** -3 **7.** 4 **9.** 2

Page 69 Lesson 3.4

TRY THESE

1. $-$ **2.** $\bullet$

PRACTICE

1. $-$ **3.** $\div$ **5.** $-$ **7.** $\div$ **9.** $-$ **11.** $+$

Page 71 Lesson 3.5

TRY THESE

1. $n=-11$ **2.** $18=t$

PRACTICE

1. 6 **3.** 12 **5.** 3 **7.** -15
9. -8 **11.** -4
13. -21 **15.** -5

Page 73 Lesson 3.6

TRY THESE

1. $n=-10$ **2.** $10=t$

PRACTICE

1. 30 **3.** 27 **5.** 20 **7.** -11
9. -6 **11.** -6 **13.** 12
15. -20 **17.** -16

Page 75 Lesson 3.7

TRY THESE

1. $35=n$ **2.** $t=24$

PRACTICE

1. 24 **3.** 18 **5.** -28 **7.** -20 **9.** -24
11. -50 **13.** 72 **15.** 15 **17.** 100

Page 77 Lesson 3.8

TRY THESE

1. $n=30$ **2.** $0=y$

PRACTICE

1. 7 **3.** 8 **5.** -6 **7.** -5
9. -24 **11.** -5 **13.** 10
15. -1 **17.** -8

Page 79 Lesson 3.9

TRY THESE
1. $y=4$ **2.** $-16=v$

PRACTICE
1. 2 **3.** 7 **5.** -28 **7.** -2
9. 25 **11.** -16

Page 81 Lesson 3.10

TRY THESE
1. $s=2$ **2.** $1=n$

PRACTICE
1. 3 **3.** -9 **5.** 13 **7.** -8 **9.** 11

Page 83 Lesson 3.11

TRY THESE
1. -2 **2.** -3

PRACTICE
1. 3 **3.** 6 **5.** 7 **7.** -4 **9.** -3 **11.** 2

Page 85 Lesson 3.12

PRACTICE
1. yes **3.** yes **5.** yes

Page 87 Lesson 3.13

TRY THESE
1. 44 **2.** 6

PRACTICE
1. $n=.55 \bullet 80; 44$ **3.** $.25 \bullet 100=n; 25$
5. $.05 \bullet 160=n; 8$

Page 89 Lesson 3.14

TRY THESE
1. $6.00 **2.** $18.00

PRACTICE
1. $1.50 **3.** $36.00 **5.** $24.00

Unit Two
Chapter 4 Introducing Functions
Page 97 Lesson 4.1

TRY THESE
1. 5 **2.** 2 **3.** left; 2 **4.** 3

PRACTICE
1. right 1 unit, up 3 units
3. up 2 units from the origin
5. left 4 units from the origin
7. left 2 units, down 5 units
9. left 5 units, down 4 units

Page 99 Lesson 4.2

TRY THESE
1. 2; up **2.** left; 3

PRACTICE
1–15.

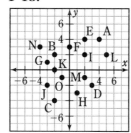

Page 101 Lesson 4.3

TRY THESE
1. $(1, 2), (2, -2), (3, -6)$ **2.** feet

PRACTICE
1. $(1, -5), (2, 0), (3, 5)$;

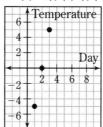

Page 103 Lesson 4.4

TRY THESE
1. $(-1, 0), (0, 3), (1, 6)$ **2.** $(-1, 2), (0, 4), (1, 6)$

PRACTICE
1. Possible answers: $(-1, -4), (0, 1), (1, 6)$
3. Possible answers: $(-1, -2), (0, 0), (1, 2)$
5. $-4; 2(0-1), -2; 2(1-1), 0; 2(2-1), 2; (-1, -4),$
$(0, -2), (1, 0), (2, 2)$

Page 105 Lesson 4.5

TRY THESE
1. is   **2.** is not

PRACTICE
1. no   **3.** yes   **5.** no

Page 107 Lesson 4.6

TRY THESE
1. $f(x) = x + 2$ **2.** $f(x) = 6(x + x^2)$ **3.** 5   **4.** 20

PRACTICE
1. $f(x) = 4 + x$ **3.** $f(x) = 3(x - 5)$ **5.** $f(0) = -9$
7. $f(8) = 24$ **9.** $f(-3) = -1$

Page 109 Lesson 4.7

PRACTICE
1. 19; $0.5(4) + 18$, 20; $0.5(6) + 18$, 21; $0.5(8) + 18$, 22

Page 111 Lesson 4.8

TRY THESE
1. $1,204   **2.** $28

PRACTICE
1. table; $16   **3.** equation; $64
5. The cost increases.

Page 113 Lesson 4.9

TRY THESE
1. 5   **2.** 2

PRACTICE
1. 3   **3.** 3

Chapter 5 Linear Equations and Functions

Page 119 Lesson 5.1

TRY THESE
1. is not   **2.** is

PRACTICE
1. yes   **3.** yes   **5.** yes   **7.** no   **9.** no
11. yes   **13.** no   **15.** yes

Page 121 Lesson 5.2

TRY THESE
1. $(-1, 4)$, $(0, 3)$, $(1, 2)$
2. $(-2, 1)$, $(0, 0)$, $(2, -1)$

PRACTICE
1.
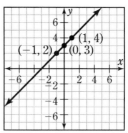

3.
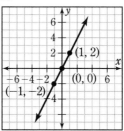

5.
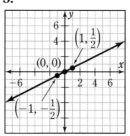

Page 123 Lesson 5.3

TRY THESE
1. $-\frac{8}{5}$ **2.** 2

PRACTICE
1. $\frac{3}{2}$ **3.** $\frac{5}{-3}$ **5.** $\frac{-5}{9}$ **7.** $\frac{8}{5}$ **9.** $\frac{1}{2}$
11. 0   **13.** 1

Page 125 Lesson 5.4

TRY THESE
1. 0   **2.** no slope

PRACTICE
1. 0   **3.** 0   **5.** $\frac{-4}{0}$; no slope
7. no slope   **9.** 0

Page 127 Lesson 5.5

TRY THESE

1. $\frac{6}{5}, \frac{6}{7}$; are not parallel

2. $3, \frac{1}{3}$; are not perpendicular

PRACTICE

1. yes   **3.** yes   **5.** yes

Page 129 Lesson 5.6

TRY THESE

1. -1 **2.** 3

PRACTICE

1. x-intercept: -1; y-intercept: 1
3. x-intercept: 2; y-intercept: -2
5. x-intercept: -2; y-intercept: 10
7. x-intercept: 6; y-intercept: -3
9. x-intercept: 0; y-intercept: 0
11. x-intercept: -3; y-intercept: 9

Page 131 Lesson 5.7

TRY THESE

1. $(1, 0)$ **2.** $(4, -3)$

PRACTICE

1.

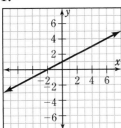

3.

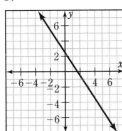

5.

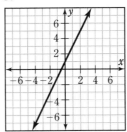

7.

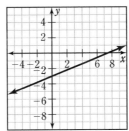

Page 133 Lesson 5.8

TRY THESE

1. $1; 5$ **2.** $\frac{3}{2}; -1$ **3.** $4; 0$ **4.** $-1; 3$

PRACTICE

1. slope: $\frac{1}{2}$; y-intercept: 3

3. slope: $\frac{-2}{3}$; y-intercept: 6

5. slope: $\frac{3}{4}$; y-intercept: 0

7. slope: -2; y-intercept: -4

9. slope: $\frac{1}{3}$; y-intercept: 1

11. slope: 3; y-intercept: 6

Page 135 Lesson 5.9

TRY THESE

1. $y = \frac{3x}{4}$ **2.** $y = 4x - 4$

PRACTICE
1. $y = -3x + 1$ **3.** $y = -5x + 10$
5. $y = -6x + 6$ **7.** $y = -3x + 10$
9. $y = \frac{-2}{3}x$ **11.** $y = -2x + 3$

Page 137 Lesson 5.10

PRACTICE
1. -13 **3.** 7 **5.** 24 **7.** 1.8 **9.** 32

Page 139 Lesson 5.11

TRY THESE
1. 8 **2.** 6 miles

PRACTICE
1. Gracie earns $40.
3. The bus could travel 300 miles.

Page 141 Lesson 5.12

TRY THESE
1. 3 **2.** $45.00

PRACTICE
1. 2 **3.** 8

Chapter 6 Writing Linear Equations
Page 147 Lesson 6.1

TRY THESE
1. $y=\frac{1}{2}x+1$ **2.** $y=3x$ **3.** $y=x+3$

PRACTICE
1. $y=-4x-3$
3. $y=-x+2$; Possible check: Use $(1, 1)$; $1=-1+2$.

Page 149 Lesson 6.2

TRY THESE
1. $y=\frac{1}{2}x+2$ **2.** $y=-3x+6$

PRACTICE
1. $y=-2x+3$ **3.** $y=\frac{3}{2}x+1$
5. $y=\frac{1}{4}x+2$ **7.** $y=x$

Page 151 Lesson 6.3

TRY THESE
1. $y=3x-1$
2. $y=\frac{-1}{2}x+4$

PRACTICE
1. $y=-\frac{1}{2}x+5$ **3.** $y=-x+10$ **5.** $y=6$
7. $y=\frac{1}{2}x$ **9.** $y=x$

Page 153 Lesson 6.4

TRY THESE
1. -1 **2.** 5

PRACTICE
1. $x=2$ **3.** $y=2$

Page 155 Lesson 6.5

TRY THESE
1. $y=\frac{1}{4}x$ **2.** $y=-2x-5$

PRACTICE
1. $y=4x+1$ **3.** $y=-\frac{1}{2}x-3$ **5.** $y=\frac{1}{2}x-6$

Page 157 Lesson 6.6

PRACTICE
1. true **3.** false **5.** false

Page 159 Lesson 6.7

TRY THESE
1. $y=x\div5$ **2.** $m=30g$

PRACTICE
1. $y=x-3$ **3.** $M=J+6$

Page 161 Lesson 6.8

TRY THESE
1. $l=\frac{2}{25}g+75$ **2.** 83

PRACTICE
1. 485 cc **3.** 700 cc

Unit 3
Chapter 7 Inequalities
Page 169 Lesson 7.1

TRY THESE
1. solid; right, 4. **2.** open; left **3.** open; right
4. solid; left

PRACTICE
1.

3.

5.

![number line with closed dot at -6, -8-7-6-5-4-3-2-1]

7.

![number line with open dot at -4, -6-5-4-3-2-1 0 1]

9.

![number line with closed dot at -5, -7-6-5-4-3-2-1 0]

11.

![number line with closed dot at -9, -13 -11 -9 -7]

13.

![number line with open dot at -6, -9-8-7-6-5-4-3-2]

15.

![number line with closed dot at -8, -12 -10 -8 -6]

Page 171 Lesson 7.2

TRY THESE
1. $x < 1$ **2.** $q \leq 1$

PRACTICE
1. $y > 2$;

![number line with open dot at 2, 0 1 2 3 4 5 6 7]

3. $b < 7$;

![number line with open dot at 7, 2 3 4 5 6 7 8 9]

5. $s > -2$;

![number line with open dot at -2, -4-3-2-1 0 1 2 3]

7. $x < 1$;

![number line with open dot at 1, -4-3-2-1 0 1 2 3]

9. $w < -9$;

![number line with open dot at -9, -13 -11 -9 -7]

Page 173 Lesson 7.3

TRY THESE
1. $x \geq -6$ **2.** $y < 3$

PRACTICE
1. $x > 8$;

![number line with open dot at 8, 6 7 8 9 10 11 12 13]

3. $f < 36$;

![number line with open dot at 36, 31 32 33 34 35 36 37 38]

5. $m \geq -30$;

![number line with closed dot at -30, -32 -30 -28 -26]

7. $x \leq -20$;

![number line with closed dot at -20, -24 -22 -20 -18]

9. $x < -20$ **11.** $f < 0$ **13.** $m \leq 35$ **15.** $x \leq -30$

Page 175 Lesson 7.4

TRY THESE
1. $x \geq 18$ **2.** $y < 3$

PRACTICE
1. $x > 12$;

![number line with open dot at 12, 10 11 12 13 14 15 16 17]

3. $x \leq -2$;

![number line with closed dot at -2, -7-6-5-4-3-2-1 0]

5. $m \geq 6$;

![number line with closed dot at 6, 4 5 6 7 8 9 10 11]

7. $x > 5$ **9.** $m \geq -21$ **11.** $a < 3$

Page 177 Lesson 7.5

TRY THESE
1. is not   **2.** is not

PRACTICE
1. yes   **3.** no
5. no   **7.** yes

Page 179 Lesson 7.6

TRY THESE
1. solid   **2.** dotted

PRACTICE
1.

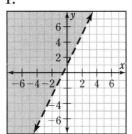

3.

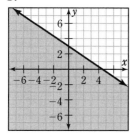

5.

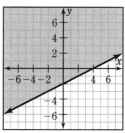

Page 181 Lesson 7.7

PRACTICE
1. $1.8 < 7.2$; yes
3. $7.2 \leq 7.2$; yes
5. $2.8 > 5.4$; no
7. $1.9 < -4.54$; no

Page 183 Lesson 7.8

TRY THESE
1. 500   2. 40

PRACTICE
1. $12t < 48$; $t < 4$ tickets
3. $7 + p \geq 15$; $p \geq 8$ pages

Page 185 Lesson 7.9

TRY THESE
1. will not   2. will

PRACTICE
1. Yes; (10, 20) is in the shaded region.
3. No; (10, 25) is on the dotted line and not in the shaded region.

Chapter 8
Page 191 Lesson 8.1

TRY THESE
1. is   2. is not

PRACTICE
1. yes   3. no   5. yes   7. yes

Page 193 Lesson 8.2

TRY THESE
1. $(-1, -2)$ 2. $(4, 2)$

PRACTICE
1. $(-1, 0)$;

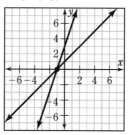

3. $(1, -1)$;

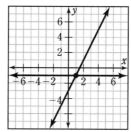

5. no solution;

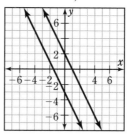

7. $(-6, -1)$;

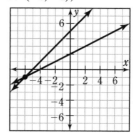

9. $(-1, 1)$;

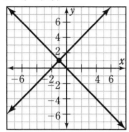

Page 195 Lesson 8.3

TRY THESE
1. $(-2, -1)$ **2.** $(3, 12)$

PRACTICE
1. $(2, 4)$ **3.** $(-3, -2)$ **5.** $(-3, -1)$

Page 197 Lesson 8.4

TRY THESE
1. $(-6, 3)$ **2.** $(-2, -5)$

PRACTICE
1. $(5, 1)$ **3.** $(-2, -1)$ **5.** $(4, 11)$

Page 199 Lesson 8.5

TRY THESE
1. $(1, -1)$ **2.** $(-2, 0)$

PRACTICE
1. $(0, 2)$ **3.** $(-3, -1)$ **5.** $(-2, -4)$

Page 201 Lesson 8.6

TRY THESE
1. $(2, 3)$ **2.** $(-2, 1)$

PRACTICE
1. $(6, -4)$ **3.** $(-5, 9)$ **5.** $(-2, 1)$

Page 203 Lesson 8.7

TRY THESE
1. is **2.** is not

PRACTICE
1. yes **3.** yes **5.** no

Page 205 Lesson 8.8

TRY THESE
1. dark shaded **2.** dark shaded

PRACTICE
1.

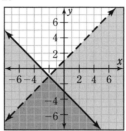

3.

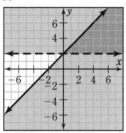

5.

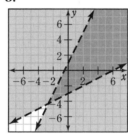

7.

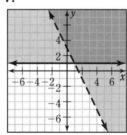

9.

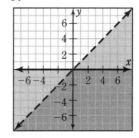

Page 207 Lesson 8.9

PRACTICE
1. yes   **3.** no   **5.** yes

Page 209 Lesson 8.10

TRY THESE
1. $4g+4a=60$ and $5g+2a=60$ **2.** $10.00

PRACTICE
1. x+y=4, x−y=2; (3, 1)
3. Tomatoes cost $1.00 a pound; Broccoli costs $3.00 a pound.

Page 211 Lesson 8.11

TRY THESE
1. $c \geq 9$; $w \geq 4$; $2c+3w \leq 36$ **2.** 12 and 4

PRACTICE
1. $b \leq 7$; $p \leq 6$; $b+p \geq 10$

Chapter 9   More About Data and Data Analysis
Page 217 Lesson 9.1

TRY THESE
1. −5   **2.** 3

PRACTICE
1. 30   **3.** 451   **5.** −10   **7.** −5
9. 30 boxes

Page 219 Lesson 9.2

TRY THESE
1. 1   **2.** 6

PRACTICE
1. −3   **3.** 16   **5.** −1 and 0   **7.** 4
9. 22   **11.** 1

Page 221 Lesson 9.3

TRY THESE
1. minimum, 1; maximum, 9   **2.** 17

PRACTICE
1. 0; 12; 12   **3.** −9; −2; 7   **5.** −6; 3; 9
7. 59; 752; 693

Page 223 Lesson 9.4

TRY THESE
1. III, 3; IIHT, 5; II, 2; 10   **2.** 2; 6–8 h   **3.** 8

PRACTICE
1. JHT I, 6; III, 3; III, 3; 12.   **3.** 1–10 years

Page 225 Lesson 9.5

TRY THESE
1. 5, 6, 8; 1, 7, 8; 25, 4
2. 550 to 559; 560 to 569

PRACTICE

1.

Stem	Leaves
1	4 5
2	1 1 3 8
3	1 3 5 6
4	2 8

3.

Stem	Leaves
72	0 4
73	5
74	8 8 8 9
75	8
76	1 4

Page 227 Lesson 9.6

TRY THESE
1. ordered pair; scatter plot
2. increase; positive

PRACTICE
1. negative correlation

Page 229 Lesson 9.7

PRACTICE
1. 714.25   **3.** 930.5   **5.** 674.8   **7.** 102.2

Page 231 Lesson 9.8

TRY THESE
1. mean; median, mode   **2.** mode; mean, median

PRACTICE

1. mean 34, median 32, modes 3 and 60; mean, median
3. mean 50, median 48, mode 15; mean, median

Page 233 Lesson 9.9

TRY THESE
1. 3, 4, 7   **2.** $27, $33, $44

PRACTICE
1. 84, 88, 94   **3.** 3, 5, 8

Unit Four
Chapter 10 Exponents and Functions
Page 241 Lesson 10.1

TRY THESE
1. n^3 **2.** xy^2 **3.** 4   **4.** 81

PRACTICE
1. g^3 **3.** a^2b^4 **5.** r^2 **7.** y^5 **9.** 64
11. -32 **13.** 1

Page 243 Lesson 10.2

TRY THESE
1. $3b^6$ **2.** $-10c^3d^2$

PRACTICE
1. c^4 **3.** x^6 **5.** x^2y **7.** $6ab$ **9.** $2x^2$
11. $-3a^4d^3$ **13.** $12ab^6$ **15.** $8h^5g^6$ **17.** $-3y^3$

Page 245 Lesson 10.3

TRY THESE
1. $10x^3y^2$ **2.** c^{12}

PRACTICE
1. x^{10} **3.** w^5x^6 **5.** b^8c^{12} **7.** $3a^4$ **9.** $30c^6q^4$
11. a^9 **13.** d^{10} **15.** y^{20} **17.** $-32n^7p$

Page 247 Lesson 10.4

TRY THESE
1. $2w$ **2.** ab^2

PRACTICE
1. b **3.** $5cd$ **5.** st^5 **7.** $6n$ **9.** $9x^2$ **11.** q^2
13. r **15.** ab **17.** $6x^4y^2$

Page 249 Lesson 10.5

TRY THESE
1. $4x^3$ **2.** g^4h^2

PRACTICE
1. b^2 **3.** $3r^4$ **5.** c^4d^2 **7.** $5m^3n^3$ **9.** x^5y^3
11. $6x^2y^2$

Page 251 Lesson 10.6

TRY THESE
1. b^2 **2.** x

PRACTICE
1. b^6 **3.** c^3d^6 **5.** t^4 **7.** y^4 **9.** xz^6 **11.** 1

Page 253 Lesson 10.7

TRY THESE
1. $\dfrac{y^3}{x^4}$ **2.** $\dfrac{a^2}{b^3}$

PRACTICE
1. b^2 **3.** $\dfrac{d^3}{c}$ **5.** $\dfrac{r^6}{q^3}$ **7.** $\dfrac{1}{m^5}$ **9.** $b^{10}c^4$
11. $\dfrac{j^5}{k^2}$

Page 255 Lesson 10.8

TRY THESE
1. .0000908   **2.** 1,300

PRACTICE
1. 161   **3.** 924,000   **5.** 274,200   **7.** .026
9. .000041   **11.** .0000047   **13.** 93,000,000

Page 257 Lesson 10.9

TRY THESE
1. (0, 1), (1, 5), (2, 25), (3, 125), (4, 625)
2. (0, 4), (1, 8), (2, 16), (3, 32), (4, 64)

PRACTICE
1.   **3.**

x	4^x	
0	1	(0, 1)
1	4	(1, 4)
2	16	(2, 16)
3	64	(3, 64)
4	256	(4, 256)

x	$-2 \cdot 5^x$	
0	-2	(0, -2)
1	-10	(1, -10)
2	-50	(2, -50)
3	-250	(3, -250)
4	$-1,250$	(4, $-1,250$)

5.

x	8^x	
0	1	(0, 1)
1	8	(1, 8)
2	64	(2, 64)
3	512	(3, 512)

Page 259 Lesson 10.10

TRY THESE
1. 4; 16; 64; 256   **2.** 1; 2; 3; 4

PRACTICE
1.

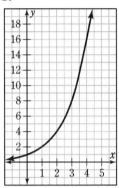

3.

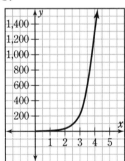

Page 261 Lesson 10.11

PRACTICE
1. 2,401   **3.** 225   **5.** 6,561   **7.** 3.24
9. 792.35   **11.** 24.39

Page 263 Lesson 10.12

TRY THESE
1.

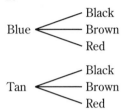

2. 6

PRACTICE
1. 6 choices;

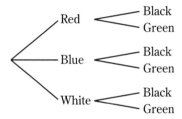

Page 265 Lesson 10.13

TRY THESE
1. $1166.40   **2.** $661.25

PRACTICE
1. $a=$1,000; r=5\%$ **3.** $a=$150; r=8\%$
5. $a=$10; r=5\%$ **7.** $385.00   **9.** $50,000.00
11. $605.00

Chapter 11   Quadratic Functions and Equations
Page 271 Lesson 11.1

TRY THESE
1. 5, 0, 8   **2.** 6, −1, 3

PRACTICE
1. 2; 3; 5   **3.** 1; 1; 1   **5.** 7; 1; 6   **7.** 3; 7; 8
9. 5; 0; −4   **11.** 2, 8, −1   **13.** −3; 0; 4
15. 1; −6; −4

Page 273 Lesson 11.2

TRY THESE
1. (2, 8), (1, 3), (0, 0), (−1, −1), (−2, 0), (−3, 3), (−4, 8)
2. (2, 8), (−1, −1)

1.

x	y
2	16
1	4
0	0
−1	4
−2	16

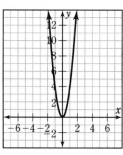

3.

x	y
2	8
1	5
0	4
−1	5
−2	8

5.

x	y
2	16
1	6
0	0
−1	−2
−2	0
−3	6
−4	16

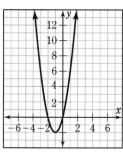

Page 275 Lesson 11.3

TRY THESE
1. upward; minimum
2. downward; maximum

PRACTICE
1. downward; maximum
3. downward; maximum
5. downward; maximum
7. upward; minimum
9. upward; minimum
11. upward, minimum

Page 277 Lesson 11.4

TRY THESE
1. 2 and −2   **2.** no zeros

PRACTICE
1. −1   **3.** 3

Page 279 Lesson 11.5

TRY THESE
1. 3, −3   **2.** 6, −6   **3.** −7   **4.** 0

PRACTICE
1. 8 and −8   **3.** 10 and −10   **5.** 1 and −1
7. 11   **9.** −3   **11.** ±9   **13.** −13
15. ±15   **17.** 25

Page 281 Lesson 11.6

TRY THESE
1. 8, −8   **2.** 4, −4

PRACTICE
1. 10 and −10   **3.** 11 and −11
5. 8 and −8   **7.** 2 and −2
9. 1 and −1

Page 283 Lesson 11.7

TRY THESE

1. $\dfrac{-b \pm \sqrt{b^2 - 4ac}}{2a}$ **2.** −2

PRACTICE
1. 1   **3.** 2 and 3   **5.** −1   **7.** −2 and −4
9. no zeros   **11.** −3 and −4

Page 285 Lesson 11.8

PRACTICE
1. .03 and −.03   **3.** 8.49 and −8.49
5. .063 and −.063   **7.** 60 and −60
9. 99 and −99   **11.** 1.1

Page 287 Lesson 11.9

TRY THESE
1. 20, 40   **2.** 11

PRACTICE
1. 12 yards

Page 289 Lesson 11.10

TRY THESE

1. 20 **2.** 5

PRACTICE

1. 10 seconds

Chapter 12 Polynomials and Factoring
Page 295 Lesson 12.1

TRY THESE

1. trinomial, -3 **2.** binomial, 0

PRACTICE

1. binomial, 0 **3.** binomial, 6 **5.** trinomial, -2
7. trinomial, -5 **9.** monomial, 0
11. binomial, 0 **13.** binomial, 0
15. trinomial, -4 **17.** binomial, -4

Page 297 Lesson 12.2

TRY THESE

1. $-3a^2 + 5a - 10$ **2.** $-x + 3y + 3$

PRACTICE

1. $4x^2 + 4x + 6$ **3.** $6s + 2t$ **5.** $-2c^2 + 6c - 5$
7. $x^2 + 7x - 3$ **9.** $2n^3 - 2n^2 - 3n - 5$ **11.** $-r^3 + 9r$

Page 299 Lesson 12.3

TRY THESE

1. $-4x^2 - x - 2$ **2.** $6p + 7q - 3$

PRACTICE

1. $-3k^2 - k + 3$ **3.** $-2m + 7n$ **5.** $-3w^2 + 2w - 2$
7. $-z^3 + 5z^2 - 4z + 4$ **9.** $-4h + 1$ **11.** $-y - 2$
13. $-x + 2$

Page 301 Lesson 12.4

TRY THESE

1. $-2a^2 + 6a$ **2.** $3x^3 - 6x^2 + 3x$

PRACTICE

1. $6b^2 + 12b$ **3.** $3y^3 + y^2$ **5.** $-2s^2 + 6s$
7. $-4x^3 + 20x^2$ **9.** $p^3 - 4p^2 + p$

Page 303 Lesson 12.5

TRY THESE

1. $x^2 - 3x - 10$ **2.** $a^2 - 9$

PRACTICE

1. $x^2 + 3x + 2$ **3.** $y^2 + 6y + 8$ **5.** $a^2 + 2a - 8$
7. $x^2 - 25$ **9.** $y^2 - 1$ **11.** $a^2 - 4a + 4$
13. $x^2 + 7x + 10$ **15.** $y^2 + 6y + 9$

Page 305 Lesson 12.6

TRY THESE

1. is **2.** is not

PRACTICE

1. yes **3.** no **5.** yes **7.** no
9. yes **11.** no

Page 307 Lesson 12.7

TRY THESE

1. $4(x + 2y)$ **2.** $2ab(3a - 1)$

PRACTICE

1. $3(x + 3y)$ **3.** $k(3k + 8)$ **5.** $a(a^2 + a - 1)$
7. $4x^2(2 - y)$ **9.** $5n(4m^2 - 1)$

Page 309 Lesson 12.8

TRY THESE

1. $(y + 3)(y + 4)$ **2.** $(a - 8)(a - 2)$

PRACTICE

1. $(x + 1)(x + 4)$ **3.** $(c + 2)(c + 2)$ **5.** $(a - 1)(a - 3)$
7. $(x - 3)(x - 4)$ **9.** $(x + 6)(x + 5)$

Page 311 Lesson 12.9

TRY THESE

1. $(x + 6)(x - 3)$ **2.** $(a - 10)(a + 2)$

PRACTICE

1. $(x - 1)(x + 5)$ **3.** $(y + 1)(y - 6)$
5. $(a - 2)(a + 4)$ **7.** $(x + 2)(x - 8)$
9. $(k + 6)(k - 2)$

Page 313 Lesson 12.10

TRY THESE

1. $(x + 6)(x - 6)$ **2.** $(10 + y)(10 - y)$

PRACTICE

1. $(x + 8)(x - 8)$ **3.** $(7 + c)(7 - c)$ **5.** $(a + 9)(a - 9)$
7. $(x + 20)(x - 20)$ **9.** $(b + 13)(b - 13)$
11. $(25 + n)(25 - n)$

Page 315 Lesson 12.11

TRY THESE

1. $y = 5$ and $y = 0$ **2.** $x = -2, x = -3$

PRACTICE

1. $x = 0$ and $x = -3$ **3.** $y = 0$ and $y = 7$
5. $y = -2$ and $y = 2$ **7.** $z = -4$ and $z = -2$
9. $x = 4$ and $x = 5$

Page 317 Lesson 12.12

TRY THESE

1. $y=0$ or $y=-4$ **2.** $x=5$

PRACTICE

1. $y=-1$ **3.** $y=4$ **5.** $a=7$ or $a=-7$
7. $y=3$ or $y=-5$ **9.** $a=9$ or $a=-4$
11. $n=-7$ or $n=4$

Page 319 Lesson 12.13

PRACTICE

1. yes   **3.** yes   **5.** yes

Page 321 Lesson 12.14

TRY THESE

1. -3 **2.** $24, -5$

PRACTICE

1. $x=-18$ or 3   **3.** $x=16$ or 3   **5.** $x=0$ or 15

Page 323 Lesson 12.15

TRY THESE

1. 53   **2.** 89

PRACTICE

1. 60 meters   **3.** $37°F$ **5.** 27 diagonals

Unit Five
Chapter 13 Radicals and Geometry
Page 331 Lesson 13.1

TRY THESE

1. $2, 3$ **2.** $3, 4$

PRACTICE

1. 2 and 3   **3.** 4 and 5   **5.** 2 and 3   **7.** 3 and 4

Page 333 Lesson 13.2

TRY THESE

1. $2\sqrt{5}$ **2.** $3\sqrt{2}$

PRACTICE

1. $2\sqrt{6}$ **3.** $2\sqrt{7}$ **5.** $2\sqrt{15}$ **7.** $2\sqrt{11}$
9. $2\sqrt{13}$ **11.** $4\sqrt{5}$ **13.** $3\sqrt{10}$ **15.** $4\sqrt{6}$

Page 335 Lesson 13.3

TRY THESE

1. $3\sqrt{6}+4\sqrt{7}$ **2.** $6\sqrt{3}-\sqrt{2}$

PRACTICE

1. $10\sqrt{2}$ **3.** $6\sqrt{5}+8\sqrt{6}$ **5.** $3\sqrt{2}+3\sqrt{6}$
7. $\sqrt{2}$ **9.** $6\sqrt{5}$ **11.** $\sqrt{7}+\sqrt{6}$

Page 337 Lesson 13.4

TRY THESE

1. $24\sqrt{5}$ **2.** $\dfrac{1}{4}$

PRACTICE

1. $9\sqrt{10}$ **3.** 5   **5.** $6\sqrt{6}$ **7.** $9\sqrt{7}$
9. $12\sqrt{5}$ **11.** 2

Page 339 Lesson 13.5

TRY THESE

1. 8   **2.** 3

PRACTICE

1. $x=4$ **3.** $x=3$ **5.** $n=2$ **7.** $p=11$ **9.** $k=2$
11. $x=4$ **13.** $w=7$ **15.** $t=12$

Page 341 Lesson 13.6

TRY THESE

1. hypotenuse is t, legs are r and s **2.** x, y

PRACTICE

1. Legs: a, b; Hypotenuse: c
3. Legs: s, t; Hypotenuse: r
5. Legs: d, e; Hypotenuse: f

Page 343 Lesson 13.7

TRY THESE

1. $\sqrt{13}$ **2.** 12

PRACTICE

1. 5 m   **3.** 5m

Page 345 Lesson 13.8

TRY THESE

1. $2\sqrt{2}, 4$ **2.** $6\sqrt{2}, 6\sqrt{2}$

PRACTICE

1. $b=3$ cm; $c=3\sqrt{2}$ cm
3. $a=5\sqrt{2}$ in.; $b=5\sqrt{2}$ in.

Page 347 Lesson 13.9

TRY THESE

1. 5   **2.** $5\sqrt{3}$

1. long leg $= 4\sqrt{3}$ in.; hypotenuse $= 8$ in.
3. short leg $= 7$ m; long leg $= 7\sqrt{3}$ m
5. long leg $= 12$ yd; hypotenuse $= 8\sqrt{3}$ yd

Page 349 Lesson 13.10

PRACTICE
1. yes   3. yes   5. yes

Page 351 Lesson 13.11

TRY THESE
1. are   2. are

PRACTICE
1. yes   3. no   5. no   7. yes   9. no

Page 353 Lesson 13.12

TRY THESE
1. $2\sqrt{5}$ 2. $\sqrt{41}$

PRACTICE
1. $\sqrt{53}$ units   3. $4\sqrt{5}$ units

Chapter 14 Rational Expressions and Equations

Page 359 Lesson 14.1

TRY THESE
1. $\frac{1}{2}$ 2. 2

PRACTICE
1. $\frac{1}{2}$ 3. $\frac{4}{11}$ 5. $\frac{10}{19}$ 7. -1 9. 12

Page 361 Lesson 14.2

TRY THESE
1. 3   2. 0, 4

PRACTICE
1. -6 3. 0   5. 0 or -5 7. 0 or -5

Page 363 Lesson 14.3

TRY THESE
1. $\frac{2}{3}$ 2. $\frac{1}{a-2}$

PRACTICE
1. $\frac{1}{4}$ 3. $\frac{7}{10}$ 5. $\frac{1}{4y}$ 7. $\frac{a-1}{a}$ 9. $\frac{p+5}{p-5}$
11. $\frac{2}{5x}$ 13. $\frac{1}{a+2}$ 15. $\frac{x-3}{2}$

Page 365 Lesson 14.4

TRY THESE
1. $20x^2y$ 2. $a(a+1)$

PRACTICE
1. 12   3. x^2 5. $2x^2y$ 7. $x(x+6)$ 9. $18x^2$
11. $(x-1)(x+1)$

Page 367 Lesson 14.5

TRY THESE
1. $\frac{5}{3x}$ 2. $\frac{4x-3xy}{y^2}$

PRACTICE
1. $\frac{9}{10}$ 3. $\frac{17}{24}$ 5. $\frac{5a}{14}$ 7. $\frac{13b}{30}$ 9. $\frac{4y-6x}{xy}$
11. $\frac{2p+7m}{mp}$ 13. $\frac{2x+8y}{x^2y^2}$ 15. $\frac{5a-6ab}{b^2}$

Page 369 Lesson 14.6

TRY THESE
1. $\frac{x^2-16}{4x}$ 2. $\frac{10x+6}{(x+3)(x-3)}$

PRACTICE
1. $\frac{8y+18}{y(y+3)}$ 3. $\frac{7y+15}{(y+1)(y+3)}$
5. $\frac{2a^2+a+10}{(a+2)(a-2)}$ 7. $\frac{-x+18}{x(x-3)}$

Page 371 Lesson 14.7

TRY THESE
1. $\frac{4}{5a}$ 2. $\frac{4}{3xy}$

PRACTICE
1. $\frac{1}{4}$ 3. $\frac{4}{5}$ 5. $\frac{5}{6}$ 7. $\frac{3y^2}{20}$ 9. $\frac{2m^2}{3}$
11. $\frac{4}{9a}$ 13. $\frac{a}{8}$ 15. $\frac{7}{4y}$

Page 373 Lesson 14.8

TRY THESE
1. $\frac{2}{9a}$ 2. $\frac{25}{x(x+3)}$

1. $\frac{12y}{5}$ 3. $\frac{6}{35x}$ 5. 6   7. $\frac{1}{15}$ 9. $\frac{3}{5(x+1)}$

Page 375 Lesson 14.9

TRY THESE
1. 5   2. -15

PRACTICE
1. $y=2$ 3. $m=36$ 5. $n=4$ 7. $n=7$ 9. $b=5$
11. $v=2$ 13. $n=4$ 15. $z=2$

Page 377 Lesson 14.10

TRY THESE
1. 5   2. -3

PRACTICE
1. $x=12$ 3. $n=-2$ 5. $y=15$ 7. $x=2$
9. $n=6$ or $n=-1$

Page 379 Lesson 14.11

PRACTICE
1. true   3. true   5. true   7. false

Page 381 Lesson 14.12

TRY THESE
1. 5   2. 24 s

PRACTICE
1. 7 miles   3. 24 days of band

Page 383 Lesson 14.13

TRY THESE
1. 3 cm   2. 2 cm

PRACTICE
1. 9 h   3. 8 cm

Chapter 15 Probability
Page 389 Lesson 15.1

TRY THESE
1. 30   2. 12

PRACTICE
1. 16   3. 12

Page 391 Lesson 15.2

TRY THESE
1. 90   2. 24

PRACTICE
1. 6   3. 30

Page 393 Lesson 15.3

TRY THESE
1. 20   2. 21

PRACTICE
1. 10   3. 120   5. 6

Page 395 Lesson 15.4

TRY THESE
1. $\frac{4}{6}$ 2. $\frac{3}{6}$

PRACTICE
1. $\frac{1}{5}$ 3. $\frac{3}{5}$ 5. $\frac{2}{5}$

Page 397 Lesson 15.5

TRY THESE
1. $\frac{1}{5}$ 2. $\frac{1}{3}$

PRACTICE
1. $\frac{9}{11}$ 3. $\frac{11}{11}=1$ 5. $\frac{2}{5}$

Page 399 Lesson 15.6

TRY THESE
1. $\frac{3}{30}$ 2. $\frac{6}{30}$

PRACTICE
1. $\frac{2}{30}$ 3. $\frac{3}{30}$

Page 401 Lesson 15.7

TRY THESE
1. $\frac{20}{30}$ 2. 0

PRACTICE
1. $\frac{2}{20}$ 3. $\frac{6}{20}$

Page 403 Lesson 15.8

PRACTICE

1. 362,880 **3.** 175,560 **5.** 12,650

Page 405 Lesson 15.9

TRY THESE

1. 62.5% **2.** 30%

PRACTICE

1. 92%

Page 407 Lesson 15.10

TRY THESE

1. 45 **2.** 2.4

PRACTICE

1. 12 people **3.** 10 defective spark plugs
5. 1 pearl

Additional Practice
Page 413 Chapter 1

1.

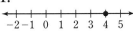

2. 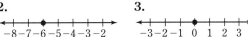 **3.**

4. < **5.** > **6.** < **7.** 8 **8.** 13 **9.** 20
10. ⁻14 **11.** 4 **12.** ⁻9 **13.** 3 **14.** ⁻2
15. 5 **16.** ⁻13 **17.** 21 **18.** −12 **19.** 5
20. −3 **21.** 25 **22.** 140 paper; 70 cloth
23. August

Page 414 Chapter 2

1. 13 **2.** 6 **3.** −4 **4.** 42 **5.** 10
6. −16 **7.** −4 **8.** 3 **9.** 0 **10.** 30
11. −12, −12, equivalent
12. 36, 40, not equivalent
13. Identity Property of Addition
14. Identity Property of Multiplication
15. Associative Property of Multiplication
16. Commutative Property of Addition
17. $8x$ **18.** $-2ab$ **19.** $16-16a$ **20.** $15x-4y$
21. $7c+1$ **22.** $13a-3$ **23.** $3x+12$
24. $10n-30$ **25.** $-a-7$ **26.** $-5+x$
27. $20x-20$ **28.** $-3-x$ **29.** $j=m+4$
30. 20 cm **31.** 66 ft

Page 415 Chapter 3

1. yes **2.** no **3.** no **4.** yes **5.** 14 **6.** −8
7. 9 **8.** 20 **9.** −12 **10.** 20 **11.** 3 **12.** −7
13. 3 **14.** 0 **15.** −11 **16.** 4 **17.** 2 **18.** 1
19. −16 **20.** −1 **21.** 36 **22.** 1 **23.** $17.00
24. $2.00

Page 416 Chapter 4

1–3.

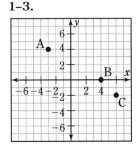

4. (1, 3), (2, 7), (3, 12);

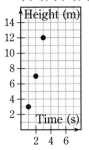

5. 14; $12-2(0)$, 12; $12-2(1)$, 10; $12-2(2)$, 8
6. yes **7.** no **8.** yes **9.** no **10.** $f(4)=12$
11. $f(-2)=6$ **12.** 185 **13.** 1997

Page 417 Chapter 5

1. no **2.** yes **3.** yes
4.

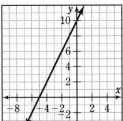

5.

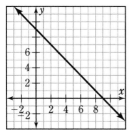

6.

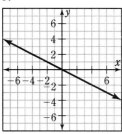

7. 3 **8.** 0 **9.** no slope **10.** perpendicular
11. parallel **12.** x-intercept: 3; y-intercept: -24
13. x-intercept: 14; y-intercept: -14
14. x-intercept: 2; y-intercept: 18
15.

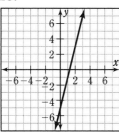

16.

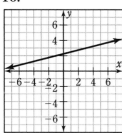

17. $y=-6x+12$ **18.** $y=x+4$ **19.** $y=4x-2$
20. 25 mile mark **21.** 3

Page 418 Chapter 6

1. $y=x+7$ **2.** $y=\frac{1}{2}x-4$ **3.** $y=-x-3$ **4.** $y=4$
5. $y=4x+5$ **6.** $y=-x+5$ **7.** $y=x+6$
8. $y=2x+1$ **9.** $y=2x-4$ **10.** $y=-2x+2$
11. $y=-3$
12. Multiply pints by 8 to find gallons. $8p=g$
13. Add 2 to x to find y. $x+2=y$ **14.** $l=115$ mm

Page 419 Chapter 7

1.

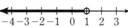

2.

3.

4.

5.

6.

7.

8.

9.

10. no **11.** yes **12.** no
13.

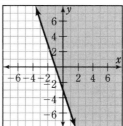

14.

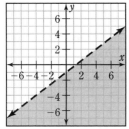

15.

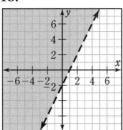

16.

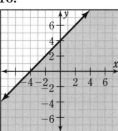

17.

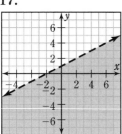

18.

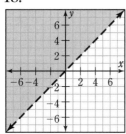

19. $2b \geq 30$; $b \geq 15$; Marcus needs to sell at least 15 books.

20. No; (3, 3) is not in the shaded region.

Page 420 Chapter 8

1. no **2.** no **3.** yes

4. $(-2, 2)$;

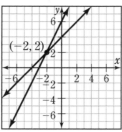

5. $(6, 6)$;

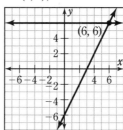

6.

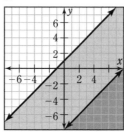

7.

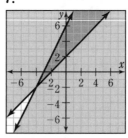

8. $(2, 10)$ **9.** $(2, 2)$ **10.** $(-5, 0)$
11. $(7, 2)$ **12.** $(-2, -7)$ **13.** $(3, -3)$
14. $(-2, 1)$ **15.** $(2, 6)$ **16.** $(2, -4)$

17. He received 4 $20 bills and 2 $10 bills.
18. 6 pounds of pork and 7 pounds of beef yields the maximum profit.

Page 421 Chapter 9
1. mean, 7; median, 8; mode, 9
2. mean, 77; median, 80; mode, 80
3. min. 2; max. 15; range 13
4. min. 10; max. 22; range 12
5.

Grades	Frequency
A	5
B	7
C	3
F	2
Total	17

There are 17 grades: five As, seven Bs, three Cs, and two Fs .

6. 12 grades
7.

Stem	Leaves
4	0 5 9
5	4 4
6	4 5 6

8.

Stem	Leaves
6	2
7	0 5 5 7
8	0 0 4
9	1

9. positive   **10.** negative
11. 11; 3; 3; median and mode
12. 58; 62; 2; mean and median
13. 13; 17; 21   **14.** 29; 36; 49

Page 422 Chapter 10
1. x^4 **2.** ab^3 **3.** $2m^2n^3$ **4.** -8 **5.** 64
6. 100 **7.** $15x^5$ **8.** b^8c^6 **9.** a^{14} **10.** $8x^8$
11. $\dfrac{x^5}{y}$ **12.** 1 **13.** b^5 **14.** x^6y
15. $2c^{11}d$ **16.** 1 **17.** $\dfrac{1}{c^4}$ **18.** $\dfrac{z^3}{y^{10}}$ **19.** 5,000
20. 11,000 **21.** .000036 **22.** 9,400,000
23. .09 **24.** 409,000
25. (0, 3), (1, 6), (2, 12), (3, 24), (4, 48)

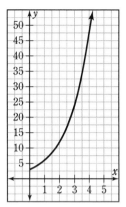

26. 6 choices;

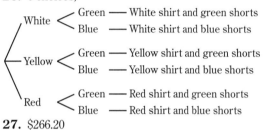

White — Green — White shirt and green shorts
White — Blue — White shirt and blue shorts
Yellow — Green — Yellow shirt and green shorts
Yellow — Blue — Yellow shirt and blue shorts
Red — Green — Red shirt and green shorts
Red — Blue — Red shirt and blue shorts

27. $266.20

Page 423 Chapter 11
1. 1, 4, 12   **2.** $-5, 3, -18$
3.

x	y
2	4
1	1
0	0
-1	1
-2	4
-3	9

4.

x	y
2	6
1	2
0	0
-1	0
-2	2
-3	6

5.

x	y
2	9
1	6
0	5
−1	6
−2	9
−3	14

6. upward; minimum   **7.** downward; maximum
8. upward; minimum   **9.** no zeros
10. 3 and −1   **11.** 7 and −7   **12.** 8   **13.** −5
14. 6 and −6   **15.** 7 and −7   **16.** 5 and 6
17. The length is 40 feet and the width is 10 feet
18. 3 seconds

Page 424 Chapter 12

1. binomial   **2.** trinomial   **3.** monomial
4. $4y^2 + 7y - 2$ **5.** $-3x^2 + 4x + 7$ **6.** $3x^2 + 15x + 18$
7. $-2a^2 + 8a$ **8.** $2b^3 - 6b^2 - 20b$ **9.** $x^2 + 11x + 30$
10. $a^2 - 10a + 9$ **11.** $y^2 + 8y - 20$ **12.** yes
13. no   **14.** $a(a+6)$ **15.** $3n(n^2+4)$
16. $6(2x^2+y)$ **17.** $(y-5)(y-6)$
18. $(x-1)(x+11)$ **19.** $(y+5)(y-6)$
20. $(x+1)(x+13)$ **21.** $(x+9)(x-9)$
22. $(y+8)(y+8)$ **23.** $x=0$ or -4 **24.** $y=5$ or 8
25. $x=-1$ or -3 **26.** $x=2$ or -2 **27.** $x=0$ or 4
28. $x=-15$ or -5 **29.** 5 diagonals

Page 425 Chapter 13

1. 4 and 5   **2.** 6 and 7   **3.** 2 and 3   **4.** $3\sqrt{2}$
5. $2\sqrt{6}$ **6.** $2\sqrt{3} + 2\sqrt{6}$ **7.** $-9\sqrt{5}$ **8.** $7\sqrt{2}$
9. $20\sqrt{6}$ **10.** $14\sqrt{30}$ **11.** $3\sqrt{3}$ **12.** 10
13. $m=21$ **14.** $y=12$ **15.** $p=5$ **16.** 6 in.
17. $\sqrt{34}$ cm   **18.** $d=10$ m; $e=10\sqrt{2}$ m
19. $w=6\sqrt{3}$ cm; $x=12$ cm
20. $m=4$ yd; $n=4$ yd   **21.** $g=9$ in.; $h=18$ in.
22. yes   **23.** 10 units

Page 426 Chapter 14

1. $\dfrac{9}{10}$ **2.** -6 **3.** 0 or 7   **4.** 8 or -9 **5.** $\dfrac{x+3}{2x}$
6. $\dfrac{8x}{x+9}$ **7.** $4y(y+7)$ **8.** $16a^2$
9. $(x+9)(x-9)$ **10.** $\dfrac{23}{20}$ **11.** $\dfrac{8y-3}{2y^2}$
12. $\dfrac{2y^2+32}{8y}$ **13.** $\dfrac{x^2-15}{9x}$ **14.** $\dfrac{b}{a}$ **15.** $\dfrac{t}{4}$
16. $\dfrac{10x}{3}$ **17.** $\dfrac{3x(x-7)}{2(x-9)}$ **18.** $x=4$ **19.** $n=7$
20. $a=-1$ **21.** $n=-6$ **22.** $a=0$ or 6
23. $y=5$ **24.** 45 seniors   **25.** 2 hours

Page 427 Chapter 15

1. 40   **2.** 24   **3.** 2,730   **4.** 35   **5.** 56   **6.** $\dfrac{4}{8}$
7. 0   **8.** $\dfrac{5}{8}$ **9.** $\dfrac{2}{8}$ **10.** $\dfrac{3}{8}$ **11.** $\dfrac{5}{8}$ **12.** $\dfrac{1}{8}$
13. $\dfrac{2}{30}$ **14.** .6%   **15.** 160 adults

INDEX

X

Y

Z

PHOTO CREDITS: